A Beatles Obsession and the
Concert of a Lifetime

CAROL TYLER

FANTAGRAPHICS BOOKS
SEATTLE, WA

EDITOR: GARY GROTH
COVER DESIGN: SEAN DAVID WILLIAMS
EDITORIAL ASSISTANCE: RJ CASEY
PRODUCTION: PAUL BARESH
ASSOCIATE PUBLISHER: ERIC REYNOLDS
PUBLISHER: GARY GROTH

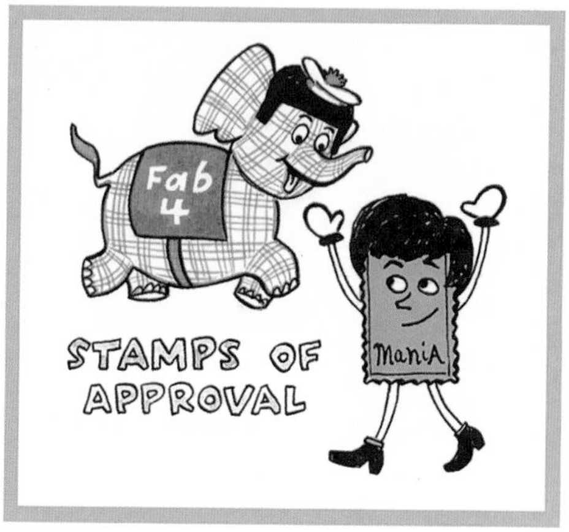
Fab 4
ManiA
STAMPS OF APPROVAL

FANTAGRAPHICS BOOKS, INC.
7563 LAKE CITY WAY NE
SEATTLE, WA 98115

OUR BOOKS MAY BE VIEWED—AND PURCHASED—ON OUR WEBSITE AT WWW.FANTAGRAPHICS.COM

FIRST PRINTING: JUNE 2018

ISBN 978-1-68396-061-4
LIBRARY OF CONGRESS CONTROL NUMBER: 2017938238
PRINTED IN CHINA

THANK YOU TO MY FAMILY, JUSTIN · JULIA · JUNIOR · TUE, MY FRIENDS, ESPECIALLY Laurie Mora Tellier. THANKS TO FANTA, STUDIO HELPERS: TYLER BALL, SAMANTHA LAKAMP, HANNAH SCHULTE, and ELLEN WANG, AND PROOFREADERS KEVIN KANN AND CAROL TILLEY. EXTRA HEARTBEATLE BEATS TO GG. AND, OF COURSE, THANKS TO THE BEATLES FOR BEING SO FAB!

THIS BOOK IS DEDICATED TO OUR YOUNGER SELVES.

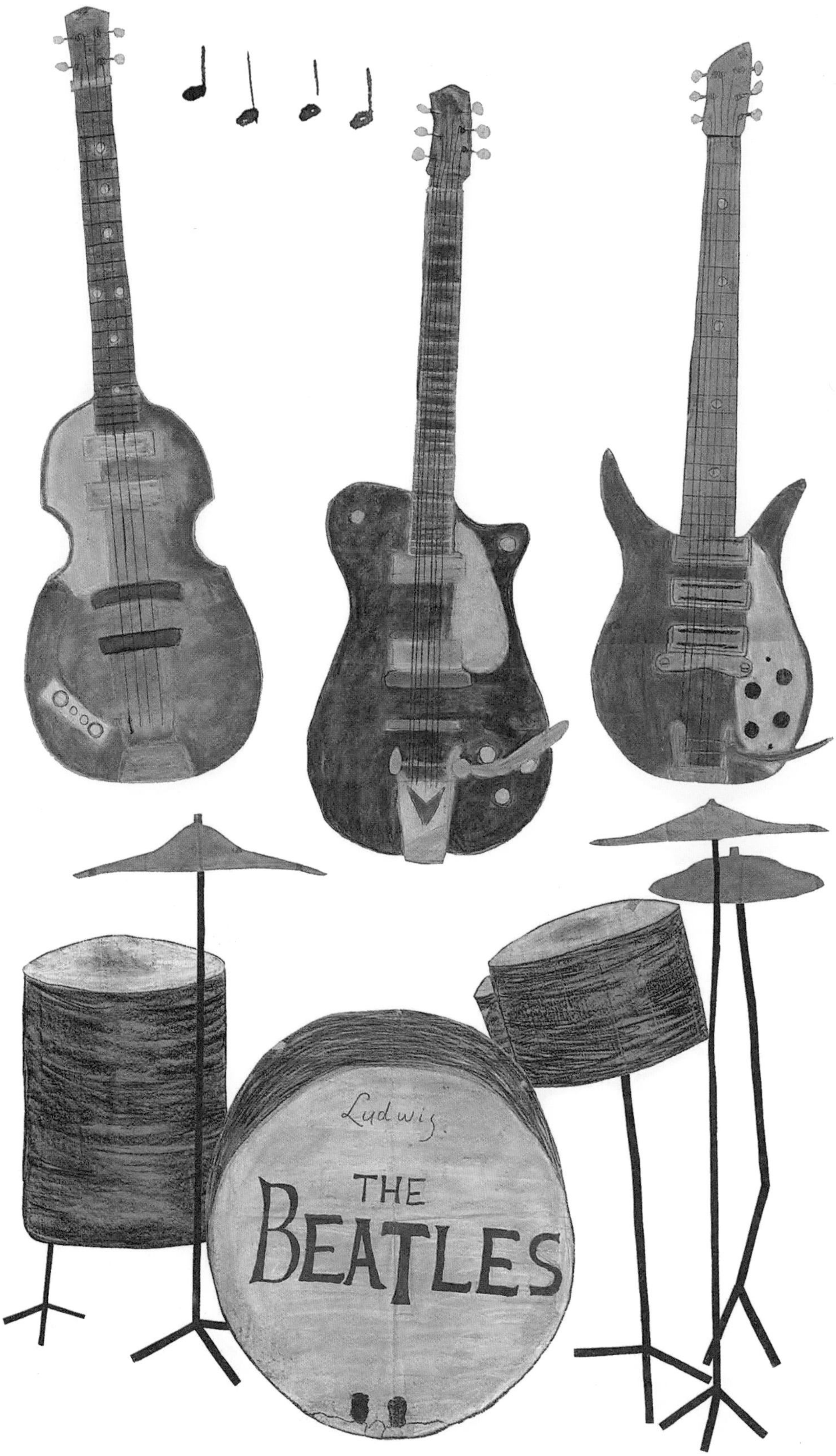
Ludwig
THE
BEATLES

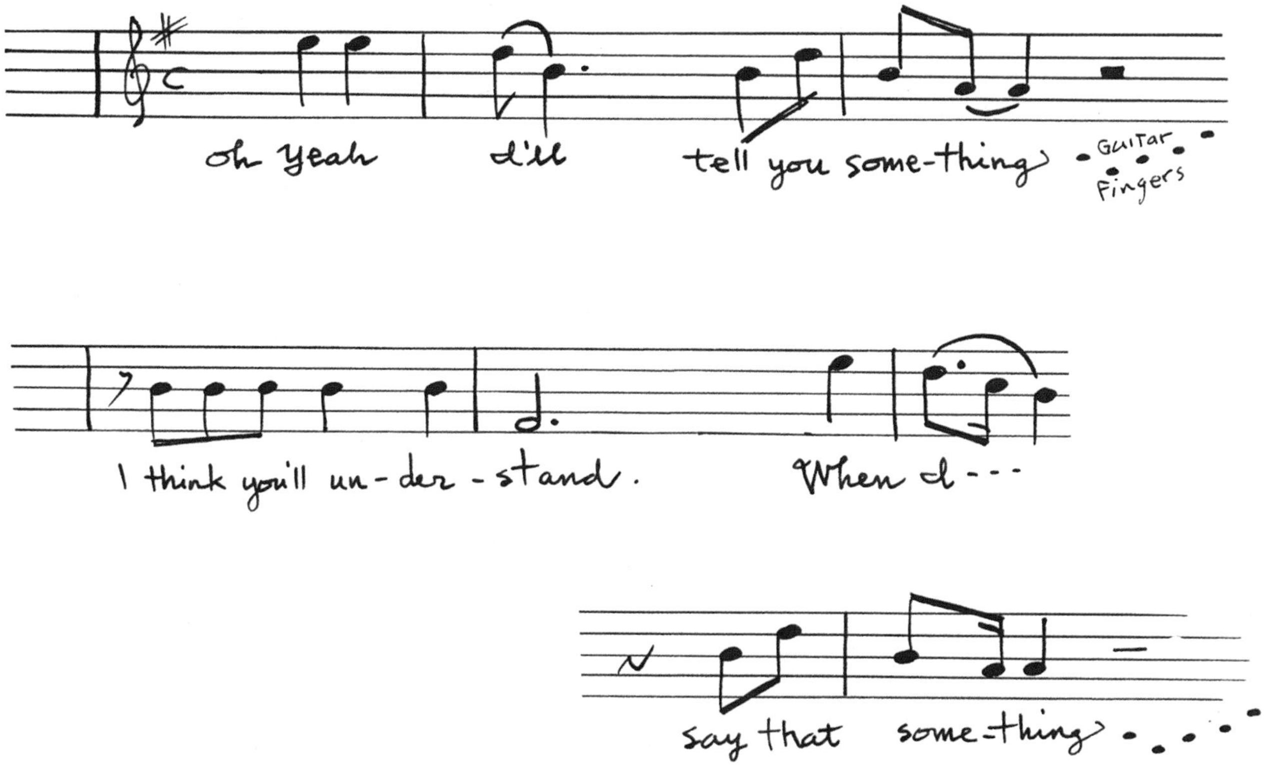
oh yeah I'll tell you some-thing
Guitar Fingers
I think you'll un-der-stand. When I - - -
say that some-thing

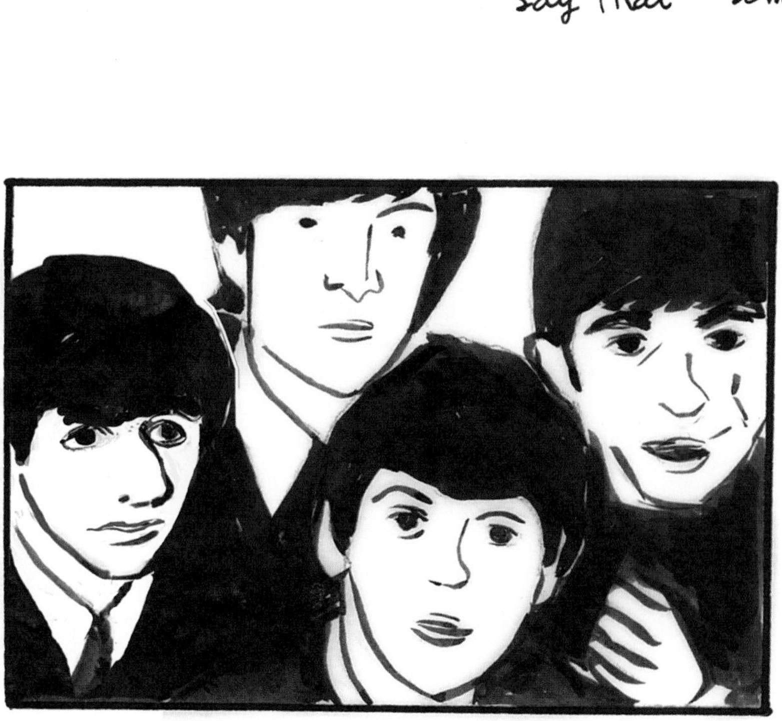

Introduction
Hunter Davies

What set the Beatles apart from other popular bands was that they attracted fans long before they were truly *The Beatles*. (the title of my biography of the group). Even before they had a record deal or went touring, they drove young girls in the Liverpool area wild. And when they hit Europe and the USA and Japan—and Mars—the mania simply spread to a larger audience.

When I was writing my book about the group, between 1966 and '69, countless fans in Liverpool, London, Hamburg, and New York shared with me their pearls of experience. Carol Tyler's memory of first hearing them, then seeing them, was echoed 'round the world. And it has never left her. That's what happens when we have passions and loves and madnesses and crushes at an early age.

Why have fans like Carol remembered those days, those feelings, so clearly and intensely? The simple answer is that it happened at a crucial stage in their early lives. But the other is that the Beatles are here forever. Back in the '60s, when they first made a splash, we could not have fathomed their staying power. I always assumed they would be superseded, that more successful groups would come along who would sell more records and have a more lasting cultural impact. But as it turns out, the Beatles were the most creative group pop music has ever known, ultimately leaving us around 100 tunes which will continue to inspire new fans as strongly as they did the young Carol Tyler in this graphic diary.

So, the Beatles are music history. Following the Beatles, writing about them, remembering how it felt to first hear them, in words and drawings and diary jottings, is social history. In this regard, I think the author of *Fab4 Mania* deserves a PhD, definitely…

Hunter Davies, one of the greatest living Beatles experts, is the author of *The Beatles Book*, *The Beatles*, *The Beatles Lyrics*, and *The Beatles – The Authorized Biography*.

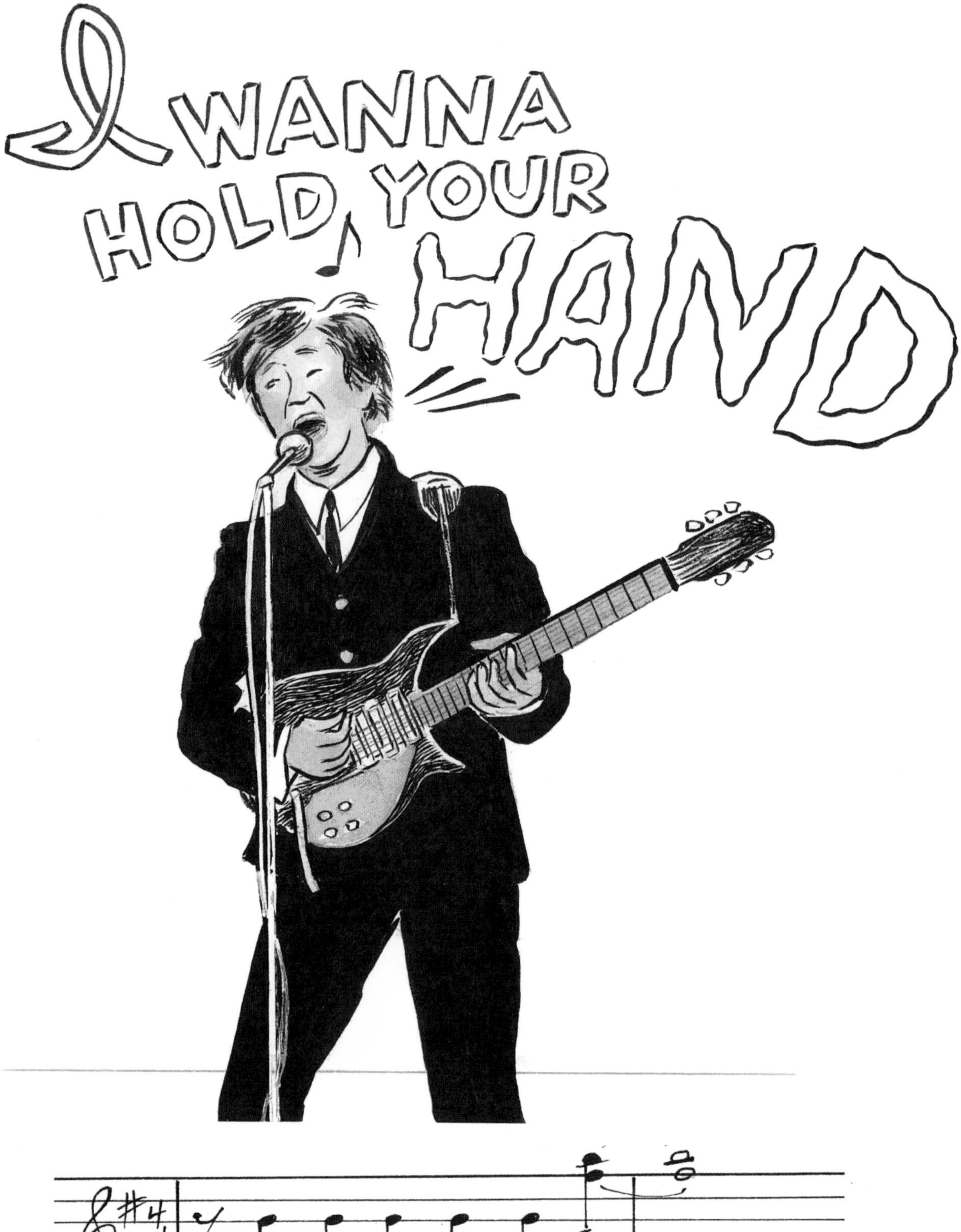
I WANNA
HOLD YOUR
HAND

♪ TABLE OF CONTENTS

♪ MUSICAL NOTE = PAGE NUMBER

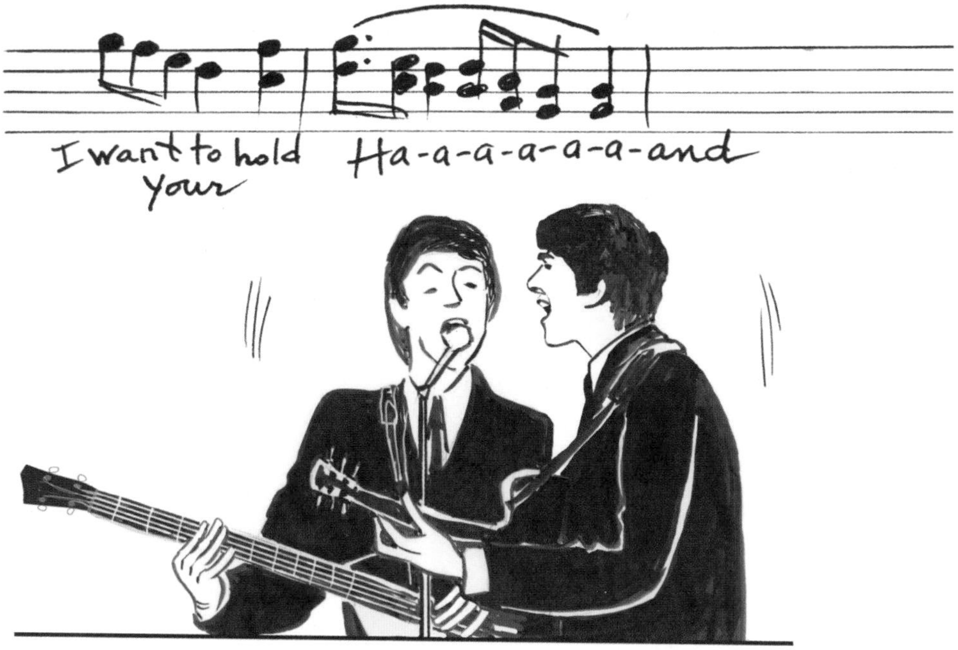
I want to hold your
Ha-a-a-a-a-a-and

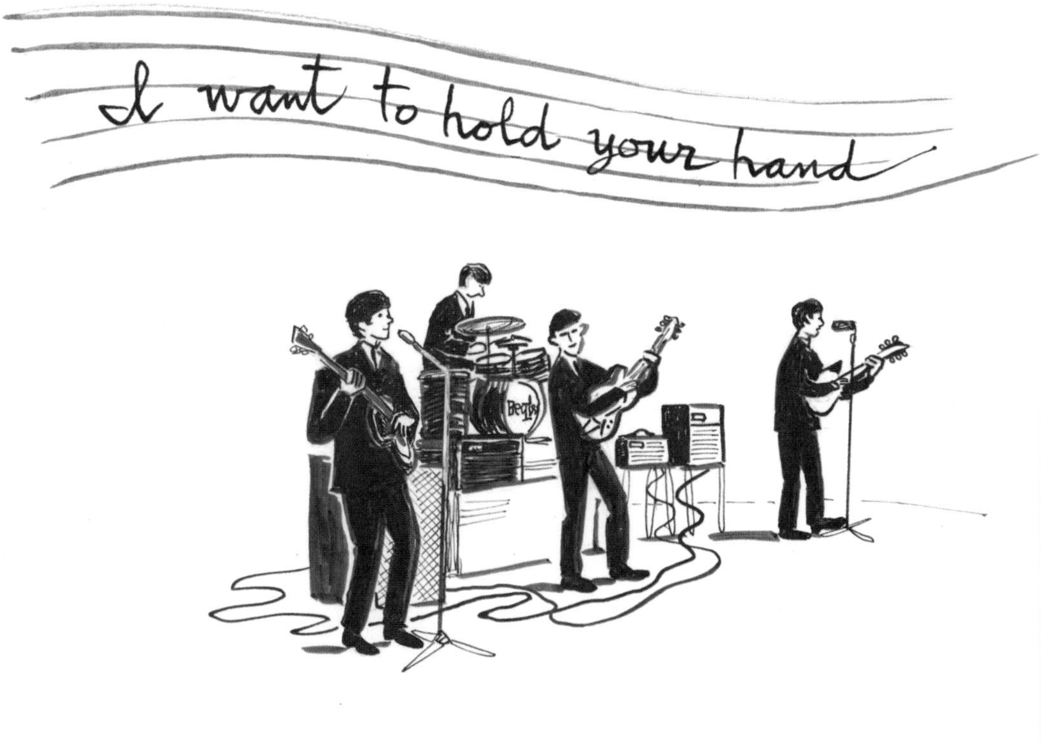
I want to hold your hand

1. IT'S LOVE, LUV

Carol Tyler

IN THE UNITED STATES.

Beatles Beatles Beatles Beatles -Beatles Beatles Beatles

Beatles Beatles Beatles Beatles Beatles Beatles Beatles

Beatles Beatles Beatles Beatles Beatles Beatles Beatles BEATLES

Beatles Beatles -Beatles Beatles Beatles Beatle Beatles BEATLES BEATLES-

Beatles Beatles Beatles Beatles Beatles Beatles Beatles BEATLES BEATLES- BEATLES

Beatles Beatles-Beatles Beatles Beatles Beatles Beatles BEATLES BEATLES- BEATLES

Beatles Beatles Beatles Beatles Beatles Beatles Beatles BEATLES BEATLES BEATLES

Beatles Beatles Beatles Beatles Beatles Beatles Beatles BEATLES BEATLES -BEATLES

Beatles Beatles Beatles Beatles Beatles Beatles Beatles BEATLES- BEATLES- BEATLES

Beatles Beatles Beatles Beatles Beatles Beatles Beatles BEATLES- BEATLES- BEATLES

Beatles Beatles Beatles Beatles Beatles Beatles Beatles BEATLES- BEATLES- BEATLES

Beatles Beatles Beatles Beatles Beatles Beatles Beatles BEATLES- BEATLES- BEATLES

Beatles Beatles Beatles Beatles Beatles Beatles Beatles BEATLES BEATLES- BEATLES

Beatles Beatles Beatles Beatles Beatle Beatles Beatles BEATLES BEATLES- BEATLES

Beatles Beatles Beatles Beatles Beatles Beatles Beatle BEATLES

Beatles Beatles Beatles Beatles Beatles Beatles Beatles BEATLES BEATLES- BEATLES

Beatles Beatles Beatles Beatles Beatle Beatles Beatles BEATLES BEATLES- BEATLCS

Beatles Beatles Beatles Beatles Beatles Beatles Beatles BEATLES BEATLES- Beatles

Beatles Beatles Beatles Beatles Beatles Beatles Beatles BEATLES BEATLES- Beatles

Beatles Beatles Beatles Beatles Beatles Beatles Beatles BEATLES BEATLES -Beatles

Beatles Beatles Beatles Beatle Beatles Beatles Beatles BEATLES BEATLES- Beatles

Beatles Beatles Beatles Beatles Beatles Beatles Beatles BEATLES BEATLES- Beatles

Beatles Beatles Beatles Beatles Beatles Beatles Beatles BEATLES BEATICS- Beatles

Beatles Beatles Beatles Beatles Beatles Beatles Beatles BEATLES BEATLES- Beatles

Beatles Beatles Beatles Beatles Beatles Beatles Beatle BEATLES BEATLES- Beatles

Beatles Beatles Beatles Beatles Beatles Beatles Beatles BEATLCS- Beatles

Beatles Beatles Beatles Beatles Beatles Beatles Beatles BEATLCS- Beatles

Beatles Beatles Beatles Beatles Beatles Beatles Beatles BEATLES -BEATLES

Beatles Beatles Beatles Beatles Beatles Beatles Beatles BEATLES -Beatles

Beatles Beatles Beatles Beatles Beatles Beatles Beatles Beatles BEATLES

BEATLES

Beatles Beatles Beatles Beatles Beatles Beatles Beatles Beatles
Beatles Beatles Beatles Beatles Beatles Beatles Beatles Beatles
Beatles Beatles Beatles Beatles Beatles Beatles Beatles Beatles

Beatles

(2)

beatles Beatles Beatles Beatles Beatles Beatles Beatles Beatles Beatles BEATLES
Beatles Beatles Beatles Beatles Beatles Beatles Beatles Beatles Beatles Beatles
Beatles Beatles Beatles Beatles Beatles Beatles Beatles Beatles Beatles Beatles
BEATLES Beatles Beatles Beatles Beatles Beatles Beatles Beatles Beatles Beatles
Beatles Beatles Beatles Beatles Beatles Beatles Beatles Beatles Beatles BEATLES
Beatles Beatles Beatles Beatles Beatles Beatles Beatles Beatles Beatles Beatles
Beatles Beatles Beatles Beatles Beatles Beatles Beatles Beatles Beatles Beatles
Beatles Beatles Beatles Beatles Beatles Beatles Beatles Beatles Beatles Beatles
Beatles Beatle Beatles Beatles Beatles Beatles Beatles Beatles Beatles Beatles
Beatles Beatle Beatles Beatles Beatles Beatles Beatles Beatles Beatles BEATLES
Beatles Beatles Beatles Beatles Beatles Beatles Beatles Beatles Beatles Beatles
Beatles Beatles Beatles Beatles Beatles Beatles Beatles Beatles Beatles Beatles
Beatles Beatles Beatles Beatles Beatles Beatles Beatles Beatles Beatles
Beatles Beatles Beatles Beatles Beatles Beatles Beatles Beatles Beatles Beatles
Beatles Beatles Beatles Beatles Beatles Beatles Beatles Beatles Beatles Beatles
Beatles Beatles Beatles Beatles Beatles Beatles Beatles Beatles Beatles Beatles
Beatles Beatles Beatles Beatles Beatles Beatles Beatles Beatles Beatles Beatles
Beatles Beatles Beatles Beatles Beatles Beatles Beatles Beatles Beatles Beatles
Beatles Beatles Beatles Beatles Beatles Beatles Beatles Beatles Beatles Beatles
Beatles Beatles Beatles Beatles Beatles Beatles Beatles Beatles Beatles Beatles
beatles Beatles Beatles Beatles Beatles Beatles Beatles Beatles Beatles Beatles
Beatles Beatles Beatles Beatles Beatles Beatles Beatles Beatles Beatles Beatles
Beatles Beatles Beatles Beatles Beatles Beatles Beatles Beatles Beatles Beatles
Beatles Beatles Beatles Beatles Beatles Beatles Beatles Beatles Beatles Beatles
Beatles Beatles Beatles Beatles Beatles Beatles Beatles Beatles Beatles
Beatles Beatles Beatles Beatles Beatles Beatles Beatles Beatles Beatles Beatles
Beatles Beatles Beatles Beatles Beatles Beatles Beatles Beatles Beatles Beatles

Beatles Beatles Beatles Beatles Beatles Beatles
Beatles Beatles Beatles Beatles (2)

Beatles Beatles Beatles Beatles Beatles Beatles Beatles Beatles Beatles Beatles
Beatles Beatles Beatles Beatles Beatles Beatles Beatles Beatles Beatles Beatles
Beatles Beatles Beatles Beatles Beatles Beatles Beatles Beatles Beatles Beatles
BEATLES Beatles Beatles Beatles Beatles Beatles Beatles Beatles Beatles Beatles
BEATLES Beatles Beatles Beatles Beatles Beatles Beatles Beatles Beatles Beatles
BEATLES Beatles Beatles Beatles Beatles Beatles Beatles Beatles Beatles Beatles
Beatles Beatles Beatles Beatles Beatles Beatles Beatles Beatles Beatles Beatles
Beatles Beatles Beatles Beatles Beatles Beatles Beatles Beatles Beatles Beatles
Beatles Beatles Beatles Beatles Beatles Beatles Beatles Beatles Beatles Beatles
Beatles Beatles Beatles Beatles Beatles Beatles Beatles Beatles Beatles Beatles
Beatles Beatles Beatles Beatles Beatles Beatles Beatles Beatles Beatles Beatles
Beatles Beatles Beatles Beatles Beatles Beatles Beatles Beatles Beatles Beatles
Beatles Beatles Beatles Beatles Beatles Beatles Beatles Beatles Beatles Beatles
Beatles Beatles Beatles Beatles Beatles Beatles Beatles Beatles Beatles Beatles
Beatles Beatles Beatles Beatles Beatles Beatles Beatles Beatles Beatles Beatles
Beatles Beatles Beatles Beatles Beatles Beatles Beatles Beatles Beatles Beatles
Beatles Beatles Beatles Beatles Beatles Beatles Beatles Beatles Beatles Beatles
Beatles Beatles Beatles Beatles Beatles Beatles Beatles Beatles Beatles Beatles
Beatles Beatles Beatles Beatles Beatles Beatles Beatles Beatles Beatles Beatles
Beatles Beatles Beatles Beatles Beatles Beatles Beatles Beatles Beatles Beatles
Beatles Beatles Beatles Beatles Beatles Beatles Beatles Beatles Beatles Beatles
Beatles Beatles Beatles Beatles Beatles Beatles Beatles Beatles Beatles Beatles
Beatles Beatles Beatles Beatles Beatles Beatles Beatles Beatles Beatles BEATLES
Beatles Beatles Beatles Beatles Beatles Beatles Beatles Beatles Beatles Beatles
Beatles Beatles Beatles Beatles Beatles Beatles Beatles Beatles Beatles BEATLES
Beatles Beatles Beatles Beatles Beatles Beatles Beatles Beatles Beatles Beatles
Beatles Beatles Beatles Beatles Beatles Beatles Beatles Beatles Beatles Beatles

Beatles Beatles Beatles Beatles Beatles Beatles Beatles Beatles Beatles Beatles
Beatles Beatles Beatles Beatles Beatles Beatles Beatles Beatles Beatles Beatles
Beatles Beatles Beatles Beatles Beatles Beatles Beatles Beatles Beatles Beatles
Beatles Beatles Beatles Beatles Beatles Beatles Beatles Beatles Beatles Beatles
Beatles Beatles Beatles Beatles Beatles Beatles Beatles Beatles Beatles Beatles
Beatles Beatles Beatles Beatles Beatles BEATLES Beatles Beatles Beatles Beatles
Beatles Beatles Beatles Beatles Beatles Beatles Beatles Beatles Beatles BEATLES
Beatles Beatles Beatles Beatles Beatles Beatles Beatles BEATLES

Beatles Beatles Beatles Beatles Beatles Beatles Beatles Beatles BEATLES
Beatles Beatles Beatles Beatles Beatles Beatles Beatles Beatles BEATLES
Beatles Beatles Beatles Beatles Beatles Beatles Beatles Beatles BEATES BEATLES
BEATLES Beatles Beatles Beatles Beatles Beatles Beatles Beatles BEATLES Beatles Beatles
Beatles Beatles Beatles Beatles Beatles Beatles Beatles Beatles Beatles Beatles
Beatles Beatles Beatles Beatles Beatles Beatles Beatles Beatles Beatles
Beatles Beatles Beatles Beatles Beatles Beatles Beatles Beatles Beatles BEATLES
Beatles Beatles Beatles Beatles Beatles Beatles Beatles Beatles Beatles BEATLES
Beatles Beatles Beatles Beatles Beatles Beatle Beatles Beatles Beatles BEATLES
Beatles Beatles Beatles Beatles Beatles Beatles Beatles Beatles Beatles BEATLE
Beatles Beatles Beatles Beatles Beatles Beatles Beatles Beatles BEATLES Beatles
Beatles Beatles Beatles Beatles Beatles Beatles Beatles Beatles Beatles Beatles
Beatles Beatles Beatles Beatles Beatles Beatles Beatles Beatles Beatles
Beatles Beatles Beatle Beatles Beatles Beatles Beatles Beatles Beatles Beatles
Beatles Beatles Beatles Beatles Beatles Beatles Beatle Beatles Beatles Beatles
Beatles Beatle Beatles Beatles Beatles Beatles Beatles Beatles Beatles Beatles
Beatles Beatles Beatles Beatles Beatles Beatle Beatles Beatles Beatles Beatles
Beatles Beatles Beatles Beatles Beatles Beatles Beatles Beatles Beatles Beatles
Beatles Beatles Beatles Beatles Beatles Beatles Beatles Beatles Beatles Beatles
Beatles Beatles Beatles Beatles Beatles Beatles Beatles Beatles Beatles Beatles
Beatle Beatles Beatles Beatles Beatles Beatles Beatles Beatle Beatles Beatles
Beatles Beatle Beatles Beatles Beatles Beatles Beatles Beatles Beatles Beatles
Beatles Beatles Beatles Beatles Beatles Beatles Beatles Beatles Beatles BEATLES
Beatles Beatles Beatles Beatles Beatles Beatles Beatles Beatles Beatles Beatles
Beatles Beatles Beatles Beatles Beatles Beatles Beatles Beatles Beatles Beatles
Beatles Beatles Beatles Beatles Beatles Beatles Beatles Beatles Beatles BEATLE
Beatles Beatles Beatles Beatles Beatles Beatles Beatles Beatles Beatles BEATLES BEATLE

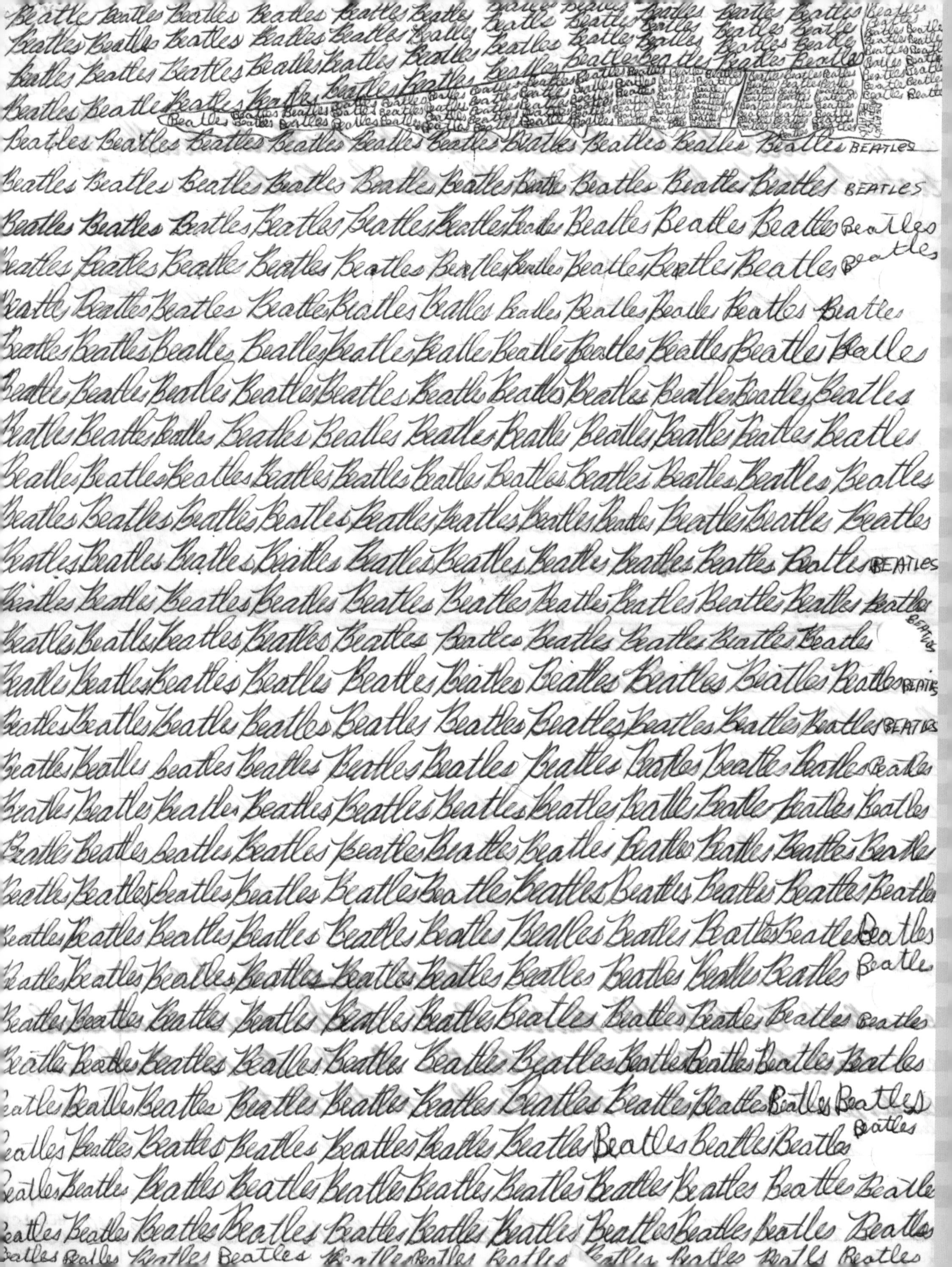
Beatles Beatles Beatles Beatles Beatles Beatles Beatles Beatles Beatles Beatles Beatles
Beatles Beatles Beatles Beatles Beatles Beatles Beatles Beatles Beatles Beatles Beatles
Beatles Beatles Beatles Beatles Beatles Beatles Beatles Beatles Beatles Beatles Beatles
Beatles Beatles Beatles Beatles Beatles Beatles Beatles Beatles Beatles Beatles Beatles
Beatles Beatles Beatles Beatles Beatles Beatles Beatles Beatles Beatles Beatles BEATLES
Beatles Beatles Beatles Beatles Beatles Beatles Beatles Beatles Beatles Beatles BEATLES
Beatles Beatles Beatles Beatles Beatles Beatles Beatles Beatles Beatles Beatles Beatles
Beatles Beatles Beatles Beatles Beatles Beatles Beatles Beatles Beatles Beatles Beatles
Beatles Beatles Beatles Beatles Beatles Beatles Beatles Beatles Beatles Beatles Beatles
Beatles Beatles Beatles Beatles Beatles Beatles Beatles Beatles Beatles Beatles Beatles
Beatles Beatles Beatles Beatles Beatles Beatles Beatles Beatles Beatles Beatles Beatles
Beatles Beatles Beatles Beatles Beatles Beatles Beatles Beatles Beatles Beatles Beatles
Beatles Beatles Beatles Beatles Beatles Beatles Beatles Beatles Beatles Beatles BEATLES
Beatles Beatles Beatles Beatles Beatles Beatles Beatles Beatles Beatles Beatles Beatles
Beatles Beatles Beatles Beatles Beatles Beatles Beatles Beatles Beatles Beatles BEATLES
Beatles Beatles Beatles Beatles Beatles Beatles Beatles Beatles Beatles Beatles Beatles BEATLES
Beatles Beatles Beatles Beatles Beatles Beatles Beatles Beatles Beatles Beatles BEATLES
Beatles Beatles Beatles Beatles Beatles Beatles Beatles Beatles Beatles Beatles Beatles
Beatles Beatles Beatles Beatles Beatles Beatles Beatles Beatles Beatles Beatles Beatles
Beatles Beatles Beatles Beatles Beatles Beatles Beatles Beatles Beatles Beatles Beatles
Beatles Beatles Beatles Beatles Beatles Beatles Beatles Beatles Beatles Beatles Beatles
Beatles Beatles Beatles Beatles Beatles Beatles Beatles Beatles Beatles Beatles Beatles
Beatles Beatles Beatles Beatles Beatles Beatles Beatles Beatles Beatles Beatles Beatle
Beatles Beatles Beatles Beatles Beatles Beatles Beatles Beatles Beatles Beatles Beatles
Beatles Beatles Beatles Beatles Beatles Beatles Beatles Beatles Beatles Beatles Beatles
Beatles Beatles Beatles Beatles Beatles Beatles Beatles Beatles Beatles Beatles Beatles Beatles
Beatles Beatles Beatles Beatles Beatles Beatles Beatles Beatles Beatles Beatles Beatles
Beatles Beatles Beatles Beatles Beatles Beatles Beatles Beatles Beatles Beatles Beatles
Beatles Beatles Beatles Beatles Beatles Beatles Beatles Beatles Beatles Beatles Beatles
Beatles Beatles Beatles Beatles Beatles Beatles Beatles Beatles Beatles Beatles Beatles

Beatles Beatles

=101

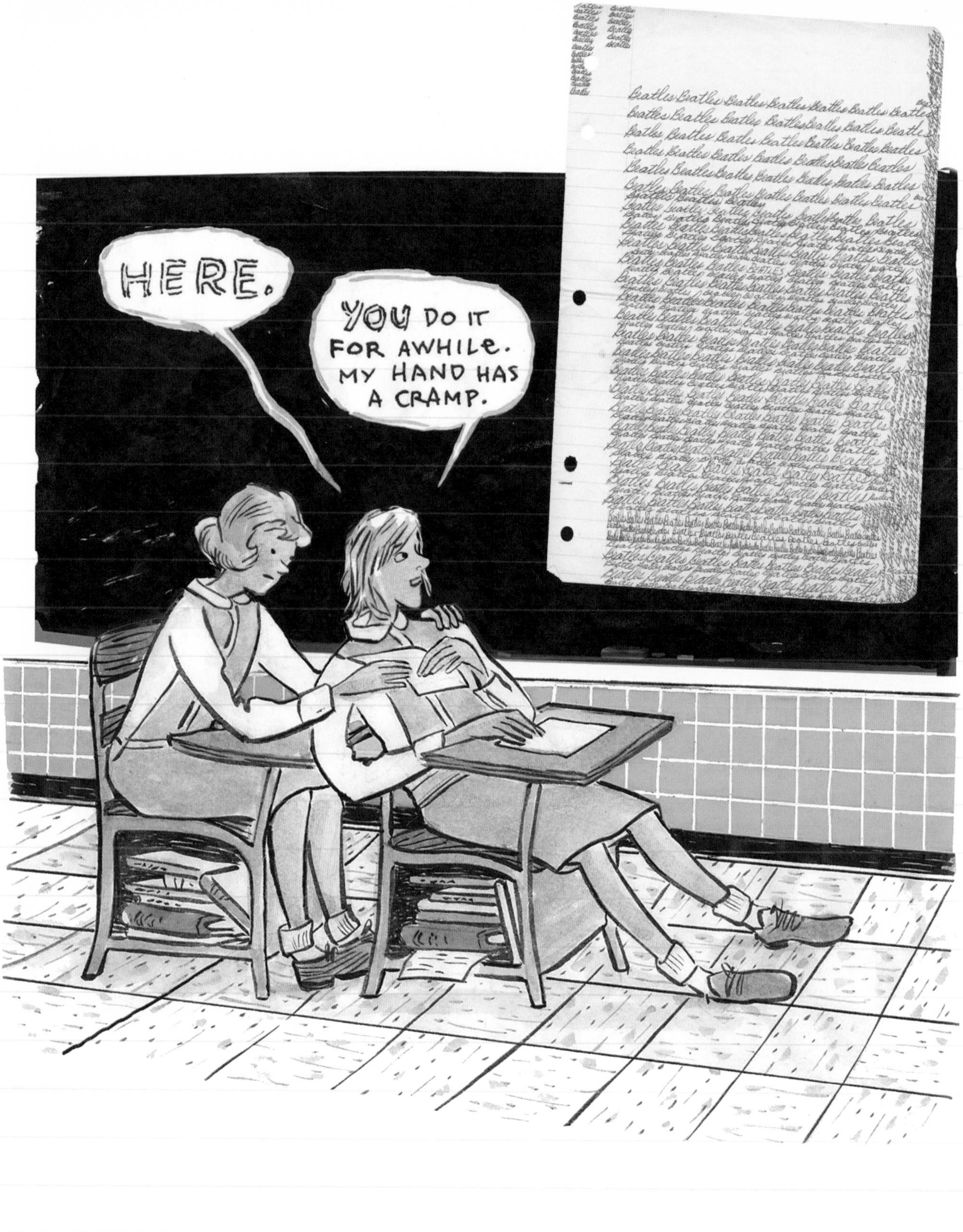
HERE.
YOU DO IT FOR AWHILE. MY HAND HAS A CRAMP.

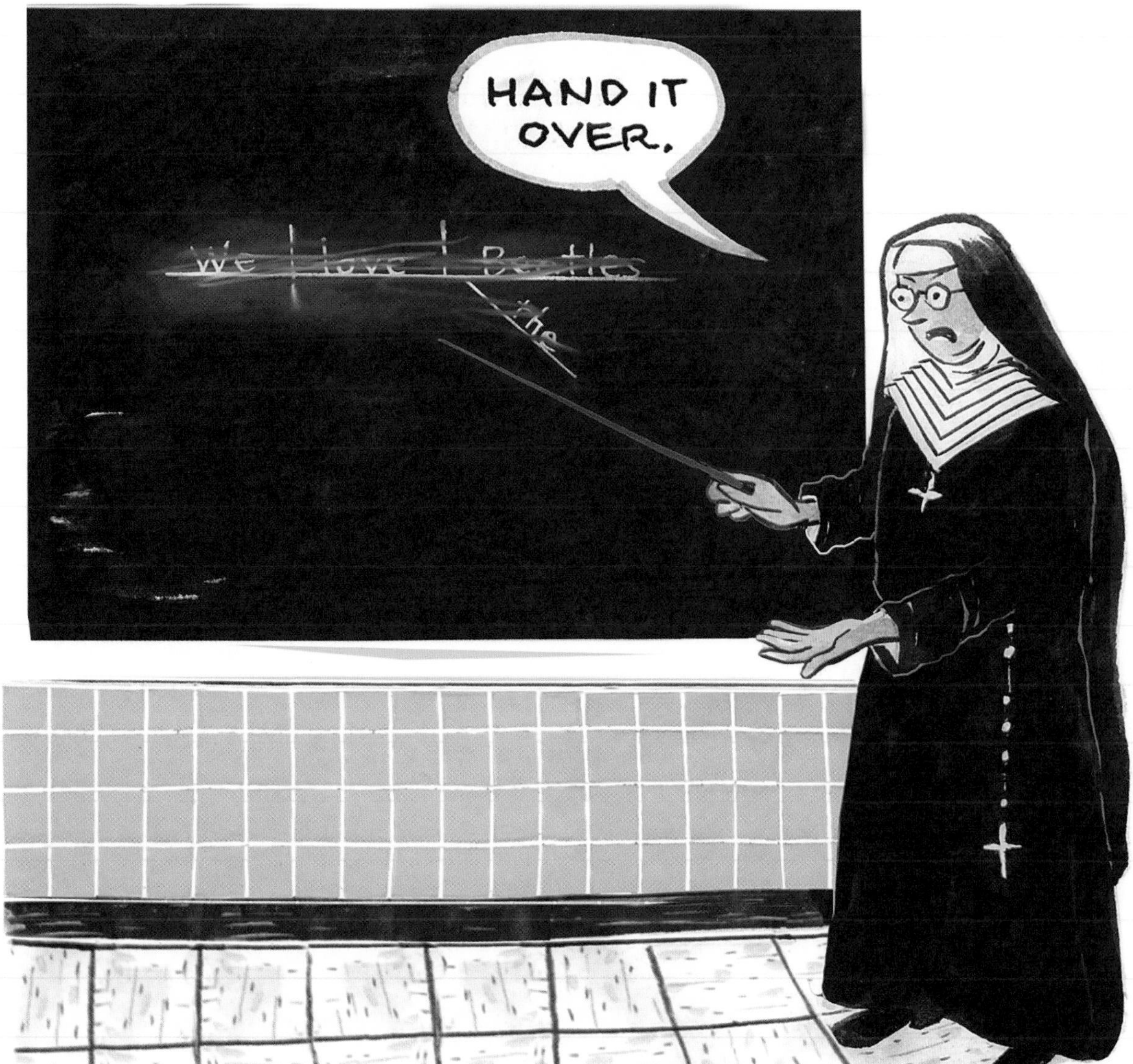
HAND IT OVER.
We love Beatles
the

All My Loving

Yup! That's the way it was last year with my OBSESSION. My life as a Beatlemaniac began on February 9, 1964. Ever since then, my life has revolved around the **FAB 4**, their music, everything English, and anything mod or British styled. At school, at home, at supper — every moment of every day.

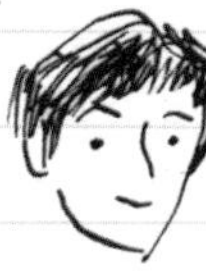

Why do I *Love* them so much? For starters, they're so Cute. And the music is so Good! Like nothing I've ever heard before. SO much *Style and Talent*. The *Beatles* make me feel like I'm alive. I actually exist! I feel so happy inside, but I can hide it — I Must. I must keep it private. It's **LOVE**, Luv.

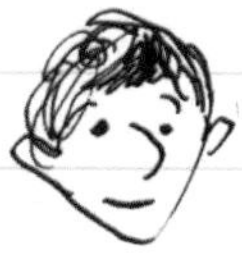

I remember my life before Feb. 9, '64. Pretty BLAH. Pretty much who cares about that 3rd kid in the family. Mom's busy and pays no attention. Dad's busy, too. My big sister Ginia works, too, at *Jewel Foods*. She's a cashier. She's mean to me. So is my big brother Joe. They either ignore me or tell me to shut up and go away. Why would I share ANY feelings with them? My baby brother Jim is pals with our dog Gu (say 'Guh.') I have no idea what anyone thinks about my boys ♥ John ♥ Paul ♥ George ♥ Ringo.

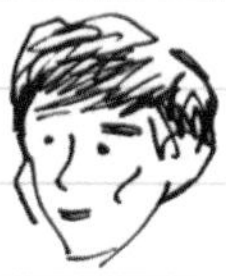

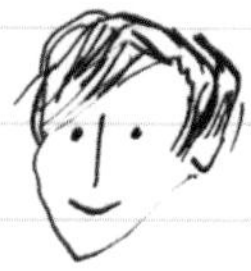

On the night I mentioned, Feb 9 '64, I was sitting in the living room with my family and we were watching the Ed Sullivan Show.

THEN THE LIGHTNING STRUCK, RIGHT AFTER I HEARD PAUL SING "Close your eyes and I'll kiss You..." THE BOLT OF LIGHTNING WAS SO BRIGHT, NOBODY ELSE WAS IN THE ROOM, IT BLANCHED THEM OUT, LEAVING ME ALONE WITH THEM. I MEAN JUST THOSE WORDS DELIVERED STRAIGHT TO ME IN OUR LIVING ROOM, I WAS AWESTRUCK!

Giant arrows pointing at them all around.

ED SULLIVAN SAID IT LIKE THIS:

The BEAT-les.

BeaTles

ON THE DRUMS, THE "T" WAS LONGER THAN THE OTHER LETTERS.

Me, stunned and ecstatic.

It WENT BY SO QUICKLY AND YET THIS WHITE-HOT HEAT INSIDE ME HAS NOT FADED. NOR WILL IT EVER BECAUSE THE LEVEL OF MY DEVOTION IS REALLY BIG AND CENTRAL. Here is a list of what they sang that night:

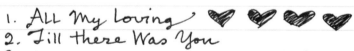

1. ALL My Loving ♥ ♥ ♥ ♥
2. Till there Was You
3. SHE Loves You — Yeah Yeah Yeah
4. I Saw Her STANDING There
5. I Want to Hold Your HAND.

I HAD TO GET UP FOR SCHOOL THE NEXT DAY BUT I COULD HARDLY SLEEP. I COULDN'T TAKE MY EYES OFF THE PICTURE. What Picture? LET ME EXPLAIN.

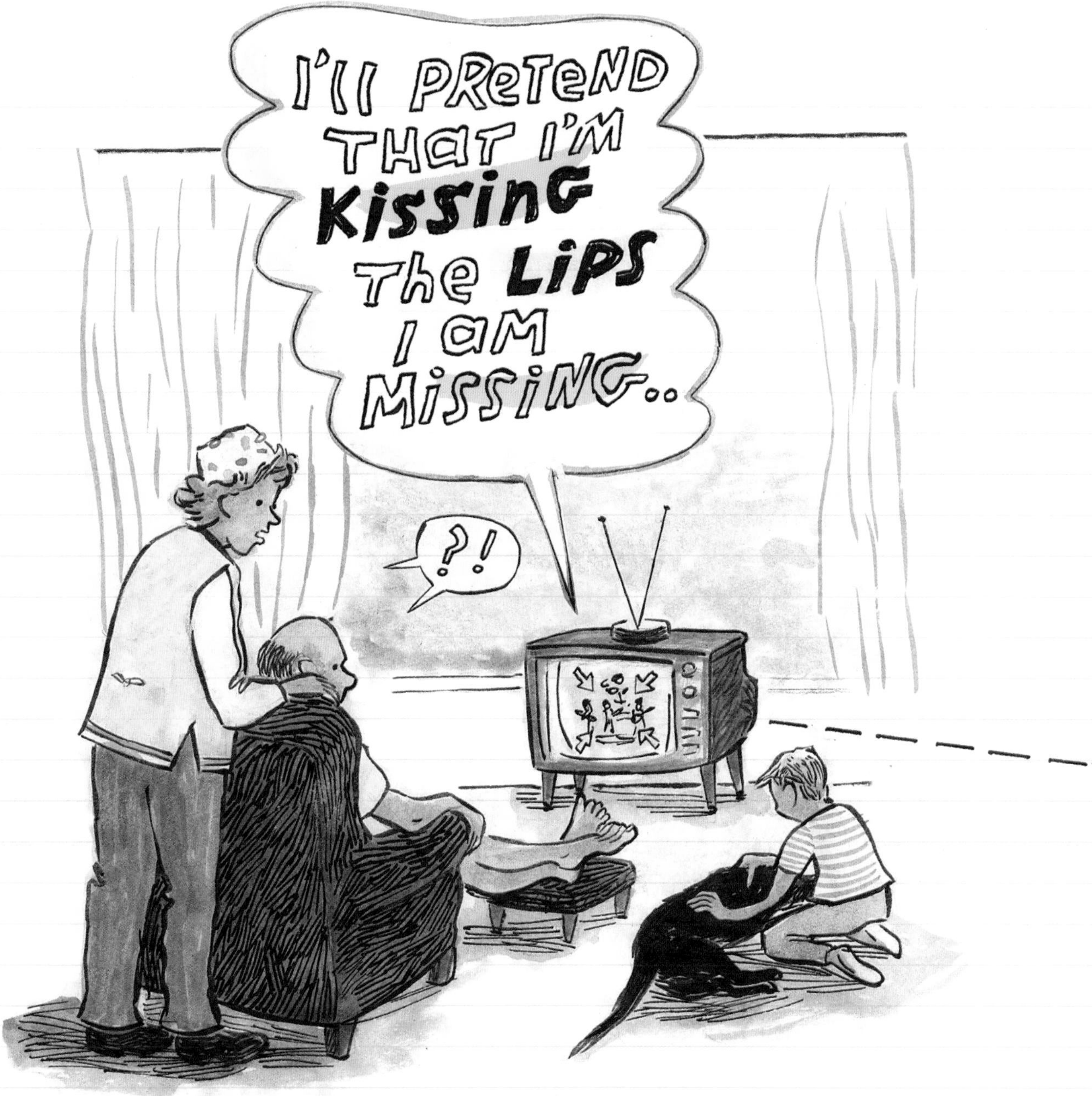
I'll PRETEND THAT I'M KISSING The LIPS I am MISSING..
?!

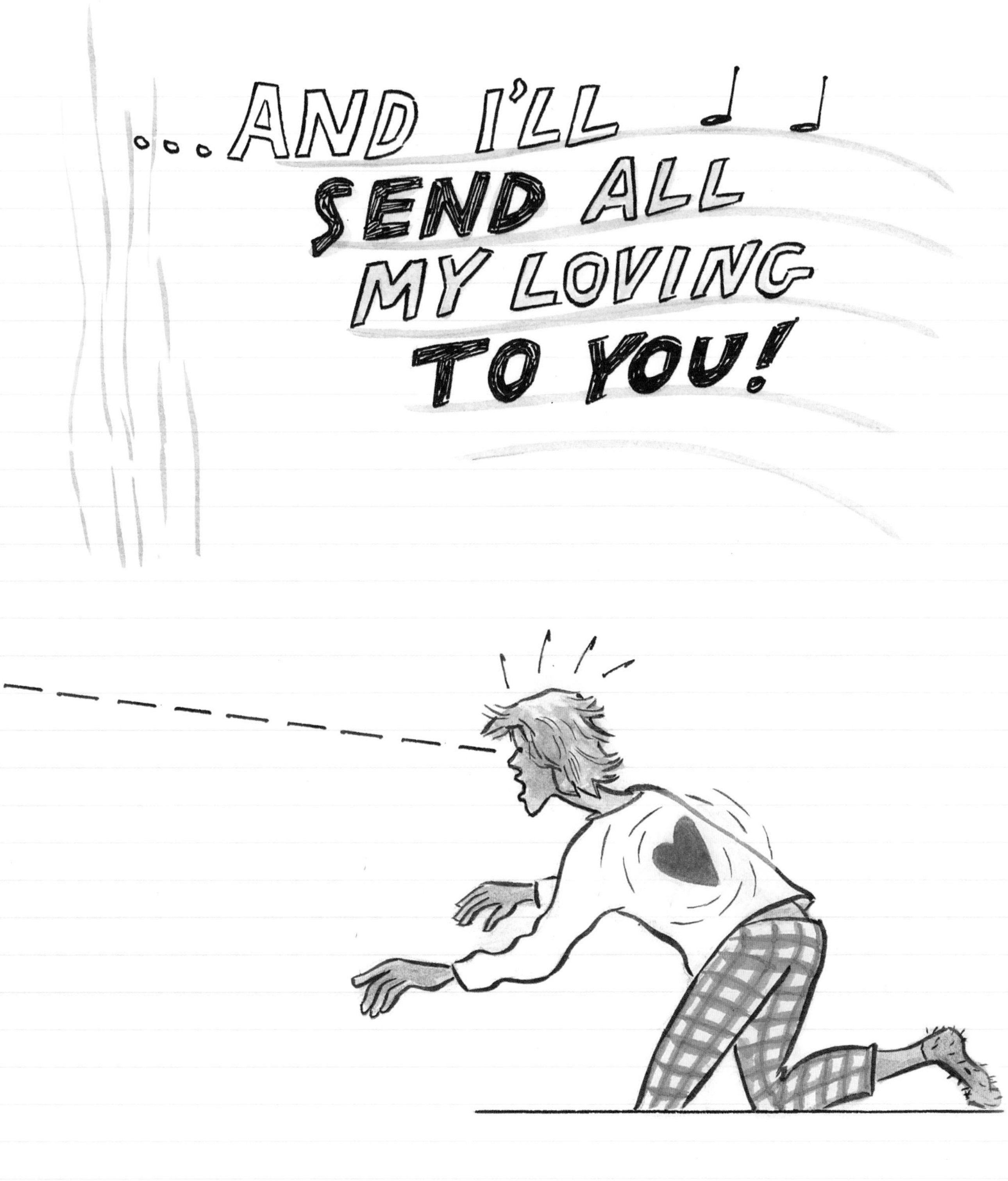
...AND I'LL
SEND ALL
MY LOVING
TO YOU!

My BROTHER JOE HAS 2 FRIENDS FROM SCHOOL. THEY ALL PLAY FOOTBALL AT Carmel, THE CATHOLIC HIGH SCHOOL, BOYS ON ONE SIDE, GIRLS ON THE OTHER LIBRARY, CAFETERIA, AND GYM ARE SHARED. BRAND NEW SCHOOL. I'M SUPPOSED TO GO THERE NEXT YEAR. LONG COMMUTE, BUT IT'S THE ONLY CATHOLIC SCHOOL IN THE COUNTY AND THE **COOLEST** SCHOOL AROUND, ALL SURFS GO THERE, NO GREASER PUNKS. COLLEGE PREP. JOE AND HIS FRIENDS ARE ALWAYS UP TO STUFF. SO MANY TIMES THEY HEARD "You three" or "You three boys" (as in troublemakers), that THEY DECIDED TO CALL THEMSELVES THE "TRINITY." THEY'RE LIKE A PACT, Joe, Jamie, and Rudy. They do EVERYTHING TOGETHER. Jockaholics.

Anyway, Jamie came over after supper with HIS NEW 45. IT WAS THE Beatles RECORD THAT HAD "I Want to Hold your Hand" on one side and on the other "I Saw Her Standing There." I WAS DOING CLEAN UP AFTER SUPPER, CLEANING OFF THE TABLE AND THEY STARTED GOOFING AROUND, Joe AND HIS PALS. I DIDN'T REALLY ACTUALLY SEE THE JACKET COVER AT FIRST. HE STARTED TO PLAY THE RECORD BUT THEN MY DAD SAID TO TURN THAT CRAP OFF. I HEARD A LITTLE OF IT, JUST THE FIRST PART OF "Hand" AND WAS STOPPED IN MID PLATE STACKING. I WAS STANDING THERE AND JAMIE HOLLERED OUT "Sorry Mr. Tyler. They're going to be on Sullivan tonight anyway." IF Jamie WOULD'VE LOOKED OVER AT ME, HE'D'VE SEEN ME STANDING THERE WITH MY Mouth wide open!

Right Away THE PROGRAM CAME ON. LIKE I SAID, WHEN PAUL STARTED WITH "Close Your Eyes," I WAS FOREVER THEIRS. THEIR HAIR, THE WAY THEY SHOOK THEIR HEADS AROUND, THE LOOKS THEY GAVE, THEIR SUITS, THEIR BOOTS TAPPING TIME, THEIR SMILES, HOW THEY BOUNCED AND WERE HAVING FUN, AND WERE **NEW** — — ALL OF THIS COMING AT ME AT ONCE ----- I HAD NEVER BEEN IN LOVE BEFORE, BUT NOW I HAD NEW HEARTBEATS.

Anyway, BETWEEN THE FIRST SET OF SONGS AND THE SECOND HALF, I WENT OVER TO THE STEREO AND TOOK THE RECORD JACKET FROM WHERE IT WAS LYING THERE ON TOP OF THE CONSOLE. NOBODY WAS AROUND. **I HAD TO HAVE A PICTURE OF THE BEATLES!** I BROUGHT IT OVER TO WHERE I WAS SITTING ON THE COUCH, STUCK IT UNDER THE CUSHION, AND PLOPPED ON TOP OF IT TILL THE END OF THE SHOW. I WAS <u>SO</u> THRILLED. AND I COULDN'T SHOW IT OR GET UP OFF THE COUCH AFTER, BECAUSE THE TRINITY WAS TEARING THE HOUSE UP, LOOKING FOR THAT JACKET. I JUST SAT THERE LIKE I WAS SO BORED, BUT INSIDE I FELT LIKE THIS:

I PUT ON A BIG BOREDOM ACT SO I COULD KEEP THAT PICTURE. LATER, AFTER EVERYONE LEFT, I STARED AT IT UP IN MY ROOM UNTIL MY EYE-

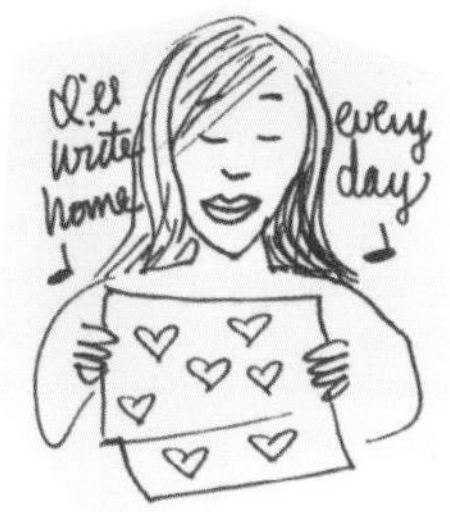
I'll write home every day

BALLS JUST ABOUT FELL OUT. TOOK IT TO SCHOOL THE NEXT DAY BUT HAD TO BE CAREFUL. THE NUNS SPENT THAT WHOLE REST OF THE YEAR TAKING AWAY KIDS' BEATLES PICTURES, CARDS, (especially cards) AND MAGAZINES. (The nuns have a LOT of cards.) I FIGURED OUT HOW TO FOLD IT UP AND HIDE IT INSIDE MY UNIFORM. I NEVER TOOK IT OUT AT SCHOOL, JUST HAD IT WITH ME IN CASE OF A BEATLES EMERGENCY. OTHERWISE, IT WAS UNDER MY PILLOW WHEN I SLEPT.

EVENTUALLY I GOT LOTS MORE PICTURES OUT OF MAGAZINES, AND SOMETIMES MOM WOULD FIND ONE IN THE NEWSPAPER. THEN I STARTED BUYING CARDS. 5¢ PACKS, AND THEY CAME WITH BUBBLE GUM THAT WAS LOUSY.

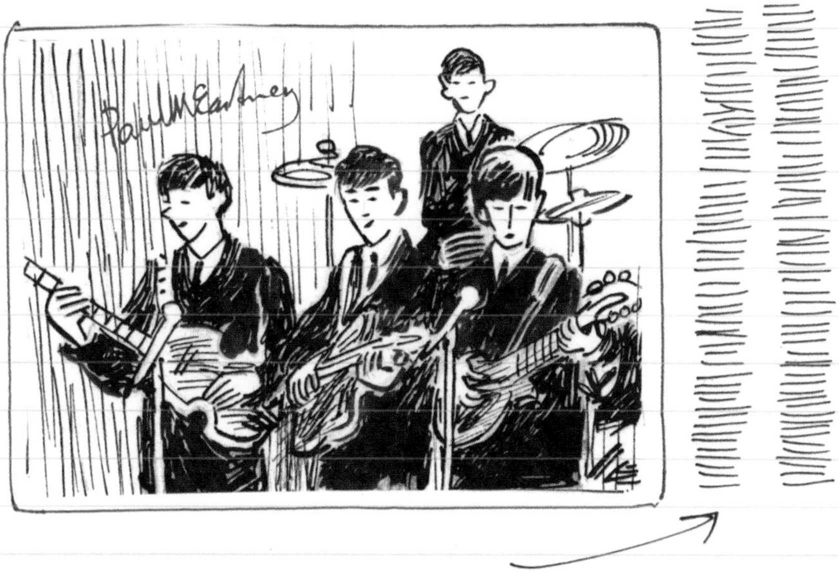
Paul McCartney

2 GIANT STACKS OF CARDS, THAT'S WHAT I HAVE NOW THAT I SORT THROUGH EVERY SO OFTEN

THE BIG SEEK

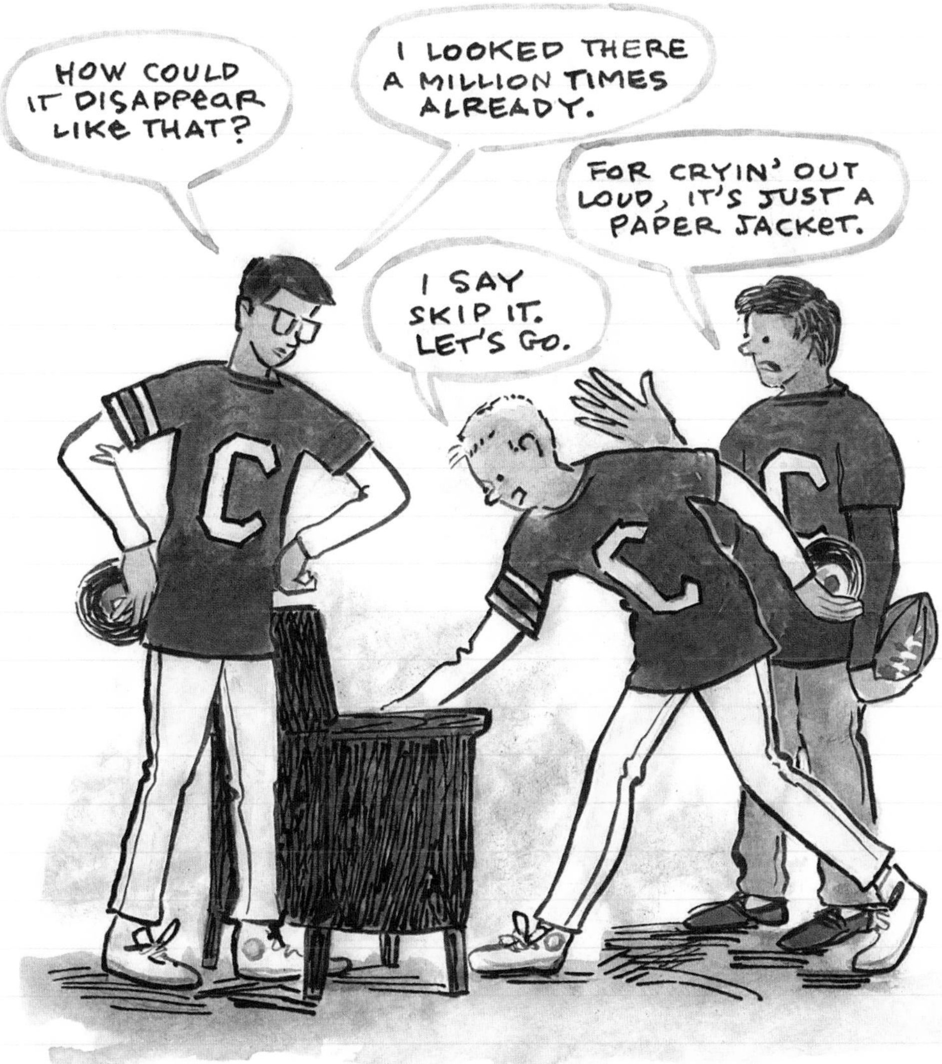
HOW COULD IT DISAPPEAR LIKE THAT?
I LOOKED THERE A MILLION TIMES ALREADY.
FOR CRYIN' OUT LOUD, IT'S JUST A PAPER JACKET.
I SAY SKIP IT. LET'S GO.

WAITING IT OUT

THE BEATLES
I SAW HER STANDING THERE
I WANT TO HOLD YOUR HAND

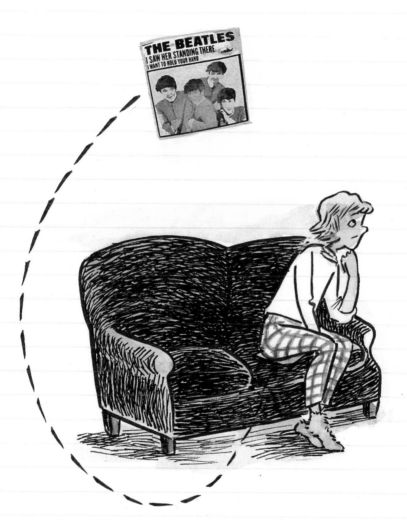

Little Miss Muffet Sat on a Beatles picture!

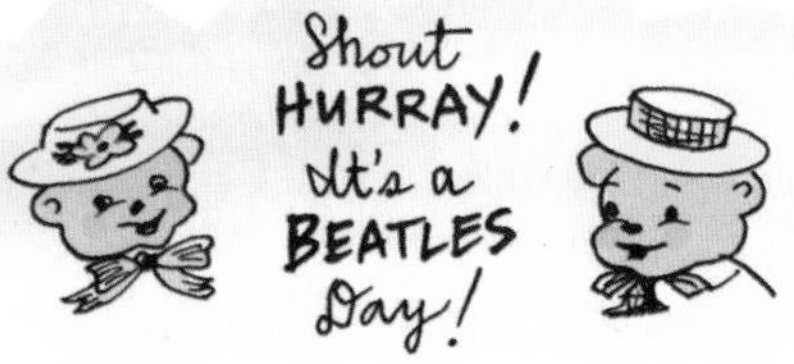
Shout
HURRAY!
It's a
BEATLES
Day!

like the card catalog at the library. I can't stop looking at their sweet faces.

I've got so many pictures on my walls now a year later. It's hard to believe just how many I have. Big posters, small magazine pics and cards filling in the spaces where the bigger pictures didn't fit. Mom brings her card club ladies up to see the progress. I'm aiming to cover every wall. e-ventually.

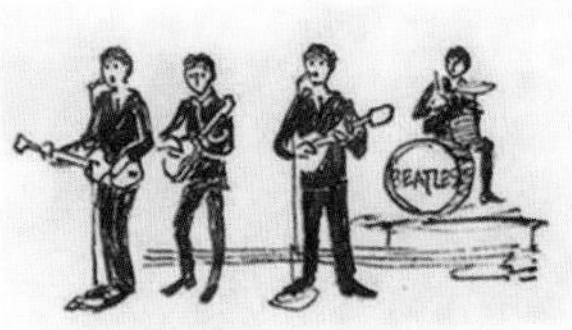
BEATLES

Our school is brand new and we are the very first eighth grade. That's why everything in the next six months is **VERY** important. You see, Sister Immaculata told us that when there's an event or something big that happens, you should make it into a keepsake booklet. Last year, she had our class make Vatican II books. We put all the information down on paper in our best handwriting and then made nice covers with a dove on the front.

Vatican II is about changes in the church. Like open the window, things are fresh and new. Our school, St. Bedes, has lots of windows, and all the classrooms are built around a small, open courtyard, like a square donut, it has a hole in the middle. Nice colors, too. Blue and aqua and silver and white mosaic pieces are on the

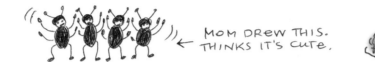 MOM DREW THIS. THINKS IT'S CUTE. ←  ←Saturday Food

WALLS WHEN YOU FIRST COME IN. THE ONLY OTHER TIME I SAW THOSE PRETTY, SHIMMERY COLORS TOGETHER LIKE THAT WAS IN THIS COOL DREAM. I WAS ON AN AIRPLANE AND I WAS GOING SOMEWHERE — ALL GROWN UP. MAYBE SOMEDAY I'LL GET TO GO ON A PLANE.

So — WHAT I'M TRYING TO SAY IS, EVERYTHING IS ABOUT NEW. We're NEW TO THE AREA, SORT OF (WE LIVED IN BROWN OLD BRICK CHICAGO FOR A long TIME. POLLUTION, TRAFFIC, AND NOISE. MY BABY BROTHER WAS BORN IN 1960. THAT'S WHEN WE MOVED OUT HERE.) I LIKE IT OUT HERE, SO CLEAN AND NEW. THE CHURCH CHANGES ARE NEW. And the BEATLES! FRESH and NEW. THEY COME FROM England WHICH IS New TO ME. IT SEEMS LIKE A CHEERFUL PLACE. EVERY TIME I PASS THE TILES UP THERE IN THE LOBBY, everything FEELS NEW AND AHEAD OF ME, AND I AM IN THE FIRST EIGHTH. I HOPE MY FIRST PLANE RIDE IS TO Liverpool! GONNA GRADUATE IN June.

Back to booklet making for a sec: MOM said to GO AHEAD AND MAKE A BOOKLET ABOUT 8th GRADE AND "BEETLE-MANIA" (she calls it), BUT I CAN'T USE MY SCHOOL PAPER. GOTTA USE THE PAPER FROM DAD'S OLD PLUMBING BUSINESS THEY HAD BACK IN CHICAGO. AND USE UP THE OFFICE SUPPLIES. I'LL HAVE TO COVER UP THE TOP PART WITH GUMMED LABELS AND SOME OTHER STUFF THEY HAD. BOXES AND BOXES OF IT. HE WORKS FOR SOME GUY NOW. PLENTY OF WORK. PLENTY OF LABELS AND PAPER. AND PANCAKES. TIME TO GRAB A STACK!

CHARLES W. TYLER
PLUMBING CONTRACTOR
1837 WEST ADDISON ST.
CHICAGO 13, ILL.

● 2

Tonight, a very special thing happened. I won the **TRAFFIC SAFETY POSTER CONTEST** out of the Whole REGION, which came as a shock.

A couple of months ago, Sister told us about the contest. We were each to come up with an idea and then make a poster. We're a new school and Sister wants us to get known.

So, I went home and told Mom about it. I was having a hard time coming up with an idea. Laurie right away figured hers out: an elephant with its trunk around a RR X-ing sign that says "Don't Forget to Stop and Look Both Ways." That's because the Milwaukee Road comes right through Ingleside and there are no automatic railroad gates. Some crashes have happened. I mean, that's not the worst problem out here. People falling through the ice, drownings, and boating accidents. Car crashes, too, and accidental falls also. Regardless, I thought her poster was the best because the elephant had nice eyes.

Mom was at the sink doing the dishes. Then she said, "How about *Let Safety Be Your Guiding Light.*" That sounded pretty good, so I went to my room to work on it. Then I started to feel **BAD** because I didn't come up with that idea by myself. It was **MOM'S** idea. But I don't drive, so how am I supposed to know about traffic safety? Why are they asking KIDS?!

Jan. 27, 1965

23

I'm a Loser

I went ahead and did the poster anyway with my pastels. It took me 2 evenings. I had my radio to keep me company. Worked slow and steady so it didn't smear. When I took it to school, Janice said it was really dumb and thought hers would win. Speeding. It was pretty good, so between hers and Laurie's I didn't think I would have a chance.

Then Mom said for me to dress nice like it was Sunday for church, but that I could sit with my friends. I told Barb and Janet that I wanted to be in the balcony because I felt so guilty about it being Mom's idea. Shame seating. Laurie had to sit with her younger brother and his friends.

Super cold night 10°

It came time to award the prizes. I couldn't believe it! They kept calling my name. (I call your name♩). There'd be a category and they'd call second place, first place, then top winner. I won every category, and each time I had to walk/skip/hurry-up down this long aisle to the stage and then go back to my seat. After the third time, I started crying because I couldn't believe it — there must be a mistake, and yet I couldn't stop smiling even though I felt ashamed. Nobody knew my secret except Laurie who said "Congratulations, but that was your Mom's idea."

Who?

Her again?

Wha?

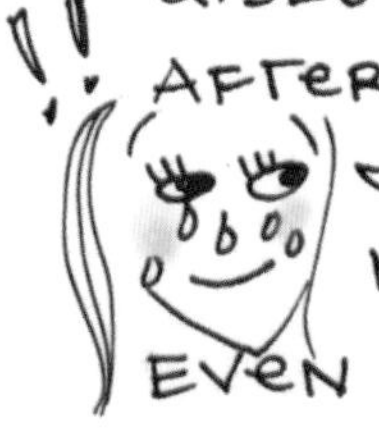

The Fox Lake Press came to school the next day and took my picture with the trophy.

GRAND PRIZE WINNER

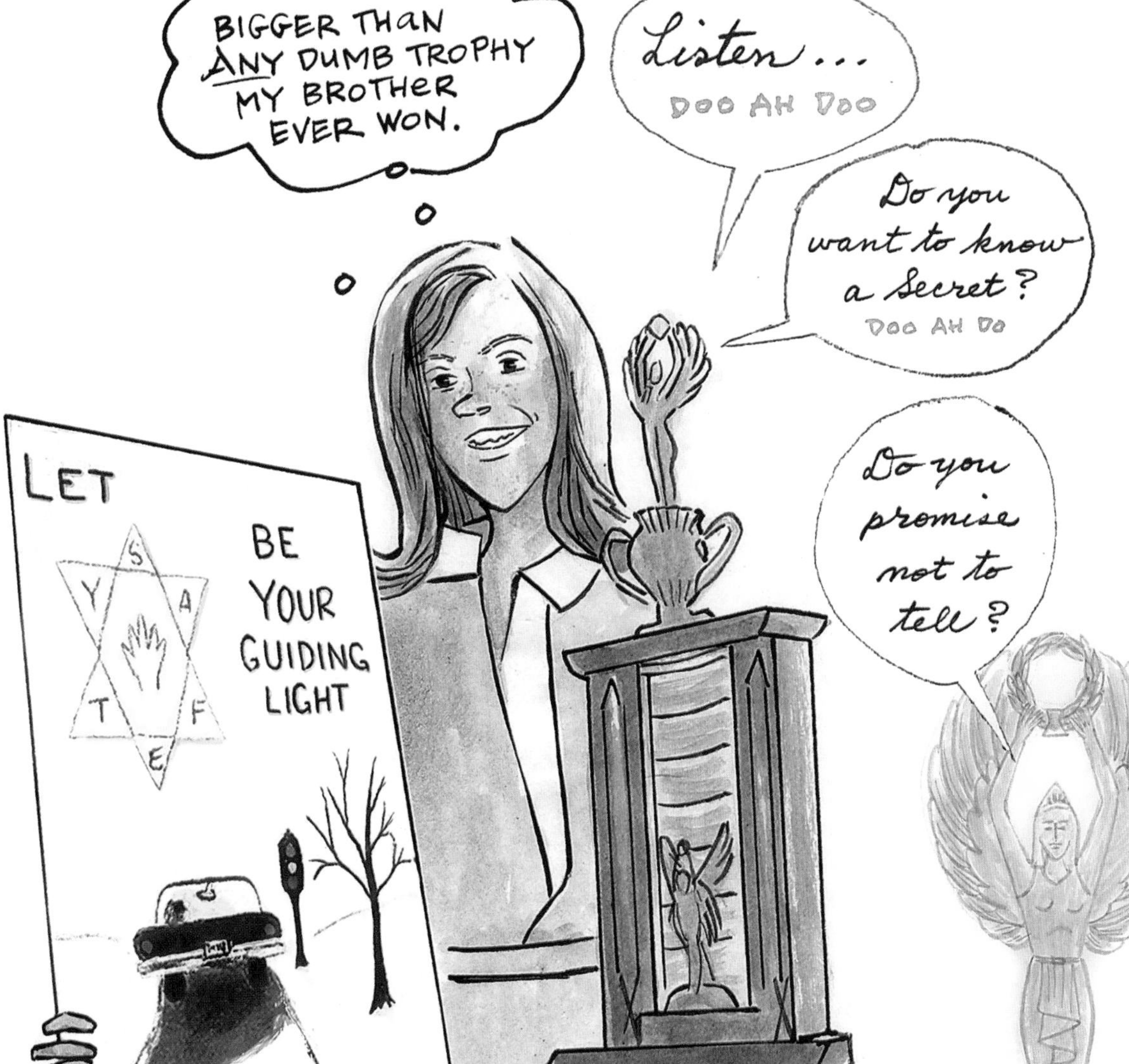

BIGGER THAN ANY DUMB TROPHY MY BROTHER EVER WON.
Listen...
DOO AH DOO
Do you want to know a Secret?
DOO AH DO
Do you promise not to tell?
LET
BE YOUR GUIDING LIGHT
S A F E T Y
C.T.

SHE SHOULD-A BEEN A AD MAN

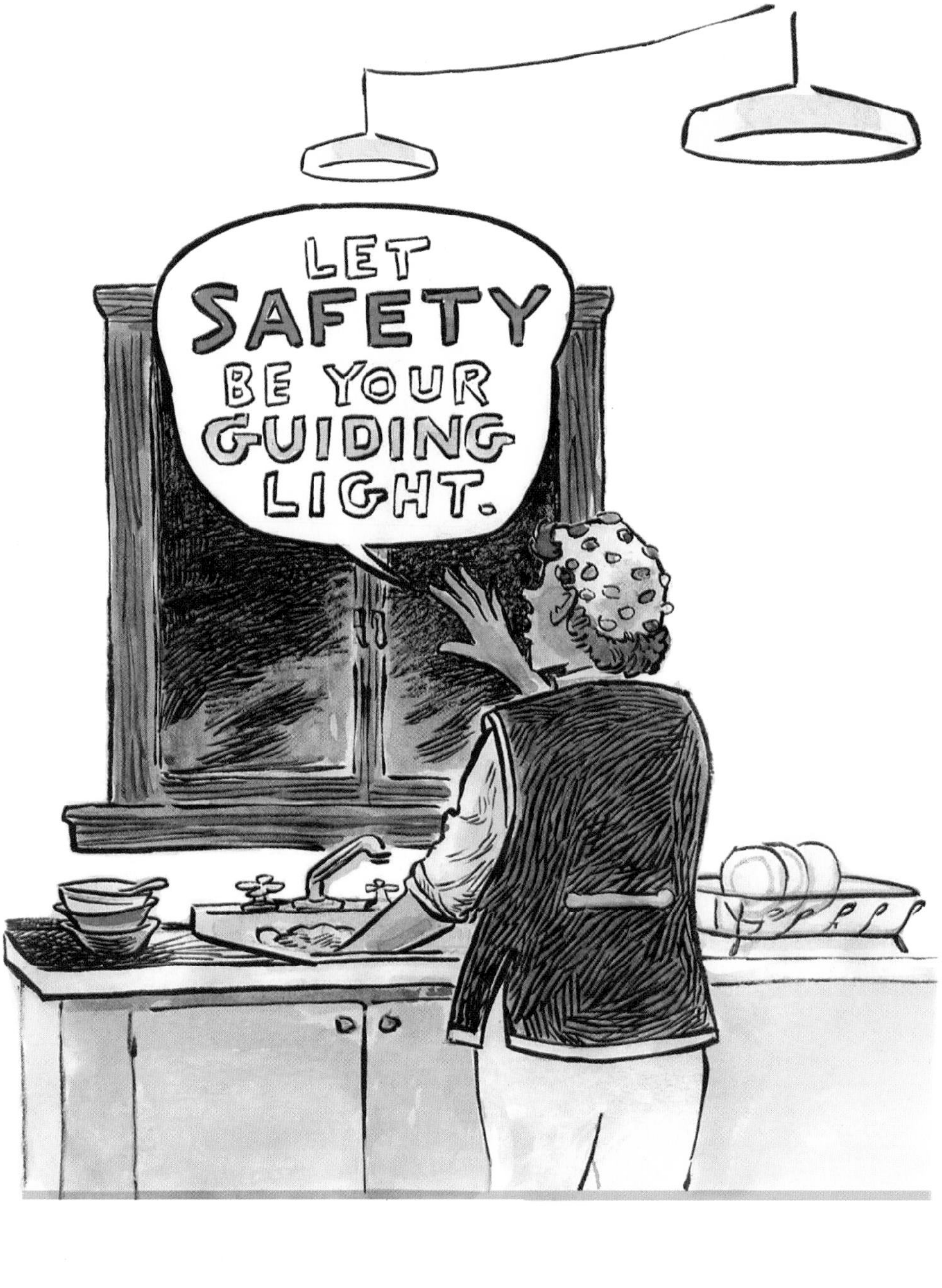
LET SAFETY BE YOUR GUIDING LIGHT.

CHARLES W. TYLER

PLUMBING CONTRACTOR
1837 WEST ADDISON ST.
CHICAGO 13, ILL.

See, turned out I won the grand prize over all. It's such a big trophy -- almost as tall as I am! I wanted to keep it at home to show up my brother Joe. But Sister said <u>No</u>, that it belonged to the school. One of the dads is going to build a display case, so that every day, kids can walk by it and feel school spirit. But I wouldn't feel that — it would remind me of what I need to take to the confessional box.

FOX LAKE PRESS 10¢

GUILTY!!!

8TH GRADE GIRL FOUND GUILTY OF CHEATING. MUST RETURN TROPHY, GIFT CERTIFICATE TO SEARS ($10), AND SEASON PASS TO DEER HAVEN.

Mother awarded Ad Agency Job.

Nuns devastated. School pride at stake. Decision to be appealed. Display case plans on hold.

?
I get my Beatles records at Sears!
I can use that gift certificate!

FAMILY SUPPORT

WHEN YOU CAN SHOW ME THAT YOU CAN KEEP YOUR ROOM CLEAN...
THEN WE'LL SEE ABOUT POSTAGE TO ENGLAND!
Bleach
49¢
16 MAG

621 Randich Rd.
Ingleside, Ill.
U. S. A.
→ ?
Beatles 4 Ever!
Anne Collingham
First Floor Service House
13 Monmouth Street
London, W. C. 2
England

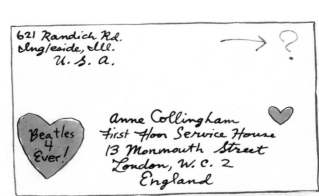

I Call Your Name

Feb. 9, 1965 — The Anniversary

I started the Beatles Fan Club of Fox Lake last year because I never heard back from Liverpool. *No Reply*. It's a good thing I started a club because this is the official one year anniversary date and we have a club in place ready to have a party. I am the president and my best friend Laurie is the V.P. We've had a sleep-over every month since last year.

When we put the club together, we asked other 7th graders. There are 8 boys and 12 girls in our class. No boys wanted to join and only 5 girls. I asked for dues, 25¢ per month, but Chris thought that was too much. This year, 8th grade, there's only 4 of us, which is good because each one of us gets to have a favorite Beatle.

Laurie loves Paul. That's perfect because they both have brown eyes. There's something going to happen between those two one day. I'm sure of it. I believe there will be 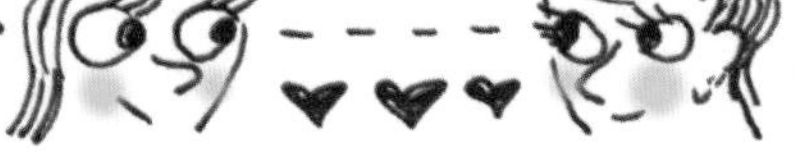 Wedding Bells.

Janet picked John even though he's married. She loves him anyway. Barb picked George. She got first choice and that's who she picked. Nobody went for Ringo since he's a bit older so it makes sense for me, the president to have him. altho I should have John. He's the leader.

* Laurie * Barbara * Janet * Carol *

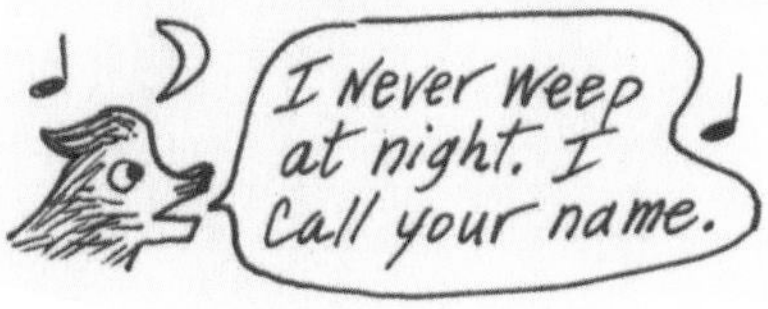
I Never Weep at night. I Call your name.

RINGO is O.K. BY ME. He WAS MY FIRST PICK. Any way, THIS PAST FRIDAY, We HAD OUR ONE Year SINCE ED SULLIVAN SLEEP-OVER PARTY. (we COULDN'T DO IT TODAY--SCHOOL NIGHT.) EVERYBODY CAME OVER RIGHT AFTER SCHOOL. We MADE a Chef-Boy-Ar-Dee PIZZA FROM THE BOX AND LISTENED TO ALBUMS. In ONE YEAR, I Have 6 OF THEM: Meet, Introducing, Second, HDsN, New, and '65. I KEEP THEM UP IN MY ROOM, NOT BY THE STEREO. Joe likes to toss RECORDS He DOESN'T LIKE OUT THE WINDOW LIKE FLYING SAUCERS. — DAD TURNED ON THE FLOODLIGHT IN THE FRONT SO JANET, BARBARA, LAURIE, and I COULD SKATE. NOBODY ELSE OUT THERE BUT SOME ICE FISHERMEN. AS SOON AS WE GOT OUT THERE, WE SHOUTED REALLY LOUD UP AT THE SKY TOWARDS ENGLAND:

We Love You Yeah, Yeah, Yeah!

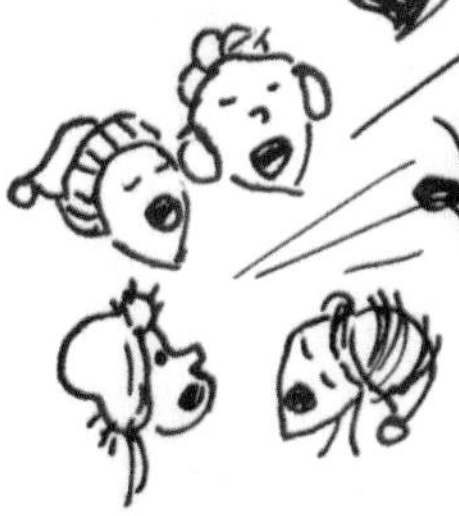

It WAS SO COLD AND CRISP THAT NIGHT, I THINK IF ENGLAND DIDN'T HEAR US, SURELY THE FISH DID.

My SISTER HATES THE BEATLES. SHE HAS ABSOLUTELY **NO** USE FOR THEM, SHE LIKES TO REMIND ANYONE WHO WILL LISTEN. Really, SHE HATES THEM SO MUCH -- BUT I CAN'T

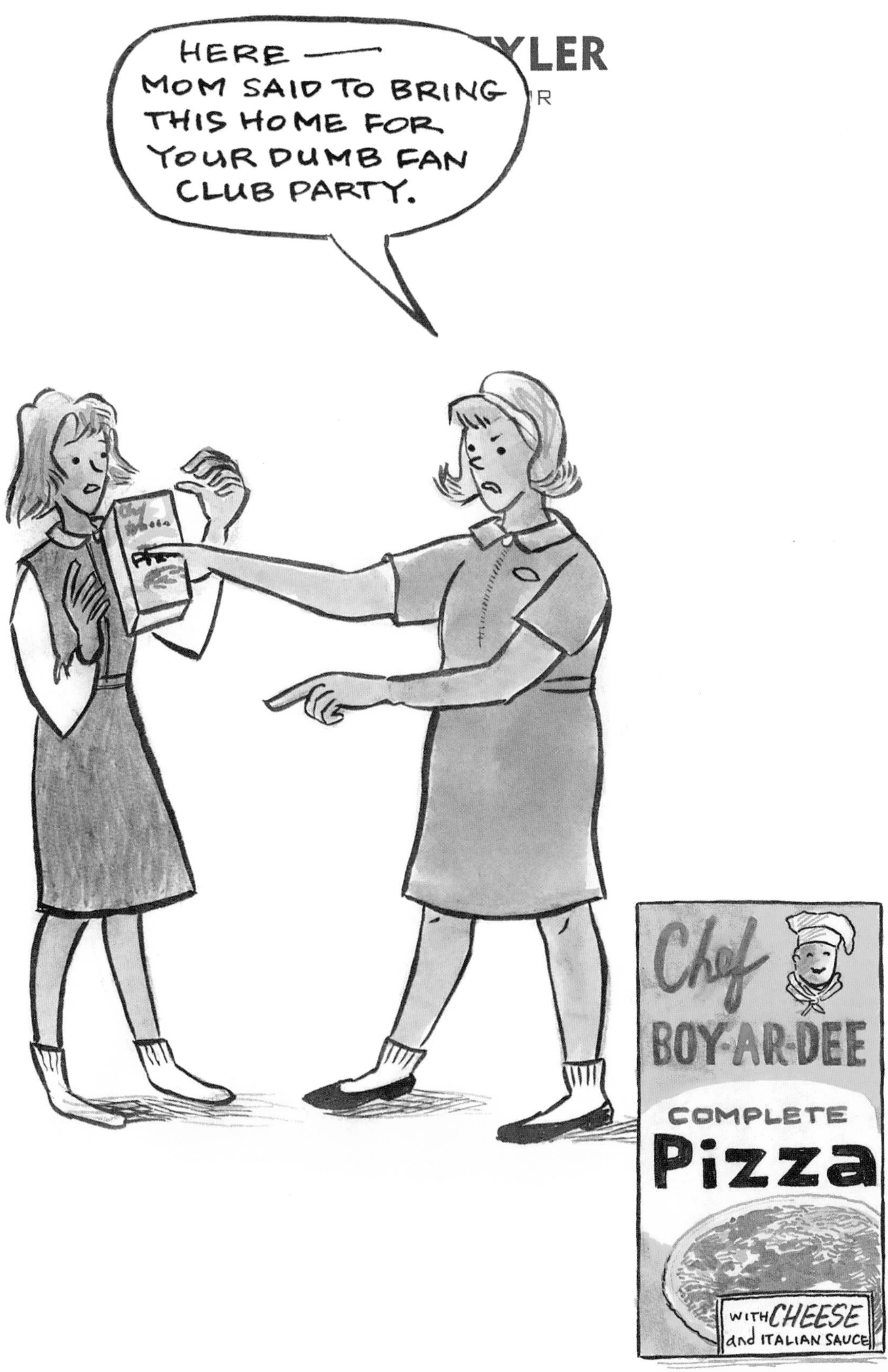
HERE — MOM SAID TO BRING THIS HOME FOR YOUR DUMB FAN CLUB PARTY.
Chef BOY-AR-DEE
COMPLETE Pizza
WITH CHEESE and ITALIAN SAUCE

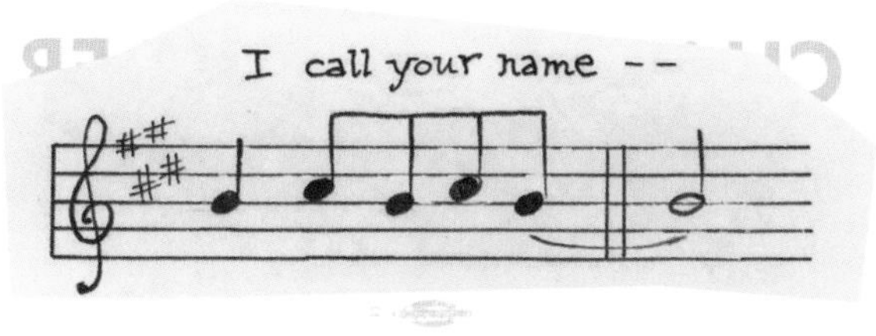
I call your name --

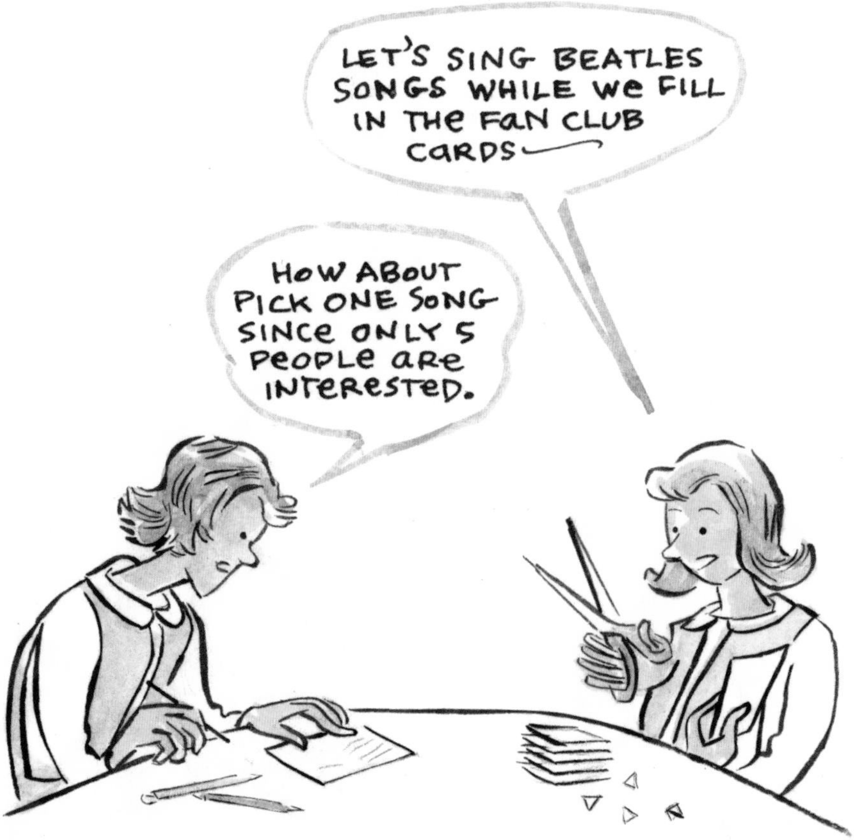
LET'S SING BEATLES SONGS WHILE WE FILL IN THE FAN CLUB CARDS
HOW ABOUT PICK ONE SONG SINCE ONLY 5 PEOPLE ARE INTERESTED.

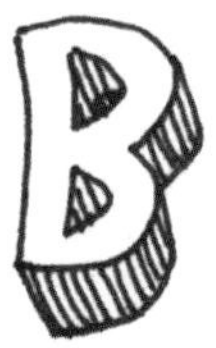
B

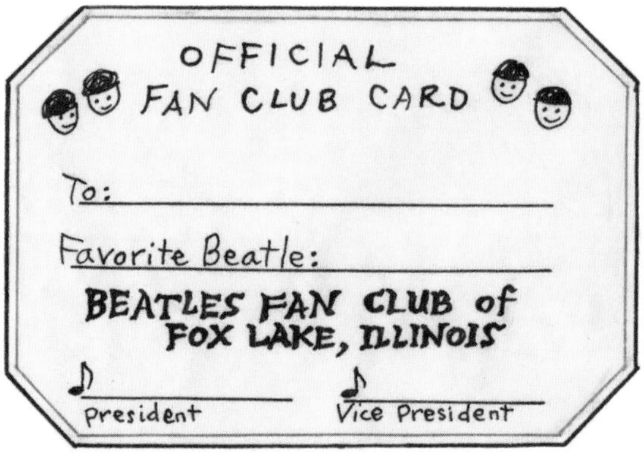
OFFICIAL
FAN CLUB CARD
To:
Favorite Beatle:
BEATLES FAN CLUB of FOX LAKE, ILLINOIS
President
Vice President

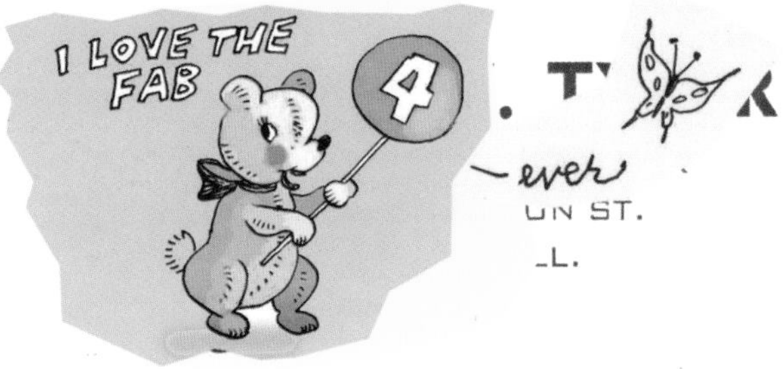
I LOVE THE FAB 4
~ever
UN ST.
L.

really say anything bad about her because she's getting ready to go into the convent. She wanted to go last year but Dad begged her to wait a year, have fun, and maybe change her mind before the cloister. I don't know what's so fun about working at the Jewel as a cashier. I wish she still was over at Patty's Lounge dishwashing. Every weekend when we picked her up after work, she got to bring home all the left-over french fries. And ketchup. But all she does now after the Jewel is lay in bed and eat candy bars. And holler at me to turn the radio off because she's trying to read *Life*, or pray, or set her hair. I like WLS more than WCFL. She's a crab. Our rooms connect. I have to go past her to get to my room. No short cut. She gets to go to Calif. to Disneyland before entering the noviciate. Dad and Grandma Tyler are taking her. That is OK. by me. I'm no longer interested in Mickey Mouse.

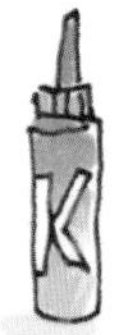
K

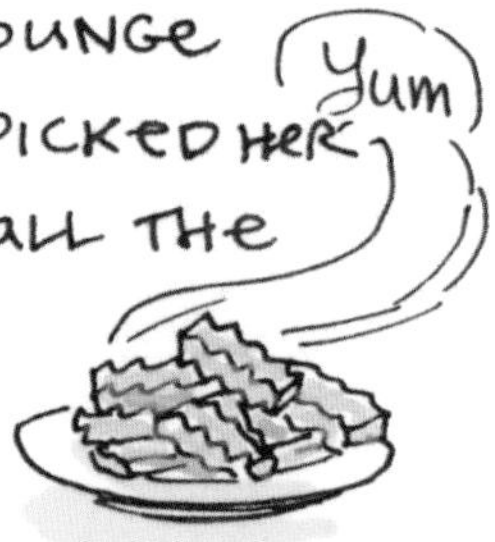
Yum

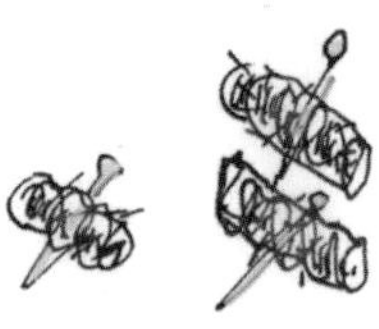

her curlers. mesh barrels with pink picks.

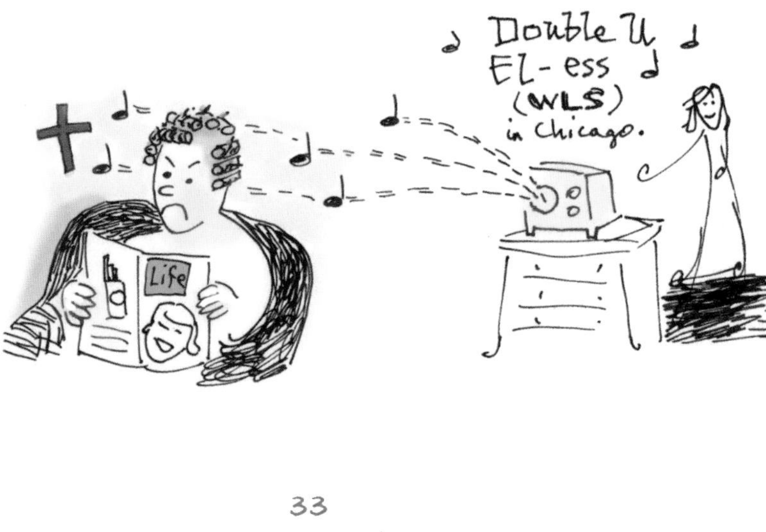
Double U
El-ess
(WLS)
in Chicago.
Life

'E PUTS THE BEAT IN BEATLES, 'E DOES

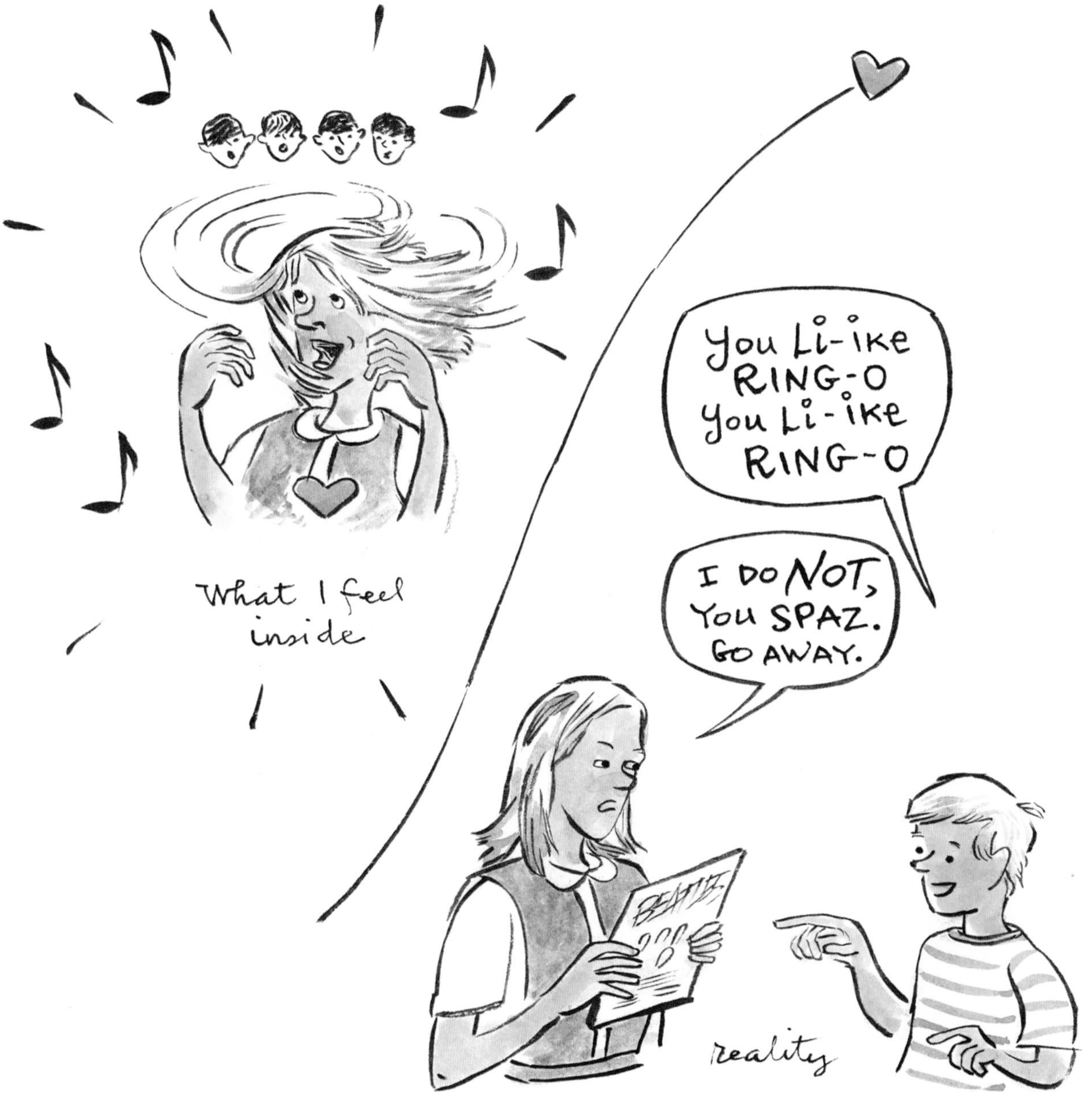

What I feel inside
You Li-ike RING-O You Li-ike RING-O
I DO NOT, You SPAZ. GO AWAY.
reality

100% PURE R

What 👁 Go 4 in 8TH GRADE

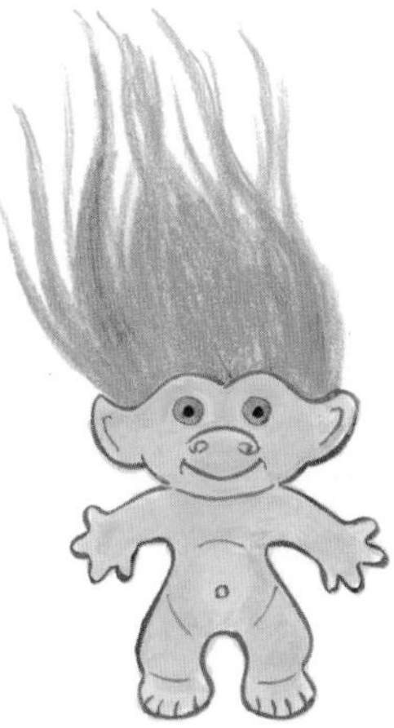

FAVORITE:

SINGERS – The Beatles (John, Paul, George, Ringo)
PROGRAMS – Shindig, Patty Duke, Ed Sullivan, Man from U.N.C.L.E., Combat, Bullwinkle.
RECORDS – All Beatles Records. Some English bands.
HAIR STYLE – Long flip or straight English – I Got
COLOR – Blue, Madras, White, Brown, Green (Dark Colours) English spelling
MASCOT – Zeke my troll
HIGH SCHOOL – Carmel
FOODS – Steak + French Fries, Spaghetti
CANDY – Sweet Tarts
SEASON – Summer
Radio Station – WLS
MONTHS – July, December, June, August
P.I.C. (Partner in crime) Laurie.

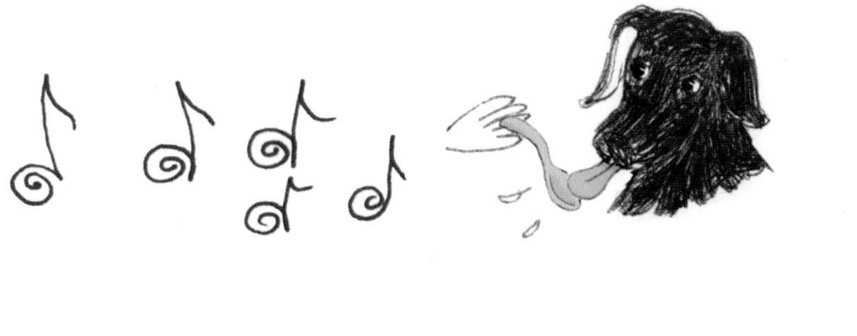

More black! More black!
Ai-Yi-Yi
YOU HAVE TO PUT A THICK BLACK LINE AROUND EVERYTHING. SEE?
LIKE THIS. TOO MUCH BEAT BUSINESS YOU GIRLS DON'T KNOW HOW TO DO ANYTHING...
SEE?
What?
No!
IT
LOOKS TERRIBLE
LOVE ME DO
Oh-o— Love Me Do!

C ER

Thank You, Girl

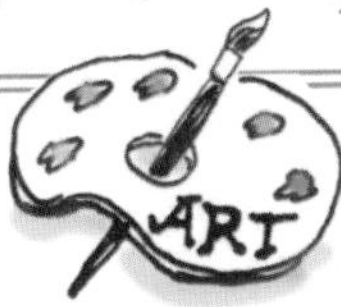
ART

Feb. 19

I LOVE Fridays because THAT'S WHEN WE HAVE ART. FROM 2-2:45. We PUT OUR BOOKS AWAY AND TAKE OUT OUR PASTELS. The BOYS DON'T WANT TO DO ART, SO THEY GO OUTSIDE WITH MR. WHITE FOR SPORTS. Sister Bernadette IS THE ART TEACHER. She HANDS OUT GREETING CARDS, SO WE EACH GET ONE TO COPY. If WE GET FINISHED IN TIME, WE GET TO DO ANOTHER. Today I GOT TO DO 2 cards.

I'M NOT CRAZY FOR CRAY-PAS. I LIKE NUPASTEL. THEY BLEND SO NICE WITH A KLEENEX. THAT'S HOW I GET MY NICE AREAS. Sister HAS BEEN COPYING CARDS AND MAKING NICE PASTEL PICTURES FOR MANY YEARS NOW, SHE TOLD US. SHE STARTED BACK IN THE OLD COUNTRY. All THE NUNS HERE HAVE ACCENTS FROM SOME COUNTRY. NOT SURE WHERE. CZECHOSLOVAKIA MAYBE? IT WAS TAKEN OVER BY THE SOVIET UNION. SISTER ALSO PAINTS POPPIES ON THE CORNER OF SILK SCARVES. AND OTHER FLOWERS. I SAW A LADY IN A PEW WITH HER HEAD DOWN, PRAYING REAL HARD FOR OVER AN HOUR WEARING A SISTER BERNADETTE SCARF. SOMETHING SERIOUS MUST HAVE HAPPENED TO HER BECAUSE SHE'S ALSO BEEN AT MORNING MASS EVERY DAY FOR MONTHS IN THAT SCARF.

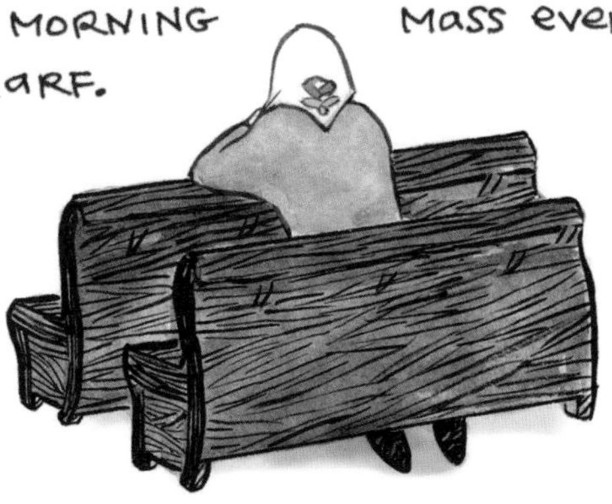

I'll Get You!

Feb 22 Laurie and I have a secret word when we can't talk on the phone. She'll call me or I'll call her on important fan club business or any Beatles news. So when any of that stuff comes up or a rumor or boy talk and there are parents or other nosy people around, we'll say "I'm in the dining room" or "Are you in the dining room?" Dining Room is the code.

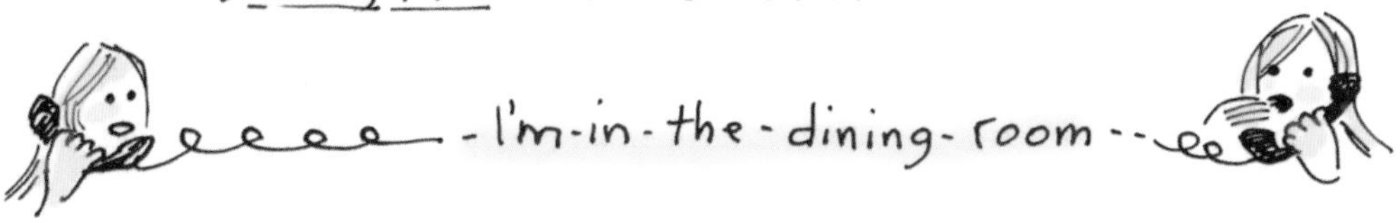
I'm-in-the-dining-room

Most of the juicy stuff we save for Friday nights. Either I go to her house or she walks home with me. She can't **STAND** Tureki (lives by me and from our class). When we get together, just her and me, we call it a *Session*. That's what the Beatles call getting together to record. We try on each others outfits, we draw, plus we work on our hairstyles. And makeup. We are both blondes. She is very good looking and eventually will be Paul's wife. This is why I can't stand Tureki:

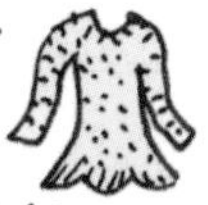

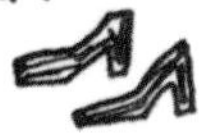

Laurie and I have been sharing this booklet back and forth that was my sister's. It's all about The Curse — a.k.a. periods. So stupid! Cathy's mom said it was a badge of womanhood to be proud of. YUCK. It ruins clothes and furniture. And stinks. I told Laurie about how Tureki kept bugging me on the way home about the booklet, then he stole it.

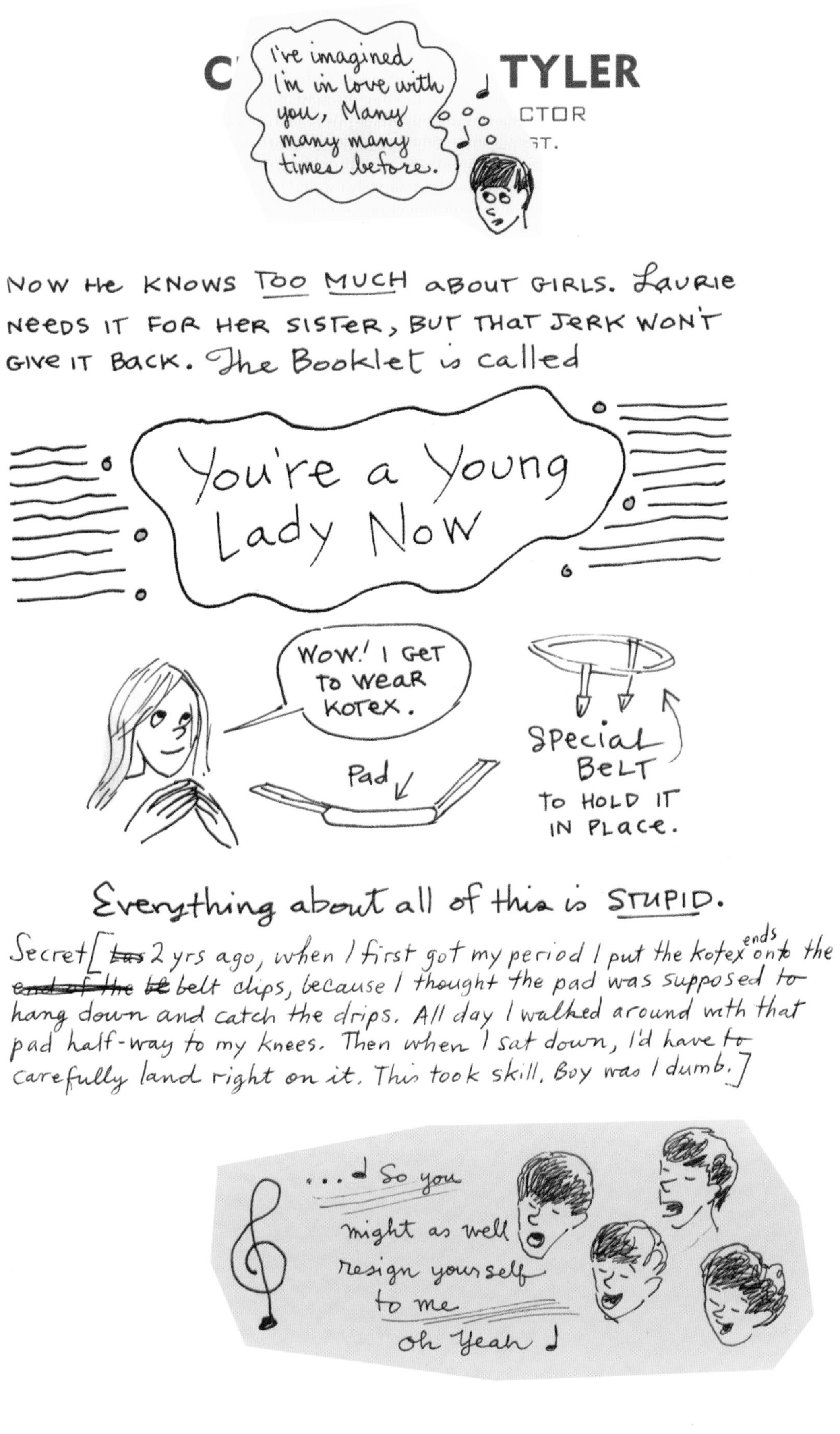
TYLER
CTOR
ST.
I've imagined I'm in love with you, Many many many times before.
NOW HE KNOWS TOO MUCH ABOUT GIRLS. Laurie NEEDS IT FOR HER SISTER, BUT THAT JERK WON'T GIVE IT BACK. The Booklet is called
You're a Young Lady Now
WOW! I GET TO WEAR KOTEX.
Pad
SPECIAL BELT TO HOLD IT IN PLACE.
Everything about all of this is STUPID.
Secret[~~las~~ 2 yrs ago, when I first got my period I put the kotex ends onto the ~~end of the~~ ~~be~~ belt clips, because I thought the pad was supposed to hang down and catch the drips. All day I walked around with that pad half-way to my knees. Then when I sat down, I'd have to carefully land right on it. This took skill. Boy was I dumb.]
... So you might as well resign yourself to me oh Yeah

PARTIAC ARREST

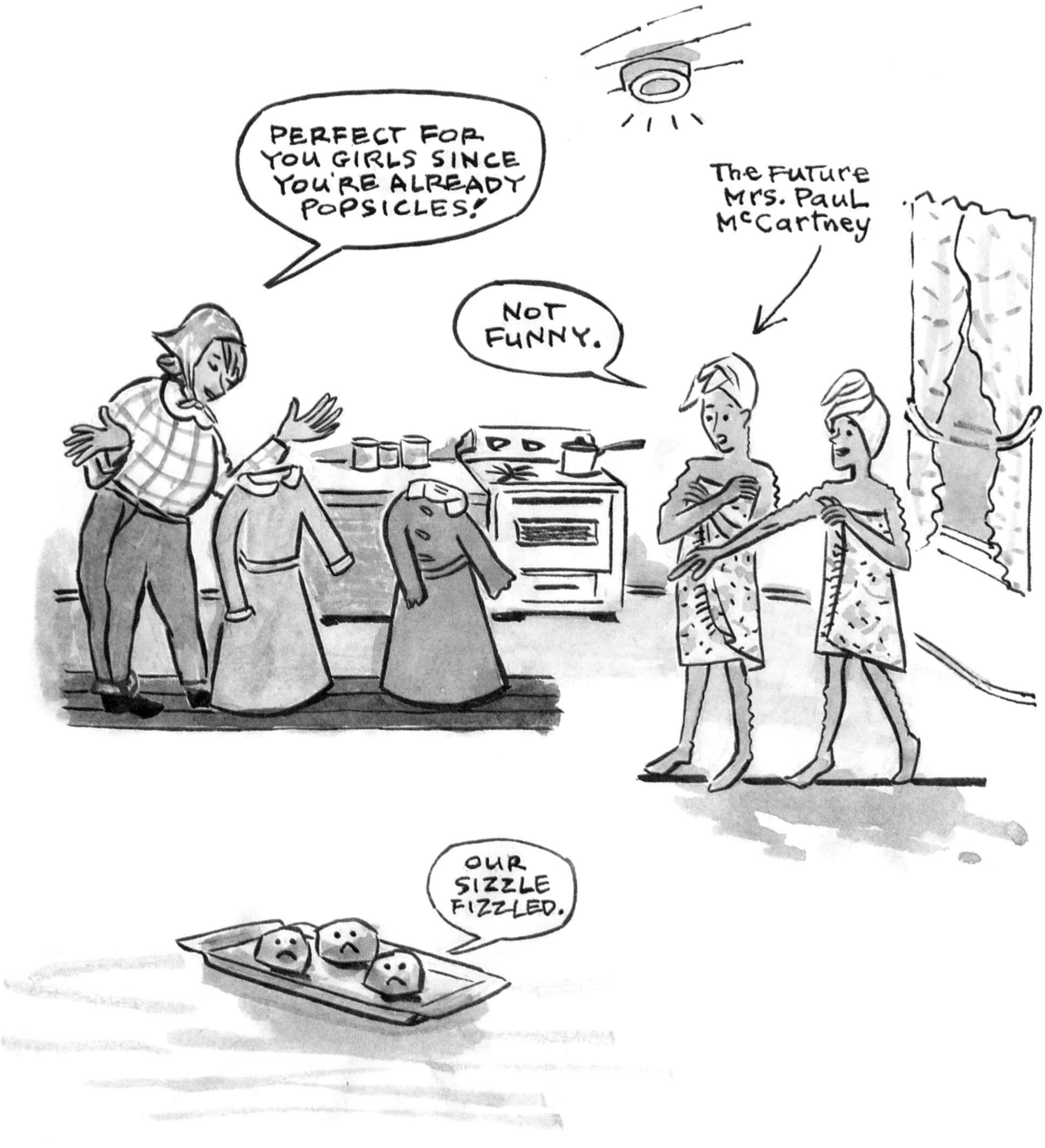
PERFECT FOR YOU GIRLS SINCE YOU'RE ALREADY POPSICLES!
The Future Mrs. Paul McCartney
NOT FUNNY.
OUR SIZZLE FIZZLED.

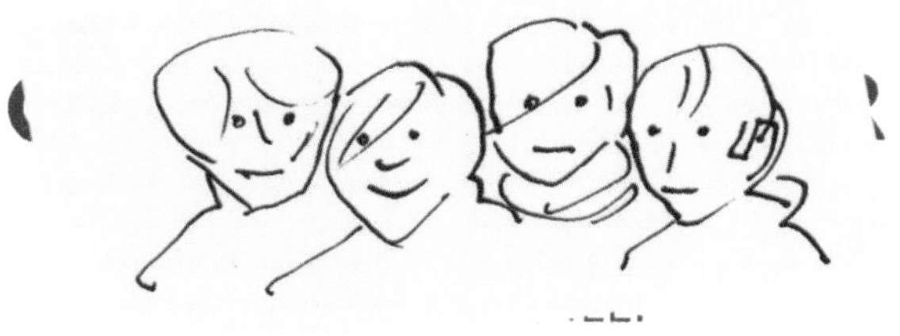

This last Friday at Laurie's she had a pretty great session planned. She read in National Geographic that at fancy resorts in Europe, they have something called "spas" at spa resorts, like in Finland or the Alps. It's for rich people. Anyway— it's a tiny room like a pantry, and it has rocks and benches. They heat up the rocks and then you go into the room naked with just a towel on, and sprinkle water onto the rocks to make steam. It's supposed to be for your health.

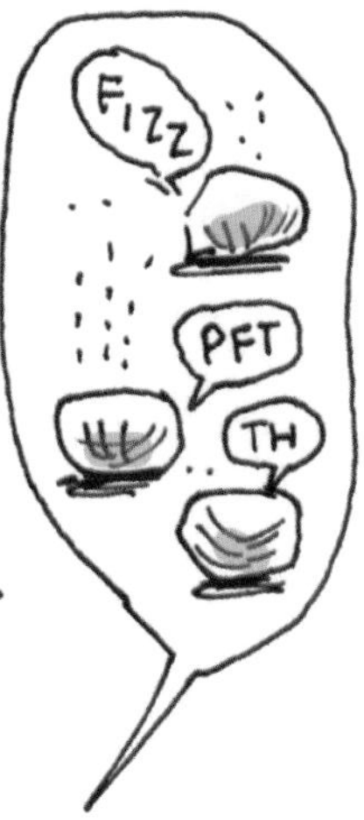
FIZZ
PFT
TH

So, we lugged in all the boulders from around her mom's flower bed and put them on baking pans in the oven. Then we got changed into our bathing suits and put on towels because her house is drafty and it's freezing cold outside. For an hour we sat in their tiny bathroom off the kitchen and sprinkled water on the hot rocks in our so-called spa. Nothing happened. We wondered if it was because Fox Lake is not in Europe.

Then, out in the kitchen, we heard her mom laughing so hard. Earlier in the day it had warmed up a bit, so her mom hung a load of wash on the line. But then a cold front came through and froze all the dresses. Her mom was laughing because they stood up by themselves. Pretty funny.

Look What You're Doing

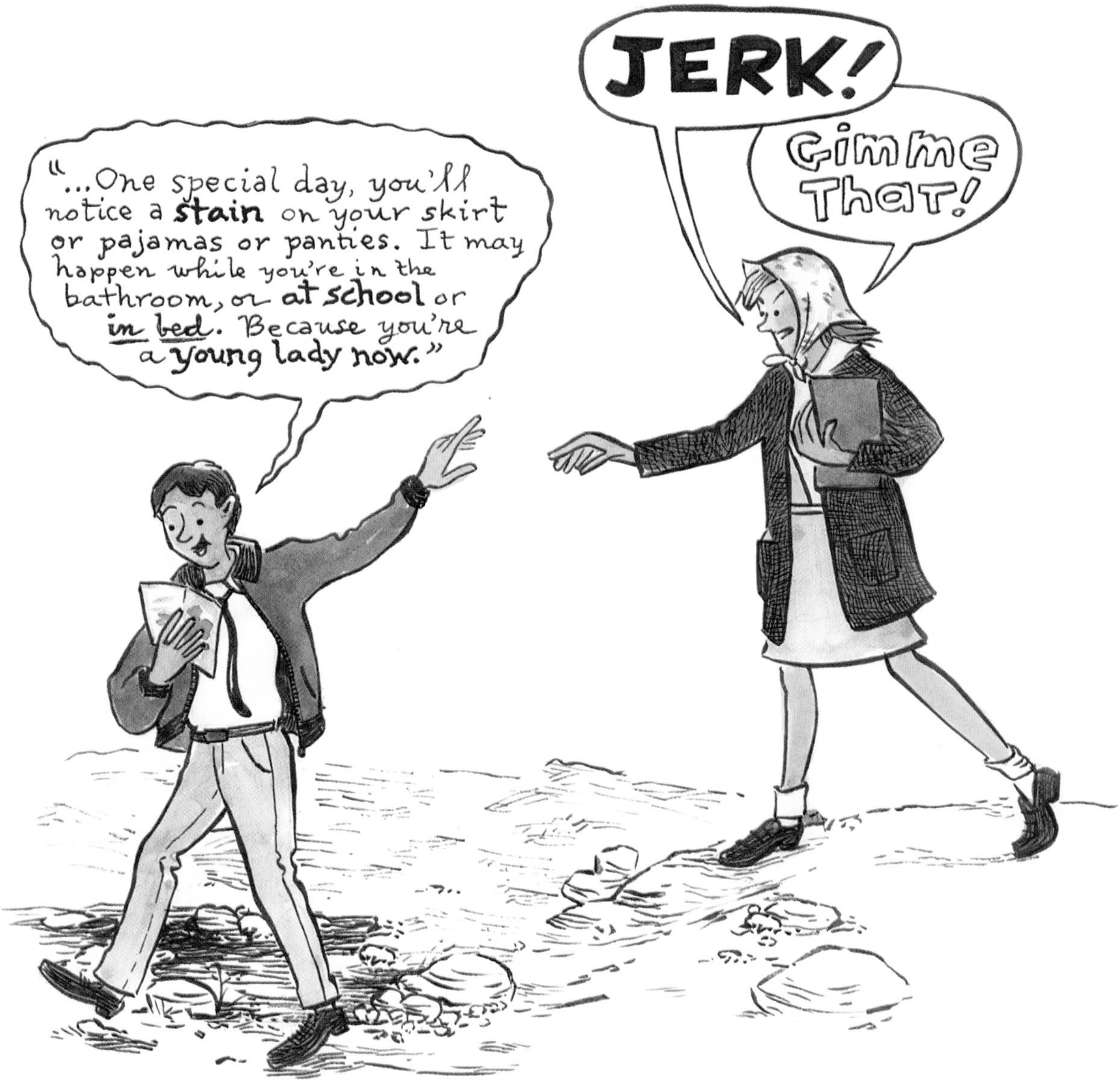
"...One special day, you'll notice a stain on your skirt or pajamas or panties. It may happen while you're in the bathroom, or at school or in bed. Because you're a young lady now."
JERK!
Gimme That!

WOTTA GENT

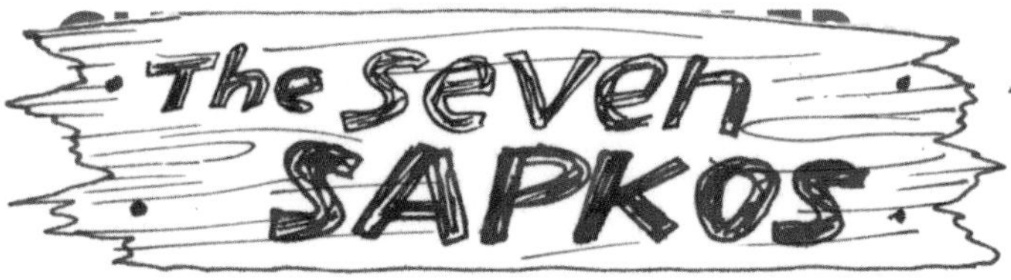
The Seven
SAPKOS

SIGN ON THEIR Garage

Feb. 28 To get money for my albums, I babysit for the Sapkos. Saturdays mostly. Just started up again after the incident last October. 5 kids, ranging from my age on down. I should say just under my age. The oldest is 10. The youngest is 2. There might be another one on the way.

Babysitting for the Sapkos is O.K. But I wish I didn't have to go there. It's a big old drafty house and the heat is turned down low to save money, so I wrap up in a blanket after the kids go to bed.

Did I say 5 kids? I meant there are 7 kids and 2 parents. The sign is old. Ages 10, 8, 7, twin 5s, 3, and just 2.

CHORES. Saturday is chores day for just about everyone I can think of. My job on Sat. is Laundry. Our washer broke so Mom takes me up to the laundromat at the plaza in town. The plaza used to be a bog a couple of years ago, with lots of stumps and frogs. But they brought in truckloads of fill, and then paved it and built stores. Sears, Woolworths, the Jewel where my sister works, the laundromat, another store, (the National), and then the Globe (ladies clothing shop). Mom loves the Globe. (expensive.) (once in awhile she gets something from there. Something nice.)

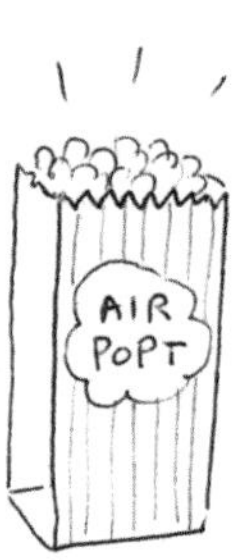
AIR
POPT

WHILE THE CLOTHES ARE IN THE WASH, I HAVE JUST ENOUGH TIME TO RUN DOWN TO WOOLWORTHS TO LOOK AT MAGAZINES AND MAKE-UP (which I'm not allowed to wear yet). I ALWAYS GET A PACK OF Beatles Cards, and THEN I GO LOOK AT ALBUMS AT Sears. I HEARD A NEW Beatles ALBUM IS COMING OUT NEXT MONTH, AND I SHOULD HAVE ENOUGH MONEY SAVED UP BY THEN. While I'M DOING ALL THIS, MOM IS GROCERY SHOPPING AT THE Jewel AND National. Things are ON SALE AT DIFFERENT STORES AND MOM LOOKS FOR SAVINGS BECAUSE Joe AND THE TRINITY eat MORE THAN THE REST OF US COMBINED! BUT THERE's No DISCOUNTS AT THE Jewel JUST BECAUSE GINIA IS A CASHIER THERE. IN FACT, MOM DOESN'T even GO THROUGH HER CHECK-OUT LINE. Mom NEVER WANTS TO DRAW SUSPICION OR EVEN A HINT AT ANY-THING Fishy.

So THOSE ARE MY CHORES. WELL, LAUNDRY ON Saturday, AND EVERYDAY IT'S CLEAN OFF THE TABLE AFTER SUPPER, FEED THE DOG, AND MAKE MY BED. BUT WHEN I GET TO THE SAPKOS FOR A COUPLE OF HOURS Saturday AFTERNOON Before THE EVENING SHIFT (I WORK 3-5 and then 8—?) WELL... LOOK AT THEIR CHORE LIST:

- Laundry   • Dishes   • Beds
- Feed Baby her bottle   • Feed Dogs AND Clean out their Pens
- Wash Windows   • Sweep and Wash Floors
- Take out Garbage   • Clean Diaper Pail
- Fix Mailbox

44

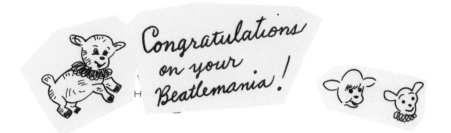
Congratulations on your Beatlemania!

MY JOB, WHEN I DO THE AFTERNOON SHIFT, IS TO MAKE SURE THE SAPKO KIDS DO ALL THEIR CHORES FROM THE LIST. THE WEE ONES CAN'T WORK, SO MOSTLY IT FALLS ON THE 3 OLDEST — AND THEY ARE ALWAYS CRABBY AND FIGHTING. TECHNICALLY, THEY HAVE UNTIL THEY GO TO BED AT 10 TO GET EVERYTHING DONE. AT 8, WHEN I GET THERE, I HEAT UP WATER FOR NOODLES AND FIX THEM SPAGHETTI. THEN I HAVE TO MAKE SURE THEY'VE DONE ALL THE CHORES WHICH NOW INCLUDES SUPPER DISHES. THEY HORSE AROUND SO MUCH, I HAVE TO YELL AND BREAK UP FIGHTS. ESPECIALLY THE TWO OLDER BOYS. THEY'RE ROUGHNECKS. THEN EVERYONE TO BED BY 10. SHEESH.

Now what do you think of that?

THOSE KIDS DON'T GO TO Catholic School AND IT SHOWS. THEY ARE WILD. As for me, I'M NOT ALLOWED TO TALK TO LAURIE ON THE PHONE. THEY DON'T HAVE 'Call Pack' (a savings package for long-winded telephone yakkers like me), SO EVERY MINUTE COSTS 7¢, WHICH WOULD BANKRUPT THEM. AND BY THE TIME I GET THOSE KIDS TO BED, I'M TOO TIRED TO ENJOY MY BEATLES MAGAZINES, SO I TURN ON TV, WATCH OLD MOVIES ON WGN, and fall asleep TILL THEY GET HOME FROM THE TAVERN SMELLY and DRUNK. FOR THIS, I MAKE 50¢ PER HOUR.

LAST OCTOBER, THE BOYS WERE SO BAD THAT I HAD TO LEAVE A NOTE FOR THEIR MOM TO READ WHILE MR. SAPKO CARRIED ME HOME IN THE DARK ON HIS SHOULDERS. HE'S A MUSCLE MAN, AND WHEN HE'S TIPSY, IT'S LIKE I'M IN A BOAT UP THERE, CARRIED.

I'LL BE BACK

OH-HO
OH-O-O

THE BOYS BROKE a LAMP, SO I WROTE IT DOWN IN THE NOTE. Well, ON MONDAY, I SAW THEM OVER AT THEIR BUS STOP. THEY WERE ALL BRUISED UP WITH BLACK EYES, AND ONE HAD A SLING. THEIR DAD HAD BEAT THEM UP, BEAT THE "H..." OUT OF THEM FOR BREAKING THE LAMP. MR SAPKO DROPPED ME OFF, WENT HOME, READ THE NOTE, GOT THE BOYS OUT OF BED AND BEAT THEM GOOD. "We're gonna GIT you for this," THEY HOLLERED AS THE BUS PULLED UP. What's a GIRL TO DO? I WAS JUST FOLLOWING ORDERS FROM Mrs. Sapko, WHO HIRED ME BECAUSE SHE SAID I WAS A "good Catholic girl from a good family." AND ON THAT NIGHT, I'D EVEN GOTTEN A 25¢ TIP, SO I HAD MADE $3.25 THAT DAY/NIGHT.

I TOLD MOM WHAT HAPPENED. SHE SAID SHE WAS GOING TO HAVE A LITTLE TALK WITH Mrs. Sapko, AND THAT I WAS TO STAY AWAY FROM THERE FOR AWHILE. TOO MUCH RESPONSIBILITY FOR A GIRL MY AGE. SO I WAS Really Really GLAD ON CHRISTMAS WHEN I GOT THE Beatles '65 ALBUM. I HADN'T WORKED BABYSITTING FOR MONTHS AND I'D SPENT THE $3.25 FROM THAT MISERABLE NIGHT ON CANDY. (I BOUGHT SUCKERS FOR THE SAPKO KIDS AND TOLD THEM I WAS SORRY.)

Beatles '65 IS GREAT. I REALLY NEEDED TO HEAR NEW MUSIC FROM MY LADS. Thank you baby JESUS FOR BEING BORN AT THE SAME TIME A NEW BEATLES ALBUM WAS RELEASED!

I Love them
SO!

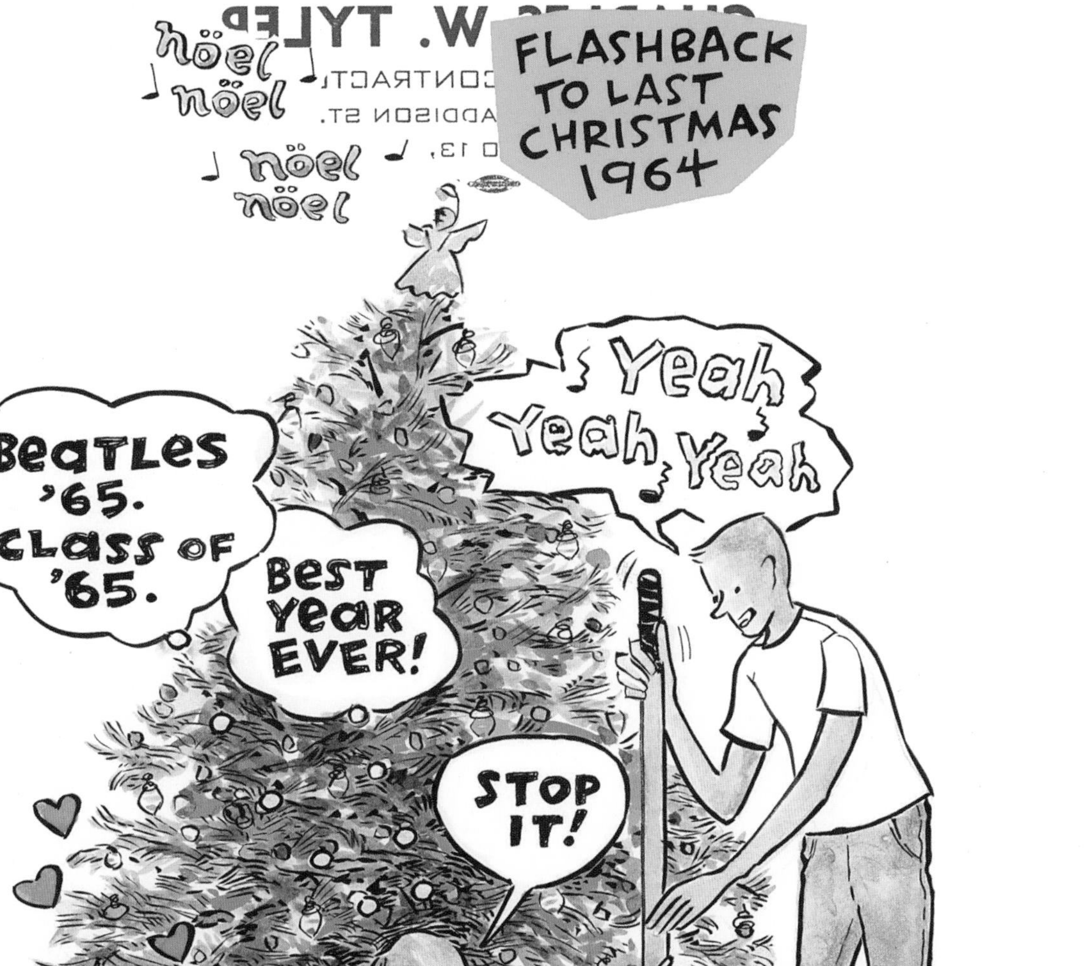

nöel nöel
nöel nöel
FLASHBACK TO LAST CHRISTMAS 1964
Beatles '65. Class of '65.
Best Year Ever!
Yeah Yeah Yeah Yeah
Stop it!
SKATES Women's Figures
MY OWN

BEST GIFT EVER

PLUMBING CONTRACTOR
1837 WEST ADDISON ST.
CHICAGO 13, ILL.

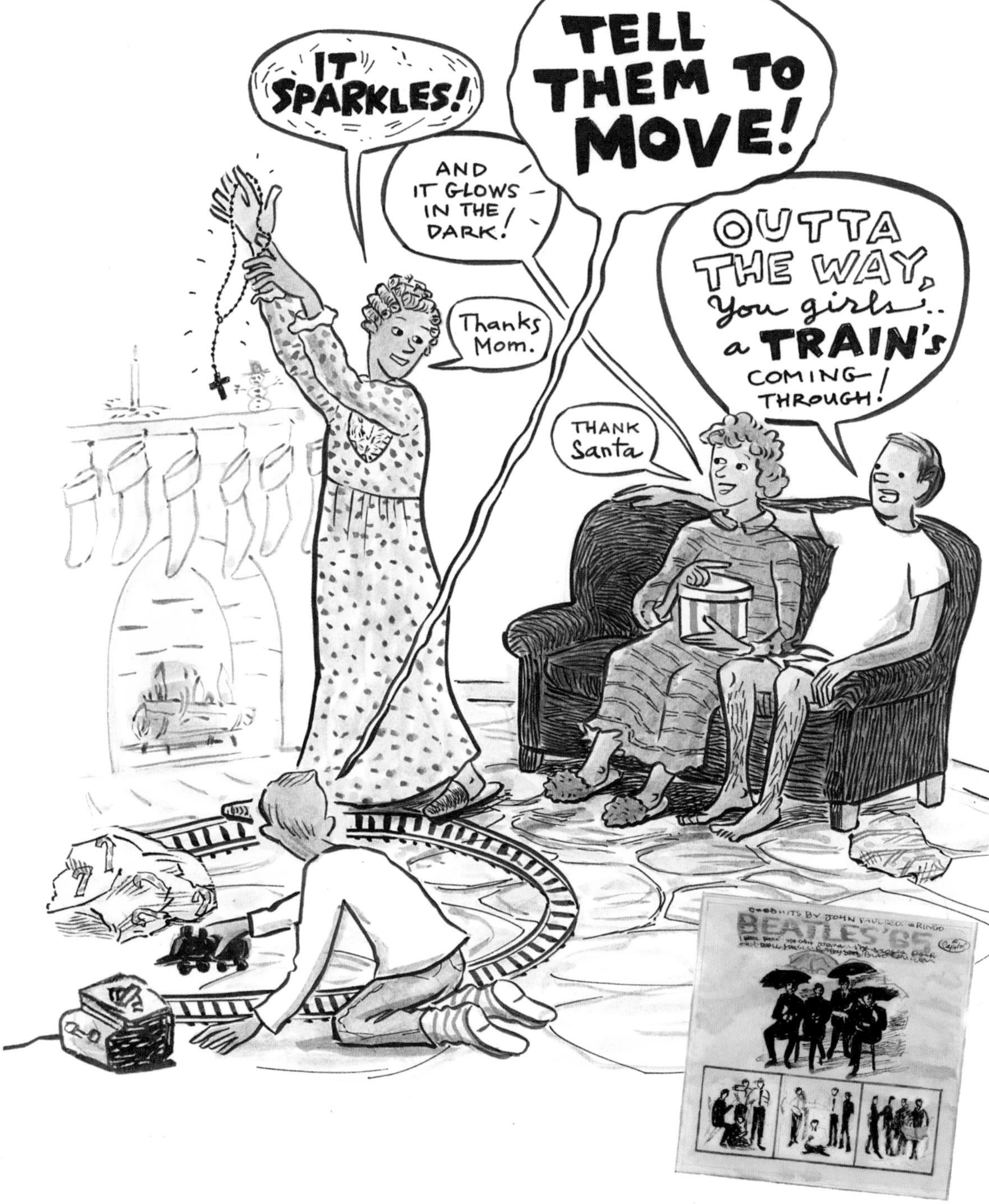
IT SPARKLES!
TELL THEM TO MOVE!
AND IT GLOWS IN THE DARK!
Thanks Mom.
OUTTA THE WAY, You girls... a TRAIN's COMING THROUGH!
THANK Santa
BEATLES '65

CHARLES W. TYLER

PLUMBING CONTRACTOR

1837 WEST ADDISON ST.

CHICAGO 13, ILL.

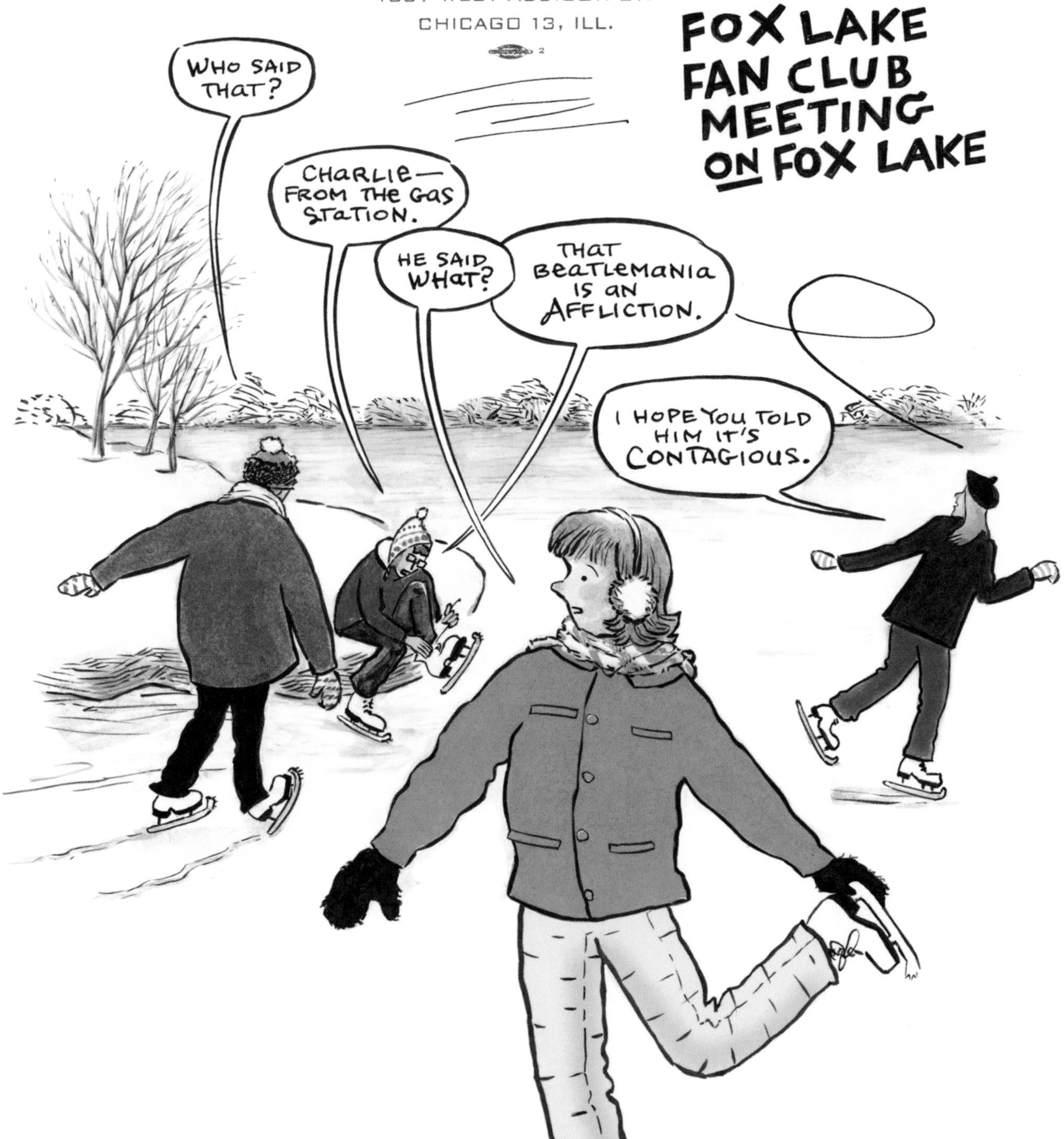
FOX LAKE FAN CLUB MEETING ON FOX LAKE
WHO SAID THAT?
CHARLIE— FROM THE GAS STATION.
HE SAID WHAT?
THAT BEATLEMANIA IS AN AFFLICTION.
I HOPE YOU TOLD HIM IT'S CONTAGIOUS.

HOLD me TIGHT

Mar. 1 Official CANDY

<u>Sweet Tarts</u> are the OFFICIAL CANDY of the Beatles Fan Club of Fox Lake.

There's ONLY one place IN TOWN TO GeT THEM. NOT WOOLWORTHS. Basts 5 & 10. THIS STORE IS NOT at Plaza MaLL, So IT'S a Separate LITTLe JaUNT. NOT THaT FaR. I CAN WALK THeRe easILY FROM THe LaUNDROMaT. I LOVe BUYING THE GOLD FOIL PaCKS. I LOVe TO SHAKe THEM IN THE PaCK. I LOVe TO FOLD IT DOWN SO I CAN SNeaK THeM aT SCHOOL. I LOVe THe ONeS THaT DISSOLVe QUICKLY, USUaLLY YeLLOW aND GReeN. a KID ON THe PLaYGROUND SaID IT WaS a PILL. IT'S NOT.
I'm SURe J P G & R LIKe THEM. ALONG WITH JeLLY BaBIeS. BuT — — (HeRe'S THe SaD PaRT) — — — Now I HaVe TO GIVe THeM UP FOR LeNT! US CaTHOLICS DeNY OURSeLVeS SOMe PLeaSURe UNTIL EaSTeR. WHaT eLSe <u>IS</u> THeRe? RaDIO? I WON'T GIVe UP THaT OR LISTeNING TO MUSIC. CaN'T GIVe UP BRICKLaYING CUZ I'M NOT a BRICKLaYeR. Har-de-har-har ALTHOUGH I <u>DID</u> HeLP DaD PuT IN OUR FIRePLaCe LaST SUMMeR. WHeN He HOLLeReD FOR a BRICK, I THReW HIM ONe. THaT JOB DIDN'T LaST LONG aT aLL.

I ♥ candy!

!
!

official Candy

SOUR CANDY
SweeTARTS
"BITE 'EM FOR A BURST OF FLAVOR"

see you at Easter.

Please
Hold Me
Squeeze
Hold Me

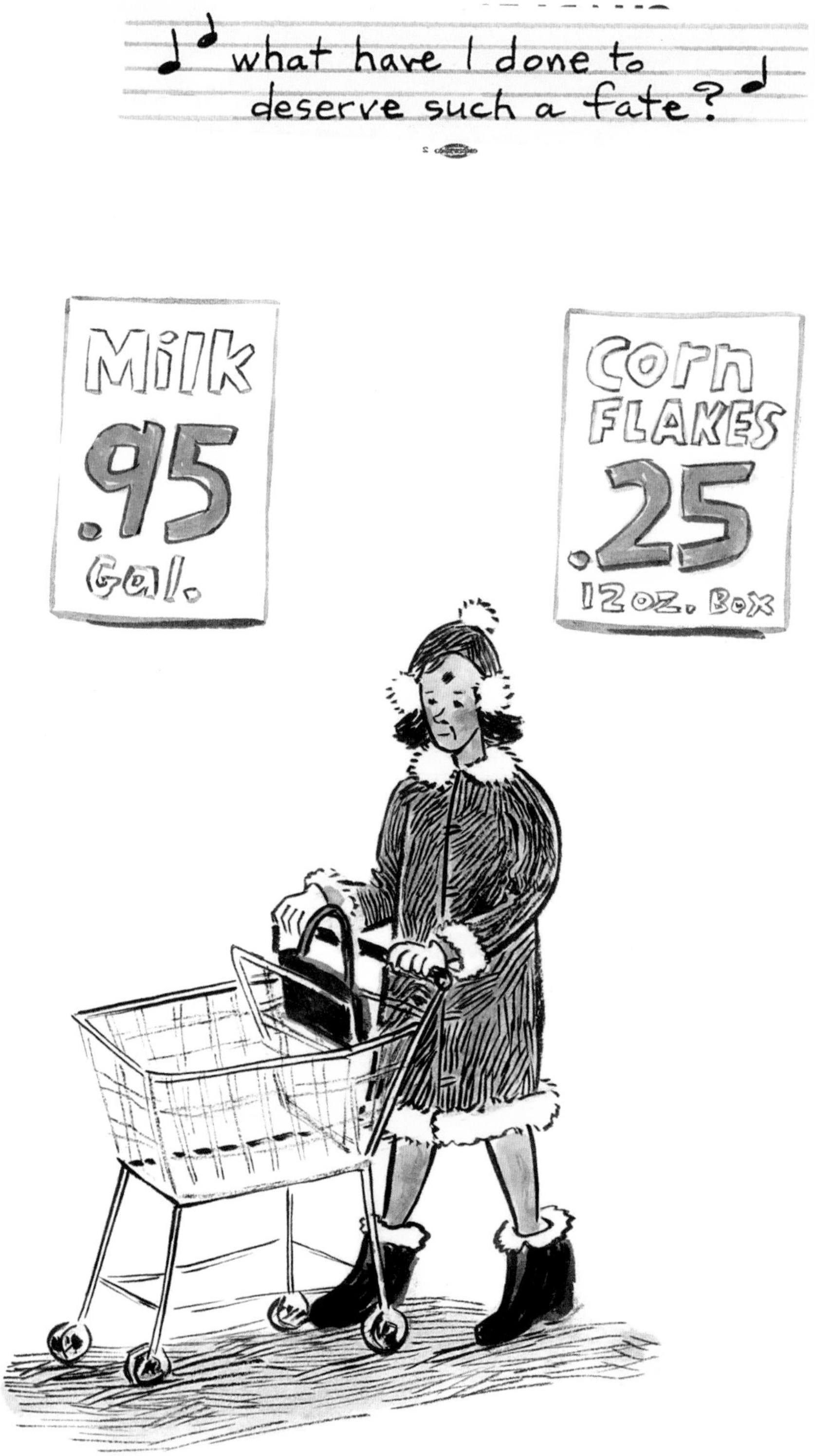
what have I done to
deserve such a fate?
Milk
.95
Gal.
Corn
FLAKES
.25
12oz. Box

CHARLES W. TYLER

PLUMBING CONTRACTOR

1837 WEST ADDISON ST.

ASH Wednesday

Mar. 3

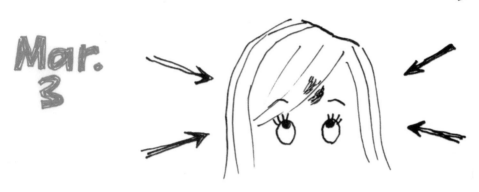

OUR CLASS WENT TO MASS FIRST THING TO GET OUR ASHES. SOME KIDS CAME BACK TO THE PEW WITH BIG ONES, THE SIZE OF BUTTER PATS. I DID. SOME GIRLS CAN COVER THEIRS WITH BANGS. FATHER COLEMAN HAS A HEAVY THUMB. I THINK IT'S UGLY. I TOSS MY HAIR AROUND WHICH THINS THEM OUT, SO IT'S NOT REALLY A COMPLETE WIPE OFF (WE'RE NOT SUPPOSED TO DO THAT). AND, YOU KNOW, IT SEEMS TO BE MEANT FOR BOYS, (THIS IS A STRETCH) BECAUSE FATHER SAID AS HE STABBED MY FOREHEAD WITH ASH "Remember Man from dust you came and to dust you shall return." HE DIDN'T SAY "Remember Young Lady," SO I THINK I'M FINE.

EVERYWHERE YOU GO -- TOWN, THE GAS STATION, GUYS COMING BACK FROM WORK, PEOPLE SHOPPING... PEOPLE EVERYWHERE HAVE ASHES. UP AT THE Jewel, GINIA SAID A LOT OF WOMEN SHOP WITH THE SPLOTCH LIKE IT'S NOTHING. Father Coleman WOULD I GUESS SAY "Remember ladies to shop at Jewel and return with milk and cornflakes."

WLS

The bright sound of Chicago Radio

SILVER DOLLAR SURVEY

Chicago's Official Radio Record Survey

MARCH 5, 1965

1. 8 DAYS A WEEK - I Don't Want to Spoil the Party Beatles
2. FERRY ACROSS THE MERSEY - Gerry + Pacemakers
3. KING OF THE ROAD ... Roger Miller - - Smash
4. THIS DIAMOND RING .... Gary Lewis - Liberty
5. LAUGH LAUGH ... The Beau Brummels - Autumn
6. CAN'T YOU HEAR MY HEARTBEAT.. Herman's Hermits
7. LITTLE THINGS ... Bobby Goldsboro -- UArtists
8. DOWNTOWN ... Petula Clark -- Warner Brothers
9. THE BIRDS AND THE BEES ... Jewel Akens -- Era
10. GOLDFINGER .... John Barry - United Artists
11. LET'S LOCK THE DOOR .... Jay and the Americans - UA
12. TELL HER NO .... Zombies - Parrot Label
13. STOP IN THE NAME OF LOVE ... Supremes - Motown
14. ALL DAY & ALL OF THE NIGHT .... The Kinks - Reprise
15. RED ROSES FOR A BLUE LADY ... B. Kaempfert - Decca
16. I GO TO PIECES ... Peter & Gordon - Capitol
17. COME HOME ... The Dave Clark Five - Epic
18. WHENEVER A TEENAGER CRIES ... Reparata & Delrons
19. MY GIRL ... The Temptations - Gordy
20. IT'S ALRIGHT ... Adam Faith - Amy
21. IF I LOVED YOU .... Chad & Jeremy - WA
22. APPLES & BANANAS ... Lawrence Welk - Dot
23. DON'T LET ME BE MISUNDERSTOOD - The Animals MGM
24. IF I RULED THE WORLD .... Tony Bennett - Columbia
25. I MUST BE SEEING THINGS .... Gene Pitney - Musicor
26. GOODNIGHT .... Roy Orbison - Monument
27. SEND ME THE PILLOW YOU DREAM ON .. Dean Martin
28. NEW YORK'S A LONELY TOWN ... The Trade - Winds
29. ASK THE LONELY .... The Four Tops - Motown
30. YEH - YEH .... Georgia Fame - Imperial
31. GO NOW .... The Moody Blues - London
32. ORANGE BLOSSOM SPECIAL ... Johnny Cash - Columbia
33. HURT SO BAD ... Little Anthony & The Imperials - DCP
34. STRANGER IN TOWN ... Del Shannon - Amy
35. NOT TOO LONG AGO ... The Uniques - Paula
36. RED ROSES FOR A BLUE LADY ... Wayne Newton
37. SHOTGUN .... Junior Walker - Soul
38. WHAT HAVE THEY DONE TO THE RAIN ... Searchers
39. APACHE '65 .... The Arrows - Tower
40. BRING YOUR LOVE TO ME .... Righteous Brothers

Brighten your evening with

Art Roberts

WLS · DIAL 890 · 24 HOURS · A · DAY

54

CHARLES W. TYLER
March 5

2

Like me, everybody in the house listens to the radio. We're 'radio ready.' They're always on "in case of a bulletin," dad says.

One in every room -- well, almost. I don't have one exclusively in my room. I have to borrow my sister's. That's such a Drag. She doesn't want me to touch it or change the dial, but that's EXACTLY what I do. Makes her mad. I don't really care. Mostly, these days, it lives on MY dresser because she's gone at work so much. But boy she can get on a tear about it, which drives me to go get mom's in the sewing room until she complains.

I listen to the good stuff in my room. WCFL and WLS mostly. After school and in the evenings. Ron Riley, Art Roberts and those guys. Dex Card with the countdown.

It's good to have so many radios. They all sport different tunes. Mom likes her 40s music, you know: big bands, bing, frank, dinah, rosemary clooney. I have to admit, I kind of like that stuff. Show tunes. Jumps. Basie and Ella. She and dad danced a lot during the war. They still go out dancing now and then. But a lot of the music is bleh. Believe me, "allegheny moon" by Patti Page is a sleeping pill. Mom calls it - 'nice music.' Yes, mom -- zzzz.

Ginia likes Neil Sedaka and stuff like that. Frankie Valli. Dion. The Platters. Joe listens to obnoxious boy songs and surf stuff. Jim's too little.

Those scruffs from Liverpool are washed up

Wally Phillips

Dad's radio listening is **LOUD** because of the saw or some pounding. In the morning it's Wally Phillips on WGN. **REALLY LOUD.** I think bombs went off in his ears in the war. 6 AM it blares to get everybody 'up and at 'em.' I Hate Wally Phillips — Talk Talk Talk. Traffic Talk. Weather Talk. News. Toilet Paper Talk. That Stupid Unicorn Song they Play over and over. What's with that? And he's Anti-Beatle. I have to wake up to that garbage. I HATE IT!

However -- it's pointless to complain. Nobody listens to me or cares about my opinion. All who live at my house share a negative view of the 4 Liverpool lads, except me, of course. All I ever say is "I want my **OWN** radio."

2 summers ago, my sister liked this boy on our road. Robert Orczekowiczki or something. Too hard to say. I called him Robert Big-O. He got my sister into listening to the radio. —— Here's what I heard about it from her friend Janice's sister who's my age: So Big-O said to listen to the songs, and whenever someone sings about a kiss or kissing, she's to meet him up at the big pole, and they would do just that -- kiss. And since so many songs are about kissing and loving, she met him up there just about everyday. He was only here for 2 weeks at his grandma's cottage. Then it was

OVER. SHE QUIT GOING UP TO THE POLE. HE FORGOT
TO TELL HER HE WAS LEAVING. IF SHE WAS SAD,
YOU WOULDN'T KNOW IT. I WONDER WHAT SHE
THINKS, GOING PAST THAT POLE EVERY DAY ON
HER WAY TO THE JEWEL. PROBABLY NOTHING.
SHE'S SUCH A CRAB. SHE DOESN'T REALLY EVEN
LISTEN TO HER RADIO ANYMORE EITHER.

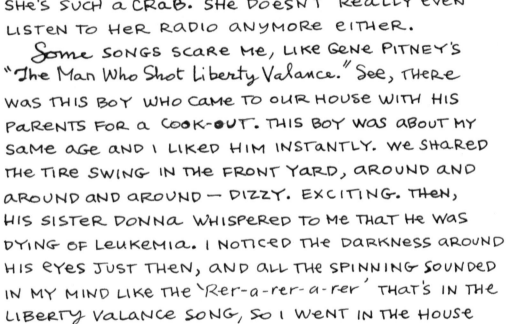

Some SONGS SCARE ME, LIKE GENE PITNEY'S
"The Man Who Shot Liberty Valance." See, THERE
WAS THIS BOY WHO CAME TO OUR HOUSE WITH HIS
PARENTS FOR A COOK-OUT. THIS BOY WAS ABOUT MY
SAME AGE AND I LIKED HIM INSTANTLY. WE SHARED
THE TIRE SWING IN THE FRONT YARD, AROUND AND
AROUND AND AROUND — DIZZY. EXCITING. THEN,
HIS SISTER DONNA WHISPERED TO ME THAT HE WAS
DYING OF LEUKEMIA. I NOTICED THE DARKNESS AROUND
HIS EYES JUST THEN, AND ALL THE SPINNING SOUNDED
IN MY MIND LIKE THE 'Rer-a-rer-a-rer' THAT'S IN THE
LIBERTY VALANCE SONG, SO I WENT IN THE HOUSE
AND STAYED IN MY ROOM THE REST OF THE DAY, AFRAID
I'D CATCH LEUKEMIA. I DIDN'T EVEN EAT.

Later that night after they all left, MY
SISTER TOLD ME THAT SHE AND DONNA COOKED UP
THAT LEUKEMIA STORY BECAUSE WE WERE HOGGING
THE SWING. BUMS!!!

"I Remember You" IS ANOTHER SCARY TUNE.
WHEN I WAS REAL LITTLE, I HAD TO SIT IN THE FRONT
IN THE CAR BETWEEN MY PARENTS, WHO IGNORED ME.
I COULDN'T SIT IN THE BACK BECAUSE DAD'S CEE-GAR

LOVE ME DO

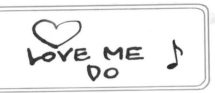

SMOKE MADE ME SICK, AND I THREW UP ALL OVER JOE AND GINIA. DAD SAID HE **HAD** TO SMOKE. HE NEEDED A FLAME HANDY FOR EMERGENCIES. (?). MOM HATED THE SMOKE, TOO. SHE'D INSIST "*Chuck, open your window,*" THAT LITTLE TRIANGLE VENT IN THE FRONT. HE COULD OPEN IT JUST ENOUGH TO SUCK THE SMOKE OUT, BUT IT WHISTLED BACK AT HER AS IF SAYING, "*Shut up already!*"

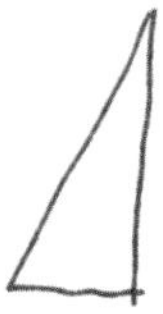

IT WAS HOT AND STUFFY UP THERE BY THE MOTOR AND THE HEATER IN MY WOOL COAT, HAT AND MUFF. I WAS TOO SHORT TO SEE ANYTHING BUT THE DASHBOARD,— I WAS SQUARE-ON WITH THE RADIO. IF I LOOKED UP, I COULD SEE INTO DAD'S NOSTRILS, COULD SEE TREE TOPS, AND ELECTRIC LINES WHIZZING BY. OCCASIONALLY, VERY SLOW IN THE DISTANCE, AND UNPLEASANT AS EVERYTHING ELSE, WERE THESE TOWERS WITH BLINKING RED LIGHTS. I FIGURED THEM TO BE RADIO TRANSMITTERS — FROM THAT 'BULLETIN and EMERGENCY' STUFF THAT DAD KNEW ABOUT. FRIGHTENING AND NECESSARY TO BRING THE MUSIC, TO FORCE IT OUT THROUGH THE SLOTS ON THE FRONT. GREAT SONGS PUSH PAST THE WIRES AND TUBES, BUT WHEN SOME GET TANGLED, THE RESULTS CAN BE BAD.

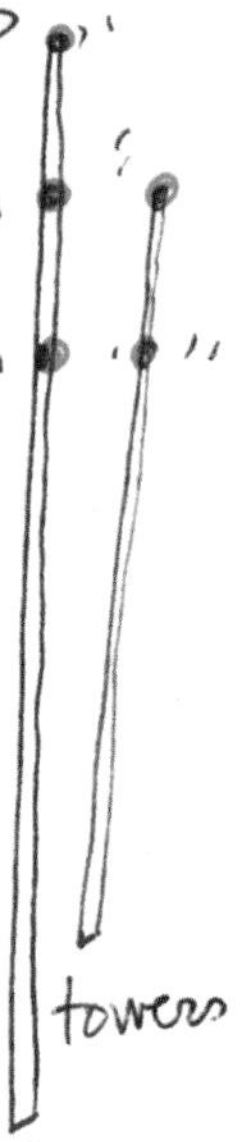
towers

I ASKED DAD WHAT THOSE TOWERS WERE, WHY THE LIGHTS WERE BLINKING, AND HE SAID "*Don't worry about it*" PUFF PUFF cigar smoke. STRAIGHT AHEAD, COMING FROM THE RADIO GRILL: yodeling. Frank Ifield, "I remember too, distant bells and stars that fell, like a rain, out of the blue-ooo-ooo . . .

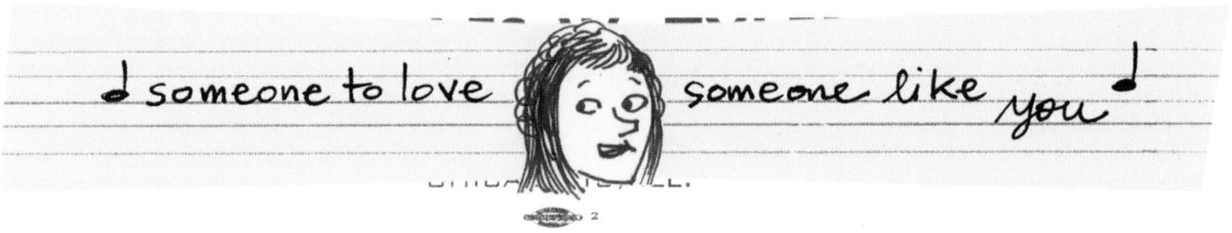
someone to love
someone like you

Then he sang "..*When my life is through*..." That made me think 'Oh no. Is he talking about when he dies?' "...*and the angels ask me to recall*..." Then I think 'Yep. Dying. Why is he singing about that?' It scared me so much, I threw up in the front this time- all over Mom.

There seems to be plenty of songs about death and sorrow and misery. I've heard them a lot in church and on the radio. I guess there *has* to be, to cover all the emotions the way Sherwin-Williams paint covers the earth. I don't understand a lot of it. Maybe when I grow up. But still, it's O.K. to like some of the music old people and even my sister listens to. (I don't have to tell them). One of Mom's radio tunes says something like "*The sweetest* sounds *I'll ever hear are still inside my head.*"

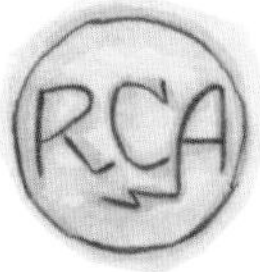
RCA

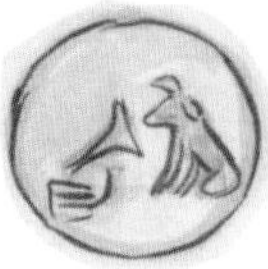

Honestly — *my head* IS full of music and sound, ALL KINDS of music, and I LOVE it. *I love it* **ALL!** *I even like* ad jingles. I've always wondered who these singers are. There are men talking, songs playing, and then these singers. WHO ARE THEY? They sing about cars, they sing about bread, they sing about carpet. They even sing phone numbers. More ladies voices than men.

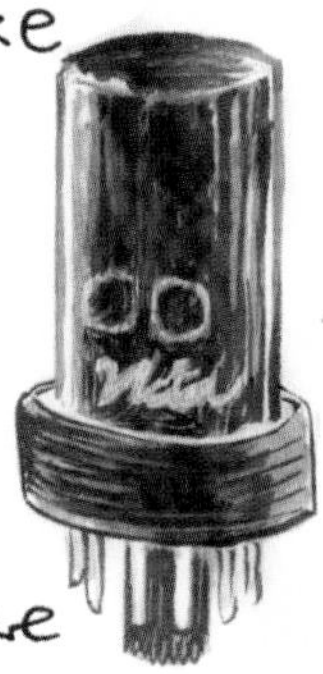

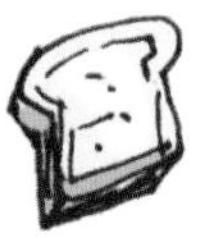

"*At 3 in the morning when you're in bed, the Holsum bakers are baking bread.*"
H-O-L-S-U-M, H-O-L-S-U-M, H-O-L-S-U-M
Holsum bread.

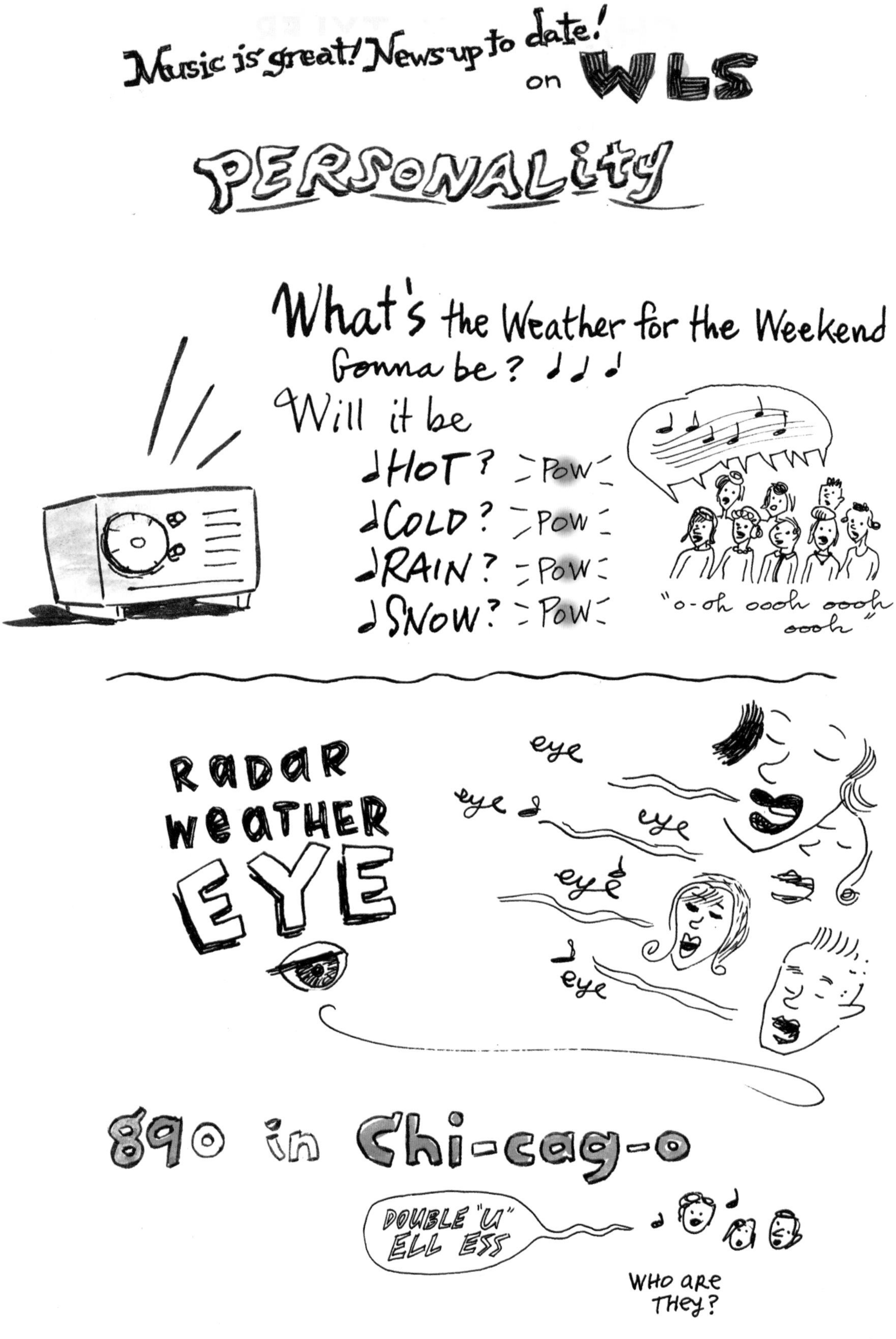
Music is great! News up to date! on WLS
PERSONALITY
What's the Weather for the Weekend Gonna be?
Will it be
HOT? POW
COLD? POW
RAIN? POW
SNOW? POW
"o-oh oooh oooh oooh"
RADAR WEATHER EYE
eye
eye
eye
eye
eye
890 in Chi-cag-o
DOUBLE "U" ELL ESS
WHO ARE THEY?

CAROL A. TYLER
RADIO READY

1. Ginia's Radio, plays Pop
2. Mom's Frank Sinatra tube radio
3. Solid state - Dad's morning WGN
4. Dad's garage/workshop radio. He made an outside shell to fit into a tight spot. Old tube radio works inside
5. Console - radio + records
   (Saturdays)

| WIND | WGN | WBBM | WENR WLS | WMAQ |

Buttons from the top of the garage radio

MARCH 10 -- I ~~THINCK~~ THINK

Ringo } I THINK RINGO IS SHARP! is sharp

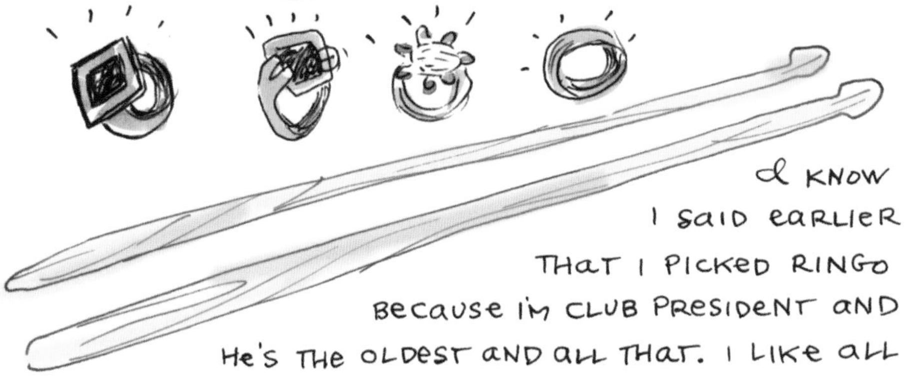

I KNOW I SAID EARLIER THAT I PICKED RINGO BECAUSE I'M CLUB PRESIDENT AND HE'S THE OLDEST AND ALL THAT. I LIKE ALL 4 EQUALLY, BUT RINGO -- WELL, I CAN'T IMAGINE A FAB 4 WITHOUT HIM. LET ME BREAK IT DOWN, NOT AS PRESIDENT, BUT AS LITTLE OLD ME.

- *John* – THE LEADER. WITTY. SMART. COULDN'T BEAT HIM IN A SPELLING BEE (and I'm <u>good</u>).
- *Paul* – COULD BE A Hollywood Star. DEFINITELY THE CUTEST, BUT I KNOW I WOULD <u>NEVER</u> HAVE A CHANCE WITH HIM.
- *George* – KINDA QUIET. KINDA LIKE DAD'S HAND TOOLS OUT IN THE GARAGE.
- *Ringo* – SHAKES HIS HEAD AROUND TO THE MUSIC. HE CAN'T HELP IT! THE BEAT MAKES HIM DO IT.

In fact – THE GUITARS ARE SO <u>ALIVE</u>, THE VIBRATIONS MAKE ME JUMP AROUND!

When they sing, PAUL IS FLIRTY, GEORGE IS BUILDING SOMETHING, JOHN AIMS RIGHT AT ME. THEY ALL SHAKE AND SHIMMY. RINGO BURSTS TO THE BEAT, AND IT'S

WOW.

CHARLES W. TYLER

PLUMBING CONTRACTOR

1837 WEST ADDISON ST.

CHICAGO 13, ILL.

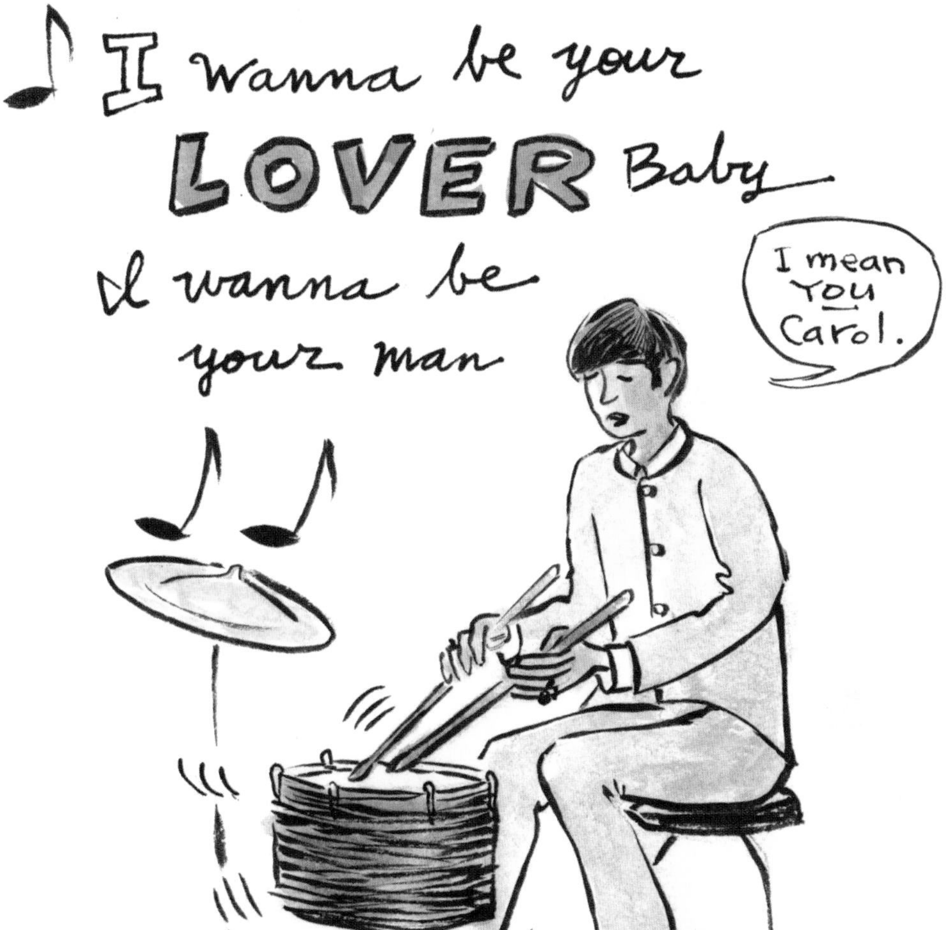
I wanna be your
LOVER Baby
I wanna be
your man
I mean YOU Carol.

ringo starr

☆ Real name = Richard Starkey. Received the name RINGO because of his many rings. When asked, "Why do you wear so many rings on your fingers?" he said "Because I can't fit them throngh my nose." Plays the drums and occasionally sings. He's the only one that doesn't write songs. He hates Donald Duck and onions.

Ringo was born on July 7, 1940. He is the oldest, leading over John by 3 months. He is 5'8" and 134 pounds, and so is the smallest. Has dark brown hair and blue eyes. One of the more popular Beatles, — although they all take the cake for that.

This Boy

THIS BOY

THAT BOY

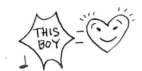

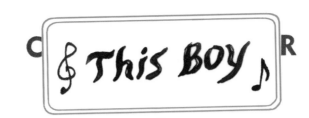

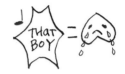

You know what a "session" is. I explained it earlier—when the Beatles get together to record. Well, last night, I had a 'session' of my own. A project. I got an idea to make all 4 of the Beatles' instruments for the walls of my bedroom. I'll be using pastels the way Sister taught me with black outlines. I got some brown paper from Mom. She has a roll.

I figured out the sizes as best I could from photographs. I used a yardstick for the neck. They are going to be pretty close to the exact size. I want it to be that they could come in my room at any time and pluck the instruments RIGHT OFF THE WALL, quickly play a song and be on their way. And, of course, I would sing right along with them because I know **EVERY SINGLE WORD TO EVERY SINGLE SONG.** Next year, if I can't go on tour with them, I can at least get a pair of drumsticks, if not an instrument for Christmas.

Here's the first result = Ringo's drum set, complete with cymbals, except I forgot to make the stool. He's the only Beatle who gets to sit down on the job.

ct + rs

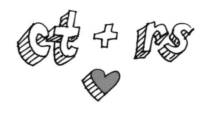

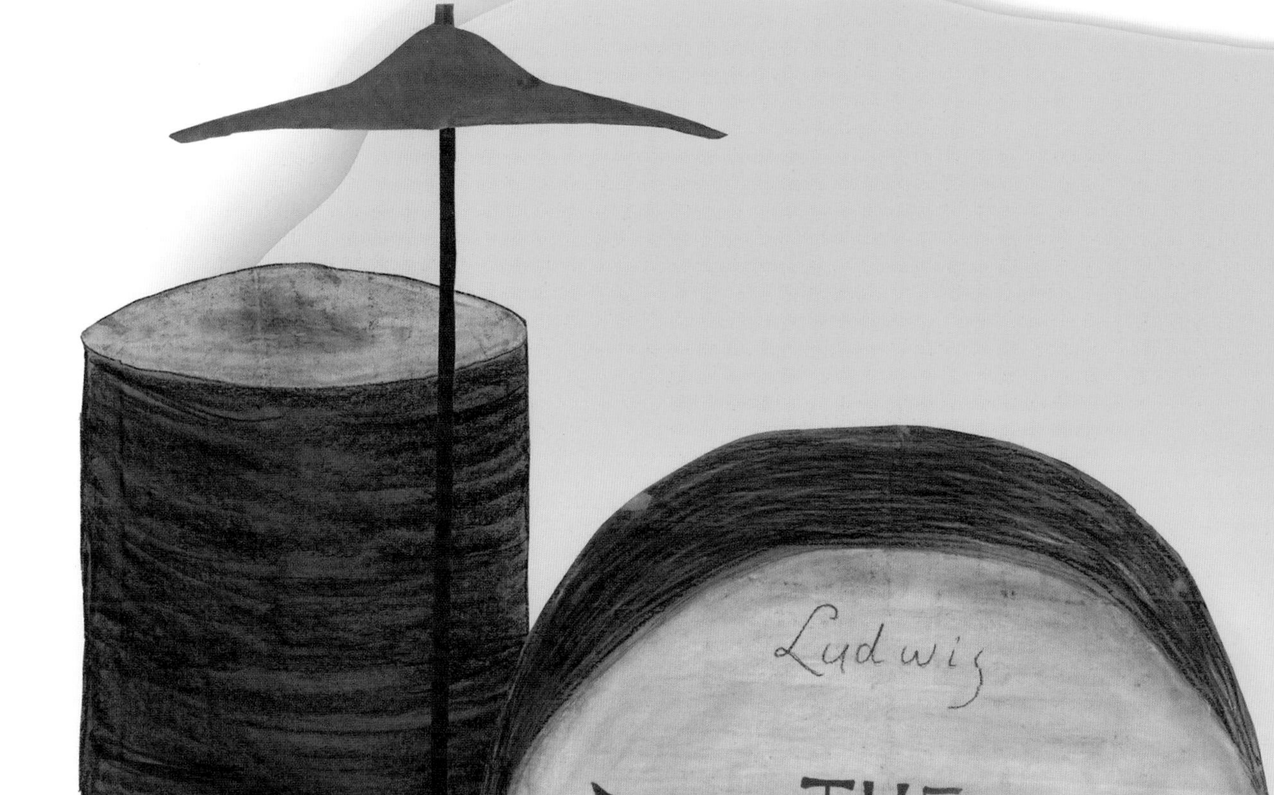
Ludwig
THE
BEATLES

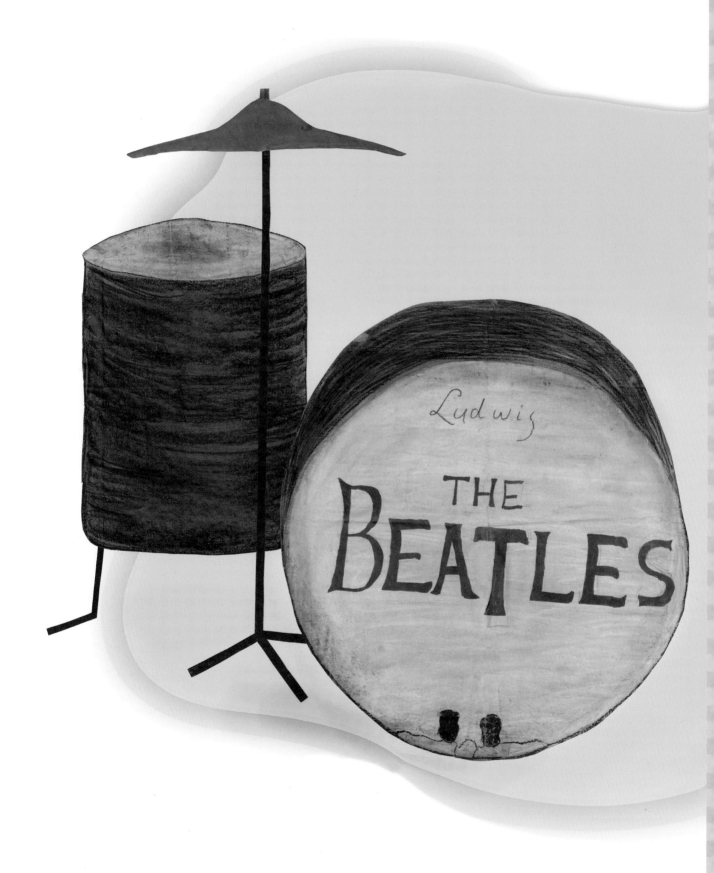

RINGO

RINGART

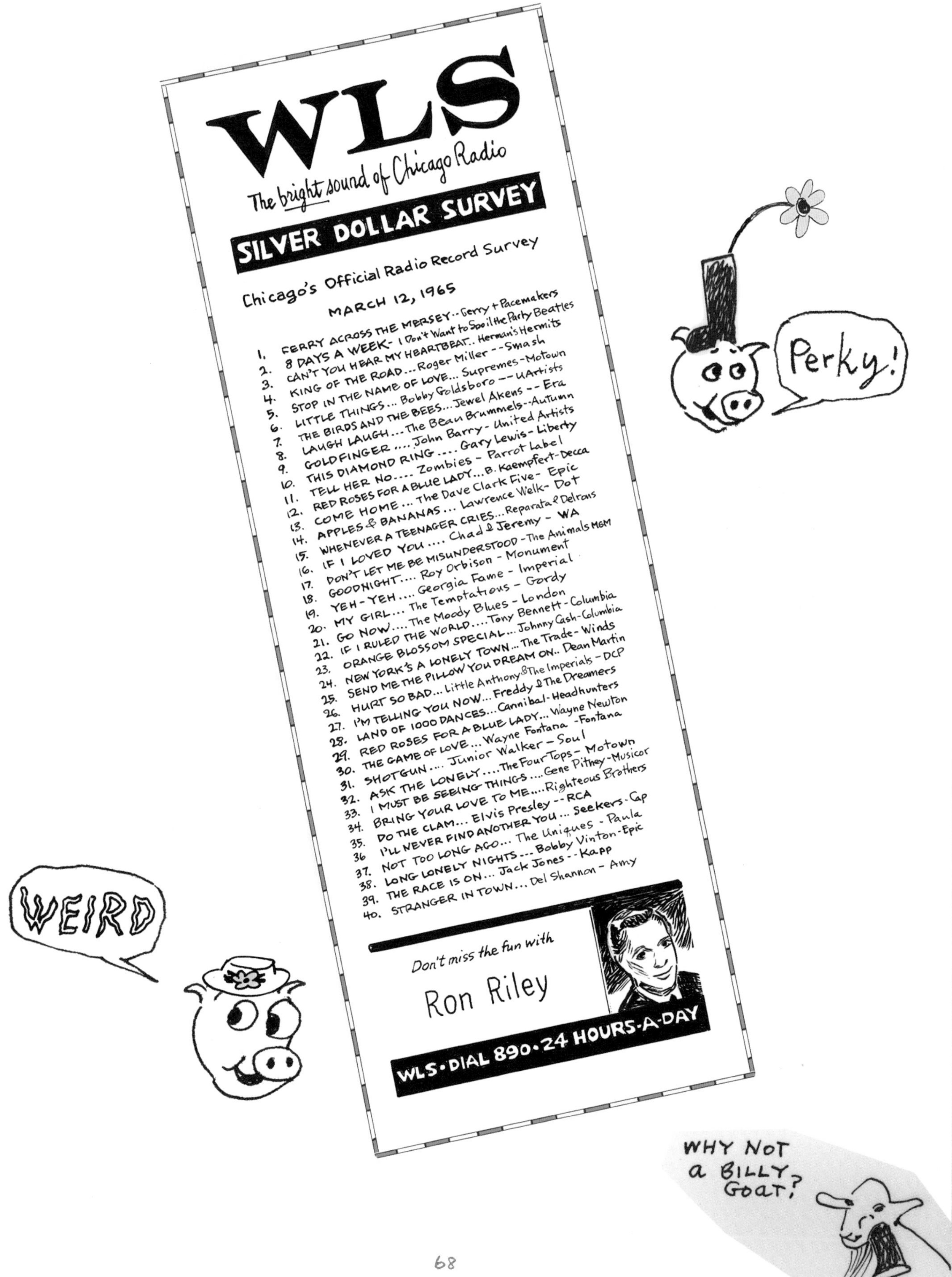

WLS
The bright sound of Chicago Radio
SILVER DOLLAR SURVEY
Chicago's Official Radio Record Survey
MARCH 12, 1965
1. FERRY ACROSS THE MERSEY.. Gerry + Pacemakers
2. 8 DAYS A WEEK- I Don't Want to Spoil the Party Beatles
3. CAN'T YOU HEAR MY HEARTBEAT.. Herman's Hermits
4. KING OF THE ROAD... Roger Miller --Smash
5. STOP IN THE NAME OF LOVE... Supremes-Motown
6. LITTLE THINGS... Bobby Goldsboro --UArtists
7. THE BIRDS AND THE BEES... Jewel Akens -- Era
8. LAUGH LAUGH... The Beau Brummels--Autumn
9. GOLDFINGER.... John Barry- United Artists
10. THIS DIAMOND RING.... Gary Lewis- Liberty
11. TELL HER NO..... Zombies - Parrot label
12. RED ROSES FOR A BLUE LADY... B. Kaempfert-Decca
13. COME HOME... The Dave Clark Five- Epic
14. APPLES & BANANAS... Lawrence Welk- Dot
15. WHENEVER A TEENAGER CRIES... Reparata & Delrons
16. IF I LOVED YOU.... Chad & Jeremy - WA
17. DON'T LET ME BE MISUNDERSTOOD -The Animals MGM
18. GOODNIGHT.... Roy Orbison - Monument
19. YEH-YEH.... Georgia Fame - Imperial
20. MY GIRL... The Temptations - Gordy
21. GO NOW.... The Moody Blues - London
22. IF I RULED THE WORLD.... Tony Bennett-Columbia
23. ORANGE BLOSSOM SPECIAL... Johnny Cash-Columbia
24. NEW YORK'S A LONELY TOWN... The Trade-Winds
25. SEND ME THE PILLOW YOU DREAM ON.. Dean Martin
26. HURT SO BAD... Little Anthony & The Imperials - DCP
27. I'M TELLING YOU NOW... Freddy & The Dreamers
28. LAND OF 1000 DANCES... Cannibal-Headhunters
29. RED ROSES FOR A BLUE LADY... Wayne Newton
30. THE GAME OF LOVE... Wayne Fontana -Fontana
31. SHOTGUN.... Junior Walker - Soul
32. ASK THE LONELY.... The Four Tops- Motown
33. I MUST BE SEEING THINGS.... Gene Pitney-Musicor
34. BRING YOUR LOVE TO ME.... Righteous Brothers
35. DO THE CLAM... Elvis Presley -- RCA
36 I'LL NEVER FIND ANOTHER YOU... Seekers-Cap
37. NOT TOO LONG AGO... The Uniques - Paula
38. LONG LONELY NIGHTS--- Bobby Vinton-Epic
39. THE RACE IS ON... Jack Jones -- Kapp
40. STRANGER IN TOWN... Del Shannon - Amy
Don't miss the fun with
Ron Riley
WLS·DIAL 890·24 HOURS·A·DAY
Perky!
WEIRD
WHY NOT a BILLY GOAT?

4 WAYS TO BE A TRUE BEATLEMANIAC.

CHICAGO 13, ILL.

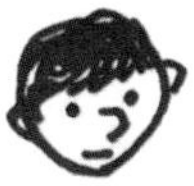
Say "Beatles" with a British accent. Emphasize the first syllable "Beat" followed by "uls" BEAT-uls.

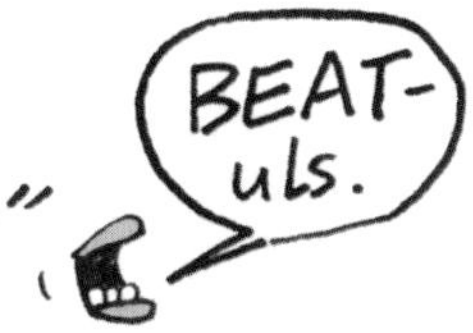
BEAT-
uls.

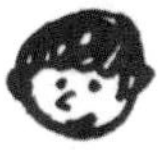
Change your clock to the Liverpool time zone.

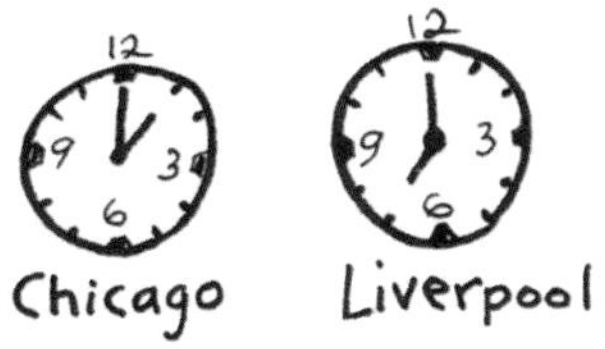
12
9
3
6
Chicago
Liverpool

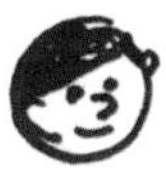
Of course write *Beatles* like this *Beatles* with the syrup on your Saturday stack.

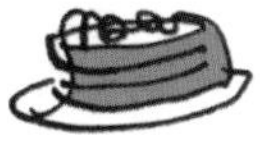

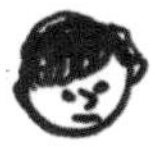
Make a cake on each Beatle birthday to celebrate. But because your family is probably sick of your Beatlemania, here's a tip: Instead of writing the name on the cake, add the numbers of the Beatle birthday and write that on top. So for John, born Oct. 9, 1940, add 10+9+40 = **59** Put that on the cake. IF anyone asks, say it's in honor of our nation's highways.

Paul — June 18, 1942 — 6+18+42 = **66**
George – Feb 25, 1943 — 2+25+43 = **70**
Ringo – July 7, 1940 — 7+7+40 = **54**

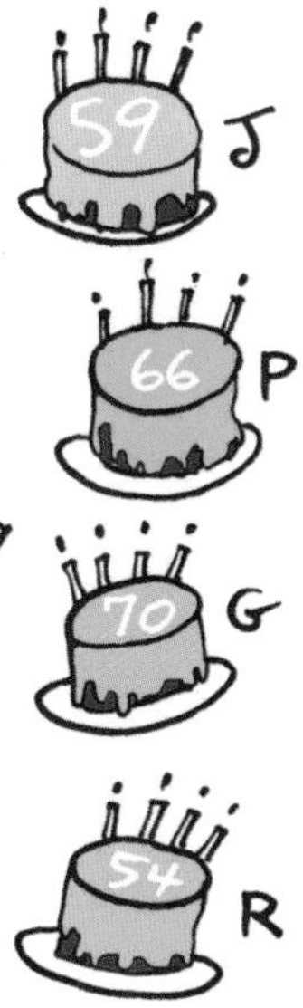
59
J
66
P
70
G
54
R

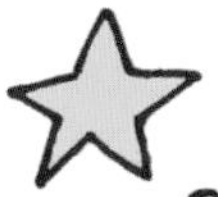
BONUS

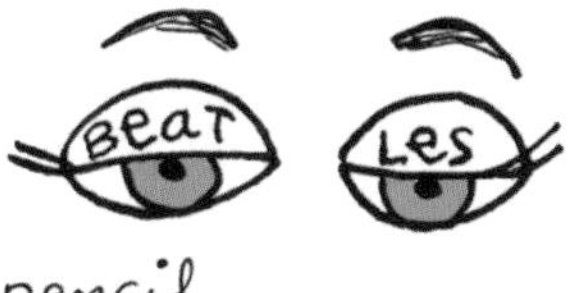
BEAT
LES

Saved the best for last:
For this you need an eyebrow pencil
Write "BEAT on one eyelid and LES on the other.
That way you can bat your eyes at people and even spell out words. Code signals. BACKWARDS ← Make sure it's Backwards to you.

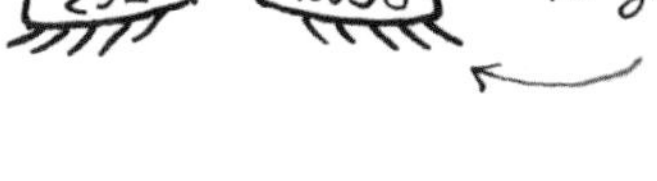
LES
BEAT

And Now -- from the 'It's just me being crazy'
DEPARTMENT - meet the new music sensation
from the other side of Liverpuke, Illinois:

The BAIN'TLES!

They ain't the Beatles

A 5 MEMBER STRING QUARTET ROCK JUG BAND.

NED ON KID PIANO
"The cute one"

FLOREENA ON a CHEESE STRING UKE
"The Clever one"

ANOTHER NED ON A KID PIANO
"The Loud one"

BOLD TONY ON A RECORDER
"The shy one"

LOOP—The DRUMMER.
"The Lucky one"

TOP 10 HITS:

 I can't Stand to Hold Your Hand.

Please PAY me, OH yeah or I'll sue you.

 It's been a HARD BOILED EGG I wouldn't feed it to a dog.

Every other day I guess I feel FINE.

She Loves You YEAH YEAH YEAH She Loves Me YEAH YEAH YEAH Which is it? YEAH yeah yeah YEAH!

 Because I told You before— OH, You CAN'T KEEP Cats.

 If I fell into a pool—

 I wanna Go To PRISON, BABY I WANNA STEAL A VAN.

 Listen... Do you WANT TO KNOW MY LOCKER COMBINATION.

 Well SHAKE The JAR BABY NOW— Shake the Jar Baby.. TWIST-OFF LID.

2. EIGHTH GRADE IS

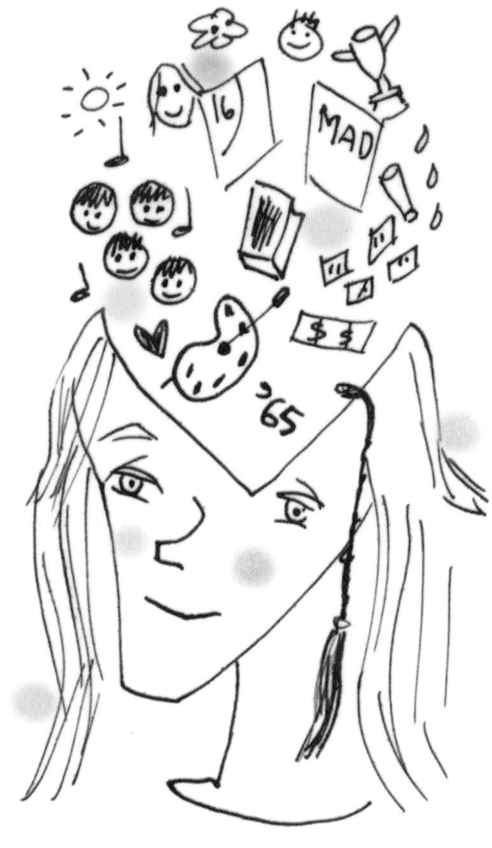
16
MAD
$$
'65

FAB GEAR

CAROL TYLER 1965

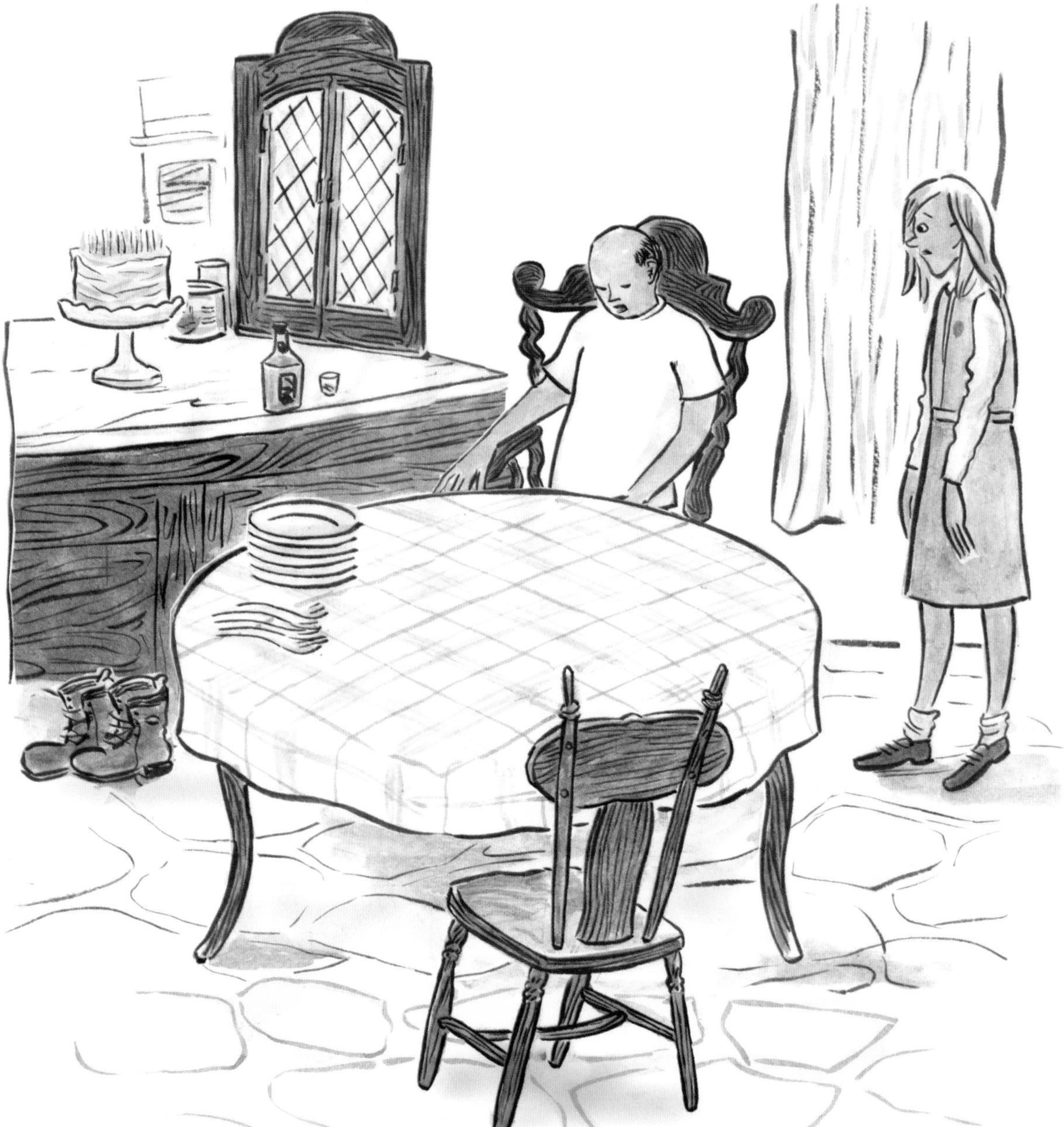

There's a Place

LER

OR

CHICAGO 13, ILL.

Mar. 13

The big 4-6

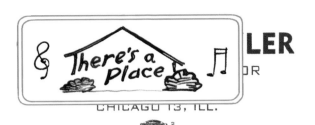

Today is Dad's birthday. I made him a cake after school. He's getting old, but I'm glad he's alive after what happened this week.

On Tuesday, he came home from work as usual. My dad works all day in a ditch at wherever there's a new something being built. He is a pipe fitter. Plumbing, you know. As they say, "If you turn on a tap or flush a toilet in the city of Chicago, you can thank a Tyler." My dad, his dad, and his dad were all plumbers. Union men. But it got too hectic in the city so we moved out here, 50 miles out, and Dad goes in to work somewhere around Chicago, western suburbs mainly. He did O'Hare.

So he came home, gave Mom a kiss, set down his lunchbox, sat in his chair, took his boots off, had a shot of whiskey and told this story.

He was in this ditch with another guy, when the dirt started to cave in. The other man was completely buried in just seconds. Dad hollered and clawed and tried to get him out but he just couldn't. Nobody could. He suffocated. A few feet over and Dad would have been gone, too. So he was pretty shook up, but he said "My number was not up yet, I guess."

Just about every day he's crabby. Yelling. Only talks to Mom. I watched him tell her all about the cave-in, over and over, shot after whiskey shot. He shook like a bare-naked sapling.

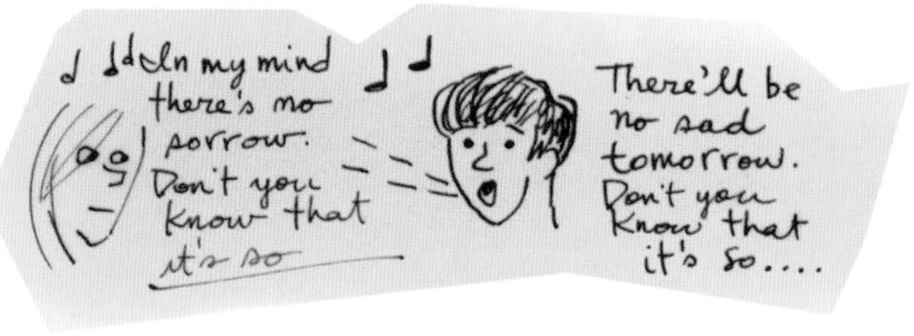
In my mind there's no sorrow. Don't you know that it's so
There'll be no sad tomorrow. Don't you know that it's so....

I WATCHED IN SECRET FROM ANOTHER ROOM. THAT'S WHY I MADE HIM A CAKE. I MEAN GINIA WOULD HAVE, SHE WANTED TO, BUT SHE'S AT WORK AND I HEARD THIS.

After HE SETTLED DOWN, THE WHISKEY PUT HIM OUT FOR A BIT. I TOOK THE CAKE OUT OF THE OVEN, STUCK IT IN THE FREEZER TO COOL, TOOK IT OUT 40 MIN. LATER AND ICED IT; THAT'S HOW LONG HE SLEPT. HE USUALLY TAKES A NAP IN HIS CHAIR AFTER WORK, AFTER A SHOT, WITH THE T.V. ON. GARFIELD GOOSE, ROCKY AND BULLWINKLE. MR. MAGOO. NO WATCHING THE NEWS. TOO GRIM.

This TIME, ON HIS BIRTHDAY, WHILE HE SLEPT, I SNUK OVER BY HIS CHAIR AND JUST LOOKED AT HIM. I STOOD THERE, AS CLOSE AS THAT BURIED MAN WAS. I LOOKED AT HIS FACE REAL HARD. SILENT. I WANTED TO TOUCH HIM -- MAYBE JUST PUT MY FINGER ON THE EDGE OF HIS T-SHIRT SOMEWHERE. BY THE ARM MUSCLE. THE WEARY, SAFEST SPOT.

AROUND HIM, MOSTLY, I FEEL INVISIBLE. IT TAKES BOLD STEPS LIKE THIS TO SEE IF I'M REAL, IF HE'S REAL. TO SEE IF I COULD GET AWAY WITH IT. I'd DIE IF I GOT CAUGHT, OR GET YELLED AT SERIOUSLY. SO I JUST STOOD THERE. IT WAS HIS BIRTHDAY. THE BIG 4-6. NO CAKE FOR ME. I GAVE UP SWEETS FOR Lent.

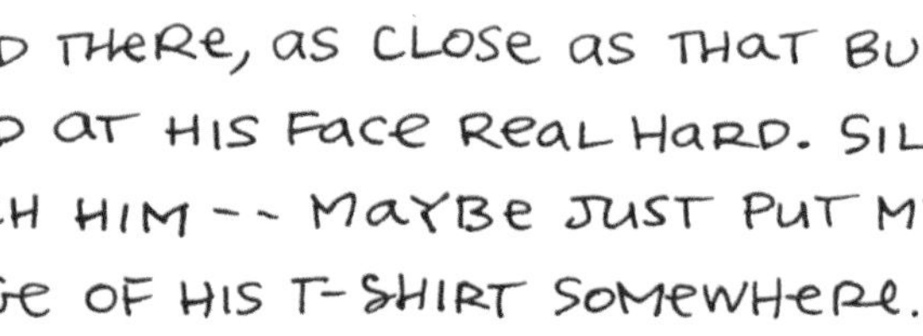
Hiya Charlie!
GG
Garfield Goose

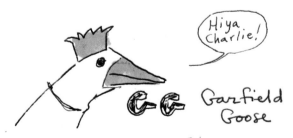

I should have known better

CHICAGO 13, ILL.

Mar. 15

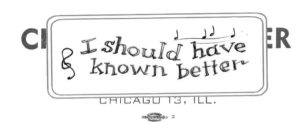

Sister Immaculata sent home a note today to tell all the parents that there's going to be a raffle and bake sale for St. Patrick's Day,

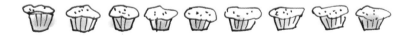

Erin Go Bragh

so I made cupcakes after supper. We need money for busses to take us on a class trip to the Museum of Science and Industry down in Chicago. I hope bunches of people have not given up cupcakes for Lent.

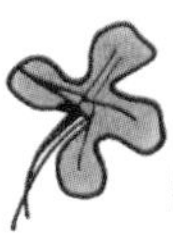

Mrs. Beets is in charge. We're all supposed to bring in a dozen or 2 dozen cupcakes. Cathy's mom is making Beatles pillows. 4 round pillows with yarn for hair. She made some last year. They went for a lot. Everything is for sale after church on Sunday. I want to buy a chance on those pillows. 25¢ each. I'll get 2 chances.

Last time we went down to the museum, I got stuck sitting next to Tureki. He kept trying to put his arm around me, but I'm tall and he's short so it didn't work. I had to scream in his face — he doesn't listen. Miller had his arm around Frances. Jekat kept looking out the window, snickering. Then he'd turn and look and quick look out the window and snicker again over and over. Nobody sat by him. Maybe I will next time just to bug Tureki.

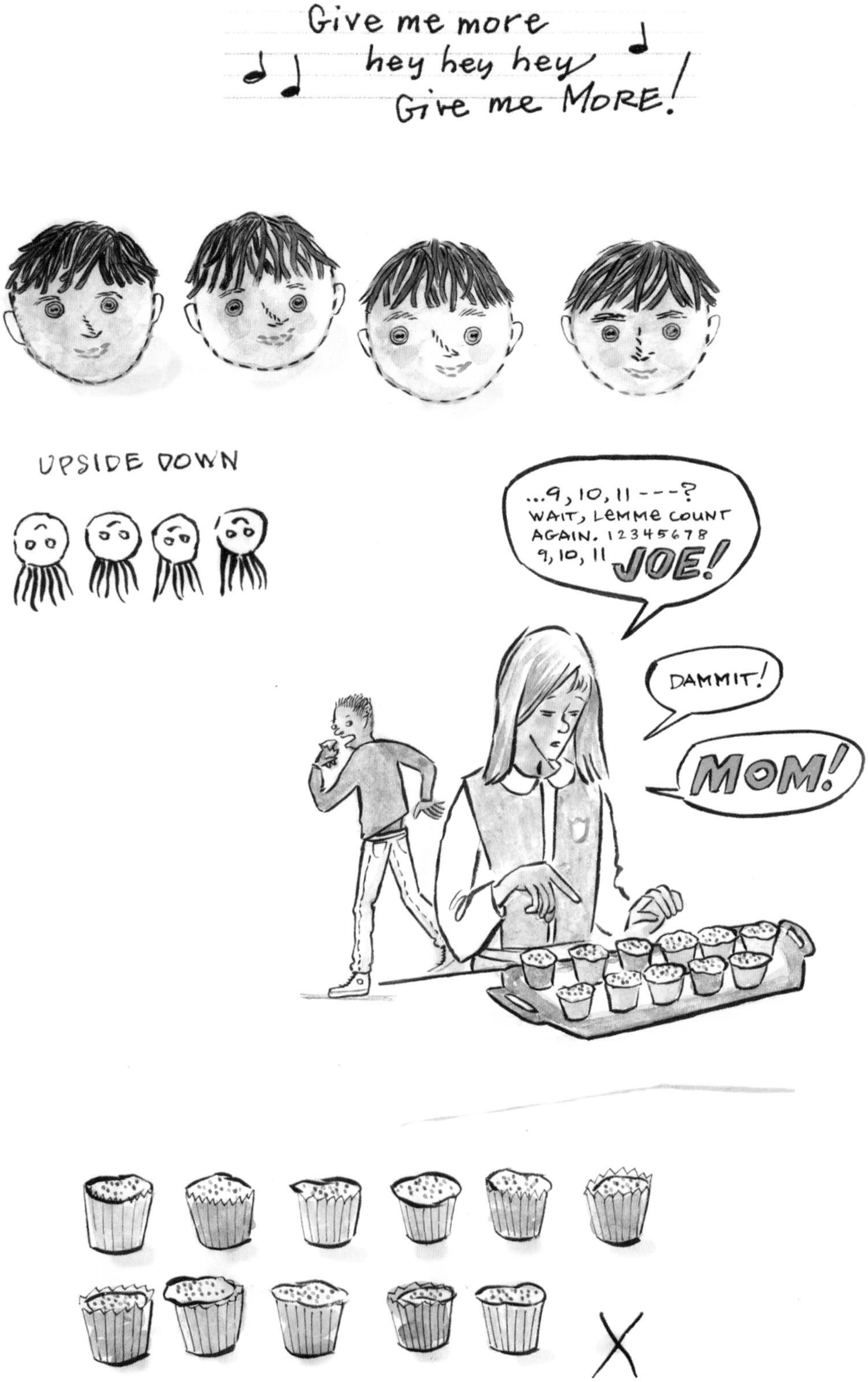
Give me more
hey hey hey
Give me MORE!
UPSIDE DOWN
...9, 10, 11 ---? WAIT, LEMME COUNT AGAIN. 12345678 9, 10, 11 JOE!
DAMMIT!
MOM!

DON'T BOTHER ME.

March 19

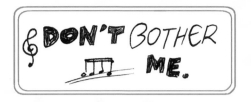

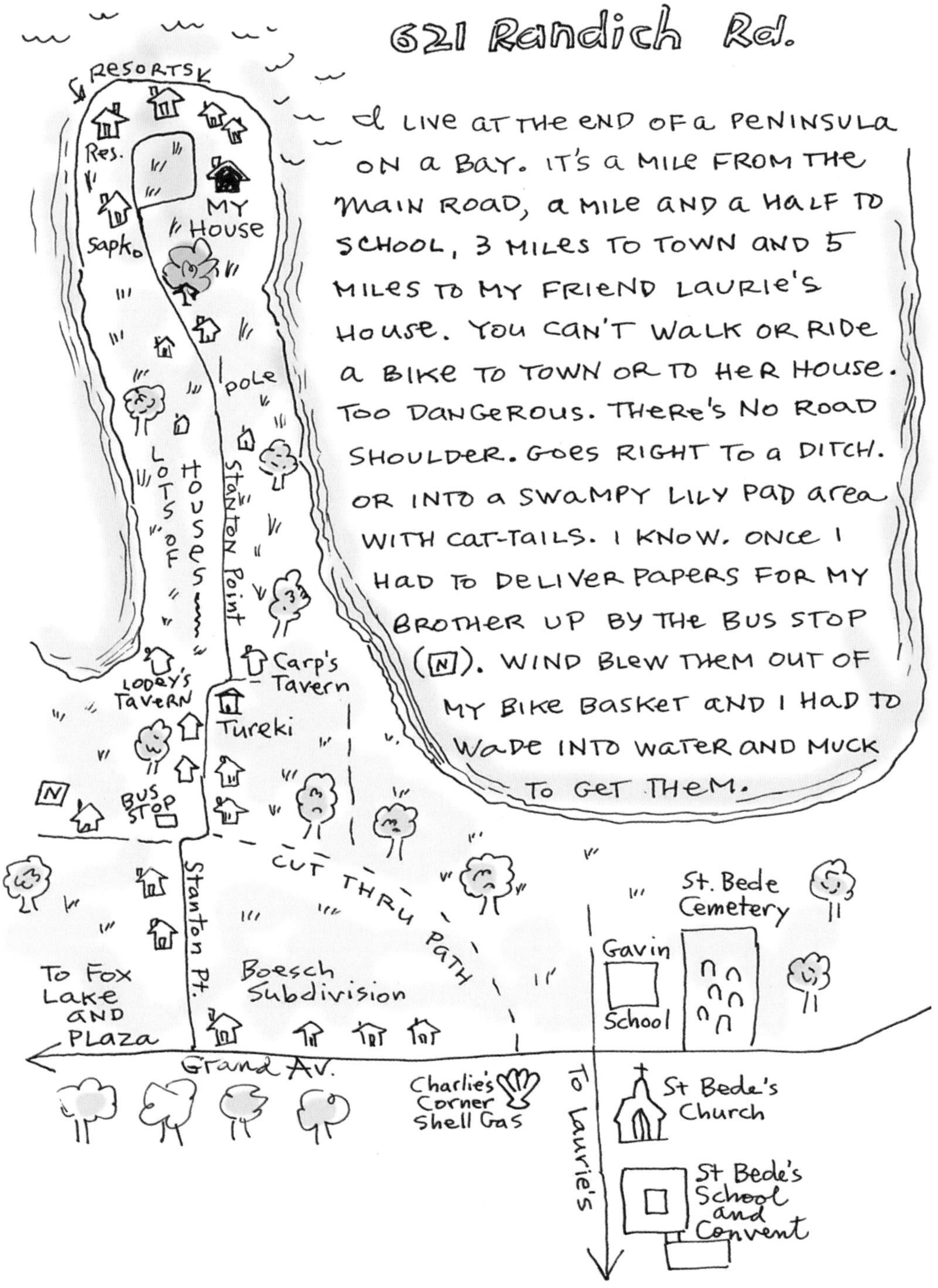
621 Randich Rd.
I live at the end of a peninsula on a bay. It's a mile from the main road, a mile and a half to school, 3 miles to town and 5 miles to my friend Laurie's house. You can't walk or ride a bike to town or to her house. Too dangerous. There's no road shoulder. Goes right to a ditch. Or into a swampy lily pad area with cat-tails. I know. Once I had to deliver papers for my brother up by the bus stop (N). Wind blew them out of my bike basket and I had to wade into water and muck to get them.
Resorts
Res.
My House
Sapko
Pole
Lots of Houses
Stanton Point
Carp's Tavern
Lodey's Tavern
Tureki
Bus Stop
Cut Thru Path
Stanton Pt.
Boesch Subdivision
To Fox Lake and Plaza
Grand Av.
Charlie's Corner Shell Gas
To Laurie's
Gavin School
St. Bede Cemetery
St Bede's Church
St Bede's School and Convent

BECAUSE I KNOW SHE'LL ALWAYS BE. THE ONLY GIRL FOR ME

MUCKY, SWAMPY, CATTAILS EVERYWHERE OUT HERE AT THE CHAIN O'LAKES. SURE IS WATERY. WE ARE SURROUNDED ON 3 SIDES BY WATER. IN WINTER, IT'S THE 'CHAIN O'ICE.' IT GETS SO THICK, PEOPLE DRIVE THEIR CARS OUT ON IT. BOYS PLAY TOO MUCH HOCKEY, AND I LIKE TO SPIN AND DO JUMPS. EVERY TIME I GO OUT THERE, I HAVE TO SHOVEL A SPOT. THERE'S SO MUCH WIND AND SNOW. IN THE SUMMER, IT'S SWIMMING AND BOATING. I PRETTY MUCH LIVE IN THE WATER. BUT THIS TIME OF YEAR, EVERYTHING **FLOODS.** THE ROAD DOWN TO OUR HOUSE FLOODS, BUT OUR HOUSE IS HIGH AND DRY. PEOPLE DRIVE THROUGH THE WATER VERY SLOW. IT'S NOT THAT DEEP. AND SINCE I WALK HOME, I WALK THROUGH IT IN UGLY RUBBER BOOTS.

LIFE OUT AT THE LAKES IS A WHOLE LOT QUIETER THAN WHEN WE LIVED IN CHICAGO. DURING FLOODING, IT SEEMS LIKE THERE'S NO LAND. JUST A FEW HOUSES ON SMALL MOUNDS HERE AND THERE. THE TREES LOOK LIKE TOOTHPICKS POKED IN ASPIC, LIKE THE CLUB GIRLS MAKE. LONELY. RIPPLES AND BABY WAVES FORM WHEN A CAR SWIMS THROUGH. THE ONLY SOUNDS ARE LOTS OF BIRDS AND CROAKING FROGS. AND CRICKETS.

I START OUT LEAVING SCHOOL ON HIGHER GROUND, USUALLY WITH TUREKI. HIS HOUSE IS THERE BEFORE WHERE THE WATER COMES OVER THE ROAD — ABOUT HALF-WAY TO MY HOUSE. WE CUT THROUGH FROM CHARLIE'S CORNER, SO WE ONLY HAVE TO CROSS THE ROAD TWICE. ONCE FROM CHURCH TO CHARLIE'S, THEN ACROSS TO BOESCH'S SUBDIVISION. NO FLOODS THERE.

MOM IS GLAD I DON'T HAVE TO TAKE THE CUT-THROUGH BY MYSELF. IT'S WEEDY AND UNDEVELOPED. BUT IF SHE EVER HEARD THAT NUMBSKULL TURCKI CARRY ON — SHE'D CHANGE HER MIND. HE'S <u>ALWAYS</u> BRINGING UP **DIRTY THINGS** YOU'RE NOT SUPPOSED TO TALK ABOUT. AND HE WON'T SHUT UP NO MATTER HOW MANY TIMES I HOLLER AT HIM TO STOP.

He said (GET THIS) "The only way those crummy Beatles will even **LOOK** at you is if you are bigger on top." THEN HE SHOWED ME THIS EXERCISE THAT GIRLS CAN DO, THAT INVOLVES PUSHING YOUR PALMS TOGETHER WITH YOUR ELBOWS OUT. SO I SET DOWN MY BOOKS AND PUT MY HARD DAY'S NIGHT ALBUM THAT JANET HAD BORROWED ON TOP, SO THAT I COULD TRY THIS. JUST THEN TURCKI GRABBED THE ALBUM AND WOULDN'T GIVE IT BACK. I KEPT LEAPING FOR IT IN THOSE DUMB FLOOD BOOTS, AND HE SAID THINGS LIKE "Yeah. Closer baby." "Ooh, I like when you leap at me." THAT MADE ME <u>SO</u> MAD, BUT THEN HE JUST PITCHED MY RECORD INTO A FLOODY SPOT AND RAN OFF TO HIS HOUSE. "It's been a hard day's wade," HE HOLLERED, AND I HAD TO SCOOT IN PAST WEEDS AND MYSTERY MUCK, JUST LIKE WITH THE PAPERS THAT TIME, QUICK REACH AND GET IT. I DRIED IT OFF AS GOOD AS I COULD WITH MY SLEEVE.

The RECORD WAS OK, BUT THE CARDBOARD JACKET WAS SATURATED. WHEN I GOT HOME I DRIED IT WITH TOWELS AND PUT IT UNDER A STACK OF ENCYCLOPEDIAS ON A WARM SPOT ON THE HEATED MARBLE FLOORS (MY DAD AND HIS COPPER TUBING!) I <u>HATE</u> TURCKI. DOESN'T HE KNOW YOU DON'T THROW MUSIC INTO FLOODED AREAS?!

♩ I've GOT NO time
for you right NOW

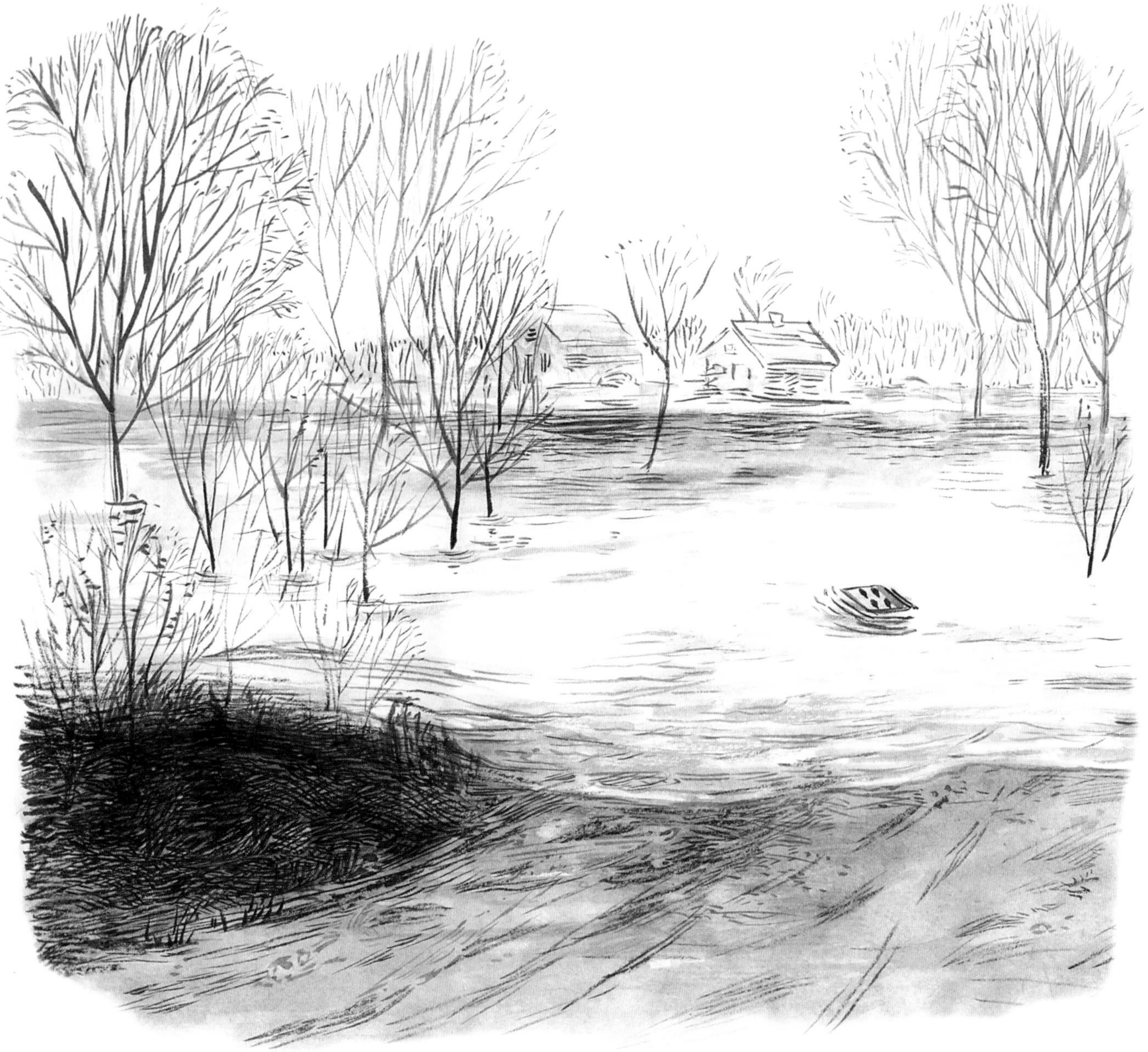

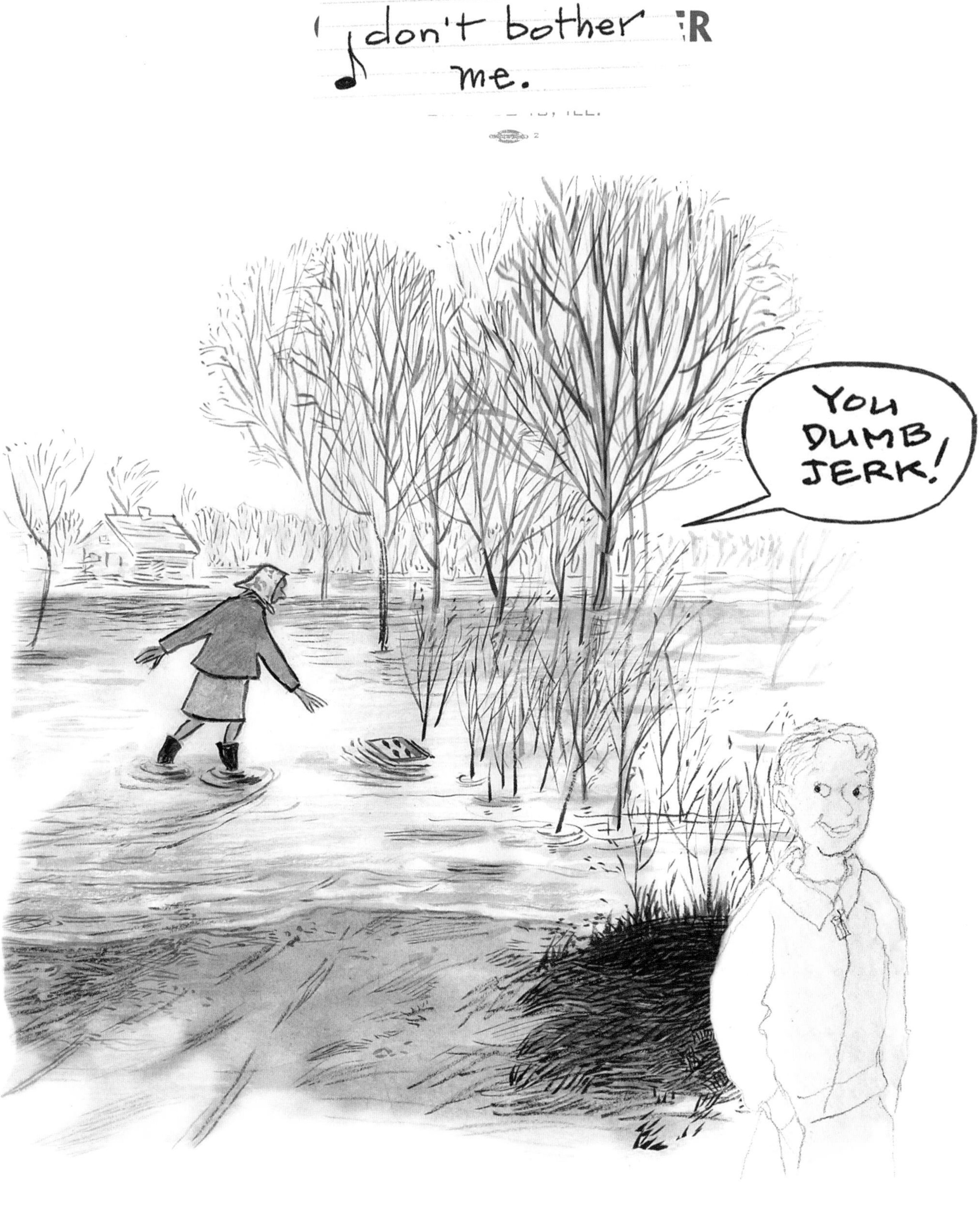
don't bother me.
YOU DUMB JERK!

4X8X16

BEATLES
4
EVER!

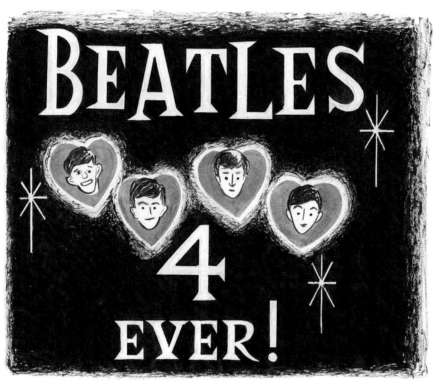

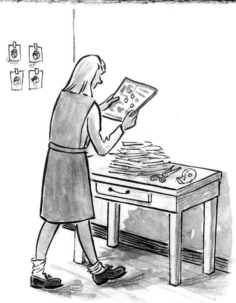

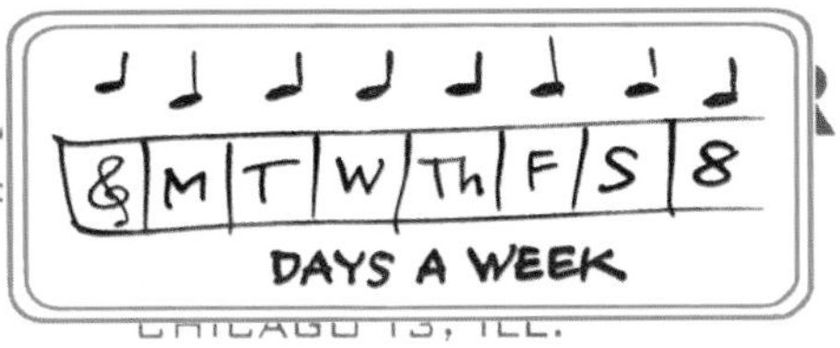
& M T W Th F S 8
DAYS A WEEK

CHICAGO 13, ILL.

M
2019
65

Ever since I got that picture from Jamie, the one I **STOLE** from him (I admit it) on Feb. 9, 1964, I have collected many pictures and came to have them HONESTLY. (Look, my brother and his friends are total **JERKS** who have made my life MISERABLE. But that **STILL** doesn't make stealing O.K. I know it's a sin, but not as bad as murder or smashing up the inside of a church with a hammer or something. Throwing a baseball at a nun. **THOSE** are sins. I'm never gonna tell Jamie, but I'll figure out some way to make up for it).

Back to pictures. I have **HUNDREDS** of pictures now, all different shapes and sizes, from posters to pins. Some are of one Beatle, but most are of all 4. All fabulous 4 of them ♥♥♥♥. And most of the pictures are on my bedroom walls. But it's not just any which way. I spend time carefully considering what goes where. I'll put up a poster and maybe a cluster of other pictures nearby. Then I'll fill in. Kind of like the way I've seen Dad had us do the mosaic of marble pieces on our floors. (Chunks he brought home from a job site —) have to fit and fill in around the larger pieces. Special stuff that's small or you have to read up close goes right above my dresser between my radio and my jewelry box which plays ♪ Fascination. That's the word Mom's friend from the card club used ("Your daughter has a fascination with the Beatles." YES I DO, Vera. Fab **4** X **8** Days a Week = **16** million heartbeats of ♫ *Fascination*

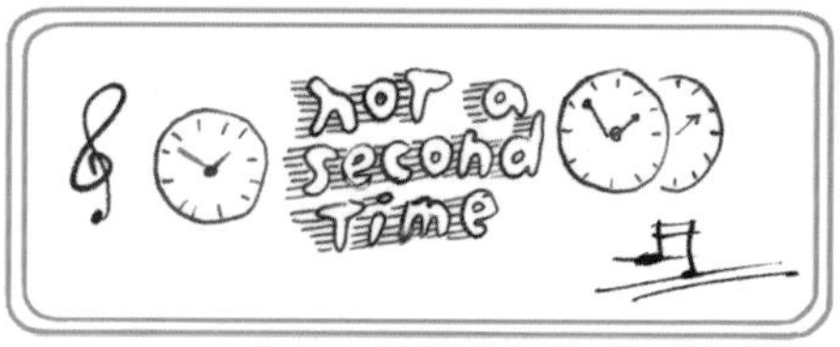
Not a
Second
Time

mar. 24

I HATE being sick and I'm sick of **COLD WEATHER!** Everything is still brown and wet and muddy. Plus, I have a little cold. It's not bad. The weather is so UP and DOWN and UP and Down. I forgot to wear a heavy coat and walked home with a ~~Bear~~ Bare head. Mom said that's why I got sick. Forgot my scarf.

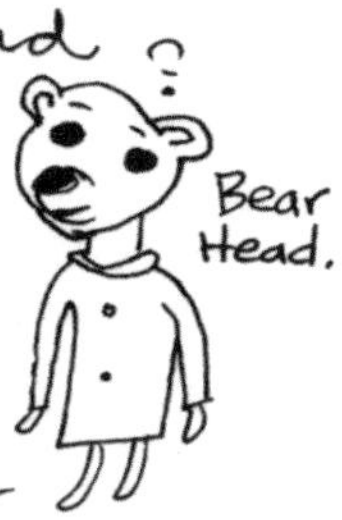
Bear
Head.

I'm so glad. "8 DAYS a WEEK" knocked 'Ferry across the Mersey' out of the #1 slot last Friday. Ferry is SUCH a **BORING** song. I mean, it's nice and everything but come on! The Fab 4 at #1 all the time is as it should be.

Ever since they were on Ed Sullivan last year, the Beatles had the #1 position on the charts with "I Want to Hold Your Hand," "I Saw Her Standing There," "She Loves You," and "Twist and Shout" in February, March, and into April, 1964. Then the streak was broken when that horrible musical mistake took over the top spot. Known as "Suspicion" Terry Stafford. GRRR! He can't sing. It was such a shock and so terrible.

At the same time, we started calling each other. The phones were hopping and popping for an hour. This had to be dealt with. We called the radio station — they said to get used to it. So we came up with a really great plan to counter the effects, because you can't simply turn off

DROWNING OUT THE DEVIL

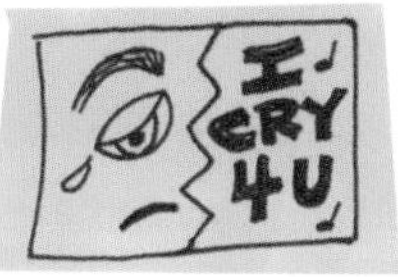
I CRY 4U

THE RADIO. ANY TIME THAT IDIOT SONG CAME ON IN THE #1 POSITION, WE'D PLUG OUR EARS AND BLAAAB OVER IT: Bla-a-a-aaa-bl-bl-bl-aaa bbbbb blaa blaa blaa blll llle bllmm.... blub blub bbbbbb a a a a a UNTIL IT WAS **OVER.** FINALLY THIS YEAR, I'M MORE GROWN UP. IF I DON'T LIKE A SONG, I CHANGE THE CHANNEL OVER TO WCFL FOR A BIT.

People SEEM TO LIKE THE Dave Clark 5. Honestly, HALF THE TIME, I DON'T KNOW WHAT'S THE MATTER WITH PEOPLE. THERE'S ONLY ONE **BEATLES.** YOU CAN'T GO SELECTING FIVE GUYS, STICK THEM TOGETHER, AND THEN EXPECT MAGIC. GIVE THEM INSTRUMENTS. **COPY CATS!** It **NEVER** WORKS. THE REAL THING CAN'T BE FAKED. Imitators DON'T LAST, THAT'S FOR SURE.

When I SAY "I Love the Beatles!" I mean it AND IT IS **REAL. NO DENYING IT.** You can SURELY TELL WHEN You ARE AROUND ME OR IN MY ROOM. THEY ARE THE GREATEST.

I THINK BETWEEN THEM BEING SO GREAT AND ME BEING SO LOYAL, I'M PRETTY SURE I WILL FEEL THIS WAY UNTIL I AM OLD AND REALLY REALLY OLD. IT'S A WHOLE LIFE "Fascination." I KNEW Falling in LOVE HAPPENED WITH Marriage AND STUFF, BUT I DIDN'T KNOW IT COULD HAPPEN WITH Musicians.

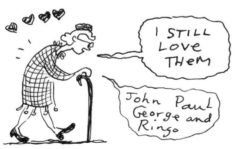

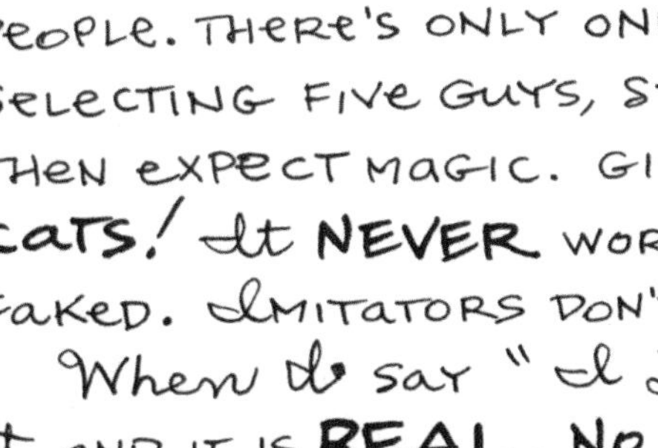
I STILL LOVE THEM
John Paul George and Ringo

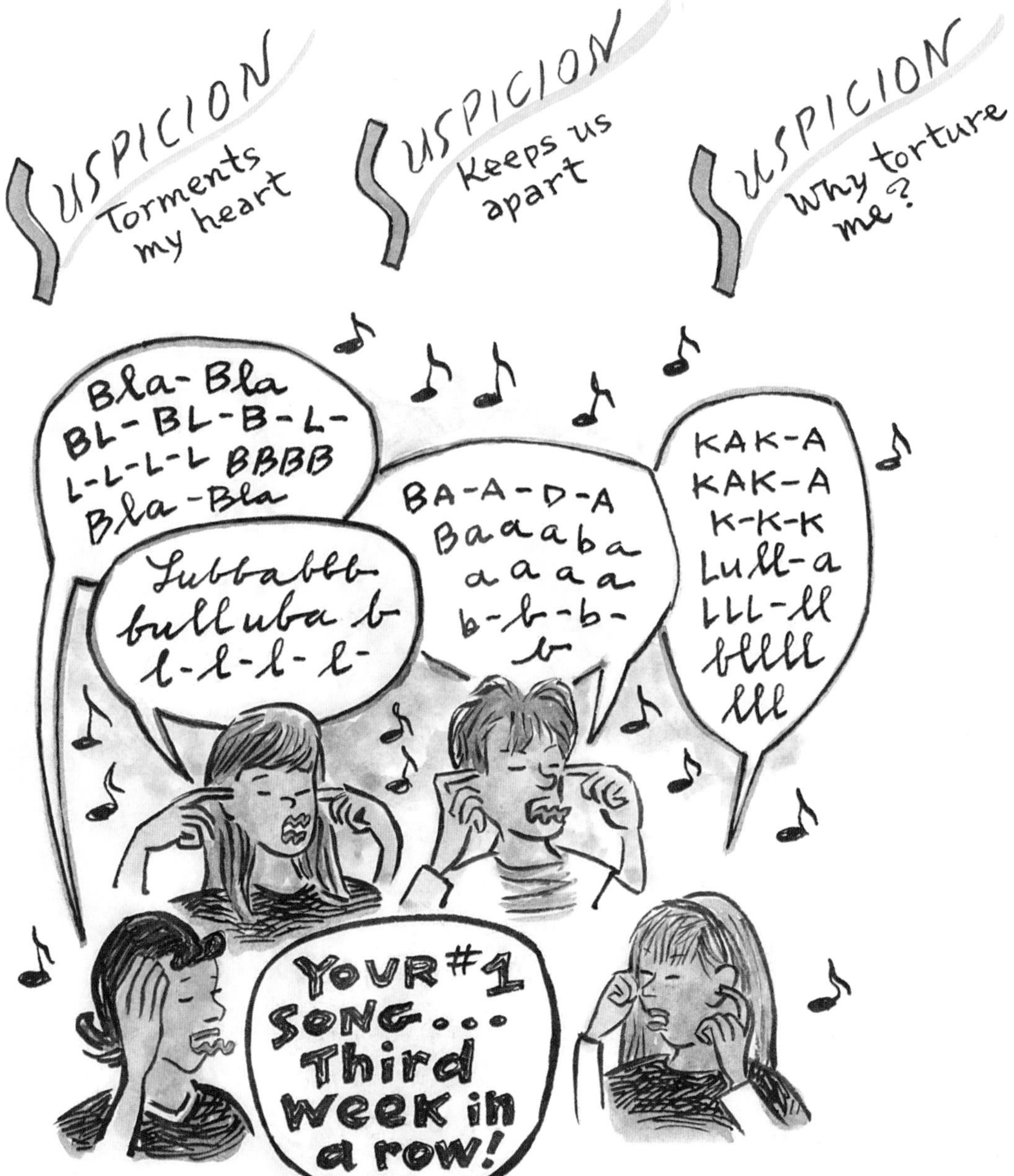
SUSPICION Torments my heart
SUSPICION Keeps us apart
SUSPICION Why torture me?
Bla-Bla BL-BL-B-L- L-L-L-L BBBB Bla-Bla
Lubbabbb bulluba b l-l-l-l-
BA-A-D-A Baaaaba aaaa b-b-b- b
KAK-A KAK-A K-K-K Lull-a LLL-ll bllll lll
YOUR #1 SONG... Third week in a row!

♪.. No no no
Not a second time.

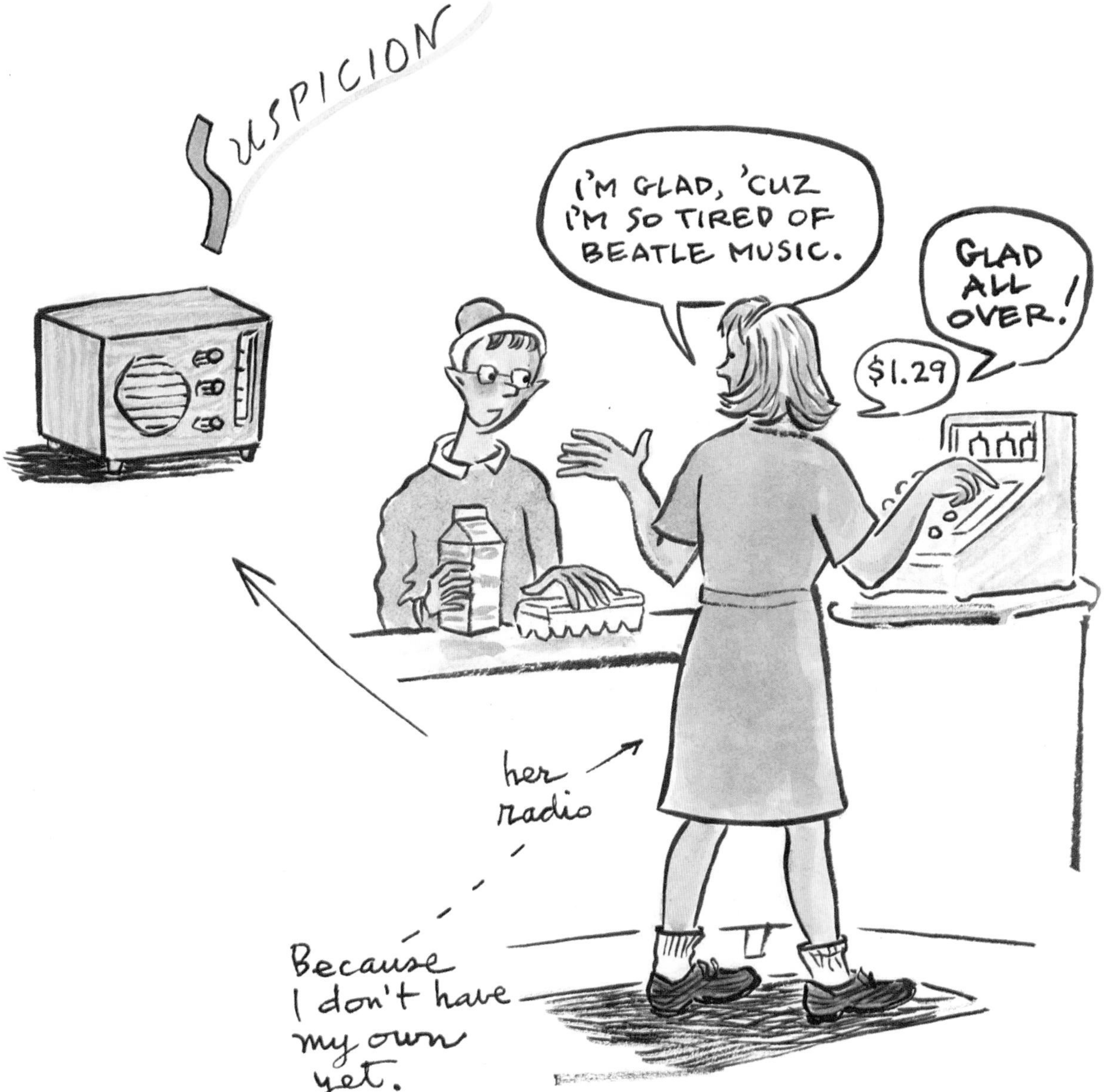
SUSPICION
I'M GLAD, 'CUZ I'M SO TIRED OF BEATLE MUSIC.
GLAD ALL OVER!
$1.29
her radio
Because I don't have my own yet.

Mar. 26

I HAVE EVERY SINGLE Beatles ALBUM SO FAR. THE FIRST ONE I BOUGHT WAS "Meet the Beatles" AND I GOT IT AT Sears UP AT THE PLAZA. Next I GOT "Introducing the Beatles: England's #1 Vocal GROUP." BOTH OF THESE I GOT IN FEBRUARY, BUT THE PICTURE OF THEM ON THAT SECOND ONE LOOKS WEIRD FOR SOME REASON. Then came "The Beatles' SECOND ALBUM," WHICH TURNED OUT TO BE MY THIRD. I GOT IT FOR EASTER '64. LAST SUMMER, THE BEST MOVIE OF ALL TIME CAME OUT, WITH A SOUNDTRACK. That would be "A Hard Day's Night." IT'S GREAT FUN AND EACH SONG IS PEPPY. WHEN I HEAR IT, MY CHEEKY BOYS COME TO MIND.

"Something New" WAS JUST THAT, AND I GOT IT WITH MY OWN MONEY ONCE I STARTED BABYSITTING. THEN FOR CHRISTMAS I GOT "Beatles '65." NOW COMES "The Early Beatles." I ALREADY HAVE A LOT OF THOSE SONGS ON 45s, BUT I'M NOT GOING TO MISS AN ALBUM.

I PLAY THEM **A LOT.** I HAVE TO KEEP THEM IN MY ROOM AWAY FROM THE NINCOMPOOPS DOWNSTAIRS. I PLAY THEM ON ANY DAY, BUT NOT Sundays. **NEVER ON SUNDAY.** Like I SAID, I HAVE MANY OF THEIR 45s, BUT ALBUMS ARE SO... THEY HAVE MORE SONGS ON THEM, AND SEEM TO ROLL ALONG TOGETHER IN A WAY. KIND OF LIKE A THEME OR A CLUB. A FAMILY. ONE SONG AFFECTS THE OTHERS LIKE SISTERS, BROTHERS, OR COUSINS. IT'S LIKE FLAVORS IN A BETTER MEAL. Except for Pork chops: (the back of a notepad that pretends to be meat.)

C R

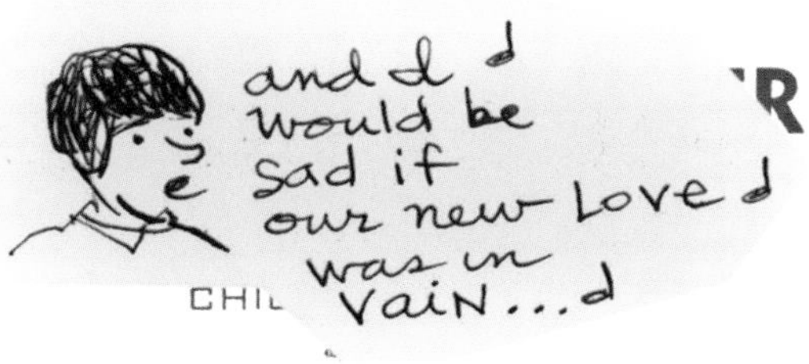
and I would be sad if our new love was in vain...

CHIL

My brother has a bunch of 45s. He stacks them up and they clunk-clunk-play one right after the other. The Trinity comes in, stand there by the stereo and sing along in unison. Or try to. Not like a nice choir, but like animals in pain. Sometimes I have to admit, it's kind of funny. They only know the most repeated words of the chorus. So they just slide over the words in the middle till they can shout what they're sure of.

It starts with "The **BIRD**" (The bird, the bird, the bird is the word, oh well the bird-bird-bird, the bird's the word, etc.). Easy for them because of that one word. So they hammer away at that one first. Then it's "You can't sit down" because honestly, you can't because of that sax.

Next (they love this one) it's "If you wanna be happy for the rest of your life, don't-a make a pretty woman your wife. So for my personal point of view **GET AN UGLY GIRL TO MARRY YOU.**" (Isn't that stupid)? "Be true to your school" is a song they believe in. They get quieter for that one. "Walk like a Man"—you can imagine. Then "Wipe Out" and "Louie Louie." <u>Ugh</u>.

My sister plays "you talk too much" (says it's about me.) She also plays "Sugar Shack" and "It's My Party."

Guess what? I like these songs, too. But I'm not going to tell them that. To me, these songs are **SILVER**. But the Beatles: **<u>GOLD</u>**.

GOLD NUGGETS

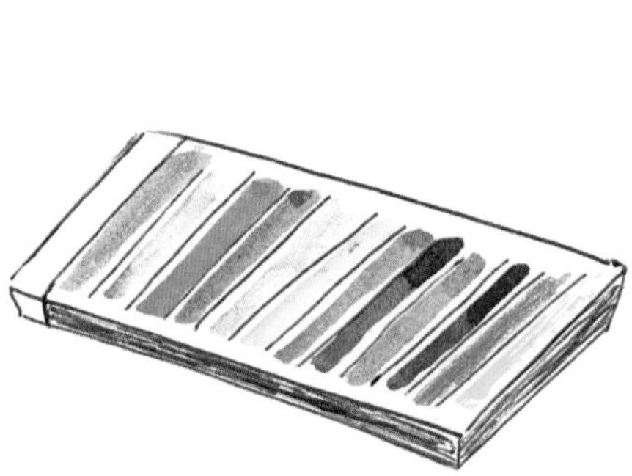

Feb 64
B
Meet
MEET THE BEATLES!
Feb 64
E
Introducing
STEREOPHONIC
THE BEATLES
Apr 64
A
Second
THE BEATLES'
SECOND ALBUM
July 64
T
Hard Day's Night
ORIGINAL MOTION PICTURE
THE BEATLES
A HARD DAYS NIGHT
Aug 64
L
Something New
Dec 64
E
'65
BEATLES'65
Mar 65
S
Early
The Early BEATLES

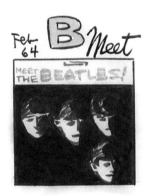

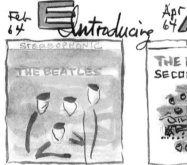

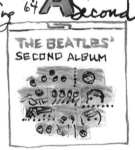

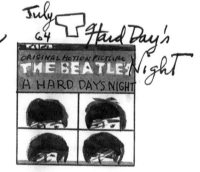

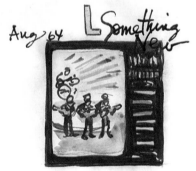

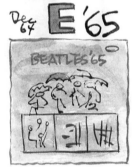

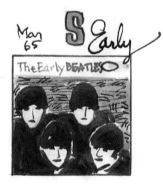

C & Misery ER

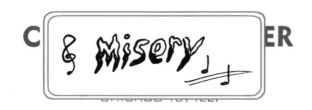

march 31

I am **so** glad basketball season is **OVER!** Let me explain why.

St. Bede's had no team until last year. We are a new school. Sister Immaculata and Father Coleman together decided that there should be a team activity for the boys, ~~so ev~~ and a team name, so we all voted in favor of the Tigers, all my friends, but **FALCONS** won. Maybe because there's more birds around the lakes area here, more than there are tigers. I've never seen a falcon either. So, why not the FISH. Mostly there's fish around here. I hear falcons are BIG.

Not like our team. Like fish, the boys are all small. Except for Mike and David. Our class has 8 boys, and they're all on the team. Anybody that wanted could join cheerleading. Only 7 out of 12 girls wanted to join and we are all TALLER than the team. They should have let us be the players.

There was no money for cheerleading uniforms. Jersey tops yes. So the moms got together and came up with a clever idea. They decided to sew these vests that we could wear over our uniforms. Yellow. Yellow V-Necked pull-over vests.

Our colors are blue and **GOLD**. But up at Basts, they only had yellow corduroy. Mine doesn't fit anymore. I've grown. I wore it for 2 years. I can hardly Breathe!

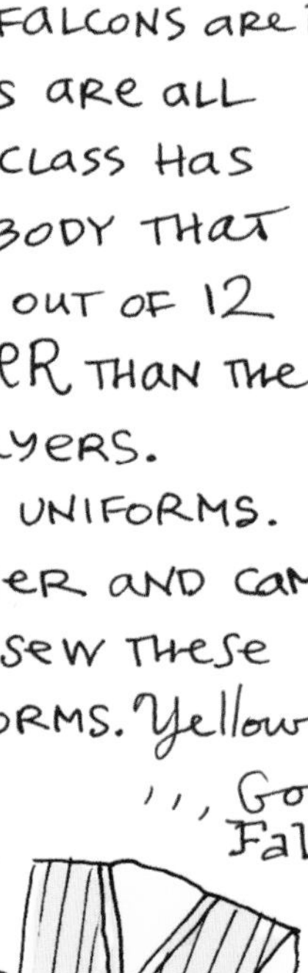
VESTS FOR VICTORY
Go Falcons

OUCH
GO Falcons TRY TO MAKE a BASKET.
Please.

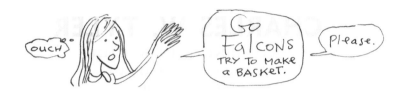

The Falcons play either at Gavin or Big Hollow because we don't have a gym. We always have to share the bathroom with girls from their school and from the other team. There's nothing that seems stranger than being with strangers in a strange bathroom while wearing a too-tight yellow vest. Some of them *say* they like the Beatles, but I don't believe them because they *also* like the Dave Clark 5 and Herman's Hermits. I consider them **FAKERS** and **PHYNQUES** (that's "finks" with fancy spelling).

Our team, the St. Bede Falcons **NEVER WIN.** We keep hollering to the others that our "team is on the beam." I'm not sure what that means but maybe they should get off because apparently, **OBVIOUSLY** being on the beam is not working out.

All 7 of us cheerleading vest girls practice after lunch in the school parking lot. And on Saturdays.

V·I·C·T·O·R·Y We each get a letter.

But we never get to **DO** that cheer, so we had to change that word victory to one that fits our great squad and our team, and that is:

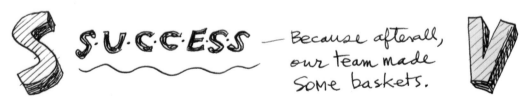

S **S·U·C·C·E·S·S** — Because afterall, our team made some baskets. **V**

♫ It's gonna be
a dra-a-a-a-ag

Misery.

THIS VEST IS PINCHING MY ARMPIT!
OOO-LOOK. SHE'S GOT A BEATLES PURSE.
IT'S STUPID.
NO, THESE VESTS ARE WHAT'S STUPID.

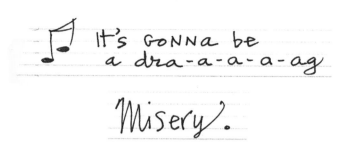

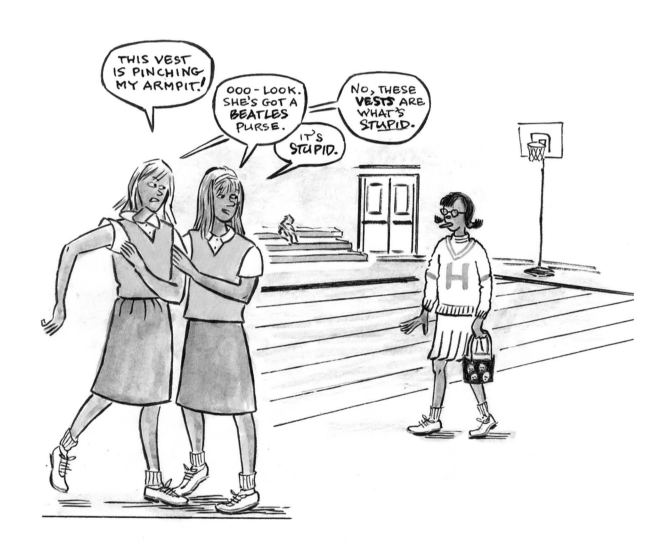

HOOP NIGHTMARE

I'll remember all the little things we've done

Here's HOW IT GOES. WE LINE UP ACCORDING TO HEIGHT ON THE CENTER LINE FACING THE BLEACHERS. JANICE IS THE TALLEST, SO SHE'S IN THE BACK. SHE'S 5'11". I'M IN FRONT OF HER AT 5'9½". THEN COMES BARB, LAURIE, AND CHRIS. Janet and Cathy come next — they're in the front. CATHY IS SO SHORT, BUT STILL AS TALL AS DAVID. We SPENT ALL OF MARCH PRACTICING THIS. SO THE FIRST GIRL, CATHY, GOES FORWARD WITH THREE LONG STEPS AND CLAPPING "S (clap) S (clap) S (clap) ESSss" and WHEN SHE SAYS "ESSss" SHE GOES DOWN ON ONE KNEE AND PUTS HER HANDS UP IN THE AIR, STRAIGHT UP THEN PUTS HER HANDS DOWN. Then Janet does THE SAME WITH U: "U (clap) U (clap) U (clap) Uuu" and SO ON. PRETTY SOON WE'RE ALL ON ONE KNEE IN A LINE — THEN WE GET UP TO MAKE a WIDE LINE WHILE STOMPING AND CLAPPING. The LAST BIG MOVE IS A SKIP-TURN IN PLACE WHILE SAYING: "That Spells Success (clap clap) for US." And WHEN WE SAY US, WE'RE BACK ON ONE KNEE WITH OUR ARMS UP. It's SHARP. WE DO THAT CHEER NOW AT THE END OF each GAME. TODAY WAS THE LAST TIME I HAD TO DO THAT CHEER. THAT Spells Success — — FOR ME!

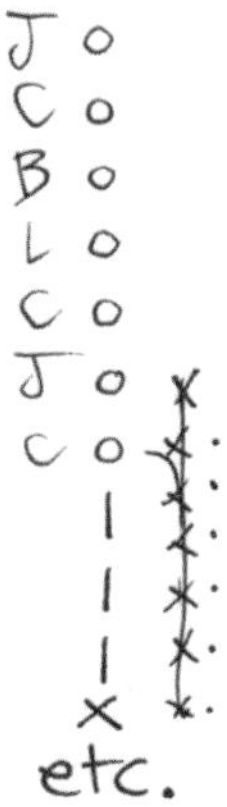

```
J  o
C  o
B  o
L  o
C  o
J  o
C  o
      x :
      x :
|     x :
|     x :
|     x :
x     x :
etc.
```

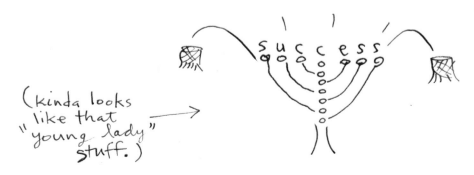

(kinda looks like that "young lady" stuff.)

C Tell Me Why ER

APR. 9

I am so excited! At 4:30 a.m. tomorrow morning, we are leaving to go visit my grandma and grandpa down in Tennessee for Easter Vacation. I'll be so happy to leave my wool coat and thick socks behind. Can't wait to lay on a blanket and work on my tan. Got to be careful, though. There are poisonous snakes and insects in Tennessee so I'd better sit in a chair to tan or put the blanket on the tin roof. Mom grew up in Tenn. She knows. We leave early because there's so

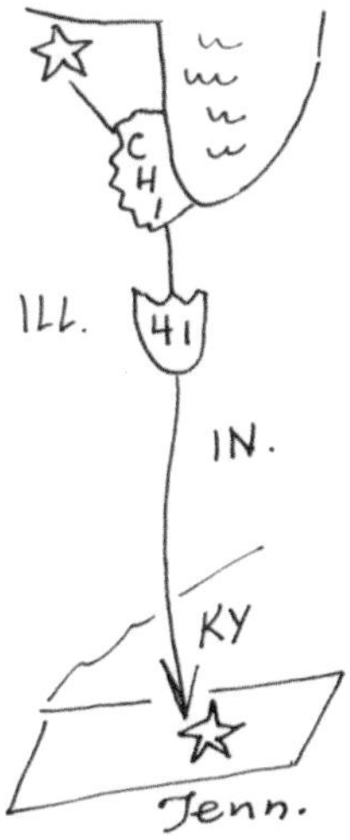

CHI
ILL.
41
IN.
KY
Tenn.

much traffic going into Chicago. Then it's boring old U.S. 41 and a thousand plain little towns like rosary beads, one

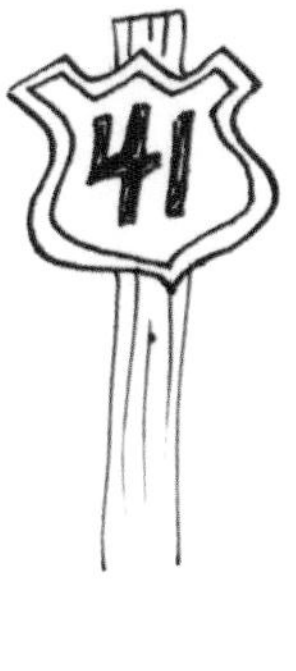

41

after another. Who lives there? Do the kids listen to the radio? I know they can get WLS—(they keep talking about 50,000 watts of power.) I mean I hope they can. Otherwise, bleak and miserable, like my town would be.

Once we get out of Nashville, that's when all the road fun begins. Curvy, wind-y up, up, up-ing the mountain toward Spencer. Those curves are called switchbacks.

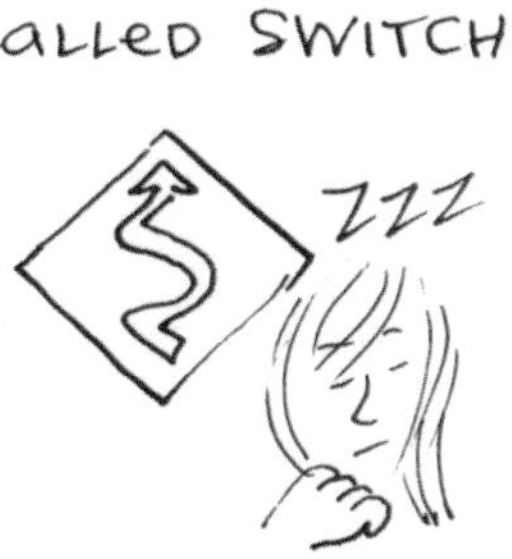

ZZZ

4:30 a.m. is much too early for me. I'm a girl who likes to stay up late, so I'm planning to sleep in the car till at least Evansville.

'cause I really can't stand it
I'm so in Love with You.

We're all going. Not Joe. He's got practice. And Ginia has to work at Jewel, so it's just me and Jim and Gu. Oh wait. Gu gets car sick, so he'll stay home with Joe and Ginia. (It's Guh, not Goo—don't forget it.) Gu has never given me a hard time about anything. He is a true friend. I tell him my secrets. The only thing he lies about is if he's been fed or not. (Usually not.) I asked him to tell me who was his favorite Beatle. He wagged his tail 4 times. So I asked "Does that mean Paul or John?" Then he wagged his tail 6 times. **LENNON.** And when I said "John Lennon?" he got up and danced around, so Gu likes John. That's sharp.

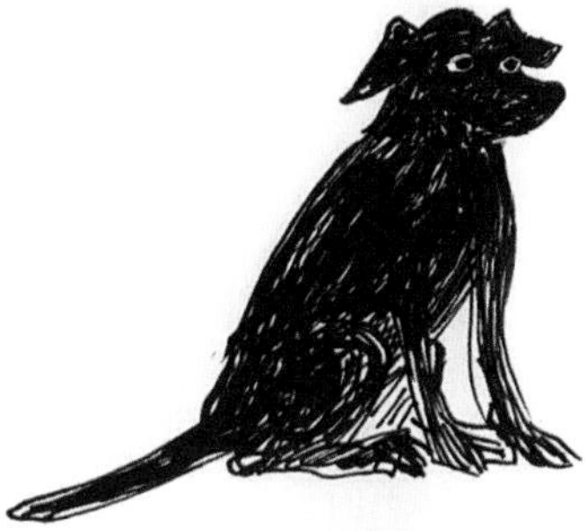

That's the thing about the Beatles. Everybody, even household pets, loves them. Stars in the sky love them, too, I bet. Maybe if I play Beatles music to the snakes they'll leave me alone.

They are 4 together smashing fellows that the worldwide loves. But each one by himself is terrific. Gu picked a good one.

John, I would say, put the band forward. He got it started. He's so witty and handsome. Wise also. Smart wisecracker. I love him. Why is he married? It was great fun to draw his guitar for my wall this week (another session.) And I tried to do a charcoal portrait of him. Don't touch, it smears.

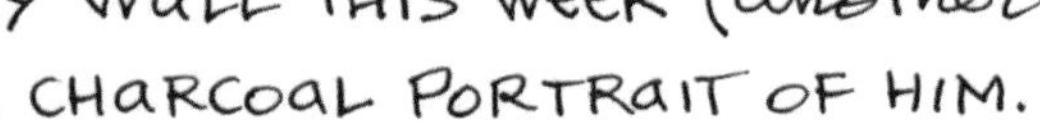
LENNON

John Lennon

Sometimes nicknamed "chief Beatle" though he often denies it. Plays rhythm guitar along with doing most of the singing and composing songs with Paul. John is also called the "literary Beatle" because of his 2 smash books of drawings, sarcasm, poems, stories and deadpan wit. John is the ideal man. He will accept you if you do your best and be yourself rather than a faker.

He was born October 9, 1940, 5'11" tall, 159 pounds. Paul calls him "fatty" because Paul is 158. He has dark brown hair and eyes and wears glasses for reading and other types. "He really can't see past the end of his nose!" George said. He hates glasses. Real name = John Winston Lennon. From Liverpool.

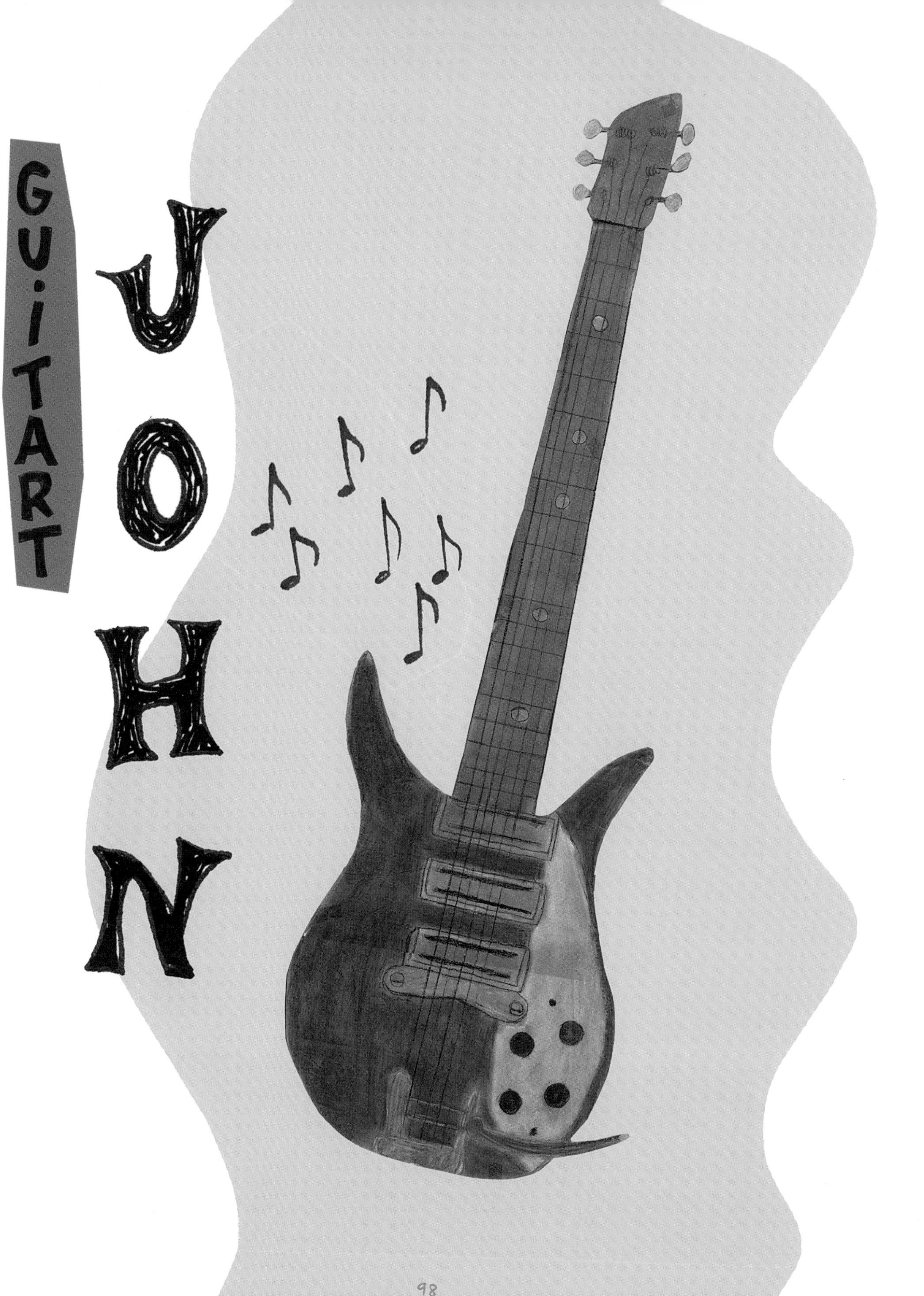
GUiTART
JOHN

It's such a *LONG* drive to be stuck in the back seat with that squirt Jummo (Jim), so I'm bringing my gum chain to work on. I've got a bag full of Wrigley wrappers. Some from me and some from Barbara and her sisters. They chew a lot of gum. More than me. I should get a lot done on this trip. I made a really really long one last year, but I took it to school to work on one time. **MISTAKE.** Sister took it away from me. Thing is, I had finished my Vatican II booklet and had nothing else to do. She said it was distracting others. Said I could have it back in a few weeks, but when I went to get it from her, she said it was missing. Probably thrown away or she kept it. It was as long as Janice is tall.

It's simple to do. You take a Wrigley's gum outside wrapper, not the foil. Doublemint, spearmint — doesn't matter. Tear it lengthwise in half, fold each half lengthwise and then weave into each other. I used to write "Beatles" inside each one.

Dad won't stop on the trip except to gas up. If I have to use the ladies room (or as dad says 'the little girl's room), I have to wait till we need fuel. Dad's gotta **GET** there, so he hollers at us to "**HURRY IT UP."** We never ever get to stop and see the sights along the way. "That's what windows are for" he'll say. "There's plenty to see." He can't see spending money on **TOURIST TRAPS.**

♪♪♪ Wo-ooh
These chains
of a-Lo-o-ove
Got a hold
on me-e
e-yeah-ah

Dad is a very fast and determined driver. He chomps that cigar, of course (unlit cuz of mom). She said she can't take that smoke anymore, and he can't seem to steer the car without it. He passes cars, trucks, convoys — everything. Mom spends most of the trip **TERRIFIED**. I trust his driving. He drove a lot during the war, and got behind the wheel at age 8. (It was obviously different back in the 1920s). Jim thinks it's cool.

That spaz, Jimmy, he likes to pump his arm up and down at semi trucks when they go by so they'll blow their air horns, and when they do, that spooks Mom. Another stupid idiot thing Jim does is to keep a count of how many cars Dad has passed. Who Cares? That's so dumb. Little kid fun. Not me. I stay busy with my chain or stare out the window as we go from flat and brown to a little hillier that turns a bit greener as we go along. Mom points out blooming things as she sees them: the forsythia bushes, crocuses, jonquils, and so many narcissus blooms. On every hillside and dale, it seems. By the time we get past Nashville, green stuff is popping out everywhere. Tulips. So pretty. Nothing is green up in Illinois.

Even though these free window sights are lovely and i'm excited about seeing Gram and Grampa, I miss seeing those faces in my room. Those Beatles are always smiling and happy. It's a different world we're going to, that is certain.

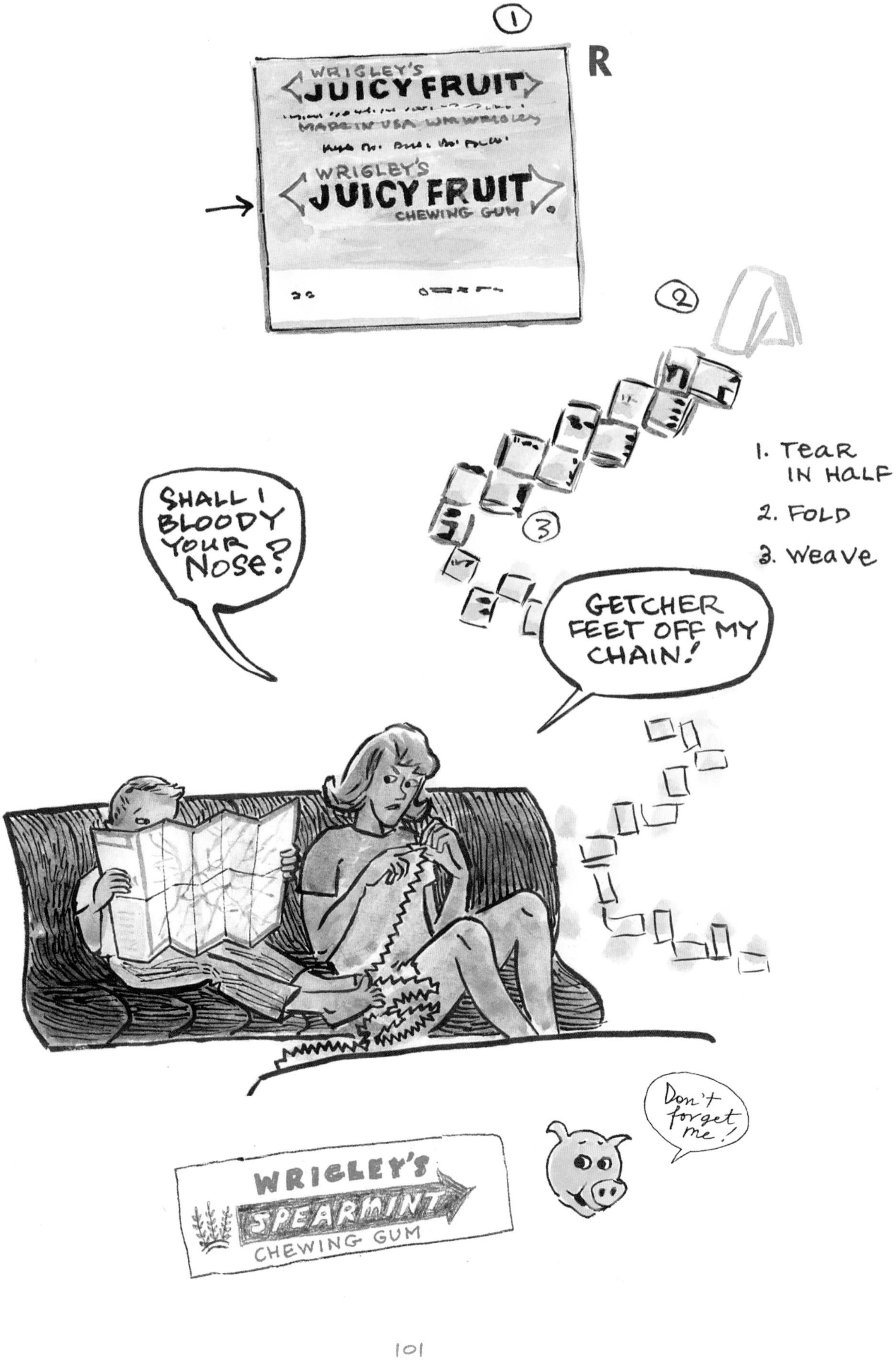

1
R
WRIGLEY'S
JUICY FRUIT
WRIGLEY'S
JUICY FRUIT
CHEWING GUM
2
3
1. TEAR IN HALF
2. FOLD
3. WEAVE
SHALL I BLOODY YOUR NOSE?
GETCHER FEET OFF MY CHAIN!
WRIGLEY'S
SPEARMINT
CHEWING GUM
Don't forget me!

APR. 16

We just got back after a whole day of in the car. I've got so much to say, but I'm **TIRED.**

17

Hello. Wooh! Back to good old still brown Illinois after a week in Green and Lovely [Tenn.] beautiful at Grandma and Grampa's little farm in Van Buren County. It's so far away from our house. can you believe the road ends at their front porch? It goes from paved to gravel to dirt then that's it. They have no neighbors, only chickens. They used to have pigs and horses, but they can't take care of animals like they used to. not even a radio at their house. Maybe it was for the best, because I just found out that Freddy And The Dreamers took over the #1 spot with that stupid hit "I'm telling you now." I know **EXACTLY** what my cousin Glenda would say about this. "They'll never be bigger than ELVIS."

In Tennessee, you wouldn't even know the Beatles existed. No pictures, no magazines, no cards, no music, no fans. I tried to explain to gramma and showed her pictures. I asked her to pick out a favorite and she picked George.

Here's how the day goes at G&G's: before the sun comes up, grampa makes a fire in the kitchen stove. That way the house is toasty and ready for breakfast. about 6, he gets us 'young-uns' up to go get eggs in the hen house. Then we get buckets and walk down this long

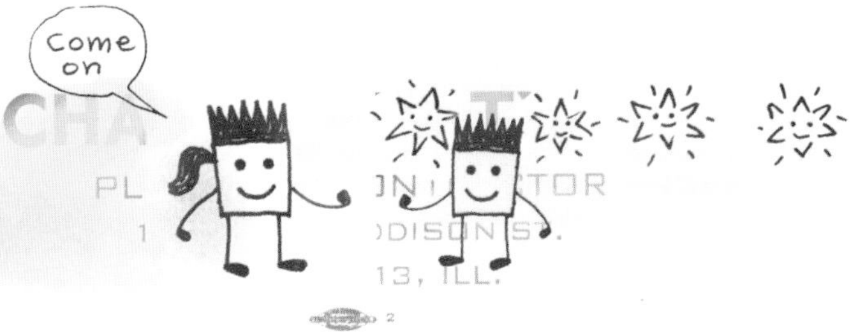
Come on

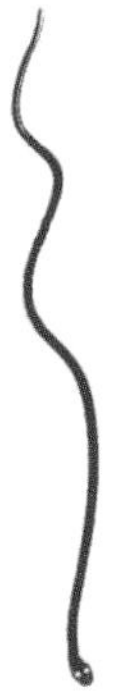

PATH WITH HIM TO THE SPRING, IN SINGLE FILE RIGHT BEHIND HIM, DOWN THE HILL. EVERY NOW AND THEN HE STOPS TO LISTEN FOR CRITTERS. "HUSH, YOU-NS." WE WENT S-L-O-W ONCE WE GOT TO THE SPRING. THAT GAVE THE BLACK SNAKE TIME TO SLITHER OFF. GRAMPA SAID IT'S GOOD HE'S THERE TO KEEP RODENTS AWAY FROM THE BUTTER HE KEEPS THERE (THEY HAVE NO REFRIGERATOR). ONCE THAT SNAKE IS OUT OF THE WAY, WE FILL OUR BUCKETS. THAT WATER IS SO **COLD**. IT SITS ON A TABLE BY THE BACK DOOR. WHEN YOU GET THIRSTY, YOU JUST DIP YOU OUT SOME WITH THE LADLE. AS SOON AS WE GET BACK WITH THE WATER, GRAMMA FRIES BACON AND SCRAMBLES UP EGGS IN THE GREASE. SO GOOD. SHE ALSO FRIES POTATOES AND MAKES BISQUITS. MMM. ALL DAY, TILL CHICKEN DINNER LATER, WE EAT them bisquits with jelly and peanut butter Mom brought. It AIN'T LIKE THIS AT HOME.

I WALKED UP THE ROAD TO TOWN WITH MY COUSINS Glenda and Larry. WE WENT TO THE LITTLE STORE THERE. NO SWEET TARTS OR 16 MAGAZINE. That's O.K. I'm BACK AND EASTER IS TOMORROW. I'm SURE THE EASTER BUNNY WILL PUT SOME IN MY BASKET. We DROVE BACK BECAUSE THERE'S NO Catholic Church IN SPENCER, AND WE HAVE SCHOOL MONDAY. It's NICE TO HAVE AN INDOOR BATHROOM.

I NEED TO SAY THAT AGAIN — THERE'S NOTHING WORSE THAN NEEDING TO GO, BUT YOU HAVE TO STEP INTO A WOODEN HUT WITH SPIDERS UP IN THE CORNER AND SIT THERE ON A BOARD WITH A HOLE, AND JIM

I GOT a whole lot of things to tell her — when I get HOME.

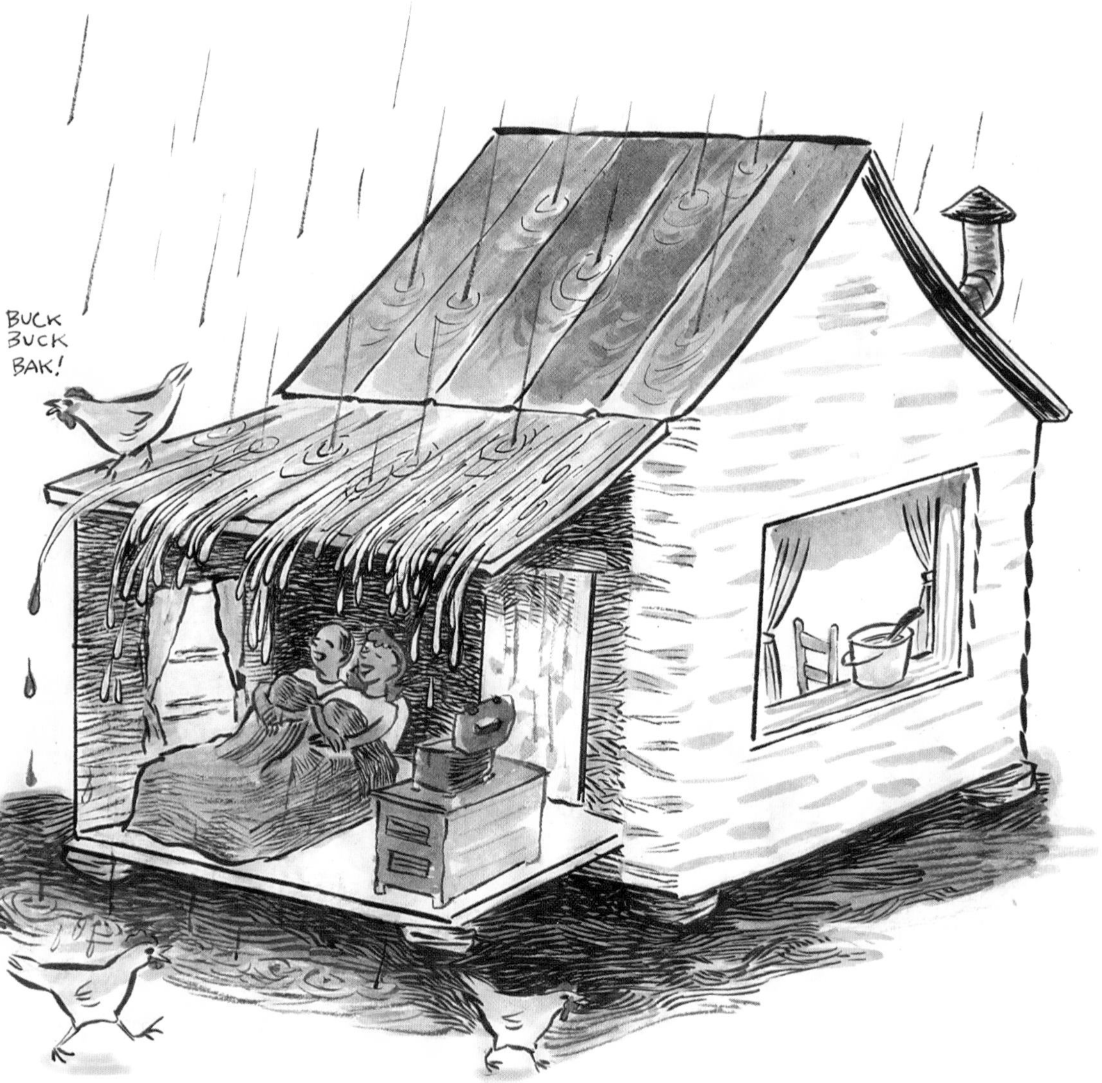
BUCK
BUCK
BAK!

NIGHT LAFFS

"WHAT IF THE RAIN MAKES THE PAINT RUN AND IT GETS ALL OVER THE CHICKENS?"

- PARENTS

AND MY LITTLE COUSIN WAYNE ARE OUTSIDE THE DOOR BLOCKING IT AND LAUGHING AT ME. PRETTY AWFUL.

OK, ON TO ANOTHER SERIOUS MATTER, AND THAT WOULD BE WHY I DON'T LIKE FREDDY AND THE DREAMERS. I am in 8TH GRADE. NEXT YEAR, I'll BE IN MY FIRST YEAR AT Carmel. SO I AM GROWN AND HAVE BIGGER THOUGHTS THAN LAST YEAR AND 6th grade. **BABIES.** THAT BAND IS FOR *BABIES* IN 6th AND 7th GRADES.

I CAN'T WAIT TO COLOR THE EGGS I COLLECTED MYSELF AT GRAMMA'S. I'M DOING 4.

Even THOUGH I'M GLAD TO BE HOME, HERE'S A LIST OF THINGS WE DID IN TENNESSEE. I miss it!

Went to a cave. And visited a rock crusher place. I GOT BLUE GYM SHOES. Saw a purple GTO. Worked on my tan. VISITED GRANDMA'S SISTER CLEO THE QUILT MAKER. Saw a tobacco barn. Swam at Fall Creek Falls. WALKED 5 MILES AND NEVER SAW A CAR. Larry had a dog bite. Went across a narrow swinging bridge. VISITED WITH Aunt LENA and UNCLE Lewey. Helped watch Dad paint the roof silver. A friend of my cousin up at the milk store kissed me on the cheek. WENT TO THE PASSION PIT (drive-in) with Glenda to see 'Girl Happy' with **ELVIS.** I wore my new blue shoes, but they weren't suede. AND everywhere along the way, I saw signs for ROCK CITY and the BLANKET STORE. We didn't go to either of those.

A NIGHT WITH THE KING

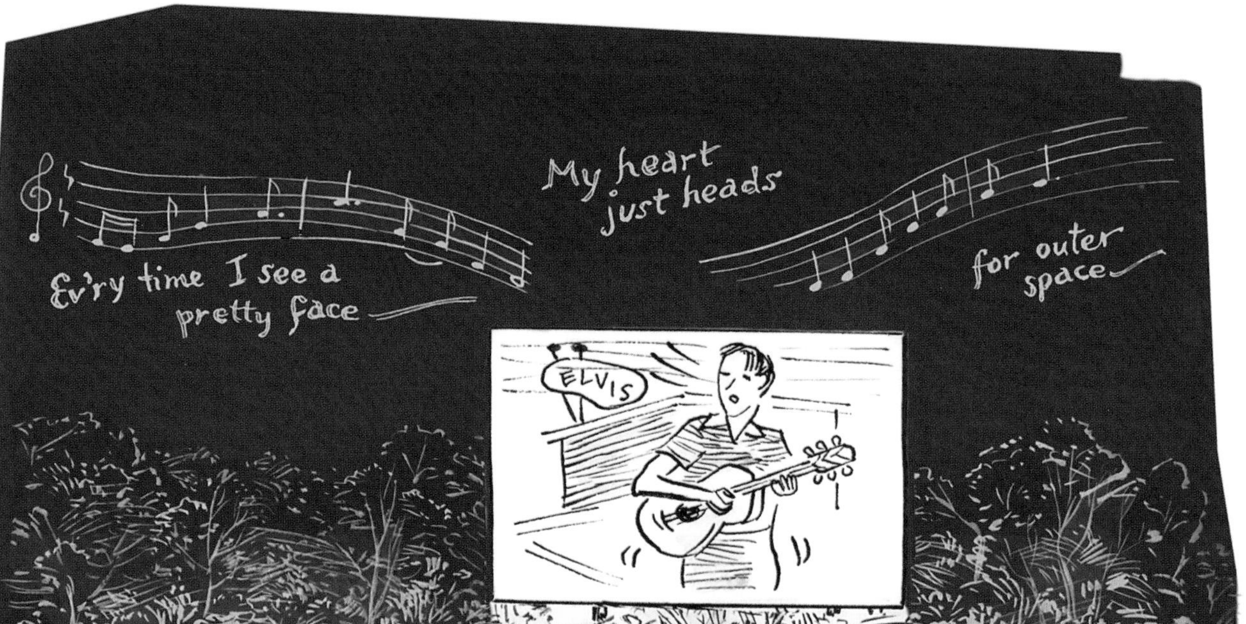
Ev'ry time I see a pretty face
My heart just heads
for outer space
ELVIS
OH ME!
HE'S MY #1 MAN FOREVER!
YOU C'N HAVE THEM MOP HEADS.
NO NO NO.

WAIT!
I STILL LOVE YOU.
NO!

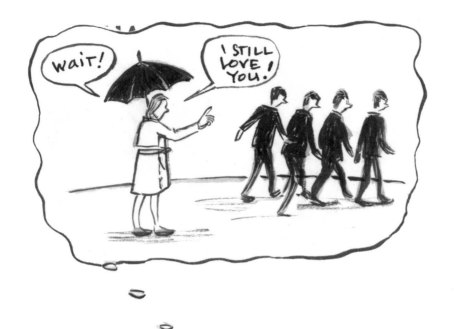

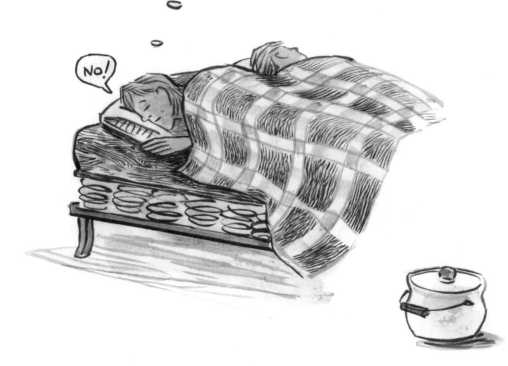

NIGHT SIGHS

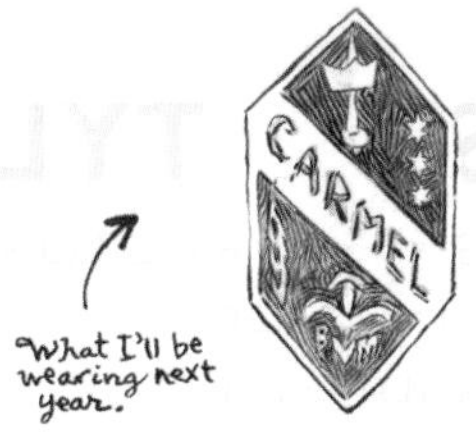
Carmel
What I'll be wearing next year.

Came home to something I was dreading: my test scores. These are the scores they will consider for my placement at Carmel next year. (Can't wait!) I **LOVE** my school now, but there's only about 6 weeks left until graduation. Class night is <u>this week</u> (yikes!) so busy. Laurie and I have a great little skit planned.

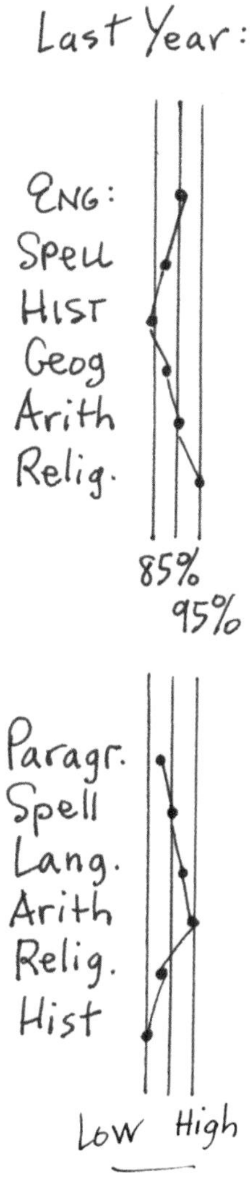
Last Year:
Eng:
Spell
Hist
Geog
Arith
Relig.
85%
95%
Paragr.
Spell
Lang.
Arith
Relig.
Hist
Low
High

Now to figure these scores. 10.2 in Paragraph meaning. That is, read a paragraph and answer questions about it after. But what happens is, I start reading and soon realize that what I'm reading is stupid, then I look out the window, then I get scared I won't finish. A lot of kids are squirming and nail biting. I've seen kids copy off each other. That's bad! 11.3 Spelling. What words did I miss? 11.4 Language. I guess I did good on that because Dad always tells me to watch my language. Biggest surprise: Arithmetic. I'm a human adding machine! But concepts in math: not so good.

Example question: "If a man has a gallon of ice cream on a hot day, and he's wearing a toupeé (did I spell that right?) and he offers his wife a cup but she refuses in matching shoes-es, how long till she beans him because he bought the wrong flavor?" She wanted black cherry.

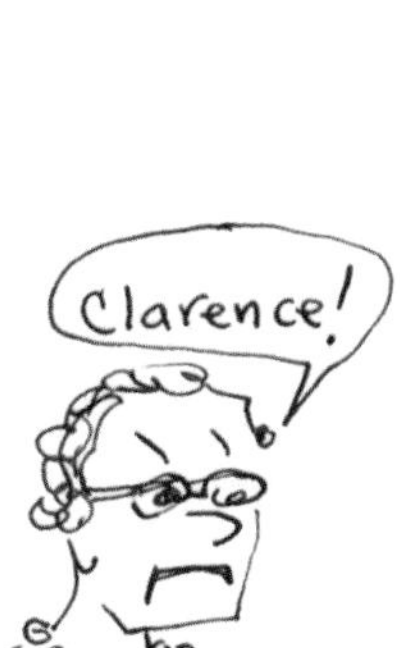
Clarence!

ADDING IT ALL UP

Mom!
JEWEL HAD 2 FOR $.79!
SERVE YOURSELF! I WAIT ON PEOPLE ALL DAY.
1.
+2.
= I hate you.
NO TALKING
7 more minutes.

Hey Girl!

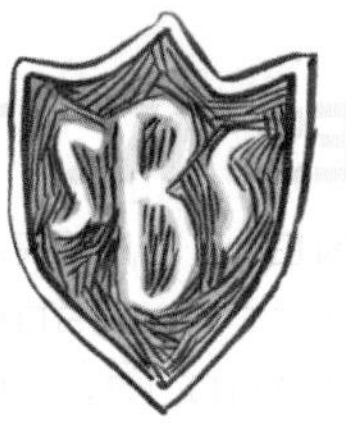
SBS

What I wear now.

I have been at St. Bede's since 5th grade. They didn't have the school built yet, so we met over at Gavin across the street. Mrs Rhodey got us excited about the space program. Tracking John Glenn all day. In 6th grade, we moved into the new school. So pretty inside, like our teacher Sister Julia. She was young. But she got sick and was replaced by old Mrs. Vrokel, who told us we had B.O. "It stinks in here — get some deodorant."

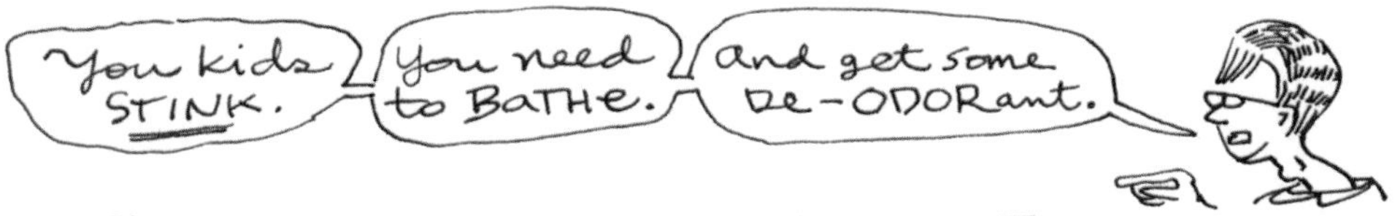
You kids STINK.
You need to BATHE.
And get some DE-ODORant.

7th grade was all about Vatican II and the worst biggest thing of all: our president was shot. John F. Kennedy. R.I.P. I found out about it at school. The speakers in our room didn't work very good, so when Sister came on to tell us, it sounded like she was saying ZRON KERNOODLE SPAT ON BED. Then she came in and told us in person. Kennedy had been shot. We got down on our knees to pray for Zron Kernoodle. Sister was in tears. We did a rosary.

Then we were shuffled off to music class. Mrs. Blair bonked out a bunch of happy tunes on the piano and we were told to sing along. "Finiculi Finicula" and "The Happy Wanderer," to name a couple. "You'll Never Walk Alone" made us all cry.

When I got home, Mom had the TV News on and Dad watched it. So sad, that week.

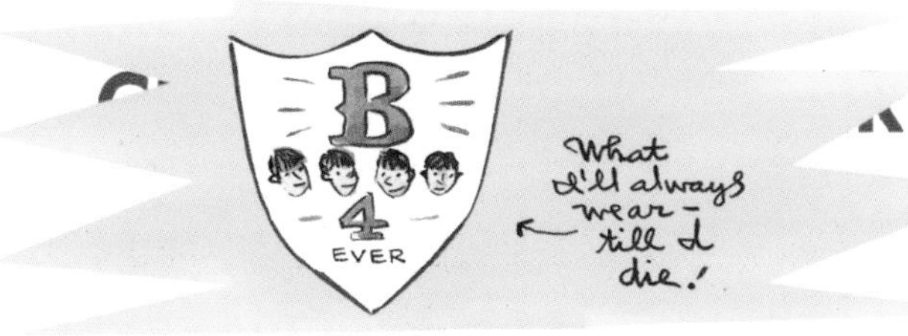
B
4
EVER
What I'll always wear – till I die!

A few months later, the Beatles came along and the mood changed. Everything seemed to get better, newer, brighter. HONESTLY. I even started getting up earlier because I wanted to sing at the 7 a.m. Mass. More music in my life. Mrs. Blair wanted singers so she asked Laurie and I, who do harmony very well. Laurie does soprano and I do alto. I have this skill: no matter what tune or melody is thrown at me, I can harmonize it. I cannot read music, but if I hear it, I know how it should go, and I never forget it. All that listening to the radio pays off in church! HAH! And some nun, when I was in kindergarten, told my mother that to send me to piano lessons would be a waste of everyone's time. What did SHE know?

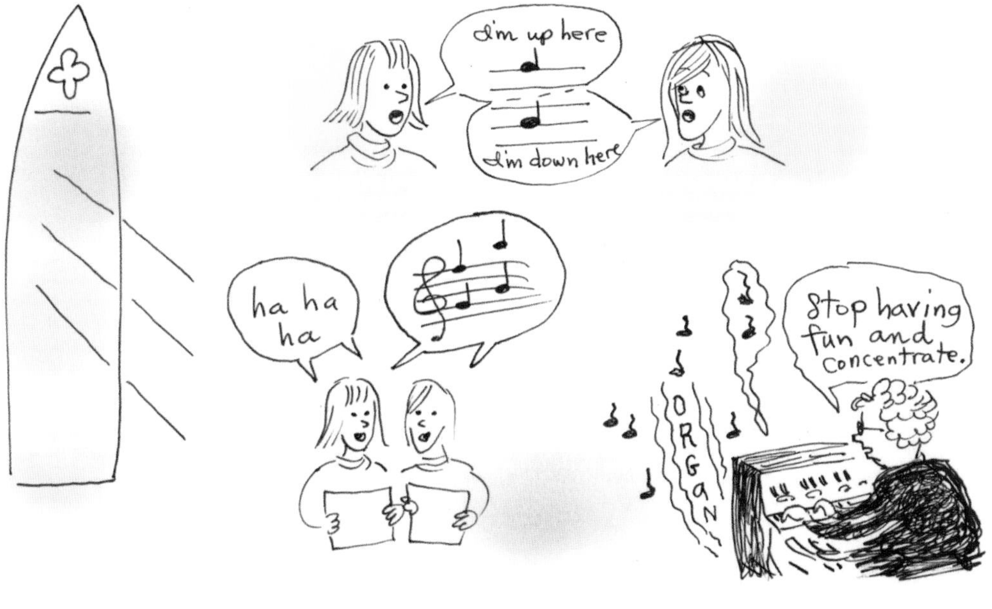
I'm up here
I'm down here
ha ha ha
Stop having fun and concentrate.
ORGAN

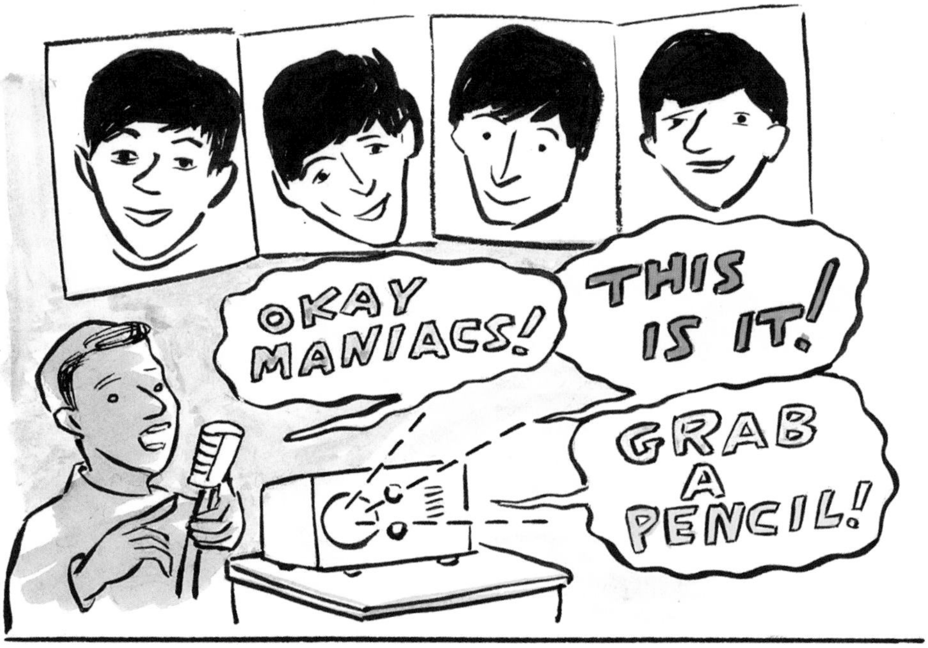
OKAY MANIACS!
THIS IS IT!
GRAB A PENCIL!

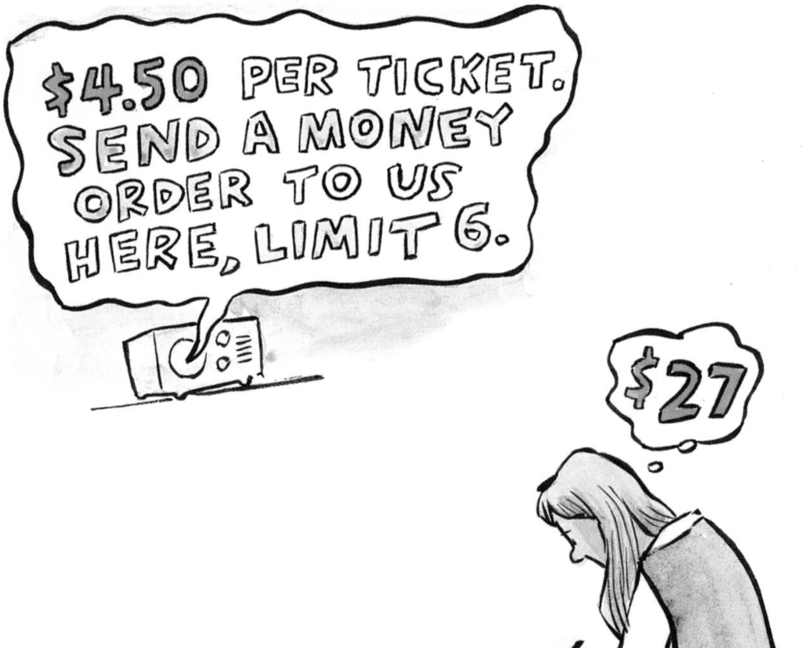
$4.50 PER TICKET. SEND A MONEY ORDER TO US HERE, LIMIT 6.
$27

 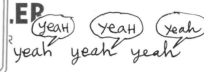

"It won't Be Long" (YEAH) (YEAH) (YEAH)
yeah yeah yeah

APR. NINETEENTH

Last year, I SENT a LETTER TO Triangle Productions REQUESTING SEATS FOR THE BEATLES SHOW AT THE AMPITHEATRE. NEVER HEARD BACK. I SAID I NEEDED FRONT ROW SEATS BECAUSE I AM FAN CLUB PRESIDENT. NO WORD.

There ARE RUMORS THAT THEY ARE COMING BACK AGAIN THIS SUMMER, AND IF I DON'T GET TO SEE THEM, IF I MISS THEM AGAIN **I WILL DIE**. I **HAVE** TO SEE THEM. IT'S LIKE *Water* or *Air*. SO I JUST CAME UP WITH ANOTHER LETTER TO SEND TO Triangle. THIS TIME THEY'RE BOUND TO SEE I'M A LITTLE OLDER WITH MUCH BETTER THOUGHTS (as an 8th grader). Here's my letter:

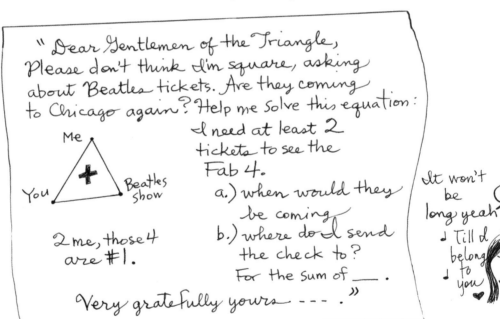

"Dear Gentlemen of the Triangle,
Please don't think I'm square, asking about Beatles tickets. Are they coming to Chicago again? Help me solve this equation:
I need at least 2 tickets to see the Fab 4.
a.) when would they be coming
b.) where do I send the check to?
For the sum of ___ .
Very gratefully yours - - - . "

Me
You   Beatles show
2 me, those 4 are #1.

It won't be long yeah (YEAH)
♪ Till I belong ♪ to you

BUT I DON'T NEED TO SEND IT, BECAUSE IT WAS JUST ANNOUNCED ON THE RADIO WHERE TO SEND IN MONEY!
SO EXCITED!! YAY!

I saw her standing there

APR. 22

How could I forget? I'm such a dunce. I forgot to tell the best part of Tennessee.

I needed a graduation dress. Mom thought it would be nice to take a run over to McMinnville to a store there. It's about an hour's drive down the mountain. Back in the '30s, she got to have a store-bought dress for her graduation. She did chores for a lady in town, in Spencer, in exchange for a room in her house (when she was in high school. Grampa thought she'd fare better up there with Mrs. Haston, whose house was closer to her school). Mrs. Haston and her sisters took Mom over there to get her dress. Mom, aka Hannah Yates, class of '36 valedictorian. Her parents could not afford a dress. They barely had enough for their own survival.

Well my heart went BOOM when I crossed that room and I held her hand in mi-eeene

I like the one I picked out. I think it would taste like a lime popsicle. I must have grown a few extra inches on my arms, because the sleeves are a bit short. So is the hemline, so my legs grew, too. Mom figured out a way to lengthen it at the waist by adding a band of trim. She also told me to put a brick on my head till June.

This is my favorite dress so far. I really love the sheer sleeves with a satin band and little pearl buttons. I bet I could even get Paul's attention.

Sorry Laurie.

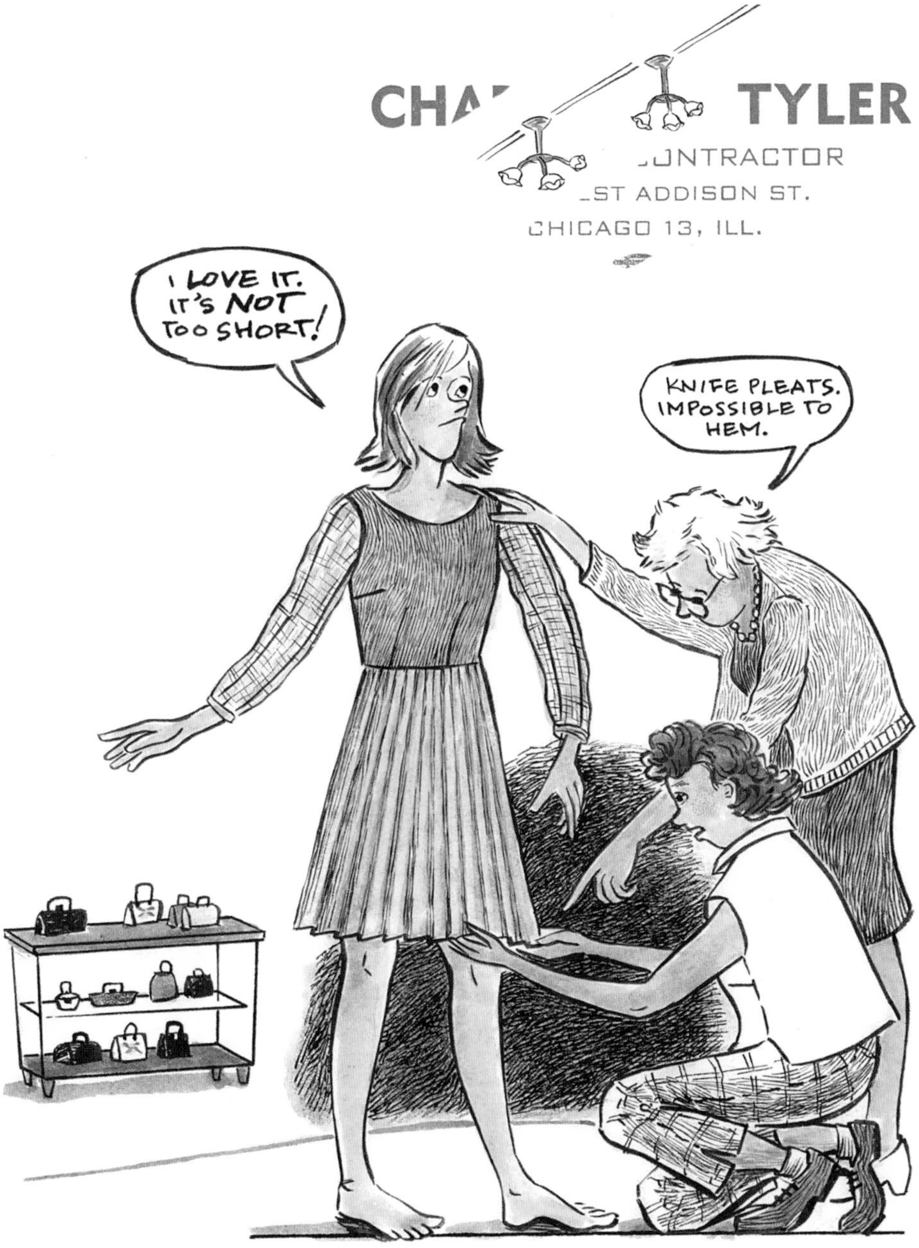
CHA TYLER
ONTRACTOR
ST ADDISON ST.
CHICAGO 13, ILL.
I **LOVE** IT. IT'S **NOT** TOO SHORT!
KNIFE PLEATS. IMPOSSIBLE TO HEM.

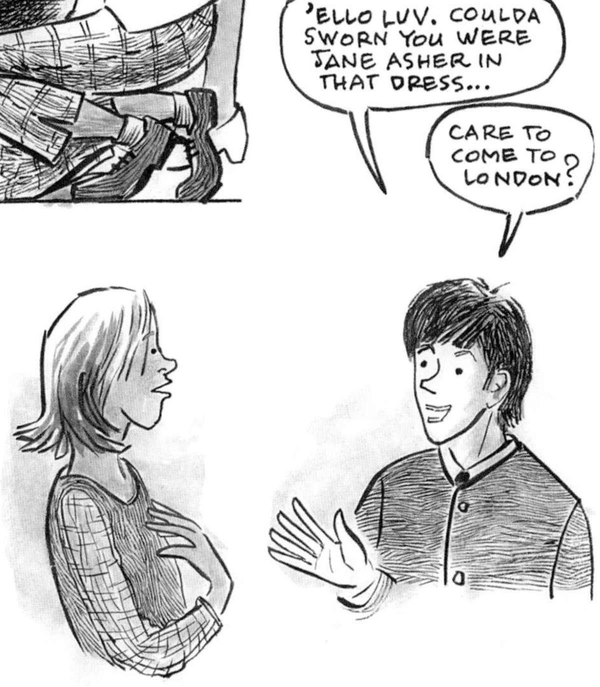
'ELLO LUV. COULDA SWORN YOU WERE JANE ASHER IN THAT DRESS...
CARE TO COME TO LONDON?

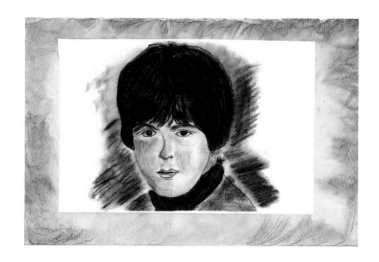

PauL McCaRTney

nicknamed "the gorgeous Beatle" because
of his good taste and extremely good looks.
He plays bass guitar. Along with composing
songs with John, he sings and harmonizes.
Hates shaving and all other types of dishonesty.
Paul is ⊥ℲℲT (Left) handed and also handles a
guitar backwards. In school, he would
write from right to left on his paper
instead of left to right.

Paul was born on June 18, 1942. 5'11" tall.
158 pounds. Dark brown hair and eyes. His
real name is
    James Paul McCartney

He is from Liverpool, England.

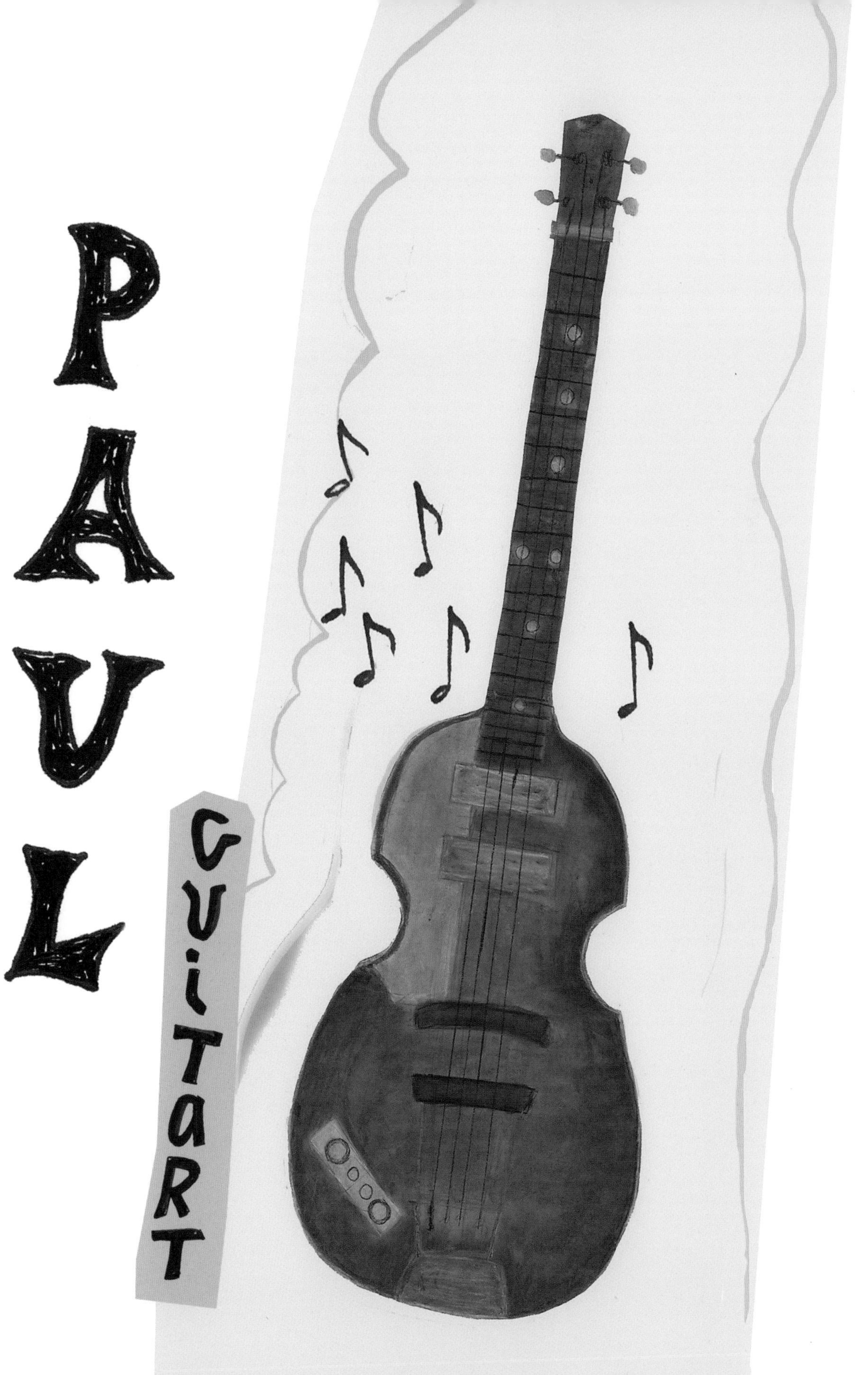
PAUL
GUiTaRT

THE ADVANTAGE

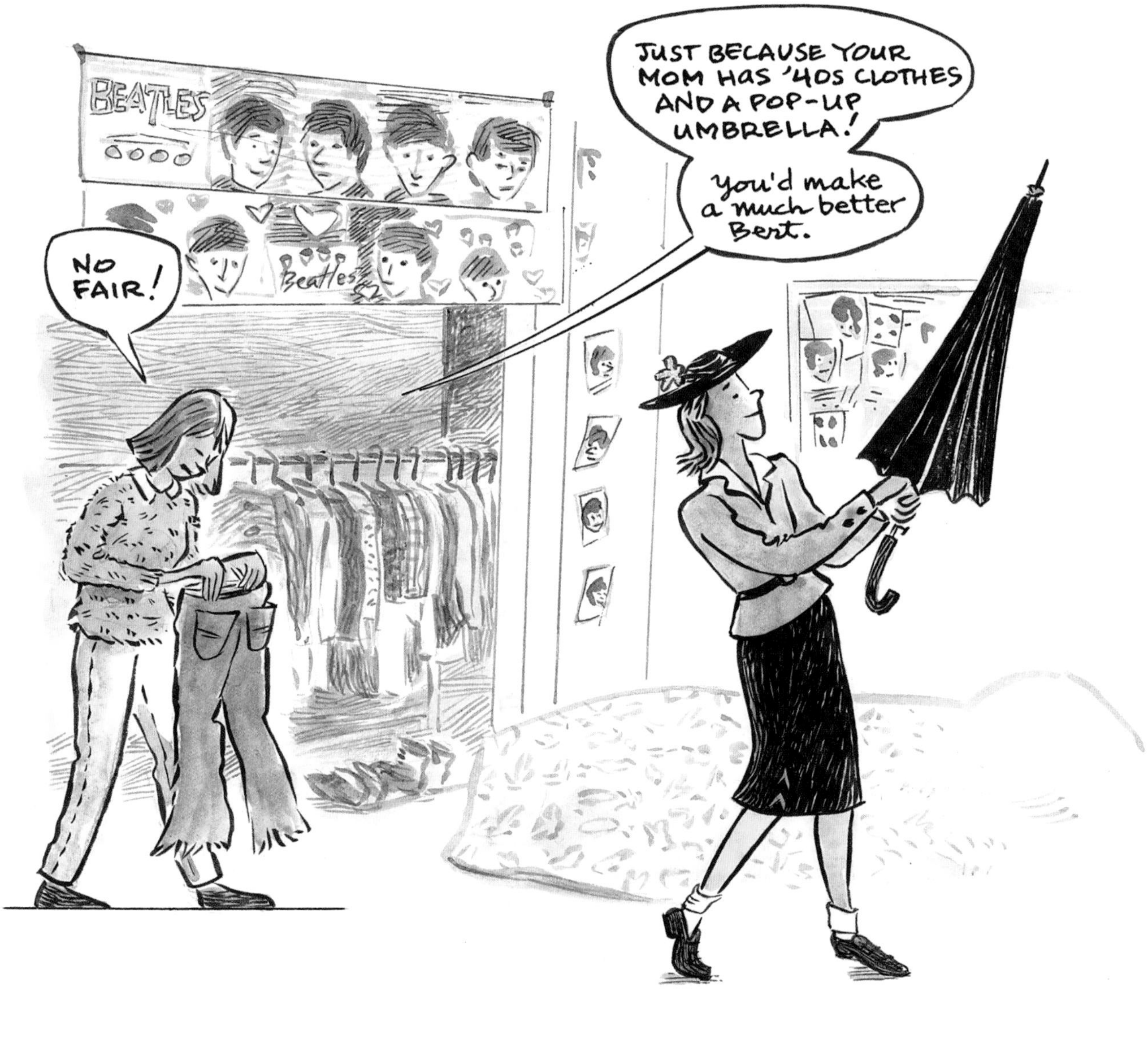

BEATLES
Beatles
NO FAIR!
JUST BECAUSE YOUR MOM HAS '40S CLOTHES AND A POP-UP UMBRELLA!
you'd make a much better Bert.

Jolly 'oliday

CLASS NIGHT

CHICAGO 13, ILL.

May 1 1965

The most EXCITING NIGHT SO FAR HAPPENS TONIGHT! IT'S Class Night FOR THE 8th Graders. CLASS OF '65. St. Bede School. A CHANCE FOR US TO SHOW OFF HOW GREAT WE ARE. TODAY WE WERE DOWN THERE IN THE CHURCH BASEMENT SETTING UP ROWS OF FOLDING CHAIRS. all 20 OF US WILL PERFORM SONGS, SKITS, AND TALENTS OF ALL KINDS FOR OUR PARENTS AND WHOEVER ELSE. Come one! Come all! AFTERWARDS, THE MOTHER'S CLUB WILL BE DOING 'Coffee and.'

Laurie AND I HAVE BEEN PRACTICING OUR ROUTINE FOR 2 WEEKS, ESPECIALLY OUR BRITISH ACCENTS. No CORNY DOROTHY SHAY SONG, WE'RE DOING Mary Poppins. Jolly Holiday. SHE DOESN'T LIKE IT THAT I PLAY MARY AND SHE'S BERT, THE CHIMNEY SWEEP. I LIKE POPPING OPEN Mom's UMBRELLA. IT'S GOT AN AUTOMATIC BUTTON. Besides, Laurie TAKES THE LEAD AT THE 7 every morning.

For a GROUP SONG, THE BEATLES FAN CLUB IS GOING TO PERFORM "This Land is Your Land." JANET'S GOING TO USE MY TAMBOURINE. We HAD ANOTHER SONG PICKED OUT AND HAD PRACTICED IT A LOT. IT INVOLVED THE COWBELL I GOT FROM GRAMPA. "You Can't Do That" WAS OUR CHOICE, BUT SISTER SAID IT WAS A LITTLE TOO WILD. WE DID A SHIMMY DANCE IN THE MIDDLE OF IT. I GUESS THAT WOULD HAVE BROUGHT THE BUILDING DOWN. CAN'T RISK ROCKING THE FOUNDATION OF THE CHURCH.

Gotta Go. I'VE GOT TO GET ALL OF MY OUTFITS TOGETHER. I'M IN 3 DIFFERENT NUMBERS. THEY ALL HAVE PROPS. I NEED A TRUNK. AND I'M TAKING THAT COWBELL JUST FOR LUCK.

WE KENN DO DAT

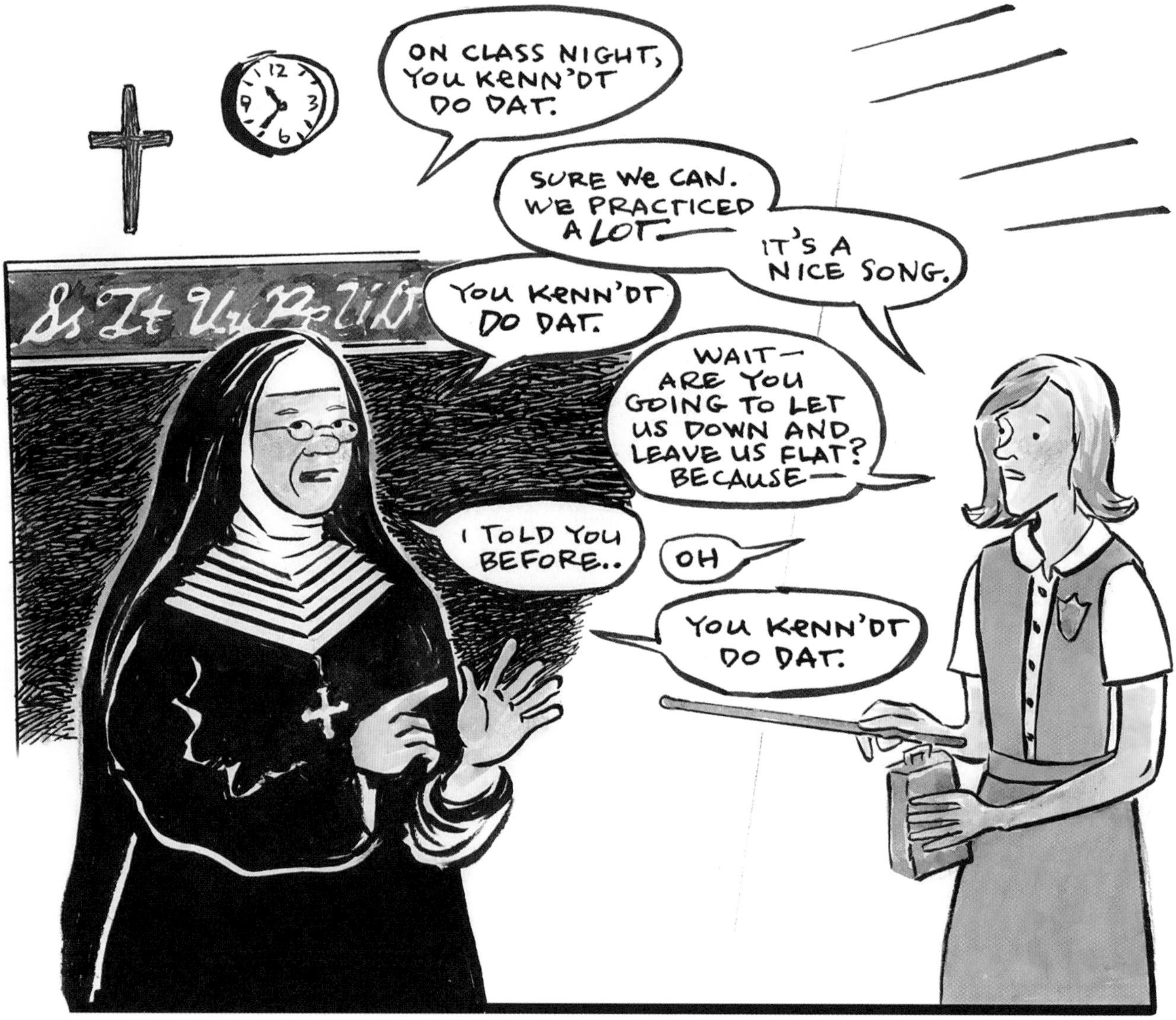
ON CLASS NIGHT, YOU KENN'DT DO DAT.
SURE WE CAN. WE PRACTICED A LOT—
IT'S A NICE SONG.
YOU KENN'DT DO DAT.
WAIT— ARE YOU GOING TO LET US DOWN AND LEAVE US FLAT? BECAUSE—
I TOLD YOU BEFORE..
OH
YOU KENN'DT DO DAT.

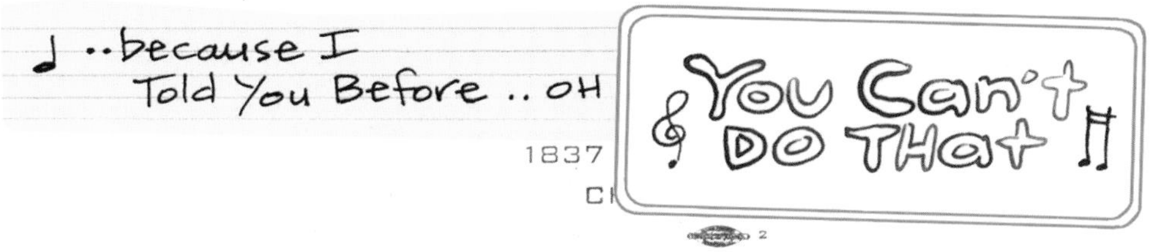
..because I Told You Before .. OH
1837
You Can't DO That

Later = **WOW!** TURNED OUT TO BE A

REALLY BIG SHEW!

(ED SULLIVAN SEZ SHEW INSTEAD OF SHOW.

Mrs. Blair kept acting like Ed. She was the evening's hostess and played piano for all the numbers. Nobody forgot the words. I was a little bit nervous. "Do the Beatles get nervous before THEY go on?" I wondered. Laurie and I hit the pivot, twirl, and umbrella pop perfectly, but the umbrella almost took my hat off, so I stepped back onto Laurie's foot. Everyone laughed, but Laurie said it proved she should've been Mary.

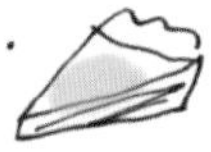

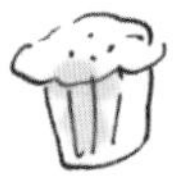

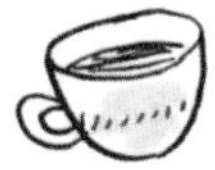

Mother's Club had the desserts laid out: cakes, pies, cupcakes, and lots of cookies. The adults drank coffee. Yuck. I hate coffee. It tastes **TERRIBLE**. Why do they **DO** it to themselves? Laurie says we have to get used to it. It's an adult beverage like beer. I hate beer too. I am **DOOMED!**

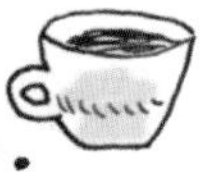

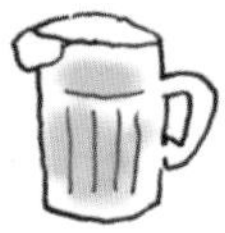

Only one kid cried during the whole show. When they sang "He" after Anna and Diane's piano duet. And guess who did an Abbott and Costello hillbilly number? Mike and Turzeki. Really dumb.

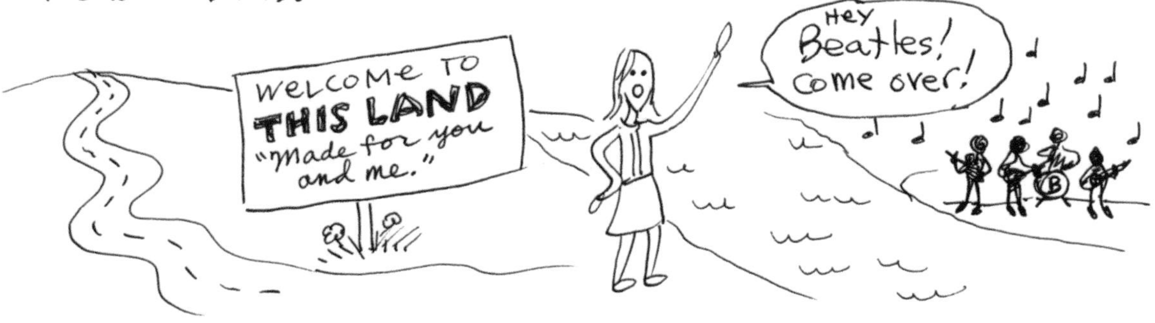
WELCOME TO
THIS LAND
"made for you and me."
Hey Beatles! come over!

What.
else is
there?

mee·u·zick

WLS
The bright sound of Chicago Radio

SILVER DOLLAR SURVEY

Chicago's Official Radio Record Survey

MAY 14, 1965

1. MRS. BROWN YOU'VE GOT A LOVELY DAUGHTER – Hermits MGM
2. SILHOUETTES ON THE SHADE – Herman's Hermits MGM
3. TICKET TO RIDE/YES IT IS – The Beatles – Capitol
4. THE LAST TIME – The Rolling Stones – London
5. HELP ME RHONDA – The Beach Boys – Capitol
6. COUNT ME IN – Gary Lewis – Liberty
7. IT'S GONNA BE ALRIGHT – Gerri & the Pacemakers – Laurie
8. TIRED OF WAITING FOR YOU – The Kinks – Reprise
9. I KNOW A PLACE – Petula Clark — WB
10. DO THE FREDDIE – Freddie & the Dreamers – Mercury
11. SAY IT SOFTLY – Bobby Whiteside – Destination
12. I'LL NEVER FIND ANOTHER YOU – The Seekers – Capitol
13. SHAKIN' ALL OVER — The Guess Who — Scepter
14. IKO IKO – The Dixie Cups – Red Bird
15. LITTLE LATIN LUPE LU – The Chancellors – Soma
16. QUEEN OF THE HOUSE – Jody Miller – Capitol
17. BACK IN MY ARMS AGAIN – The Supremes – Motown
18. ENGINE ENGINE #9 – Roger Miller – Smash
19. REELIN' AND ROCKIN' – The Dave Clark Five – Epic
20. TRUE LOVE WAYS – Peter & Gordon — Capitol
21. JUST A LITTLE — The Beau Brummels – Autumn
22. JUST ONCE IN MY LIFE – The Righteous Brothers – Philles
23. IT'S NOT UNUSUAL – Tom Jones – Parrot
24. SHE'S COMIN' HOME – The Zombies – Parrot
25. DREAM ON LITTLE DREAMER – Perry Como – RCA
26. YOU WERE MADE FOR ME — Freddie & Dreamers – Tower
27. WHAT DO YOU WANT WITH ME – Chad & Jeremy – WA
28. CONCRETE AND CLAY – Eddie Rambeau – DynoVoice
29. TOMMY – Reparata & The Delrons – WA
30. VOODOO WOMAN — Bobby Goldsboro – UA
31. SHE'S ABOUT A MOVER – Sir Douglas Quintet – Tribe
32. BABY THE RAIN MUST FALL – Glenn Yarbrough – RCA
33. OOO BABY BABY – The Miracles — Tamla
34. IT'S GROWING — The Temptations – Gordy
35. THINK OF THE GOOD TIMES – Jay & the Americans – UA
36. I'LL BE DOGGONE – Marvin Gaye – Tamla
37. I DO LOVE YOU – Billy Stewart – Chess
38. NOTHING CAN STOP ME – Gene Chandler – Constellation
39. WOOLY BULLY – Sam Sham & Pharohs – MGM
40. YOU WERE ONLY FOOLING – Vic Damone – WB

Dex Card

2:00 to 6:00 P.M.
Sunday thru Saturday

WLS·DIAL 890·24 HOURS·A·DAY

This survey is compiled each week by WLS Radio/Chicago from reports of all
record sales gathered from leading record outlets in the Chicagoland area.
Hear Dex Card play all the SILVER DOLLAR SURVEY hits daily from 2:00 to 6:00.

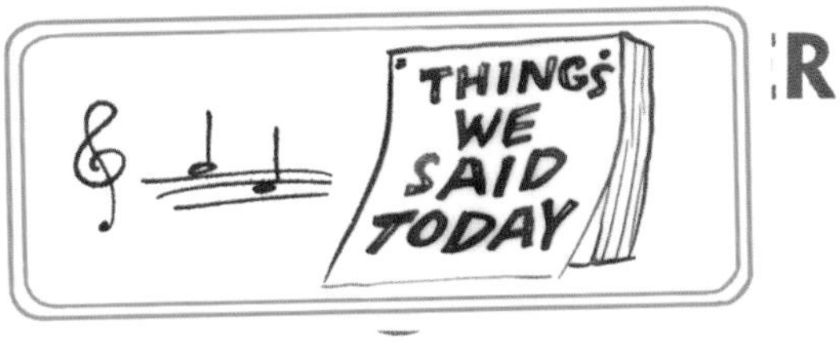
THINGS WE SAID TODAY
R

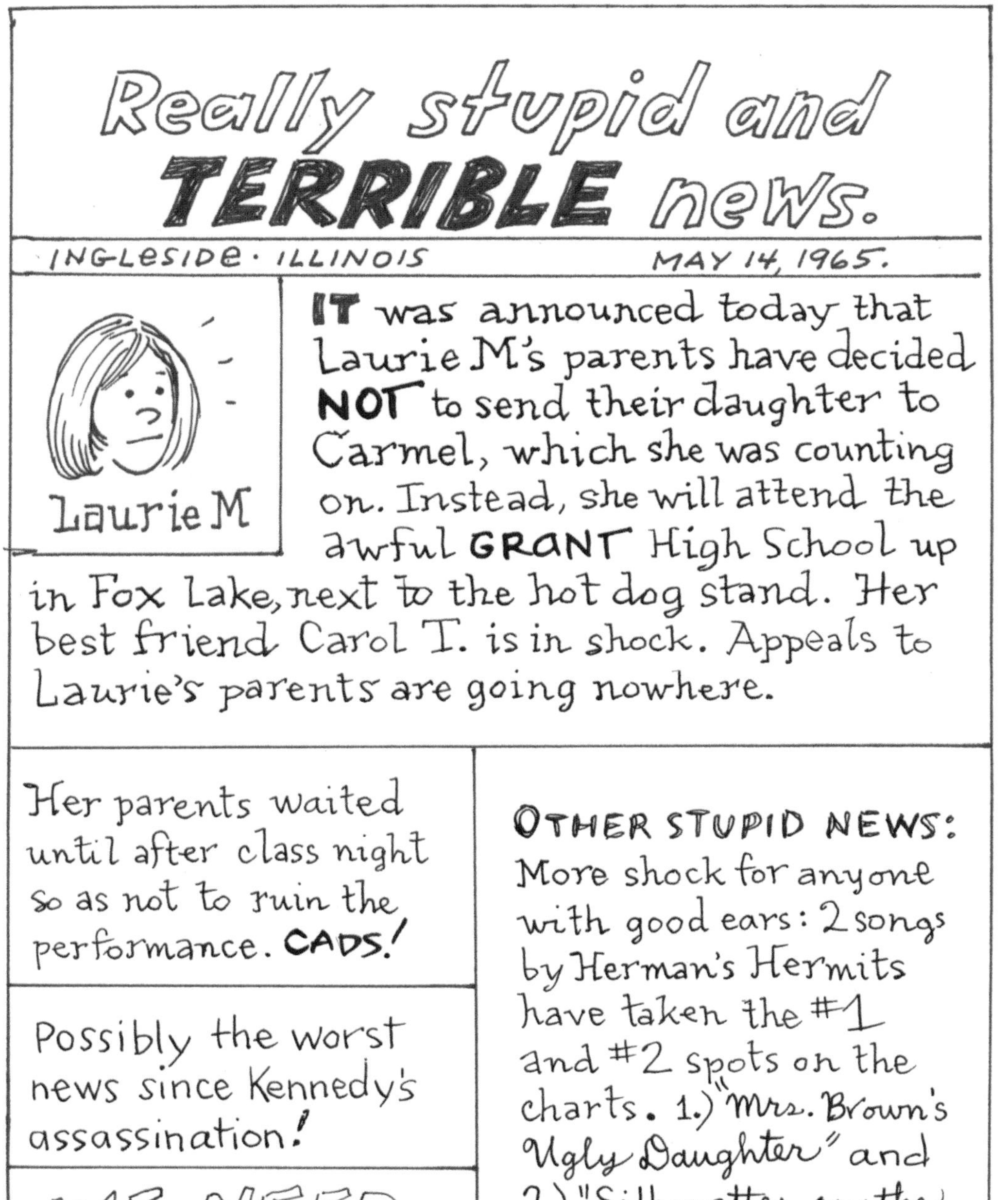
Really stupid and TERRIBLE news.
INGLESIDE · ILLINOIS
MAY 14, 1965.
Laurie M
IT was announced today that Laurie M's parents have decided NOT to send their daughter to Carmel, which she was counting on. Instead, she will attend the awful GRANT High School up in Fox Lake, next to the hot dog stand. Her best friend Carol T. is in shock. Appeals to Laurie's parents are going nowhere.
Her parents waited until after class night so as not to ruin the performance. CADS!
Possibly the worst news since Kennedy's assassination!
WE NEED MILKSHAKES!
OTHER STUPID NEWS: More shock for anyone with good ears: 2 songs by Herman's Hermits have taken the #1 and #2 spots on the charts. 1.) "Mrs. Brown's Ugly Daughter" and 2.) "Silhouettes on the Shade." This is such lousy music, folks!

♪ Me, I'm just a lucky guy
love to hear you say that love is love ♪ ♪ ♪ ♪ and though we may be blind, love is here to stay and that's enough...

Why is it that when terrible, stupid things happen, it's always at the same time? And not one person in either of our families seems disturbed by this news! How can we stay best friends and not go to the same high school? As it is now, it's hard to get together except at school. We had it all figured out, about being on the same bus. It's 35 miles to Carmel. Make that 15 miles and 35 minutes. 5 miles to Laurie's. Make that 2.5. Her parents will not change their minds. It's too expensive. Her dad works at a factory. Her mom is at home. Lots of kids. They are both friendly people. STILL WHY BREAK US UP?

We are just like those cousins on the Patty Duke Show.

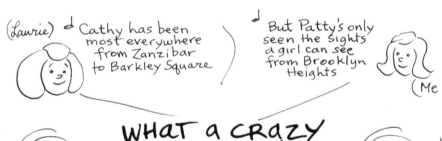

(Laurie) ♪ Cathy has been most everywhere from Zanzibar to Barkley Square

♪ But Patty's only seen the sights a girl can see from Brooklyn Heights

(Me

♪ WHAT a CRAZY PAIR! ♪ ♪ ♪

♪ cuz they're best friends. Identical best friends all the way. (ON THE SHOW, They're identical cousins)

They look alike
They talk alike
Sometimes they even walk alike

You will lose your mind!

When best friends - are 2 of a kind!

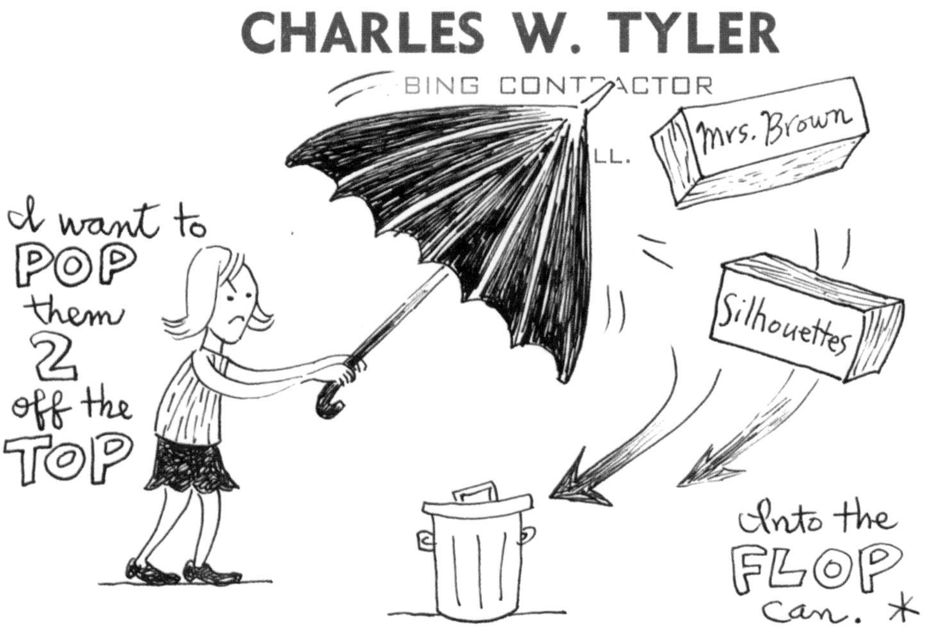
CHARLES W. TYLER
BING CONTRACTOR
LL.
Mrs. Brown
Silhouettes
I want to POP them 2 off the TOP
Into the FLOP can. *

I HATE WHEN PEOPLE SAY, THAT BECAUSE THESE 2 LOAVES OF STALE BREAD ARE ON TOP, THE Beatles are washed up. MY → [foot]. THEY'RE **NOT**. They're busy WRITING SONGS AND MAKING ANOTHER MOVIE. PLUS, THEY'RE GETTING READY TO COME TO TOUR, AND come see me IN Chicago. I WILL BE AT THEIR CONCERT Come High Hell or Water!

AND NOW THERE'S ANOTHER INSULT THAT'S COME ALONG ON THIS DAY OF STUPID NEWS: Mom says THAT over the summer, DURING TIME I COULD BE SPENDING WITH Laurie, I HAVE TO LEARN TO Type. I don't want to grow up and BE a SECRETARY. She SAID I WAS CRAZY IF I THOUGHT SHE WAS GOING TO BE TYPING ALL MY TERM PAPERS over AT Carmel. Maybe I'll go to GRANT!

(*somebody stop the old people from buying their grandkids this horrible music!)

ANY TIME AT ALL♩♩

May 18

Mister Whitel is our exercise and history instructor. He's got it set up, that before we even come in the building, unless it's severe weather, we have to do this exercise routine. He said we should do them **every morning** for the **rest of our lives.** Brand new teacher this year.

We start out at 3 rows, double arm intervals and scoot out a bit more. Then, with our arms out to the sides, we do Little Circles. 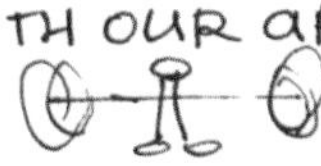 These help warm us up. Then it's toe touches, jumping jacks, torso twists, squats, side bends, running in place then 3 laps around the parking lot. If it's raining, we do this in the halls. Guess what? Many times, Laurie and I linger after the 7 to avoid this, usually arriving for that last lap.

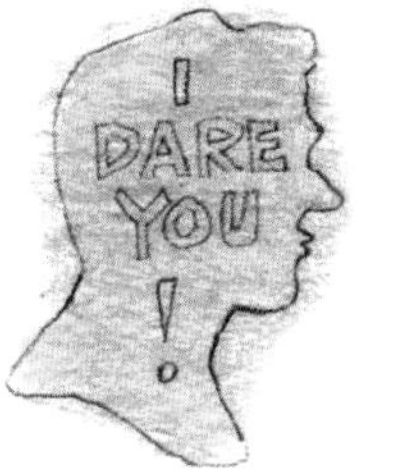
I
DARE
YOU
!

In history, Mr. Whitel talks about the communist threat in Vietnam. He gets upset when he talks about it. No more fun and games. His mouth pulls open to reveal his upset teeth in perfect alignment. He told us that even though he was out of the Marine Corps, he was ready to go sign up again and go over there. That he would probably have to go soon, and for us to promise to never stop doing our morning exercises, that we would have to lead ourselves always from now on till we are old or we die.

Then he got very serious, hung his head down, raised it up suddenly and said "I Dare You!"

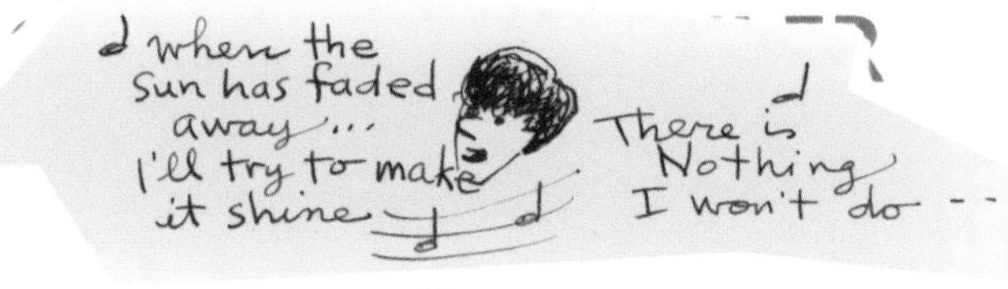
when the sun has faded away...
I'll try to make it shine
There is Nothing I won't do - -

THEN HE HANDED EACH ONE OF US 8th Graders THIS BOOK, and THE TITLE OF IT was "I Dare You." He SAID THIS WOULD HELP GUIDE US THROUGH LIFE.

On PAGE 19, IT SAYS "I want you to thoroughly fix in your mind that life is a **FOUR-SIDED AFFAIR** that will lead you to **PHYSICAL** adventures, **MENTAL** adventures, **SOCIAL** adventures, and **SPIRITUAL** adventures. You have not **ONE** but **4** lives to live. Body, brain, heart, and soul."

AND IT SHOWED THIS PICTURE:

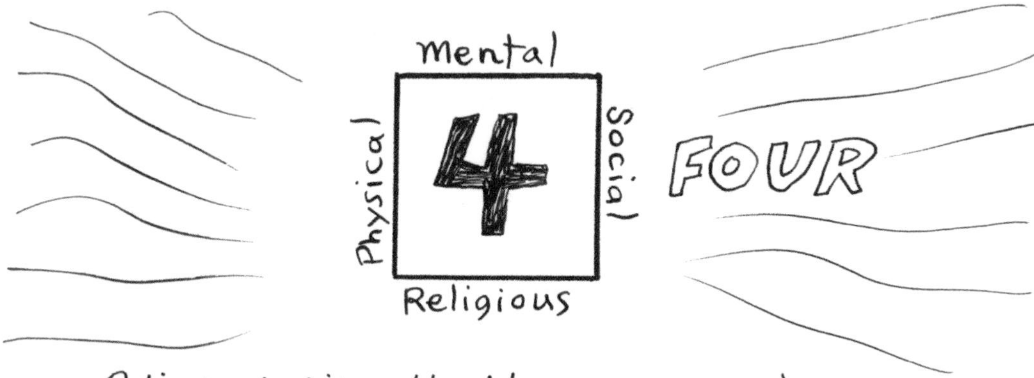
Mental
Physical
4
Social
Religious
FOUR

Kind of like 4-H:

4 is a **GREAT** NUMBER.

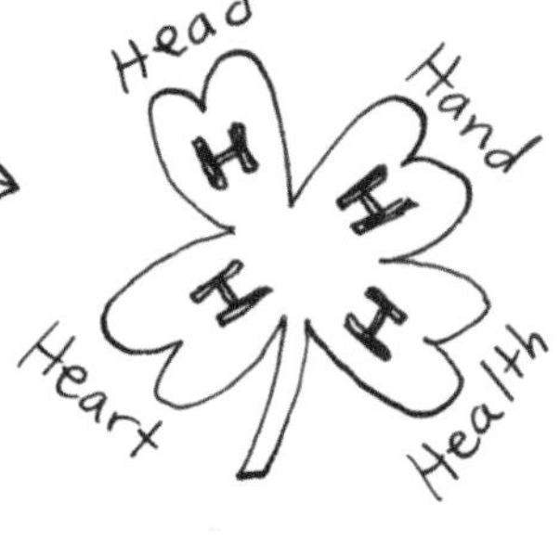
Head
Hand
Heart
Health
H
H
H
H

BIG **4**.

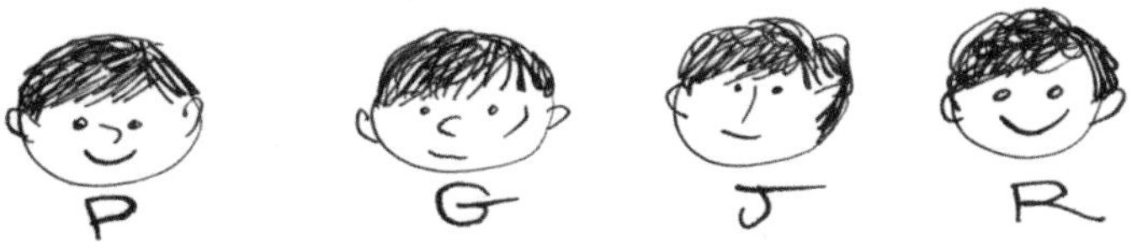
P
G
J
R

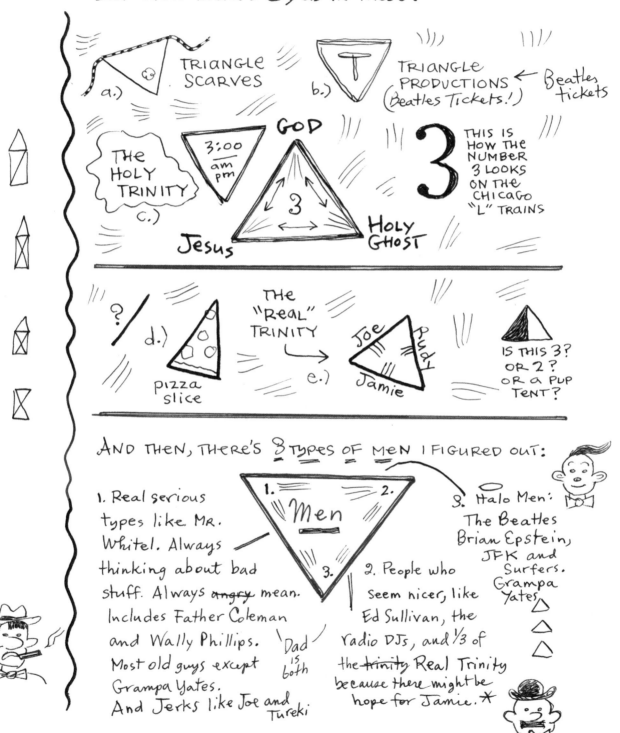

BUT THEN THERE'S **3**, AS IN THESE:

a.) TRIANGLE SCARVES

b.) TRIANGLE PRODUCTIONS (Beatles Tickets!) ← Beatles tickets

c.) THE HOLY TRINITY

3:00 am/pm

GOD
Jesus 3 HOLY GHOST

3 THIS IS HOW THE NUMBER 3 LOOKS ON THE CHICAGO "L" TRAINS

? / d.) pizza slice

THE "REAL" TRINITY → e.) Joe / Rudy / Jamie

IS THIS 3? OR 2? OR A PUP TENT?

AND THEN, THERE'S **3** TYPES OF MEN I FIGURED OUT:

1. / 2. Men 3.

1. Real serious types like MR. Whitel. Always thinking about bad stuff. Always ~~angry~~ mean. Includes Father Coleman and Wally Phillips. Most old guys except Grampa Yates. And Jerks like Joe and Tureki

Dad is both

2. People who seem nicer, like Ed Sullivan, the radio DJs, and ⅓ of the ~~trinity~~ Real Trinity because there might be hope for Jamie. ✱

3. Halo Men: The Beatles Brian Epstein, JFK and Surfers. Grampa Yates △ △ △

128

SIX minus FOUR

CHARLES W TYLER

mystery

1837 WES

CHICAGO 13, ILL.

UH

*HERE'S THE SITUATION WITH Jamie. He LIKES the Beatles, BUT HE CAN'T SAY IT OUT LOUD OR HE WILL BE
6 POUNCED ON BY JOE AND RUDY, WHO THINK THEY ARE A SISSY BAND FOR TEENIE BOPPERS. AND LISTEN TO THIS: Jamie found out I ordered 6 TICKETS TO THE SHOW. THEN HE ASKED "Who are the other 2 for?" There's only 4 in your little fan club." I TOLD HIM ONE WAS FOR GINIA, WHO
4 SAID SHE WOULD DRIVE US, AND ONE WAS FOR --- DON'T KNOW YET. THEN HE SAID "Well, maybe you DO know." So I SAID BACK "UH, only if that person drives us there
2 in his rag top Mustang," AND THAT WAS THE END OF THAT, BECAUSE HE WOULDN'T BE CAUGHT DEAD TAKING a BUNCH OF 8th GRADERS, I MEAN (By Then) FRESHMEN **ANYWHERE** IN HIS CAR. MUSTANG, NO. BUT HE'D SAY YES TO RIDING WITH US IN Mom's SKYLARK — ALTHO Maybe NOT. I'm not going to talk tickets till they get here. Back to NUMBERS COUNTDOWN.

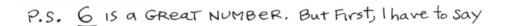

P.S. 6 IS a GREAT NUMBER. But First, I have to say

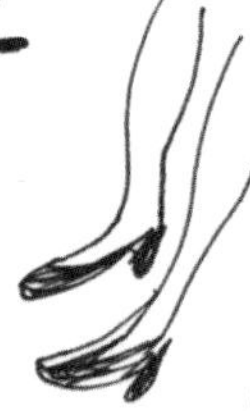

2 WILL Always BE ME AND Laurie

AND NOW, NUMBER 1 WITHOUT a DOUBT, Forever

The BeaTLes. THE 1 and only. One

One one one One one

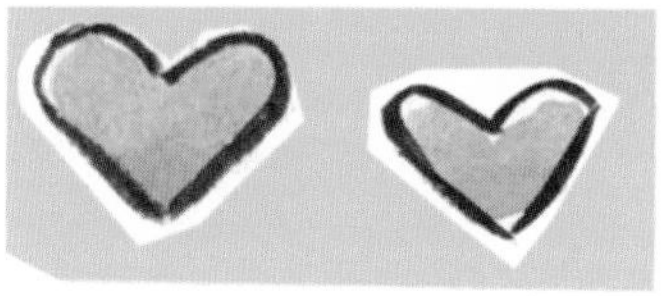

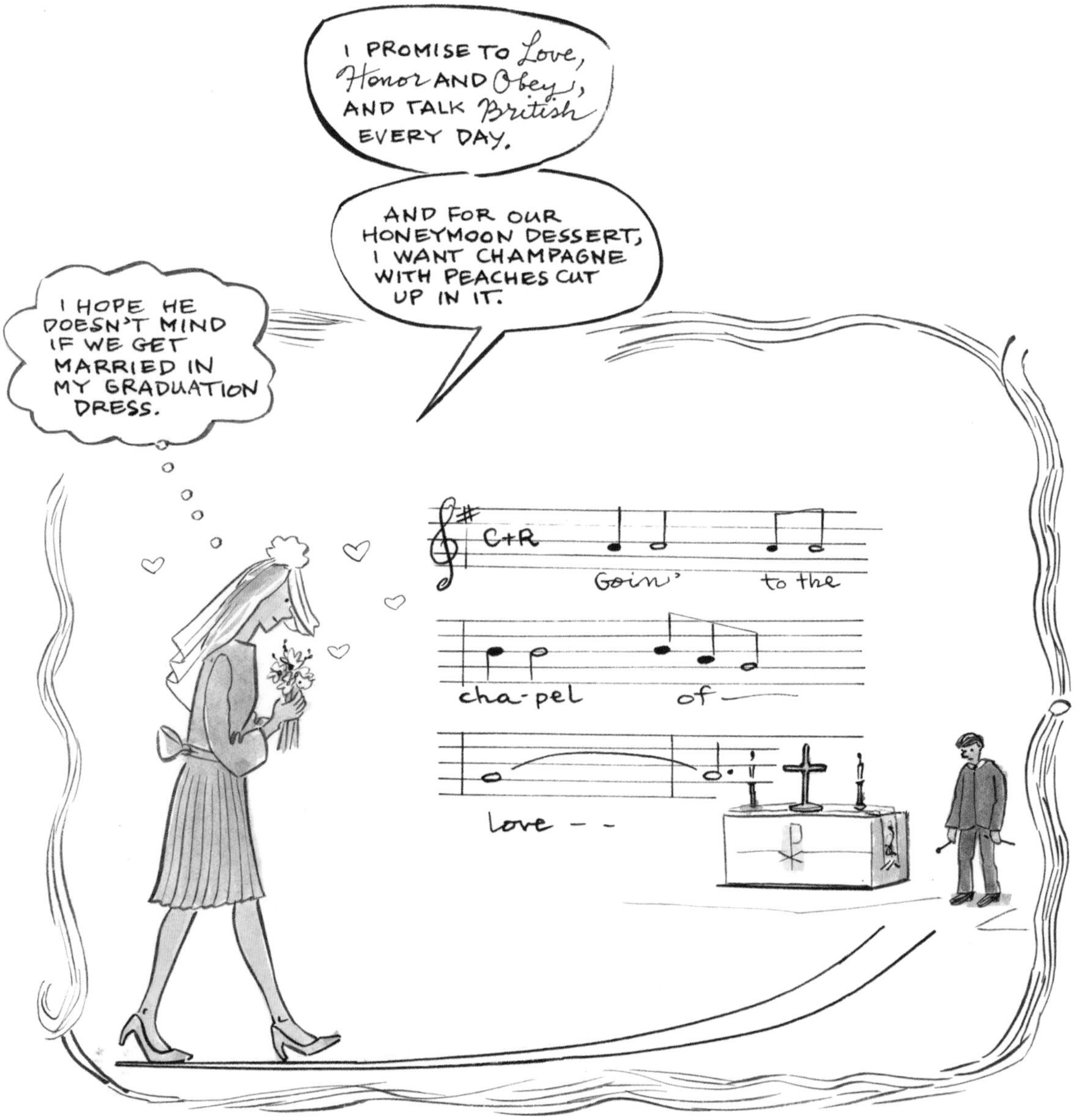
I PROMISE TO Love, Honor AND Obey, AND TALK British EVERY DAY.
AND FOR OUR HONEYMOON DESSERT, I WANT CHAMPAGNE WITH PEACHES CUT UP IN IT.
I HOPE HE DOESN'T MIND IF WE GET MARRIED IN MY GRADUATION DRESS.
C+R
Goin' to the
cha-pel of
love - -

A FEW BEATLE DREAMS   BY CAROL TYLER

One night I drempt that I was in the car with Joe,
Jamie, and Virginia.I saw this big bulding and I went
inside. Brian Epstein just then left.THE BEATLES were
siting at a long table at my left.First cme(from left
to right),PAUL, thenGEORGE, then JOHNand RINGO.I went
and talked to PAUL,AND GEORGE AND JOHN,and RINGO for about
an hour(just RINGO for an hour but the rest for I5
minutes each).Just as I was going for the door RINGO
made a drum movement and I told him I could play the
drums.PAUL said,"That is no way to say goodbye!" so
he took out a tube of lipstick and put it on real
slopy,and kissed my hand."That is the way to do it."
GEORGE followed his example.JOHN SAID "Wait",got a
cup of tea and shook hands. RINGO put it on and kissed
my cheek,and gave me the lipstick. Then I left.

One night I saw myself in a wedding gown and I
was to marry RINGO.

One night I was to go to a BEATLE CONCERT.After
the show I went to the back of the amphitheatre and
saw a door.I entered.Directly in front of me were two
stairways.One going up and the other down.I took
the one that went down.At the bottom was a door.

Inside was RINGO'S DRUMS,PAUL'S,JOHN'S&& GEORGE'S
GUITARS. Iplayed RINGO'S DRUMS(the newest ⬛⬛⬛⬛Songs)
"SHE LOVES YOU" ON PAULES BASS GUITAR "YOU CAN'T DO THAT"
ON GEORGE'S GUITAR,AND messed around with JOHN'S GUITAR.
I saw a table with 4 cups with spoons and the BEATLES'
Nanes on them.I took the spoons and put them in my
pocket & put the cups in a bag.I gave the basement one last
look when Joe came in & pulled me out.Just as we were leaving
1
(I WROTE THE BEATLES A LETTER& TOLD THEM I WAS THERE&
TOLD RINGO THAT I PLAYED HIS DRUMS& GAVE THEM MY ADDRESS.)
I heard English voices and heard footsteps.It was too late
Joe closed the door.

                    ONe night

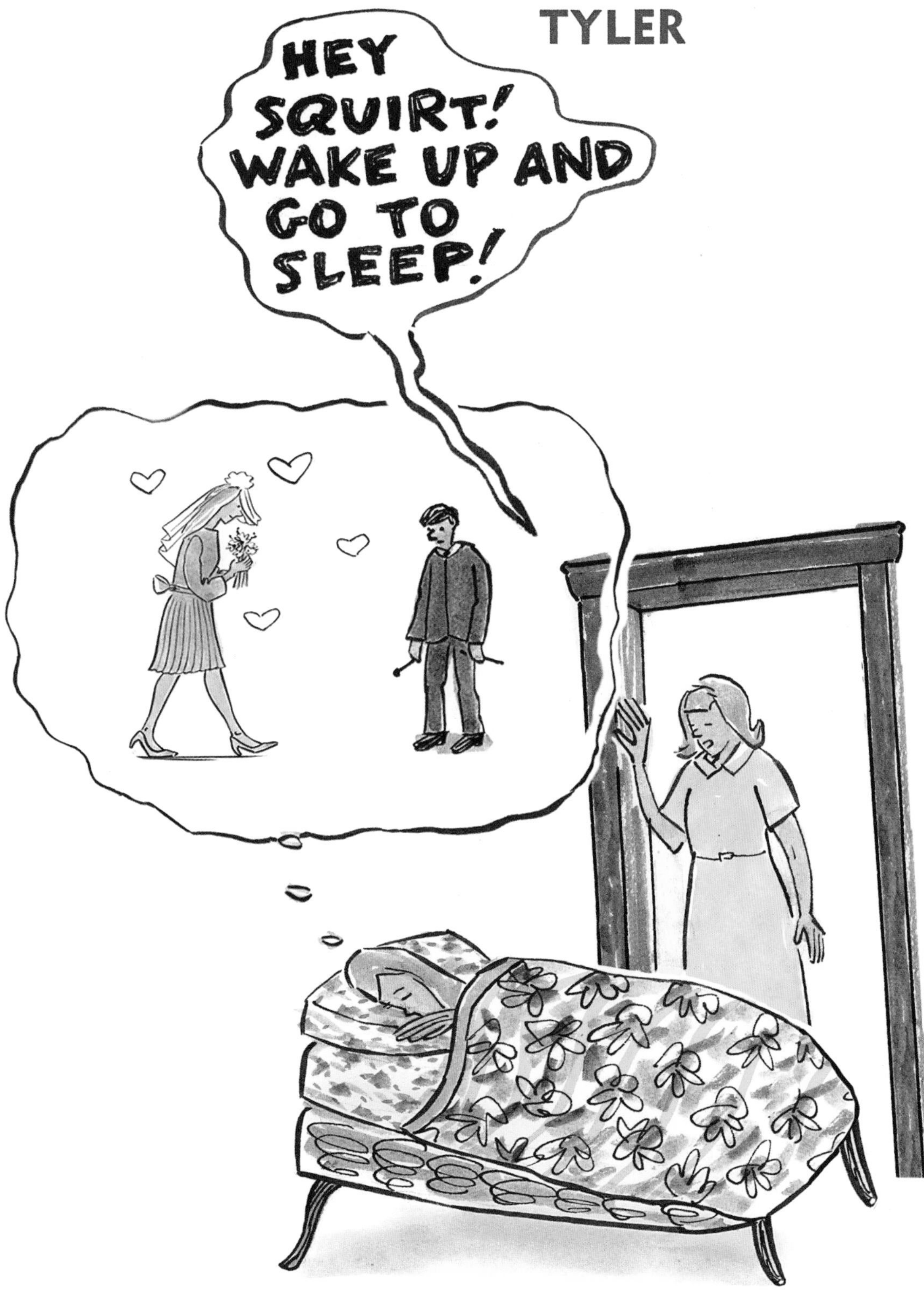
TYLER
HEY SQUIRT! WAKE UP AND GO TO SLEEP!

♪ ALL I GOTTA DO. ♪

may 28

I MAY NOT BE CONSIDERED THE Holy ONE IN OUR FAMILY, BUT I'M GOOD. I MEAN, I GO TO Catholic SCHOOL, AND I PRAY AND DO THE SACRAMENTS LIKE I'M SUPPOSED TO. PLUS, I SING IN THE CHOIR WITH Laurie every MORNING AT THE 7. It's a QUICK MASS, BUT THERE'S STILL PLENTY TO SING.

It's TRUE THAT I HAVE CAUSED A BIT OF TROUBLE HERE AND THERE. A LITTLE BIT OF LYING IS ALLOWED I THINK. I DIDN'T MEAN TO SQUASH THAT MOUSE OR LEAVE ALL THOSE PERCH FLOPPING ON THE SAND. I DON'T LIKE **SIN** AND I ESPECIALLY DON'T LIKE THE FEELING OF BEING IN TROUBLE. In fact, I'm so AFRAID OF GETTING IN TROUBLE THAT I DON'T EVEN TRY TO GET AWAY WITH ANYTHING WHICH CAN MAKE ME KIND OF **BORING**. EXCEPT I DID STEAL THAT Beatles cover from Jamie. WHAT's a Beatlemaniac to do? Besides, I keep it with me always AND TAKE GREAT CARE OF IT. →neatly folded. I DON'T EVEN WANT TO THINK OF WHAT JAMIE MIGHT DO IF HE KNEW. Sic THE Trinity on ME. They'd RANSACK MY ROOM, AND HE'D PROBABLY ACT LIKE IT WAS NEWS TO HIM, SO HE COULD COME OFF AS THE NICE GUY. I'd be in TEARS AND CLAIM I DON'T KNOW HOW IT CAME TO BE IN MY POSSESSION, AND HE COULD SAY "There There."

I DEFINITELY DON'T CHEAT IN CLASS BY COPYING SOMEONE ELSE'S ANSWERS. I DON'T TRACE ART EITHER, CHEATING IN ANOTHER FORM, I THINK. A STUPID WAY

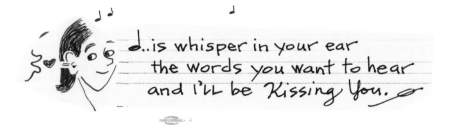

♩..is whisper in your ear
the words you want to hear
and I'll be *Kissing You.*

TO EARN A SIN. I MEAN IF YOU'RE GOING TO SIN, WHY NOT GO FOR SOMETHING *BIG* LIKE MOP THE KITCHEN FLOOR WITH A CAT, OR WATCH A FRENCH MOVIE. OO LA LA! NOT TORMENTING FISH. SEE, I HAD THIS IDEA TO MAKE IT FUN FOR FISH, WHO ALWAYS SEEM BORED AND MISERABLE. SO I DUG OUT A SAND/DIRT MAZE, ADDED A BUNCH OF LAKE WATER AND THEN DUMPED IN A WHOLE BUCKET OF MR. BOUCEK'S BLUE GILLS. HE CATCHES THEM REAL EARLY. THEY'RE IN THIS BUCKET WITH HOLES AND LEFT IN THE WATER TILL SUPPER. SO I TOOK THE LITTLEST CUTIES AND DUMPED THEM IN THE MAZE. BEFORE I KNEW IT, THE WATER SEEPED AWAY AND THE FLOPPING BEGAN. SO THEN I LAID THEM ON LILY PADS, LIKE AT A SPA RESORT. BUT THEY FLIPPED BACK INTO THE WATER AND TECHNICALLY OFF OF MR. BOUCEK'S DINNER PLATE. HE WAS SO MAD.

NO GOOD

  I THINK MAKING OUT IN THE CHOIR LOFT WOULD BE PRETTY BAD. READING MAGAZINES UP THERE IS ALSO BAD. A FEW MONTHS AGO, LAURIE AND I GOT INTO *BIG* TROUBLE AT THE 7 FOR SINGING DOWN INTO OUR HYMNALS INSTEAD OF PROJECTING OUTWARD. SECRETLY WE WERE READING OUR BEATLES MAGAZINES. RUMOR —— SOME SORT OF RUMOR GOING AROUND ABOUT THE LADS AND DUSTY SPRINGFIELD. AND SOME SINGER NAMED HELEN. DUSTY OR HELEN, WHICH WAS RUMORED TO BE THE NEWEST BEATLE BRIDE? FR. COLEMAN STOPPED MASS TO CALL US OUT. THING IS, WE CAN SING `Requiem Aeternam´ IN OUR SLEEP! OH THAT 7 CRACKS ME *UP!*

♩ You just got to call on me.

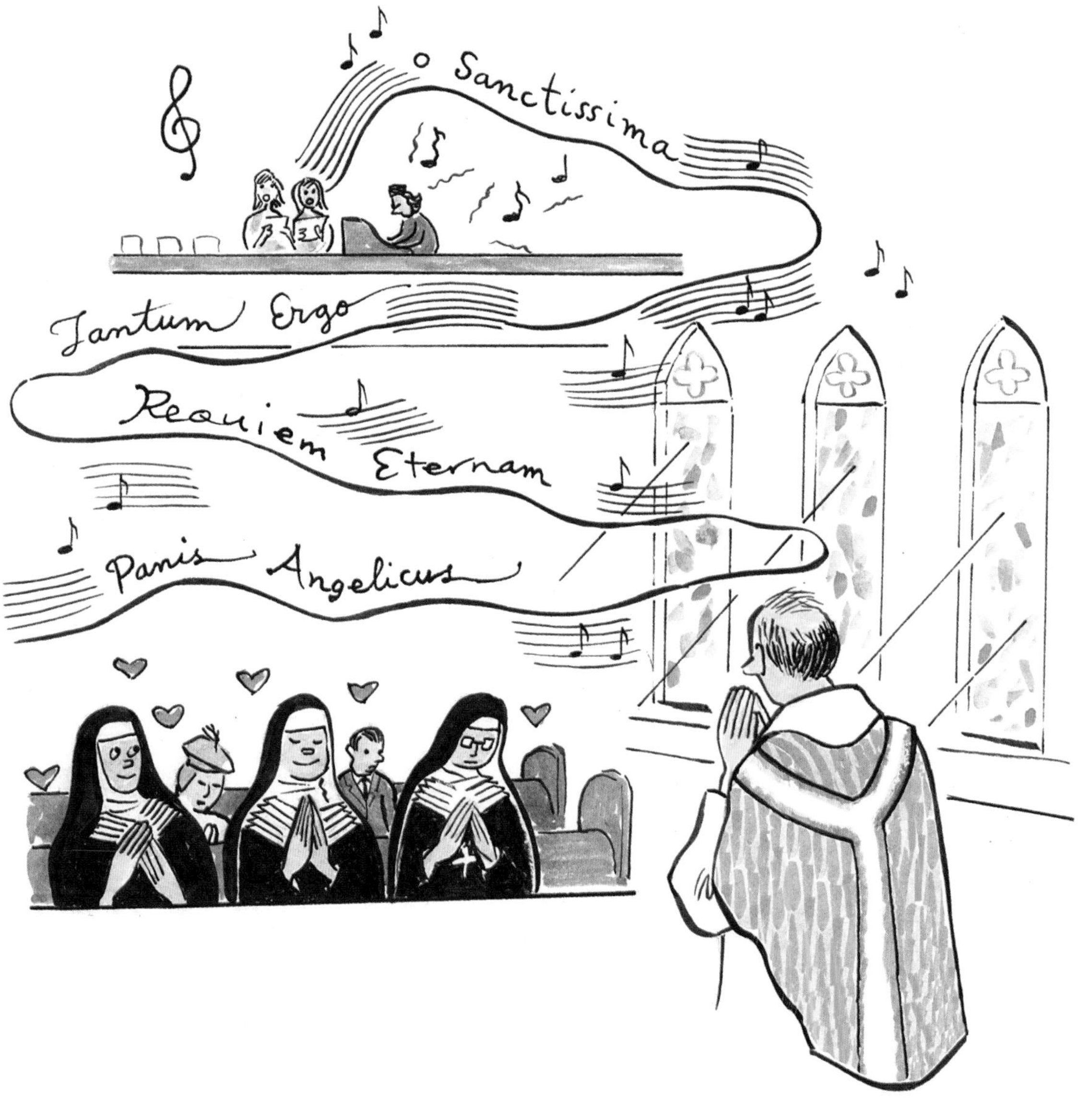
O Sanctissima
Tantum Ergo
Requiem Eternam
Panis Angelicus

HOLY US

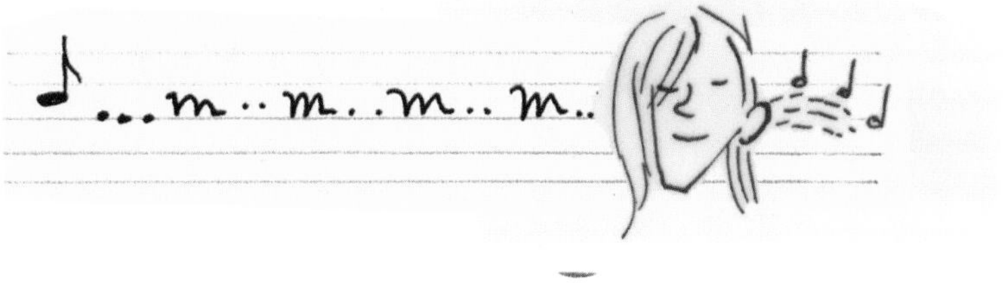
...m..m..m..m..

For example -- there's this one pew that is so old and creeky, it sounds like someone is cutting the cheese when they sit down. The same lady sits there every morning, in a lace cap and with a rosary. Doesn't she hear it? How come she's not embarrassed? Then, as soon as I stop laughing about that, Father Coleman's voice cuts the place in two like a hatchet, and the nuns jump a mile out of their seats. It's a **RIOT!** Every day, the same thing. Up in the choir loft where we're at, everything's louder. Plus, we get to **SEE** everything, like the people who *sneak* out of Mass right after communion. A Bee Line, once that obligation is fulfilled. Altar boys goof off, too. They're fun to watch.

Morning light angles in through the long windows, softened by statues, colors, and incense, weighed down by sin. So much sin. (Everyone seems nice, where is all this sin happening in F.L. Ill?)

It drives Mrs. Blair **CRAZY** when the altar boys go on too long with the "tinkling bells" during the consecration. She snorts like Gu does and harps loudly "They're **TINKLING** TOO LONG!" That makes Laurie and I laugh so hard, but we're not supposed to, so that makes it even funnier. Because we tell the altar boys before Mass to ring the bells long and slow, the sisters like it that way, just so we can watch Mrs. Blair blow her stack. — Uh oh. Is this a sin?

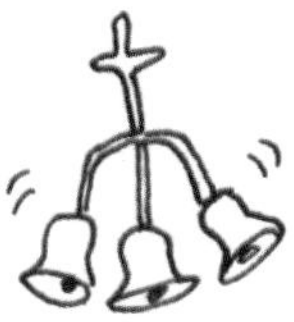

THE BELL THING WITH THE ALTAR BOYS (IT ONLY WORKS WITH THE NEW ONES OR THE YOUNG ONES) THAT'S ONE ITEM OF BUSINESS. THEN THERE'S REQUESTS. THERE'S A LIST OF THEIR FAVORITES, Mrs Blair TAUGHT US, and SO ON CERTAIN DAYS, THEY'D RATHER HEAR THIS one OR THAT one. And as a THANK YOU, ON THE WAY BACK FROM COMMUNION, OVER THEIR HUMBLY FOLDED HANDS, THEY NOD UP AT US, THE WAY CHILDREN DO WITH Santa Claus. WE SING Father Coleman's FAVORITES, TOO. Mrs. Blair KNOWS WHAT HE LIKES, AND IF HE'S ANGRY OVER THE TINKLING, SHE'LL ORGAN-UP a BIG ONE. He SITS IN THAT BIG RED CHAIR SMILING LIKE a SATISFIED RADIO LISTENER. YUP, WE CHOIRETTES CRANK OUT THE TOP 40 HITS OF THE 7, EFFORTLESSLY, AND IN Latin!

Last Year IT STARTED: A TAP ON THE SHOULDER, COME TO THE BACK OF THE ROOM, HAND OVER YOUR BEATLES ITEMS. ALWAYS DREADFUL, THAT TAP AND THEN BEING MOTIONED WITH SISTER'S BENT FINGER. BUT THIS YEAR, THE TAP/COME HERE WAS FOR SOMETHING ELSE. THE "CONVERSATION." EVERY MONTH, SOMETIMES TWICE a MONTH, EVEN WEEKLY, ALL OF US GIRLS HEARD THE SAME THING: "I THINK YOU HAVE VOCATION." Sister Immaculata, tapping out each syllable softly, SLOWLY, VO-CAY-SHUN, SHE WOULD whisper. "Nope! HOLY IS NOT FOR ME." Yes, I SING LIKE AN ANGEL, BUT I'M ALSO a FISH miserable-izer and Thief.

..I-I-I'll be here
Yes I will. Whenever
you call.

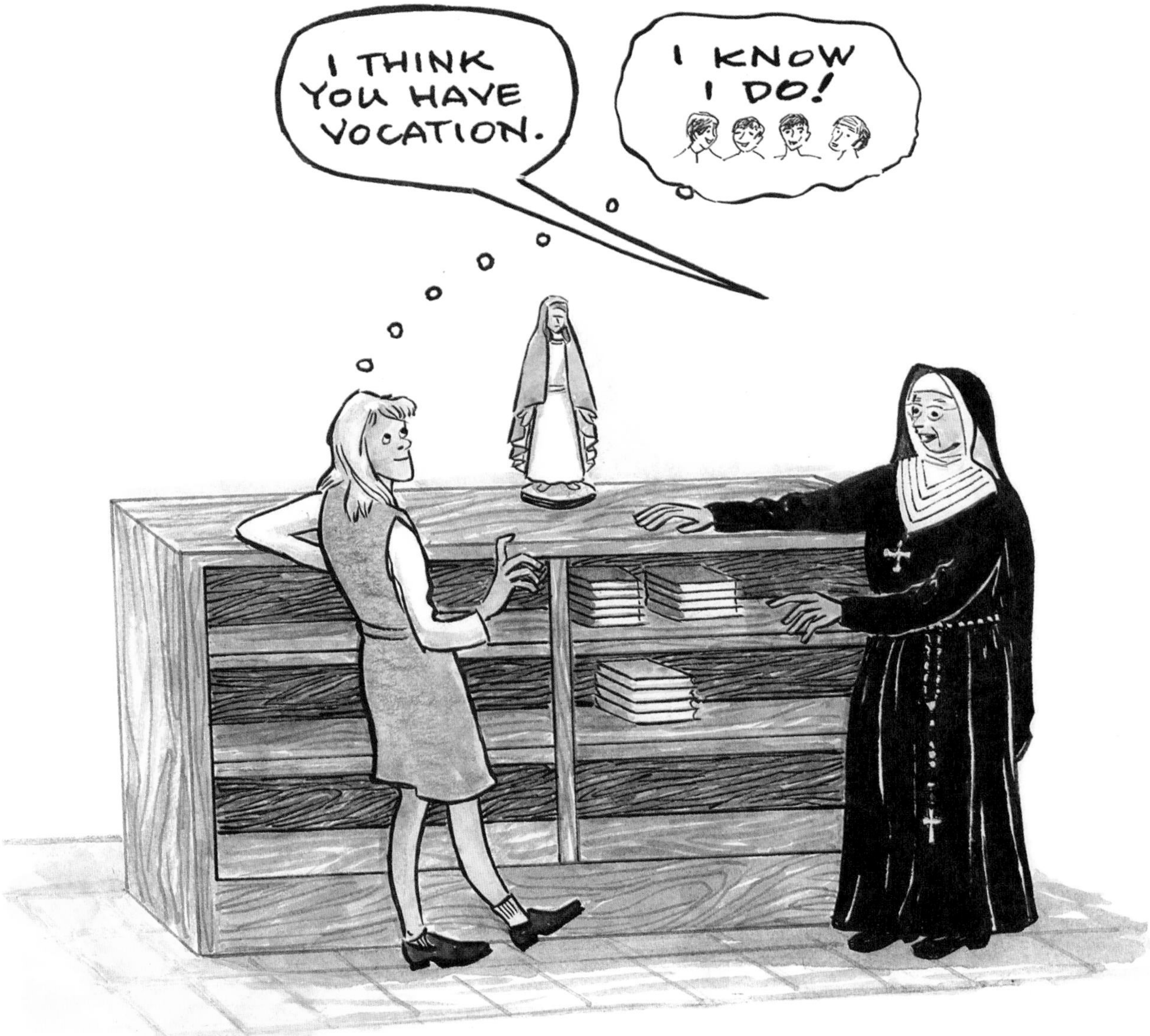
I THINK YOU HAVE VOCATION.
I KNOW I DO!

June 17

My GRAMPA DIED. NOT THE ONE IN Tennessee WHO GAVE ME THE COWBELL. THE ONE HERE. MY DAD'S DAD. A PLUMBER FROM CHICAGO. DAD LEARNED EVERYTHING FROM HIM. SO THIS WEEK WAS GRADUATION AND A FUNERAL AT THE SAME TIME. EVERYONE HERE IS GLUM. HE WASN'T SICK OR ANYTHING. JUST OLD.

GRADUATION CAME FIRST. SISTER ONLY HAD TO SLAP ME ONCE ACROSS THE BACK. IT WAS DURING PRACTICE THE DAY BEFORE. I WALKED TOO FAR BACK IN THE AISLE. SHE HOLLERED <u>STOP</u> IN HER CRANKLE VOICE, BUT I WAS BUSY WITH JANICE'S FLIP. HER SISTER IS A BEAUTICIAN. HER FLIP IS PERFECT, AND SO STIFF, A PENCIL CAN REST IN IT COMFORTABLY. IT WON'T SHAKE OUT AND YOU CAN'T SEE IT. THAT'S WHAT I WAS DOING, LAYIN' A PENCIL TO REST IN JANICE'S STIFF BLONDE CURL WHEN SISTER HIT ME AND HOLLERED "Grow Up!"

I WASN'T VERY CLOSE TO GRAMPA T. HE WAS ALWAYS TIRED. WORN OUT FROM PLUMBING. WHEN WE LIVED IN CHICAGO, HE'D SIT THERE IN THE KITCHEN BY THE BACK DOOR AND GRAB MY LEG AS I FLEW BY. "Hand me a knife, I'm gonna cut this leg OFF" HE'D SAY. HA HA VERY FUNNY, GRAMPA. THEN HE'D TAKE A BUTTER KNIFE AND PRETEND HE WAS SAWING WHILE TICKLING ME.

DAD SAID WHEN HE WAS BORN, HE WAS SO TINY, THEY DIDN'T EXPECT HIM TO LIVE. BORN AT HOME BACK IN 1880. SO, THEY PUT LITTLE AL IN AN EMPTY CIGAR BOX, DRANK BEER THEY MADE THEMSELVES, AND PLAYED CARDS ALL NIGHT WHILE ON DEATH WATCH.

Cheeri-o Old chap!

♪♪ BABY'S in BLACK ♪♪

He showed them alright, BY MAKING IT THROUGH THE NIGHT AND LIVING ON TO BE A HAPPY, PRODUCTIVE, HEALTHY, AND THEN OLD FELLOW.

I RODE WITH MY COUSINS TO THE FUNERAL. For a PRETTY GOOD WHILE THERE, WE WERE **LAUGHING**. In fact, WE LAUGHED OUR SIDES SORE! My UNCLE HOLLERED AT US TO KNOCK IT OFF, BUT MOM TOLD HIM THAT LAUGHING CAN BE A NORMAL REACTION. SHE HAD NO GREAT LOVE FOR Grampa T. HE WAS ALWAYS GRABBING HER FOR A KISS. SHE <u>HATED</u> IT. BEER, YOU KNOW.

I COULDN'T WEAR MY GRADUATION DRESS TO THE FUNERAL. TOO PRETTY. INSTEAD I WORE AN OLD WOOL SKIRT OF GINIA'S AND ONE OF MY UNIFORM BLOUSES. HAD TO PIN THE SKIRT AND FORCE MYSELF TO WEAR A WHITE BLOUSE FROM SCHOOL <u>ONE MORE TIME</u>. I SPRAY PAINTED MY LIME GREEN GRADUATION SHOES BLACK. They Still fit. Plus I wore a hat of MOM's.

After MY UNCLE YELLED AT US TO SETTLE DOWN, HE FLIPPED ON THE RADIO. THIS WAS ON:

" R-Ra-aindrops FALLIN' FROM MY eye-eyes...

♩♩

Wa-oh w-oh-oh Must be a cloud in my head. Rain fallin' from my eye-eyes..."

SHOOTIN' THE CURL

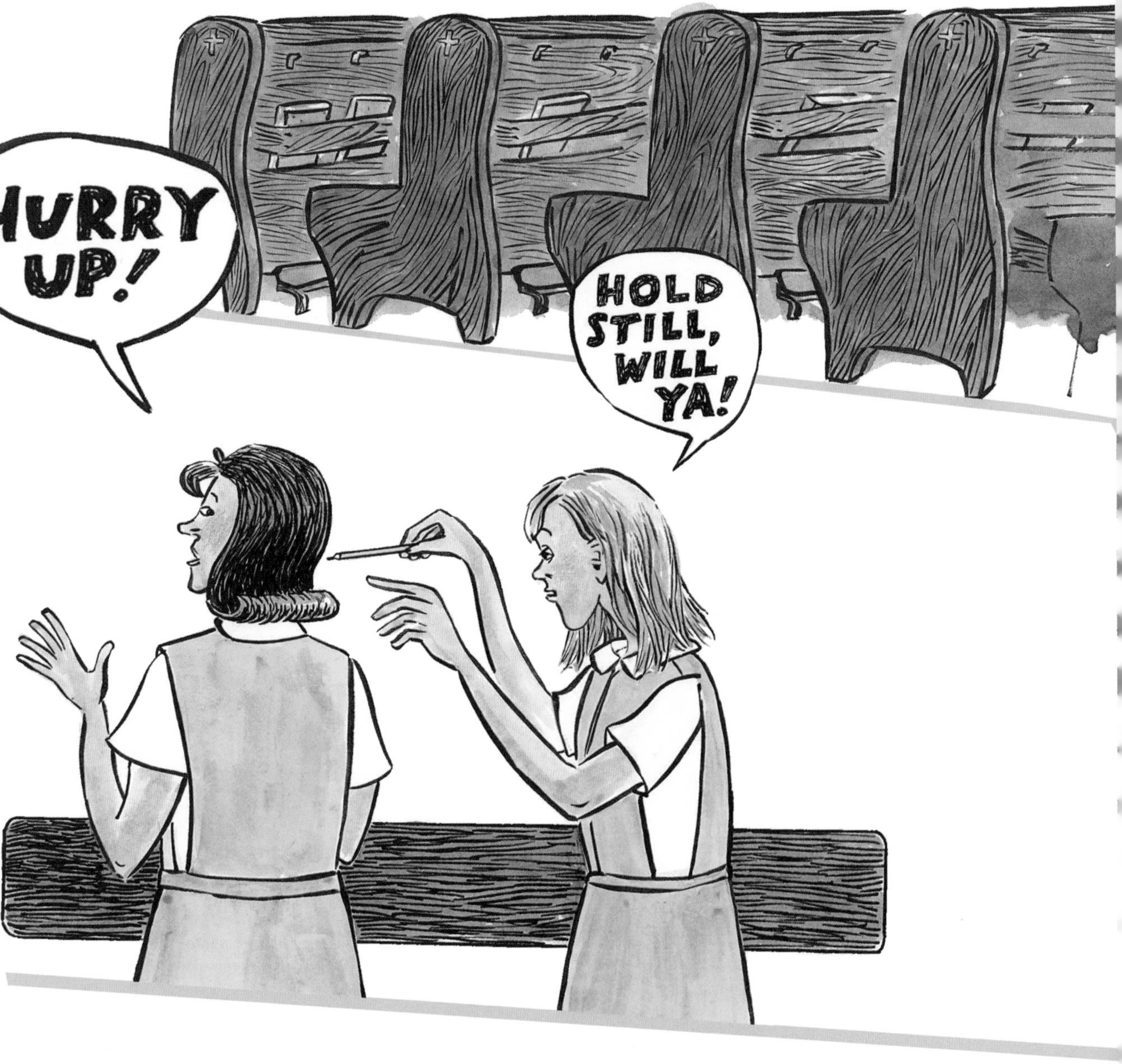
HURRY UP!
HOLD STILL, WILL YA!

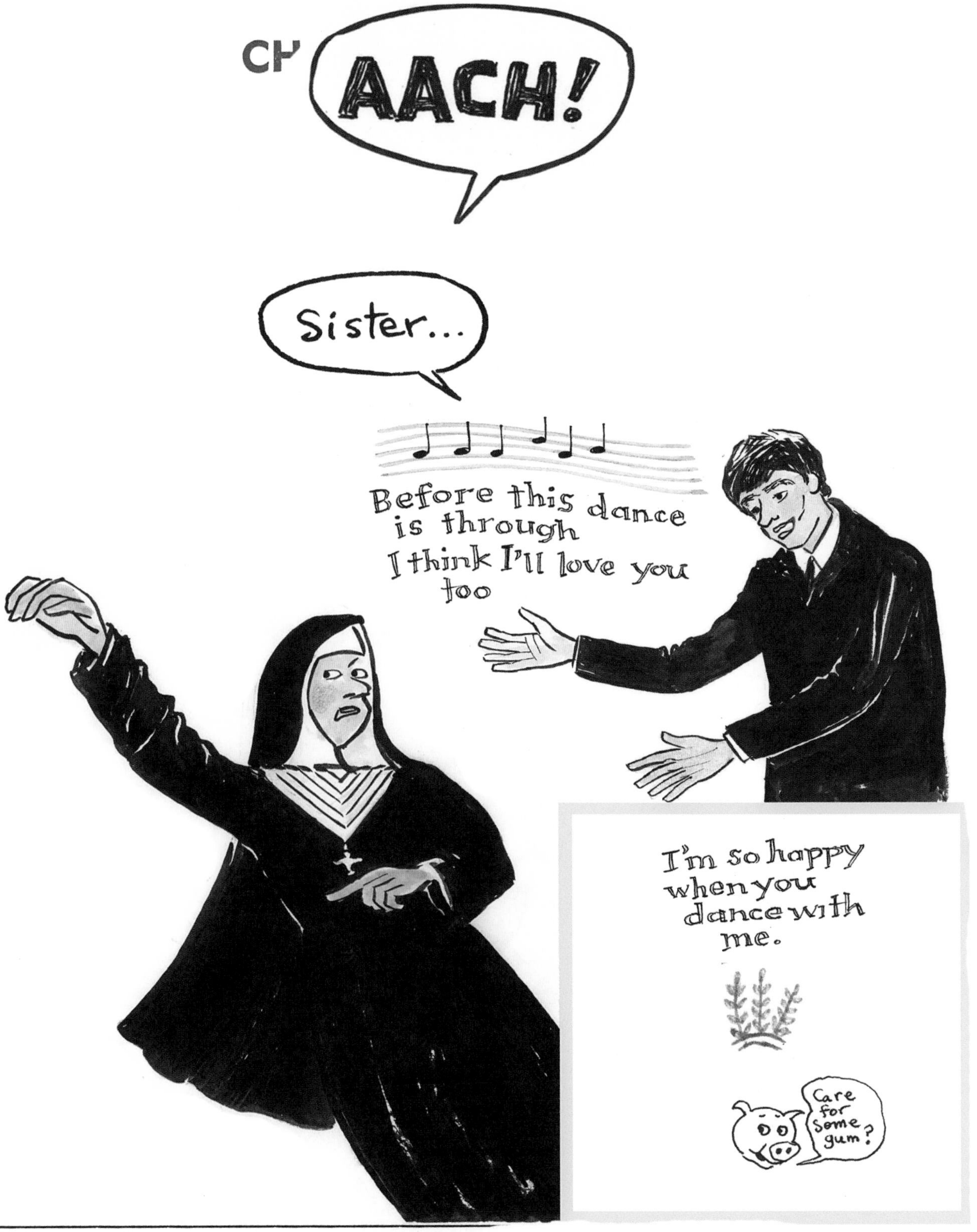
CH' AACH!
Sister...
Before this dance is through I think I'll love you too
I'm so happy when you dance with me.
Care for some gum?

george Harrison

Plays lead guitar and hates haircuts. Occasionally
sings and also had a go at writing songs. "Don't
Bother Me" and "You Like Me Too Much" show off
some of his writing talent and singing ability.
He has a much quicker wit than most people.
When asked "Did you have a haircut?" he replied
"No, I had them all cut!" He loves Chet Atkins
and Duane Eddy and would very much like to
be a guitar designer.

George was born on February 25, 1943 and is the
baby of the Beatles. He is 5'11" tall and weighs
142 pounds. He has dark brown hair and eyes,
and a big toothy smile. He has one sister living
in Illinois. His real name is

George Harrison

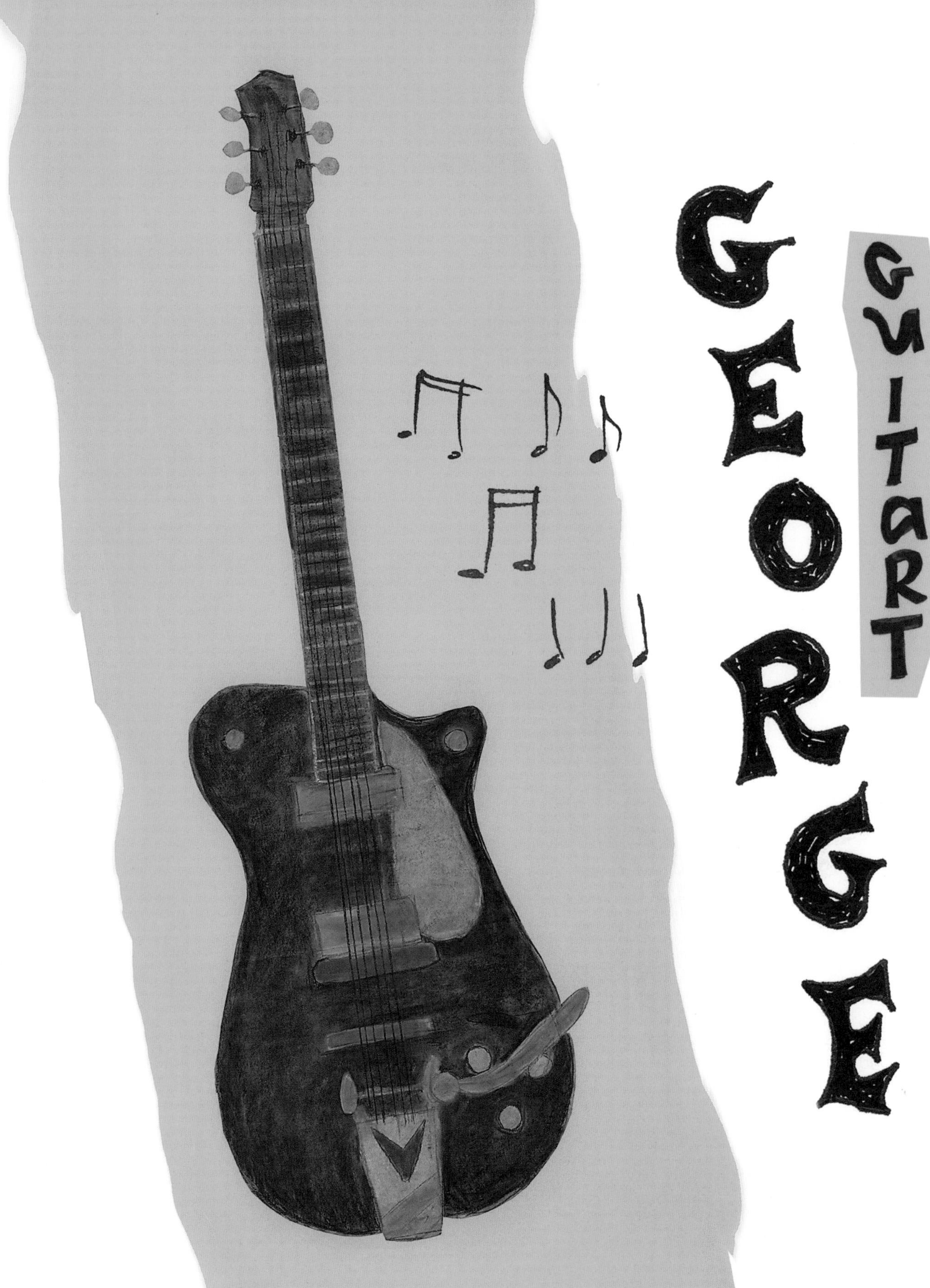
GEORGE
GUITART

C... ER

Do you want to know a Secret?

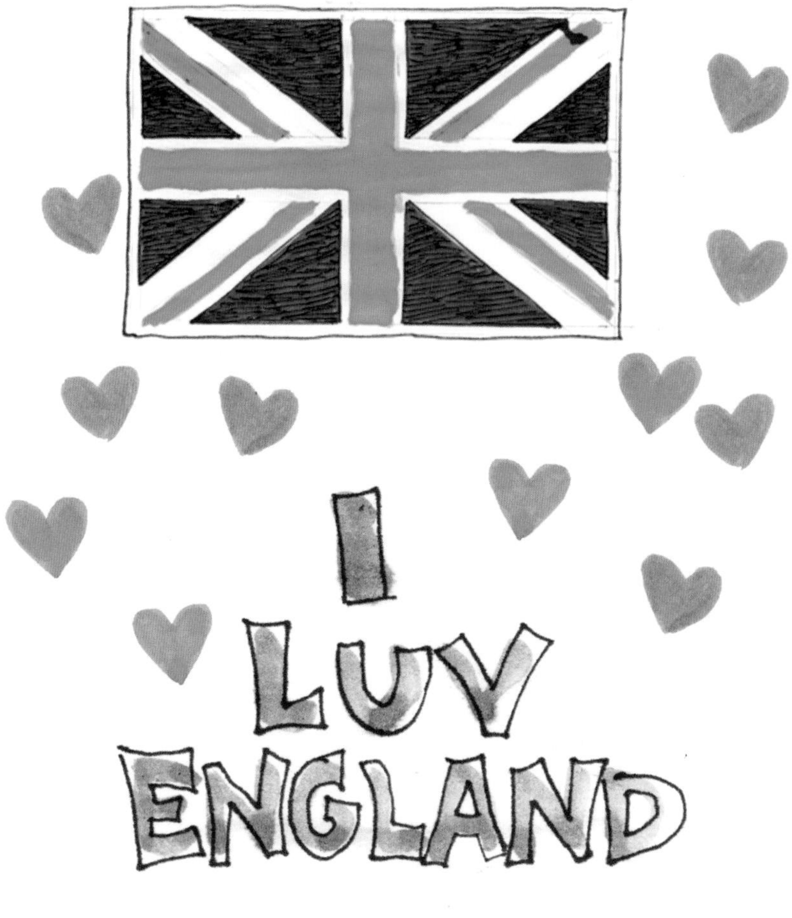
I
LUV
ENGLAND

3. BRITISH PASSPORT

SUMMER '65

CAROL TYLER

She's a Woman

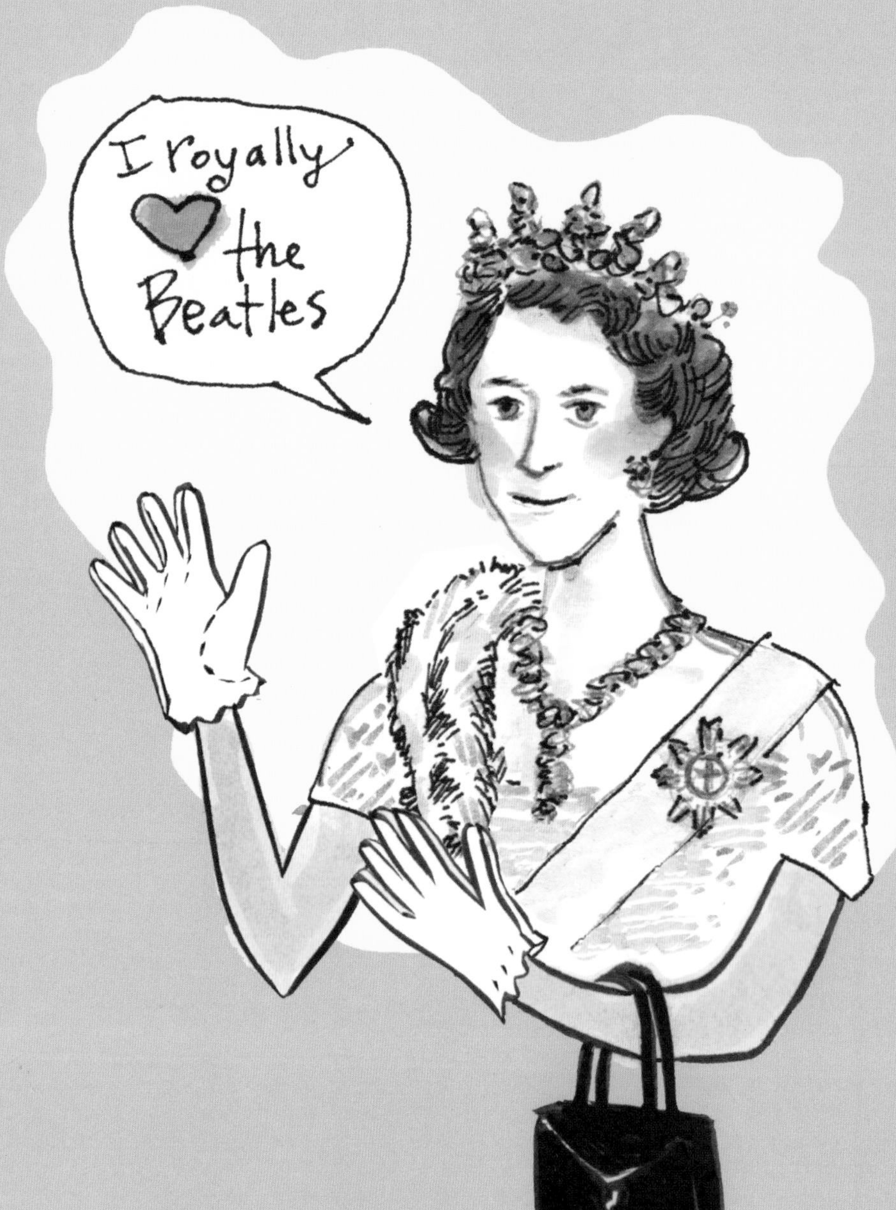
I royally ♥ the Beatles

June 21 GRADUATION Wrap Up.

I MADE OUT WITH a *Lot* OF GIFTS. BEST PART IS $5 CASH, WHICH I USED TO BUY *Beatles VI*.

The actual GRADUATION CEREMONY WAS NICE. I DIDN'T WANT TO GET HIT AGAIN, SO I DIDN'T FORGET TO STOP IN THE AISLE. THE CHURCH WAS PACKED. SOME KIDS FROM 7TH GRADE WERE IN THE CHOIR SINGING — MRS. *Blair's* NEW BATCH. AFTERWARDS, WE HAD a RECEPTION AT OUR HOUSE. PEOPLE BROUGHT FOOD AND GIFTS. *Mom* GOT a HAM FROM THE *Jewel.*

SURPRISES: I WAS GIVEN THE *American Legion* AWARD. *Honorable Mention.* I FOUND OUT LATER FROM *Mrs.* PETERSON THAT I WOULD HAVE BEEN GIVEN FIRST PRIZE, BUT THEY HAD TO GIVE IT TO a BOY. WE HAD TO WRITE an ESSAY TO BE CONSIDERED. *Mine* was CALLED "*Beautiful America: From Sea to Shining Sea.*" IT'S ABOUT OUR BEAUTIFUL LAND AND HOW WE SHOULD TAKE CARE OF IT. *The* BOY WHO WON, HIS ESSAY WAS ABOUT THE *Founding Fathers.* I ALSO GOT AN AWARD FOR HAVING *beautiful handwriting*! <u>AND</u>, AND *Laurie and I* GOT ART AWARDS.

SUMMER IS IN FULL SWING. I'M GOING TO CALL THESE DAYS MY *British Passport*, READYING MYSELF FOR a BEATLES CONCERT, PLUS WORK ON MY BRITISH ACCENT. I AM <u>SO GLAD</u> SCHOOL IS OVER. I DON'T HAVE TO GET UP AT 6.

To PAY FOR HER NEW CAR, *Mom* HAD TO GET a JOB. OTHER BILLS, TOO, NEED TO BE PAID. SHE WORKS AT *Allendale.* *It's a Buick Skylark. 1965, robin's egg blue convertible*

WITH SPINNER HUB-CAPS AND A V-8 ENGINE. IT CAN EASILY GO 100 MPH. Only a year and a half TILL I GET MY DRIVER'S PERMIT. I CAN'T <u>WAIT</u> TO DRIVE.

So THAT Mom CAN WORK THIS SUMMER, I HAVE TO BABYSIT MY BROTHER. Oh WHAT A JOY! AND I GET PAID Zero DOLLARS PER HOUR. PLUS, I HAVE TO DO DISHES, BUT MOSTLY I HAVE TO WATCH HIM, AND **HE** LIKES TO SPEND ALL DAY IN THE Water WITH HIS CHUMS. I LIKE THE WATER, TOO, SO IT'S NOT A BAD JOB.

Little problem, though. THERE'S ALGAE IN THE LAKE THAT MAKES ME BREAK OUT IN A RASH, BUT ONLY WHERE MY SUIT IS, AND GUESS WHAT? I WEAR IT ALL DAY LONG. I **LIVE** IN MY SUIT DURING THE DAY AND AT NIGHT, SAME THING TILL I GO TO BED IN A T-SHIRT. The algae water GETS UP IN MY NOSE AND IN MY EYES. Some NIGHTS, I'M SO STUFFED I CAN HARDLY BREATHE. It DIDN'T USED TO BE THIS BAD. THERE ARE SO MANY MOTOR BOATS, THEY'RE CHEWING UP THE LILY PADS AND THEY'RE DREDGING, THEY'RE MESSING AROUND WITH THE LAKE LEVELS. THE WATER WAS SO PRETTY AND CLEAR WHEN WE MOVED OUT HERE. THEY ARE ALSO FILLING IN TO MAKE LOTS. PEOPLE WANT LAKEFRONT HOUSES. IT'S CHANGED SO MUCH IN JUST A FEW YEARS.

We HAVE 7 BOATS. THE BIG SKI BOAT: A Lyman WITH A Johnson 75 MOTOR AND 2 GAS TANKS. I'm NOT ALLOWED TO DRIVE THE CAR, BUT I CAN DRIVE THE BOAT ALL OVER THE Chain-o-Lakes. We also HAVE AN ALUMINUM BOAT, ANOTHER WOODEN BOAT, THE KAYAK DAD MADE AT MY AGE BACK IN THE '30S. DAD ALSO MADE A SAILBOAT, BUT I NEVER GOT TO GO OUT IN THAT. HE USED TO SAIL

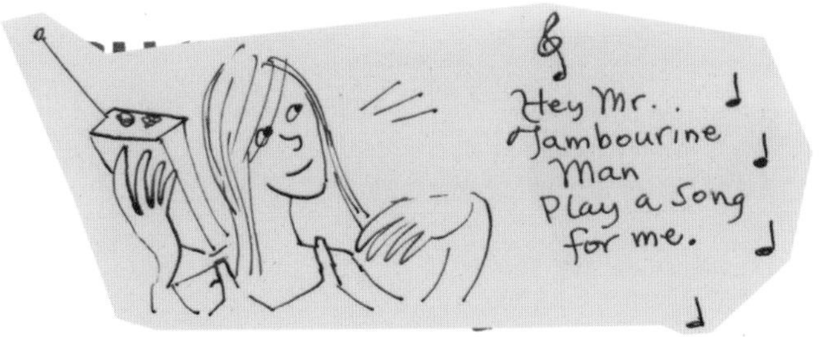
Hey Mr..
Tambourine
Man
Play a Song
for me.

OUT ON LAKE MICHIGAN WHEN HE WAS AT Lane TECH H.S. IN CHICAGO. VERY COMPLICATED, THOSE SAILS. THERE ARE 2 OTHER LITTLE BOATS AND A JOHNSON 7½ MOTOR.

The TRINITY HAVE PRETTY MUCH TAKEN OVER THE SKI BOAT. THEY GET UP BEFORE DAWN TO SKI BEFORE GOING TO PRACTICE. GINIA SKIS WITH THEM IN HER CURLERS BEFORE GOING TO WORK. THE LAKE IS SO CALM AT THAT HOUR, IT'S LIKE SLIDING ON GLASS. I WOULD LIKE TO TRY SMOOTH SKIING, BUT YOU WON'T CATCH ME UP AT THAT HOUR JUMPING INTO THE WATER. BESIDES, GOING WITH THEM WOULD ONLY RESULT IN BULLYING AND BICKERING. I HAVE MY HANDS FULL AS IT IS DURING THE DAY WITH THE TOT AND HIS BUNCH.

When JIM AND HIS LITTLE SHRIMP SQUADRON HIT THE WATER, I CAN EITHER WATCH FROM THE PIER OR ONE OF THE ROW BOATS. I LIKE THERE TO BE SOME DISTANCE FROM THE GOOFS. If I COULD, I'D SPEND ALL DAY IN THE WATER, BUT THERE ARE TIMES WHEN I CAN'T, BECAUSE, WELL--- I AM A YOUNG LADY NOW, AS THE PAMPHLET SAYS. I NEED TO BE READY BECAUSE THOSE RUNTS KICK SAND AND START FIGHTS. ESPECIALLY WHEN THE SAPKOS SHOW UP. I REALLY JUST WANT TO WORK ON MY TAN AND LISTEN TO MY NEW TRANSISTOR RADIO, A GIFT FROM MY GODPARENTS. GOD BLESS THEM.

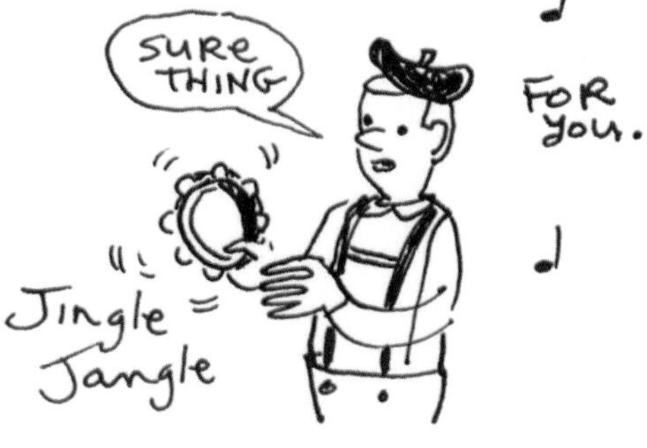
SURE THING
FOR YOU.
Jingle
Jangle

♩ But tomorrow may rain, so --

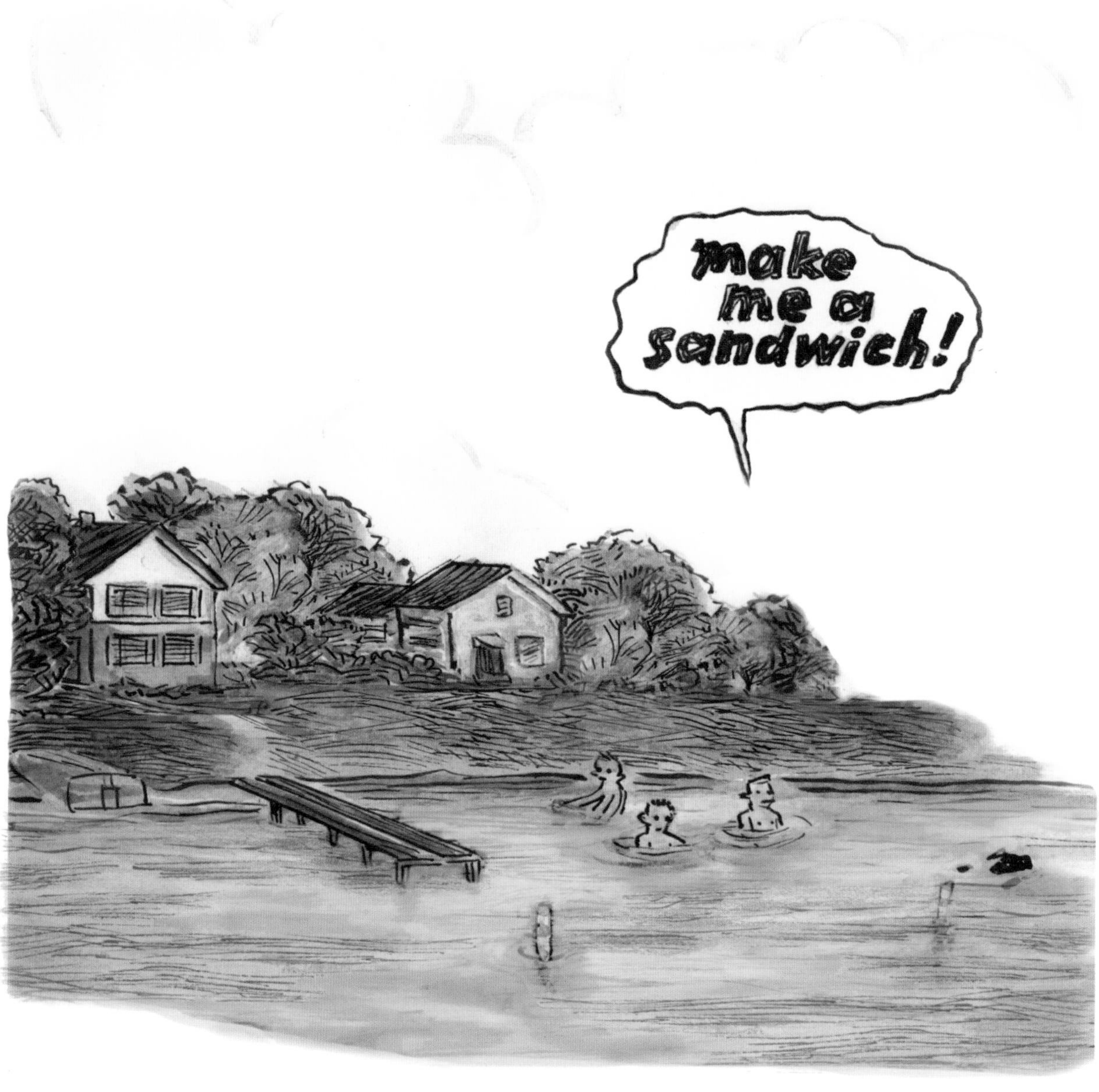
make me a sandwich!

I'll follow the sun.

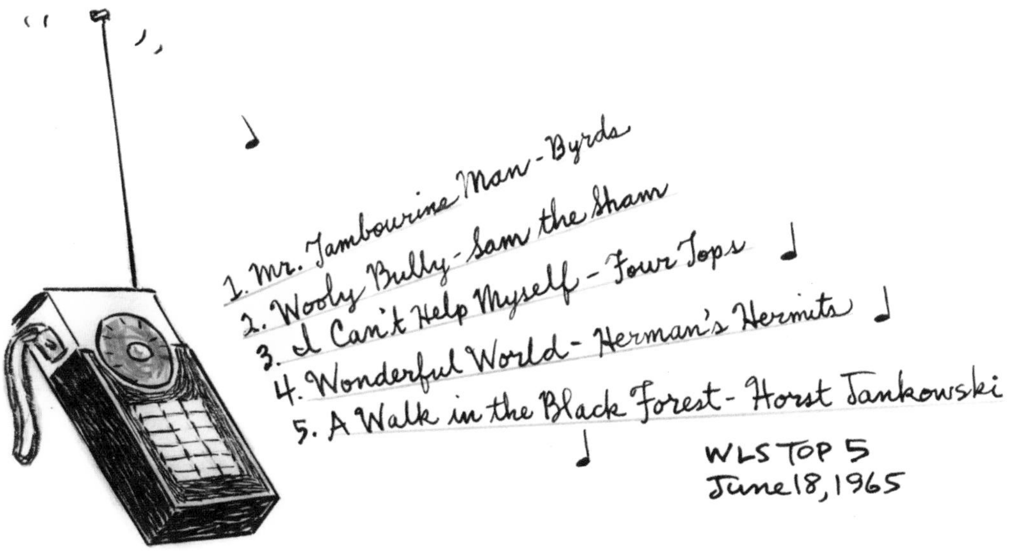
1. Mr. Tambourine Man - Byrds
2. Wooly Bully - Sam the Sham
3. I Can't Help Myself - Four Tops
4. Wonderful World - Herman's Hermits
5. A Walk in the Black Forest - Horst Jankowski
WLS TOP 5
June 18, 1965

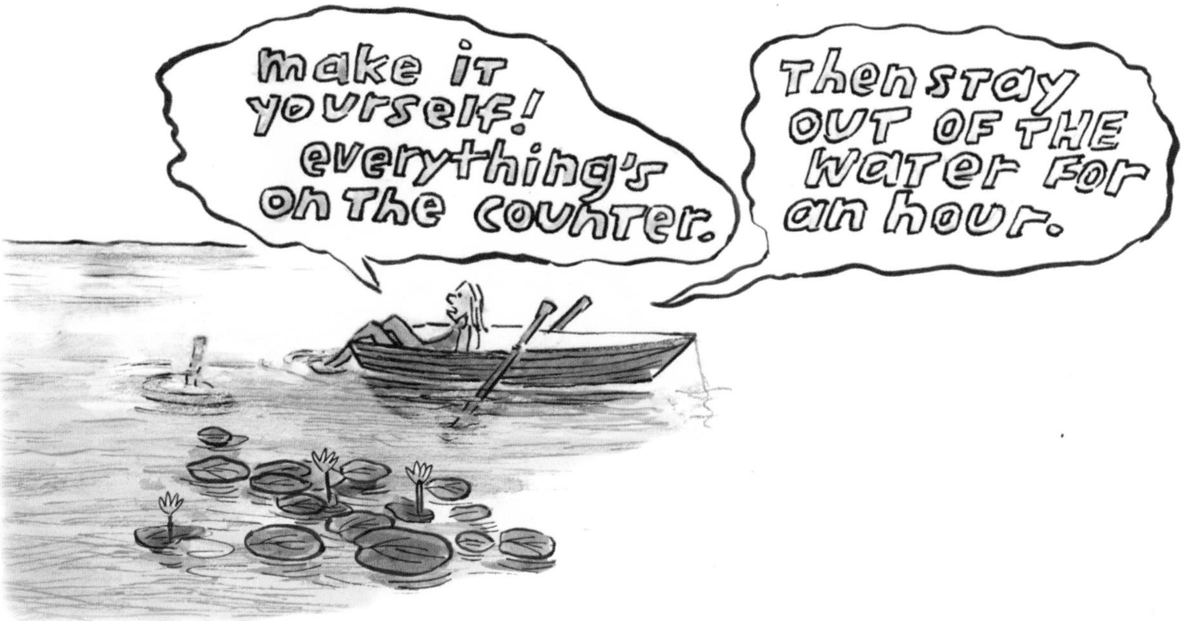
make it yourself! everything's on the counter.
Then stay out of the water for an hour.

Typing . Learning to type. Carol Tyler. Carol rTylwer

I hate typign ng hate ty Typing.
I dont want to be
a secretary , //qwerty)
assdfjkjl; asdfjk;;;oio
  Carol Tyler carol A. Tyler> I like James Cah g Cagney movies

  I don't want to do this, I would rather pound nails into cement
  blocks allll dday LLLlllllongh. that would be stuppid too"

  This is as bert---borun-ing boring. Ever watched an ant hill

  Type with a English acceñtme y limey limeye blokebloke bloke bb bb

          let me try exzop';r
    Just

        maybe I should learn to tap dance to Yankee DppdlBoodle
        Yankee Doodle

              I QUIrT!

DEVIL IN HER HEART

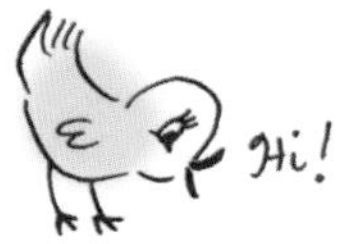
Hi!

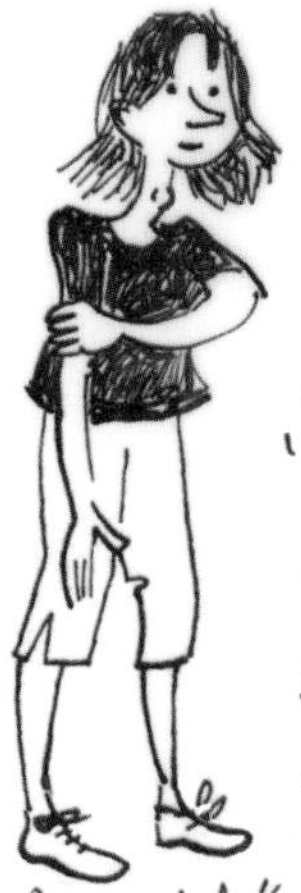

"Bisquick"

This girl came by today. Mary Bisquere. I've seen her at the bus stop with the Sapkos. Kids call her 'Bisquick' like she's a pot pie or something. She wanted to know if she and I could be friends since we live on the same peninsula. She likes the Beatles, but doesn't have any of their records. We listened during Jim's nap time.

In fact, Mary doesn't even have a swimsuit, so I gave her an old one. She's so small and skinny. She's nice and friendly. She said her mom sent her down to play with me because we are a nice family. She's got bruises. I asked her if she wanted to join the fan club, but she doesn't have the 25¢ dues. I gave her a few Beatles cards, some that I had that were doubles.

Later I called the club members to ask them if Mary could join our club without dues. Everybody said it would be okay for summer, but then she'd have to start paying to be fair. I called Mary to tell her but she wasn't allowed to talk on the phone. Maybe I'll see her tomorrow and tell her the good news.

After a long day at work, all I want to do is get back on the lake. Jim's not allowed out at night. What I like to do is slip one of those little wooden row boats into the water, just off the shore where the lily pads hang out, and I drift around. I lay down, put on more mosquito spray, and think about how I share the same sky with the Beatles. Because of the time zone, they are ahead of us — so that means the sky I see now, they already saw. It brings their lovely magic to me, drops down as starlight and moon. Even clouds.

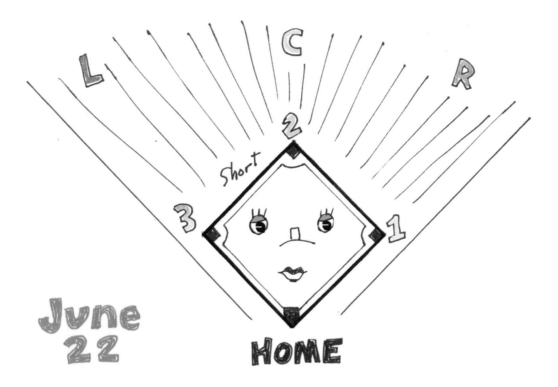

L   C   R

2

Short

3   1

June
22

HOME

Something else is going on with Mary. A boy named John asked her to the show, a friend of her brother. They sat alone together in the dark. A kid who lives on Laurie's street saw them and told Laurie what he saw them doing and she told me. John's older brother picked up Mary, dropped them off, picked them up after, and drove Mary home. Her mom didn't know this. Somehow she got the idea a bunch of us were going, me included, which is why her mom said ok.

They kissed **MANY** times during the movie I've seen before: GOLDFINGER. So John had his arm around her the **WHOLE TIME** that kid said, and they kissed a total of **7** times, which means — pay attention to this: seven times Mary went to first base!

OY YOY YOY!

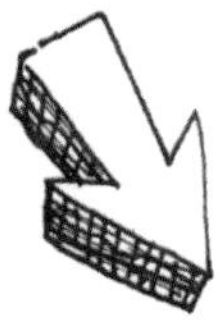

WHAT?!

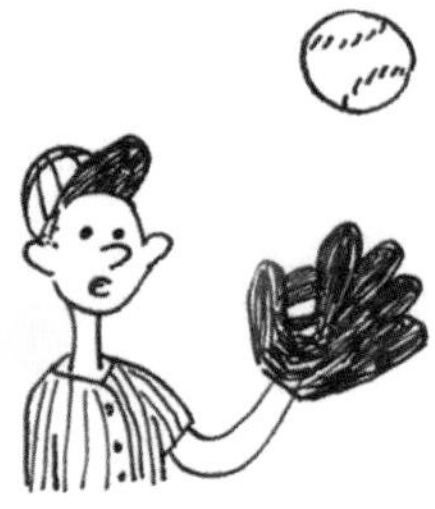

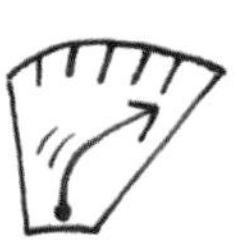
too fast!

♪ ..oh this I can't believe

I DIDN'T KNOW THIS ABOUT Mary, BUT KIND OF -- I'M *not* SURPRISED. EVERY TIME SHE COMES OVER, SHE'S GOT HER EYE ON Joe, OR SHE ASKS ABOUT HIM, AND HE COULD CARE LESS IF SHE EVEN EXISTS! SHE'S A LITTLE STRANGE. IT'S ALMOST LIKE SHE LIKES BEING BOSSED AROUND AND TALKED INTO THINGS. WHEN SHE COMES HERE, SHE NEVER WANTS TO DECIDE ON ANYTHING, SO SHE JUST GOES ALONG WITH WHATEVER I SAY OR DO. THE SAPKOS HOLLERED "BISQUICK'S A SLUT." I RAN THOSE IDIOTS OFF AND Mary JUST KIND OF IGNORED IT AND CHANGED THE SUBJECT LIKE IT DIDN'T HAPPEN. "aren't you insulted? They're stupid," I SAID. SHE SHRUGGED. I DON'T GET SOME PEOPLE.

According TO Randy (THAT'S THE NAME OF THE KID WHO WITNESSED EVERYTHING AT THE SHOW), John WAS A SLOPPY KISSER, MAKING ALL KINDS OF SLURPING NOISES. I THOUGHT KISSING WAS QUIET. PEOPLE WERE GROSSED OUT. AND APPARENTLY HE TRIED FOR SECOND BASE, BUT THE SHOW WAS OVER AND THE LIGHTS CAME ON. MARY'S CLOTHES WERE A MESS, BUT THAT'S NOT WHAT UPSET Randy. IT WAS John's SHOES. AS HE PUT IT, "Who wears 2-toned shoes to see Goldfinger. It's NOT just Wrong, IT'S **WRONG**."

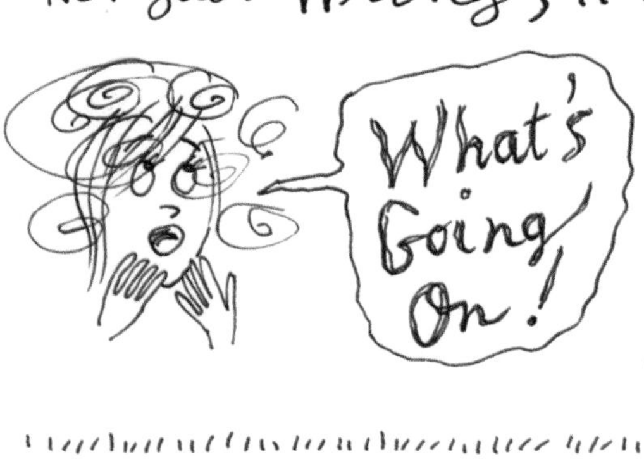
What's Going On!

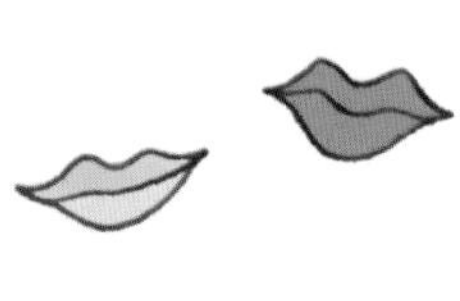

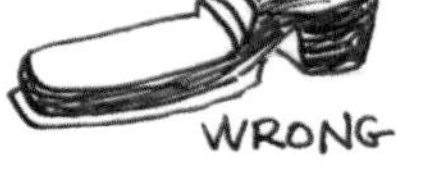
WRONG

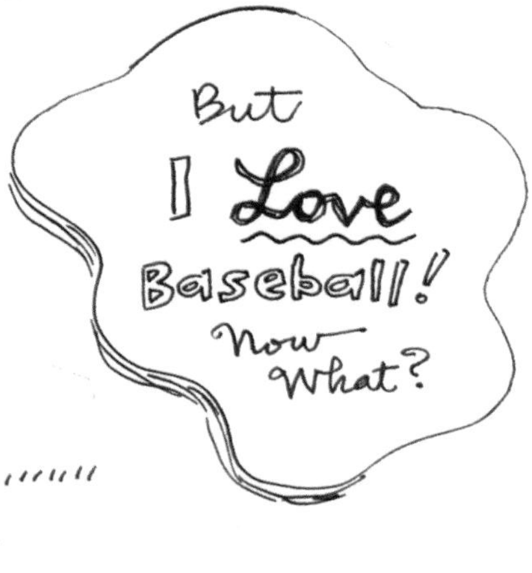
But I Love Baseball!
Now What?

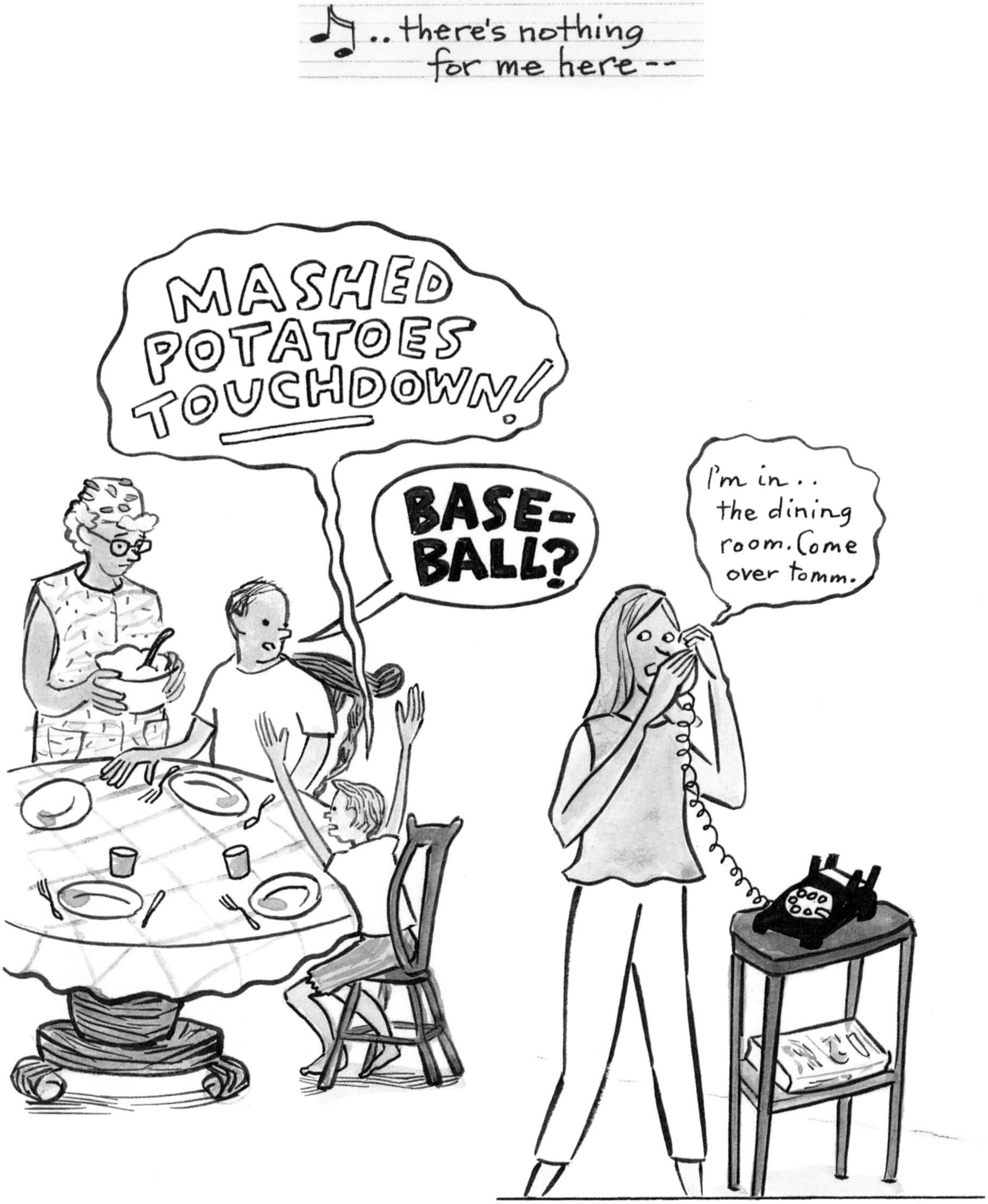
.. there's nothing for me here --
MASHED POTATOES TOUCHDOWN!
BASE-BALL?
I'm in.. the dining room. Come over tomm.

♪... so I will disappear.

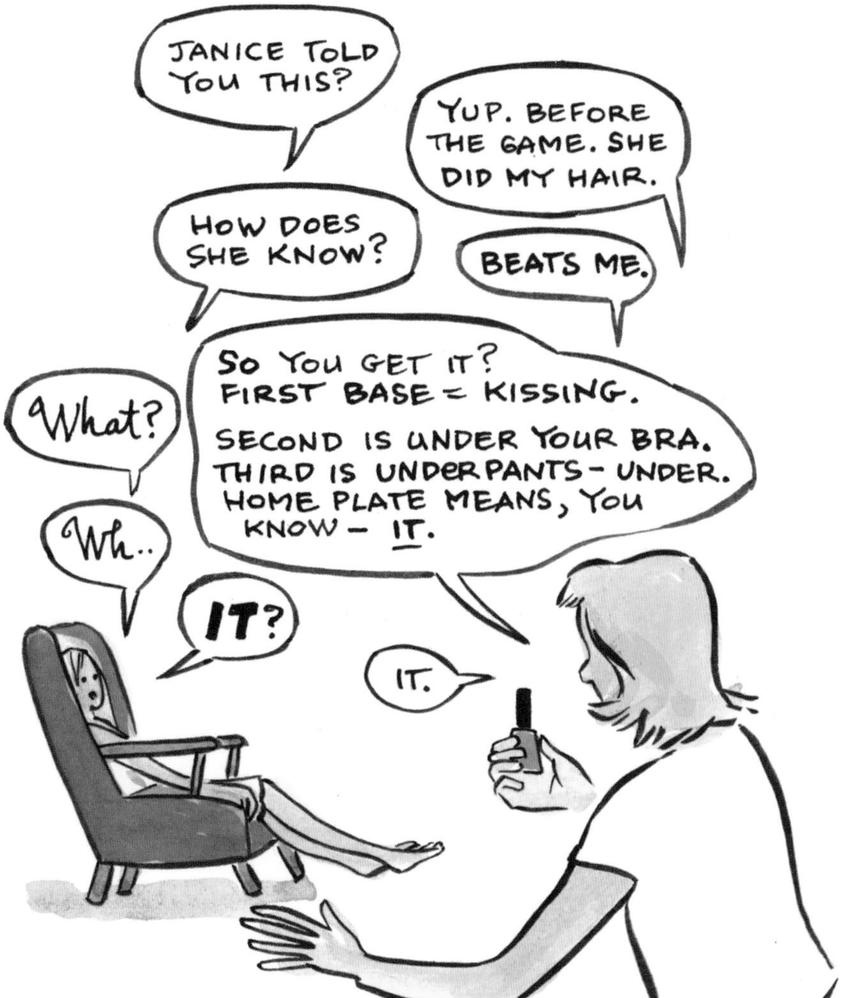

JANICE TOLD YOU THIS?
YUP. BEFORE THE GAME. SHE DID MY HAIR.
HOW DOES SHE KNOW?
BEATS ME.
SO YOU GET IT? FIRST BASE = KISSING. SECOND IS UNDER YOUR BRA. THIRD IS UNDERPANTS - UNDER. HOME PLATE MEANS, YOU KNOW - IT.
What?
Wh..
IT?
IT.

RULES OF THE GAME

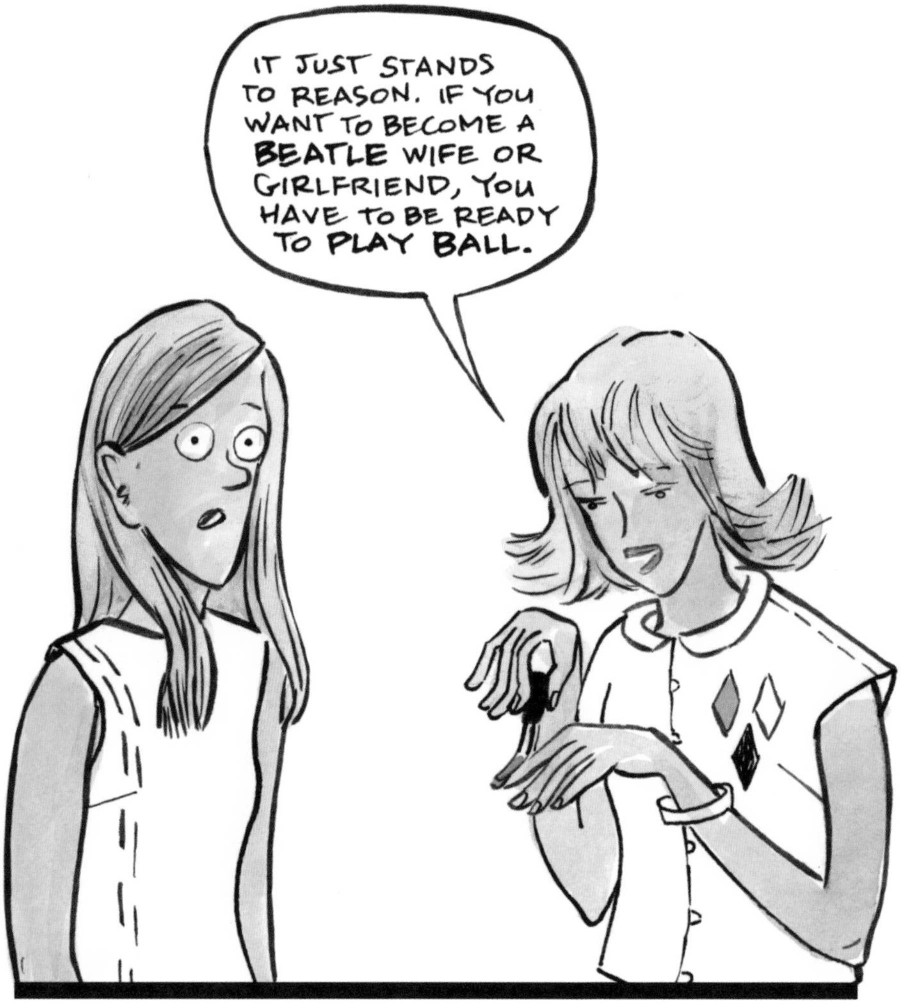
IT JUST STANDS TO REASON. IF YOU WANT TO BECOME A BEATLE WIFE OR GIRLFRIEND, YOU HAVE TO BE READY TO PLAY BALL.

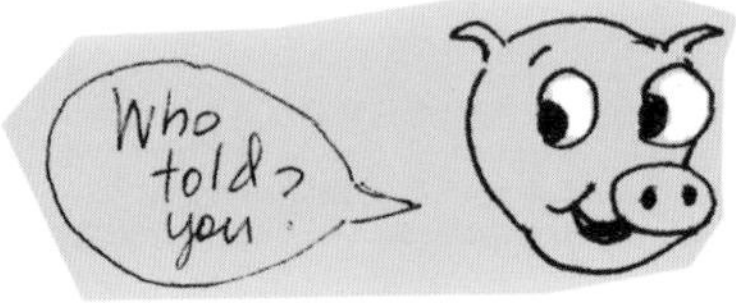
Who told you?

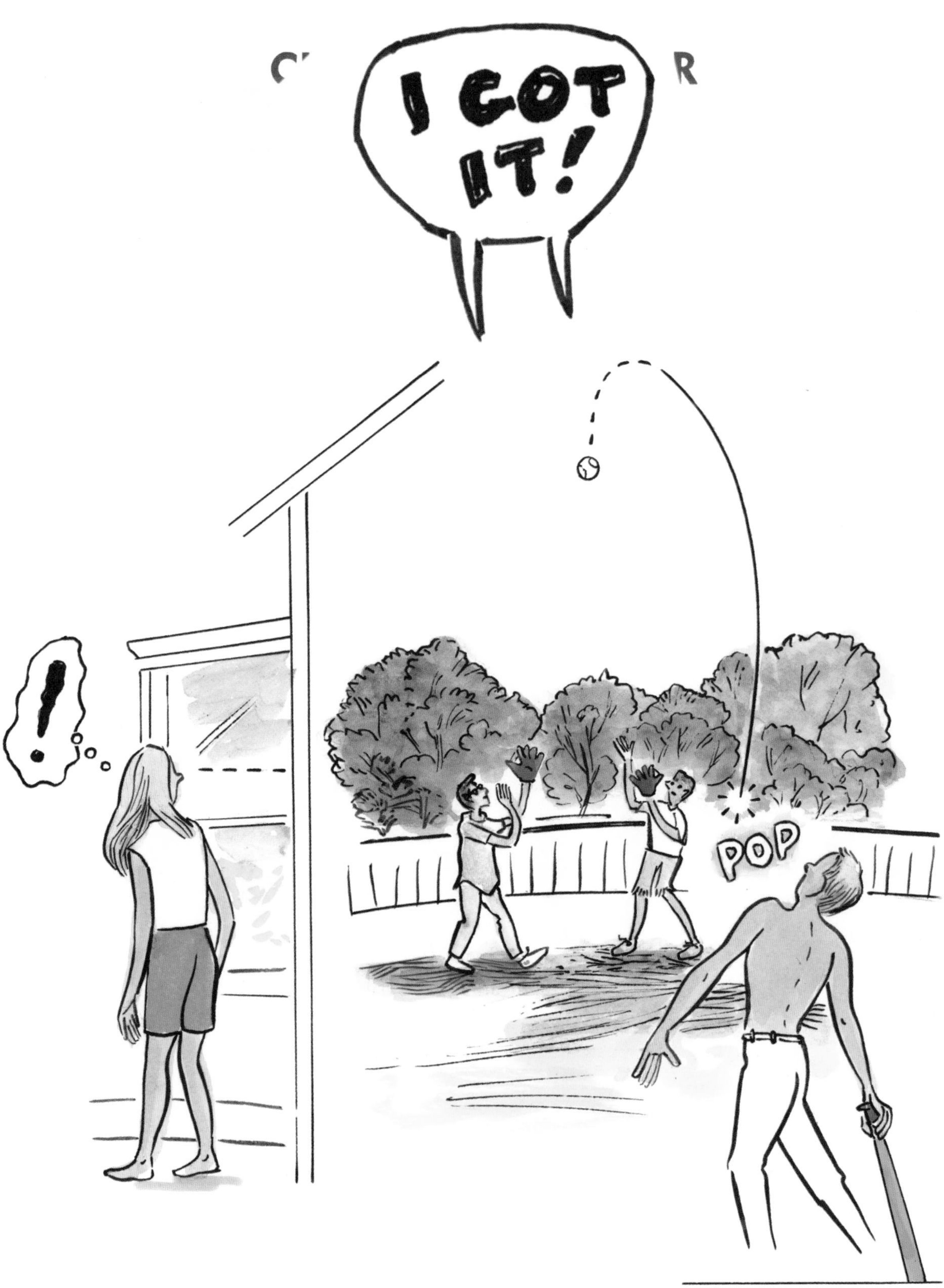
C R
I GOT IT!
!
POP

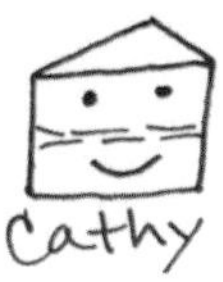
Cathy

I DON'T WANT TO SPOIL THE PARTY

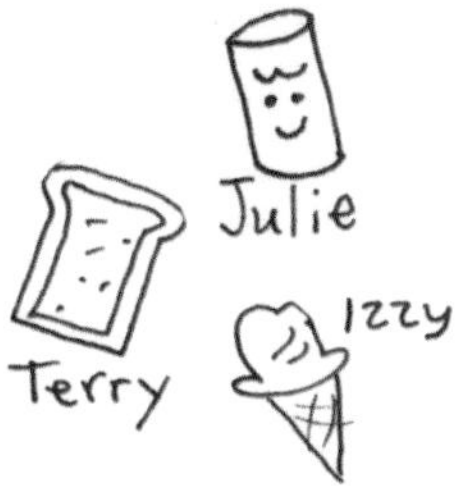
Julie
Terry
Izzy

June 24

Summer putts along like a layer of Lake Krud, taking all day to go nowhere, battery running low. When are my tickets going to come? I mailed in the money order just like they said to. Now I wait and wait and itch and wait while taking care of Little Lord Jummo. He must have algae in his butt-crack — he won't stop scratching. But I'm NOT putting ointment there!

Mary came over. She told me she was hungry so we had cornflakes. She said she never heard of baseball except for the **REAL** baseball, which I love. I've been listening to Cubs games on my transistor. "Have you ever been to first base, Mary?" I asked. "Yeah," she answered. No smile. "Anything else?" I asked. Her reply: "Another bowl of cornflakes, please."

WOOH!

All day, I try to stay calm, because there are times when it pops into my head that in 2 months or so I will be seeing the Beatles and this shakes me up like tickles in a popcorn popper. Can't show my excitement around the tyke, so what I do to hide it is, I've nick-named all the foods in the kitchen. Foods he eats like: Karen Ketchup. Terry Toast. Carrie Cucumber. Freddy Frankfurter. I do it with my accent. Madame Mildred Mustard and Pete-a Pancake. Drink your Julia Juice. Eat your Sally Sandwich so you can have some Cathy Cake and Ian Ice Cream. Or Sir William Watermelon. He hates when I talk English-y. Calls me a phoney and throws a sock in the fan. Brat. For that he gets Penelope Peanut Butter on his pups!

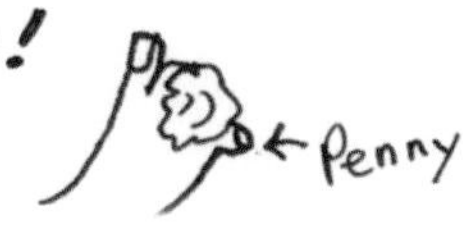
Penny

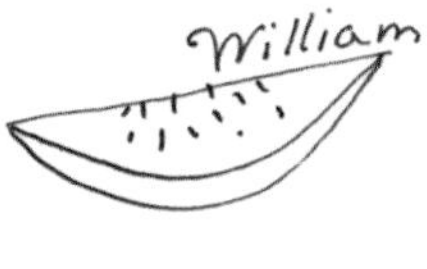
William

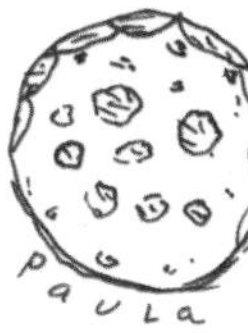
Paula
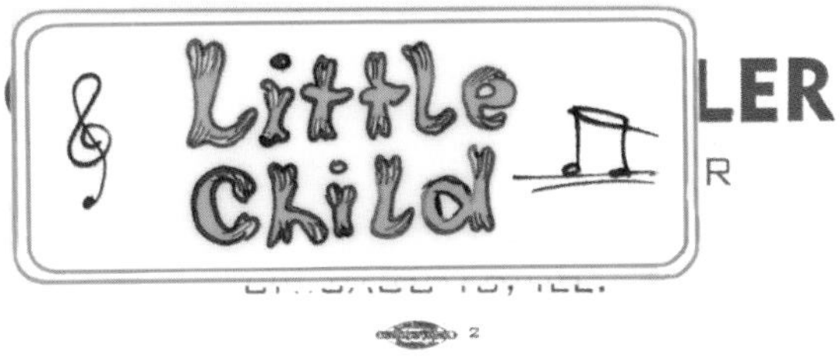
Little Child
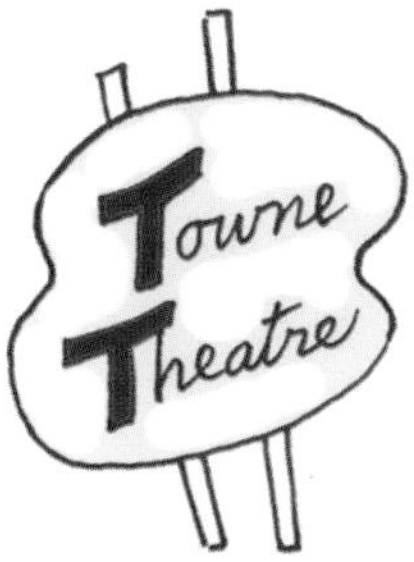
Towne Theatre
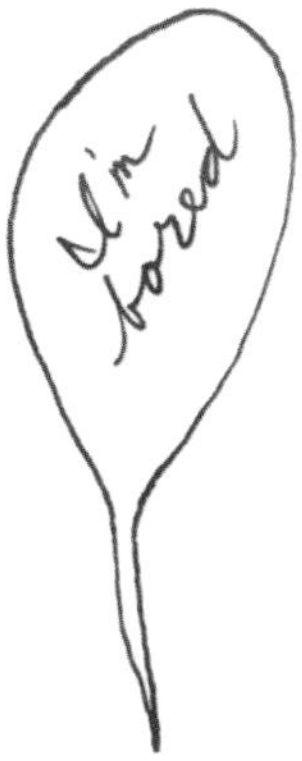
I'm bored

There's bored AND THEN THERE'S BORED AND THEN THERE'S borrD. OK, SO FIRST I KEPT THE KID HAPPY WITH NAMES FOR THE FOOD. NEXT, HE WANTED ME TO PUT FACES ON EVERYTHING, SO I SAID I'D MAKE HIM a Paula Pizza WITH PIMPLES (sausages). **HE TOLD ALL HIS FRIENDS, EVEN THE SAPKOS.** 13 KIDS LINED UP FOR a CHEESE PIE WITH ZITS! STUPID. I DON'T MIND SHARING FOOD WITH MY FRIENDS OR EVEN ONE OR 2 OF HIS PALS, BUT THIS WAS NUTTY. SO I SAID "Fine. Come in. MENU CHANGE," AND I WENT INTO Mom's OFFICE SUPPLY DRAWER AND TOOK OUT A BOX OF GUMMED STARS. I PUT OIL IN THE PAN AND FRIED THE STARS — "HEY" THEY ALL HOLLERED AND RAN OFF. "Come back, kids. I'm also serving Rolling SPIT!" THAT ENDED THAT.

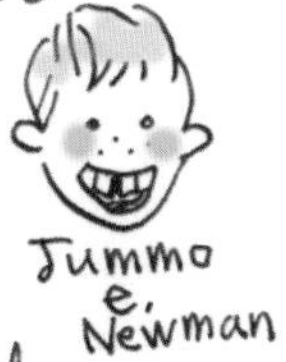
Jummo e. Newman

But NOT REALLY. Because LATER ALL THE KIDS DECIDED ON BALL TEAM NAMES FOR Baseball — TEAMS ARE ALWAYS FORMING AROUND HERE. TEAM #1 **FRIED STARS.** TEAM #2 — you guessed it **ROLLING SPIT.**

Later, Laurie AND I ARE GETTING TOGETHER TO GO TO THE SHOW — NO JOHN — JUST US. GOLDFINGER AGAIN FOR THE MILLIONTH TIME. OUR MISSION IS TO STUDY THE HAIRSTYLES AND SEND HEARTS TO OUR DREAMY **BOND. James Bond.** IF I WASN'T COMPLETELY IN LOVE WITH THE Beatles, I WOULD LOVE HIM THE MOST.

TOMORROW I'M HELPING AT Laurie's GRANDMOTHER'S. WE HAVE TO WASH ALL OF THE BASEBOARDS IN HER HOUSE. FIRST, PULL THE FURNITURE AWAY FROM THE WALLS. SHE SAID SHE'D GIVE US A DOLLAR EACH IF WE DID A GOOD JOB. Otherwise, half.

POPCORN PICK

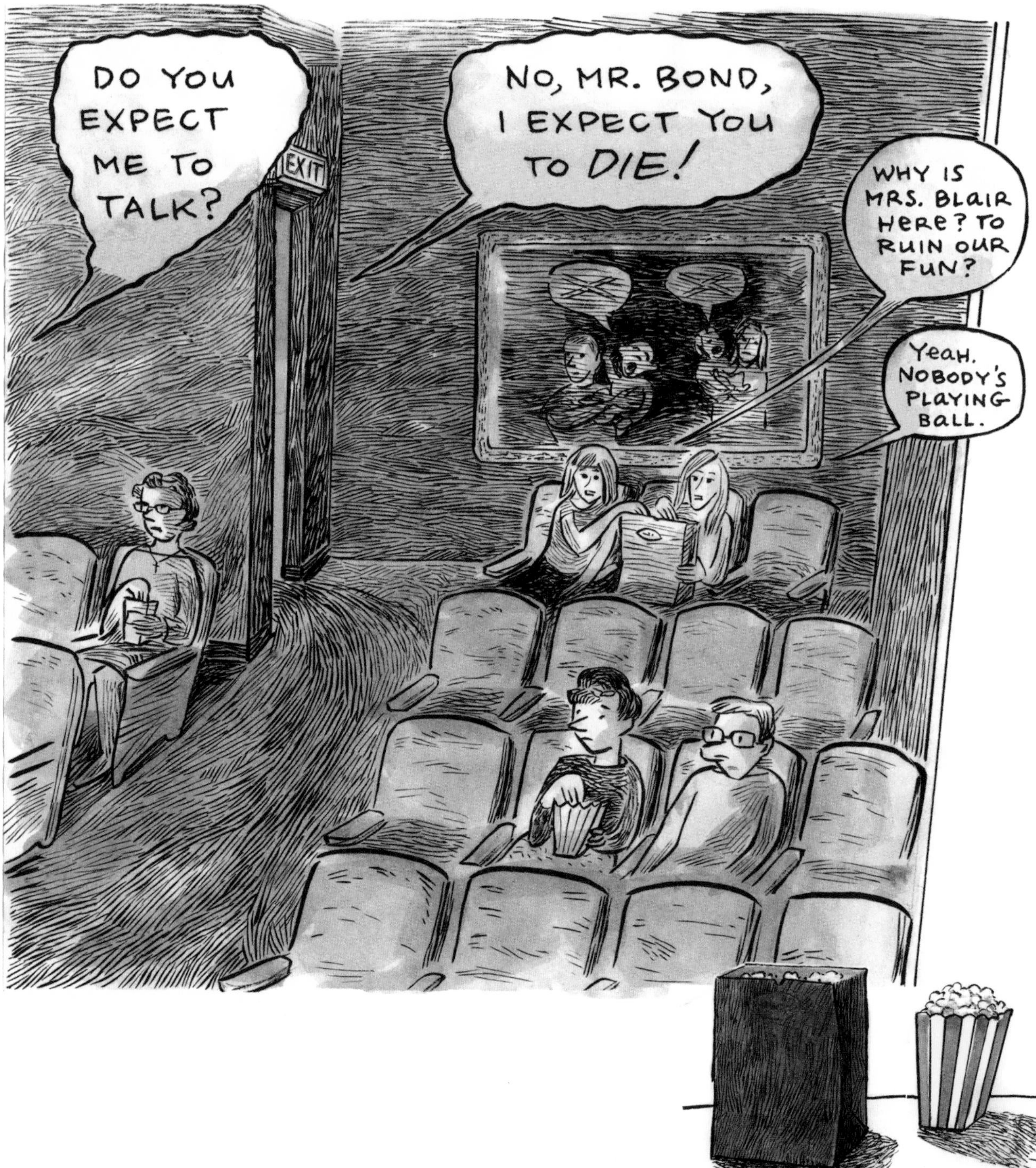
DO YOU EXPECT ME TO TALK?
EXIT
NO, MR. BOND, I EXPECT YOU TO DIE!
WHY IS MRS. BLAIR HERE? TO RUIN OUR FUN?
YEAH. NOBODY'S PLAYING BALL.

CHARLES W. TYLER

PLUMBING CONTRACTOR

1837 WEST ADDISON ST.

CHICAGO 13, ILL.

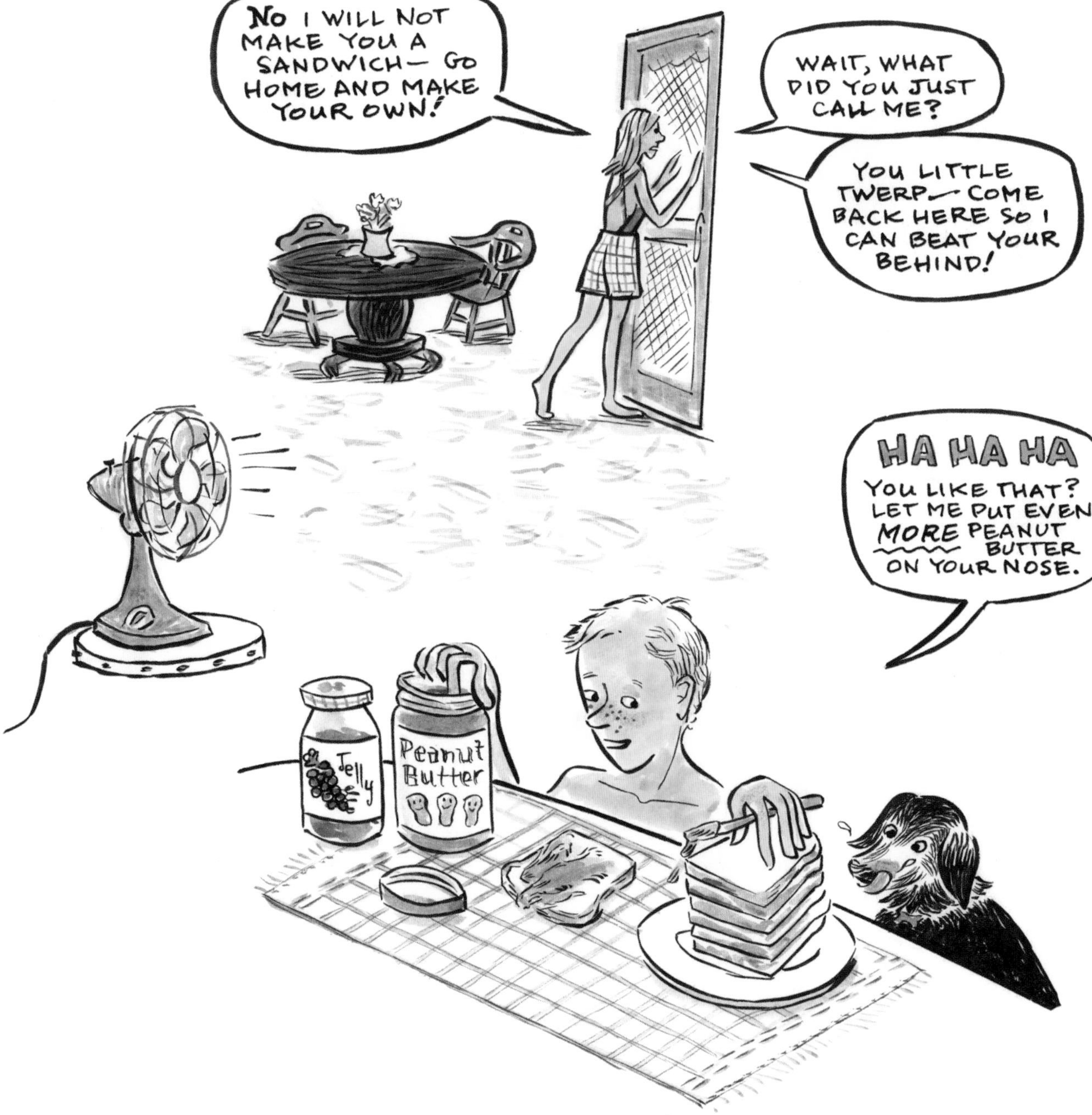

NO I WILL NOT MAKE YOU A SANDWICH— GO HOME AND MAKE YOUR OWN!
WAIT, WHAT DID YOU JUST CALL ME?
YOU LITTLE TWERP— COME BACK HERE SO I CAN BEAT YOUR BEHIND!
HA HA HA
YOU LIKE THAT? LET ME PUT EVEN MORE PEANUT BUTTER ON YOUR NOSE.
Jelly
Peanut Butter

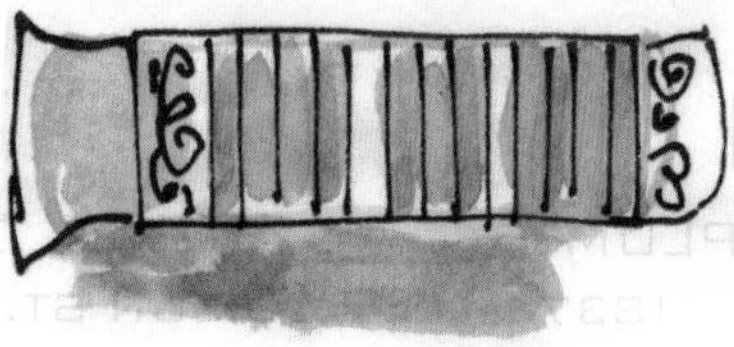

June 29

Hooray for Yardley of London! I know I am not allowed to wear make up out in public YET. Soon. But I am allowed to look and shop and try it at home. I have a secret place to keep it.

Yardley of London

Here's what I have:

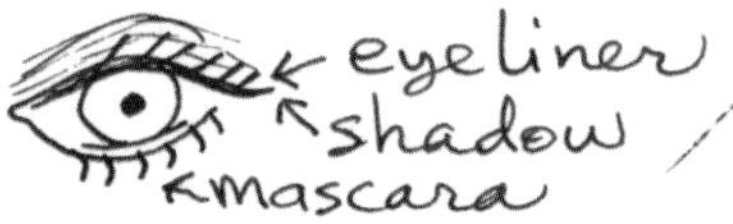
eyeliner
shadow
mascara

I practice in my room.

Don't like when I have to take it off. I look blah.

You know how I said I was good but not holy? Well, there's a little way I *bend* the rules on make-up. One of my Yardley products is this lipstick called SLICKER. It's a neutral color. You can hardly tell I've got anything on. I told Mom it's Vaseline. Is this a sin?

Before I got my Yardley stuff, I tried on my Mom's make-up (Ginia doesn't wear any). I put on her powder, rouge, and lipstick. Goodness Gracious, I looked like a Raggedy Ann Doll. Bright red lipstick is **OUT**. Very old fashioned.

I think Mom said I could wear a little eye make-up to the concert. I will anyway regardless. I need to look **SMASHING** for my boys. My hair is long and straight like Pattie Boyd. But all the products in the world cannot disguise my biggest problem: my two front teeth are broken. Little Jummo threw his baby bottle at my face. Mom ran me up to the dentist, who is also the football

COACH AT GRANT, AND HE GLUED PLASTIC CAPS ON THEM. THAT LASTED ABOUT 2 SECONDS BECAUSE I CAME HOME AND JUMPED IN THE LAKE. THIS WAS 2 YEARS AGO. I'M GLAD THEY FELL OF. IT LOOKED LIKE I WAS WEARING CORN KERNELS. EVENTUALLY, I HAD TO GET MY "FANGS" SANDED DOWN. NOT SO POINTY NOW, BUT STILL A "V" NONE THE LESS. I'VE GOT A CRAZY BITE, TOO. NEED BRACES.

I TRADED 4 BEATLE CARDS FOR THAT LIPSTICK. THIS GIRL I KNEW FROM 4-H WHO GOES TO BIG HOLLOW SCHOOL SWAPPED WITH ME AT OUR LAST BASKETBALL GAME. SHE DIDN'T CARE FOR THE *London Look*. THE CARDS WERE FOR HER SISTER. SHE ONLY USED THE LIPSTICK ONCE. THEN I HEARD SHE STOLE HER SISTER'S SLICKER LIPSTICK FOR SPITE AND TRADED IT TO ME TO MAKE HER MAD. I UNDERSTAND ALL ABOUT HOW SISTERS CAN MAKE EACH OTHER'S LIVES MISERABLE, BUT I'M **NOT** GIVING BACK THE *SLICKER*. THE COLOR IS CALLED "Good Night."

Laurie AND I SWAP MAKE-UP, AS NEEDED. ONE OF OUR BEST SESSIONS WAS LEARNING HOW TO DO EYE-LINER JUST RIGHT. IT'S NOT THAT EASY. YOU HAVE TO SLIGHTLY PULL THE EYE AT THE END, BUT NOT MUCH. IT'S NOT EASY TO DO THE WING AND THE TAPERING AT THE END.

I SAT *Mary* DOWN IN A CHAIR YESTERDAY AND TALKED TO HER ABOUT MAKE-UP AND HAIR. JUST HER LOOK IN GENERAL, I THINK SHE'S GOT TROUBLES. HER SKIN IS ––

♪ If you put your
trust in me —
I'LL MAKE BRIGHT YOUR DAY.

Red
IS 
OUT!

IN!

I'M NOT SURE IF SHE EVEN WASHES HER FACE. I GOT HER SCRUBBED UP GOOD AND FIXED HER EYES SO PRETTY. BOY WAS SHE EVER HAPPY. BIG SMILE WITH SOME TEETH MISSING. PRETTY GIRL, THOUGH. SHE'LL BE AT GRANT WITH Laurie. AND John (oh brother!).

Speaking OF BROTHERS, MARY TOLD ME HER BROTHER Steve LIKED ME, AND HE WONDERED IF HE COULD COME BY SOME TIME. "No!" I TOLD HER. "I've GOT A LOT TO GET READY FOR, AND I'M Busy All the Time." HER BROTHER IS A JUNIOR (will be a JUNIOR) AT GRANT. AND I HEARD HE HAD BEEN IN TROUBLE FOR SOMETHING. POLICE TROUBLE. POLICE CAME TO THEIR HOUSE. I DON'T KNOW. BUT I'LL HAVE TO SAY, MY OWN BROTHER AND HIS FRIENDS △ ALMOST HAD THE POLICE CALLED ON THEM FOR PUTTING CHERRY BOMBS IN PEOPLE'S MAILBOXES LAST YEAR. DAD WENT UP AND TALKED TO BOSSY OLSON, THE MAYOR. STRAIGHTENED THAT MESS OUT. STEVE AND Mary's DAD DRINKS A LOT OF BEER AT HOME. NOT VERY MUCH A STRAIGHTEN-THINGS-OUT-ER. So, BEFORE Mary left, AFTER SHE WASHED OFF HER MAKE-UP, WE ate SANDWICHES WITH THE RUNT. I HOPE SHE'S NOT MAD THAT I DON'T LIKE HER BROTHER.

THE RULES FOR eyes:

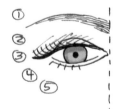

① ② ③ ④ ⑤

1. PLUCK OUT STRAY HAIRS BETWEEN THE eyes
2. HIGHLIGHT BONE ABOVE THE eye, UNDER THE END OF THE BROW.
3. SHADOW ON THE LID AND IN THE CREASE
4. eyeLINER - CLOSE TO THE LASHES. BRING TO A POINT
5. MASCARA ON LASHES

WE LOOK GOOD NOW.

Just in from Fox Lake!

THE LONDON LOOK

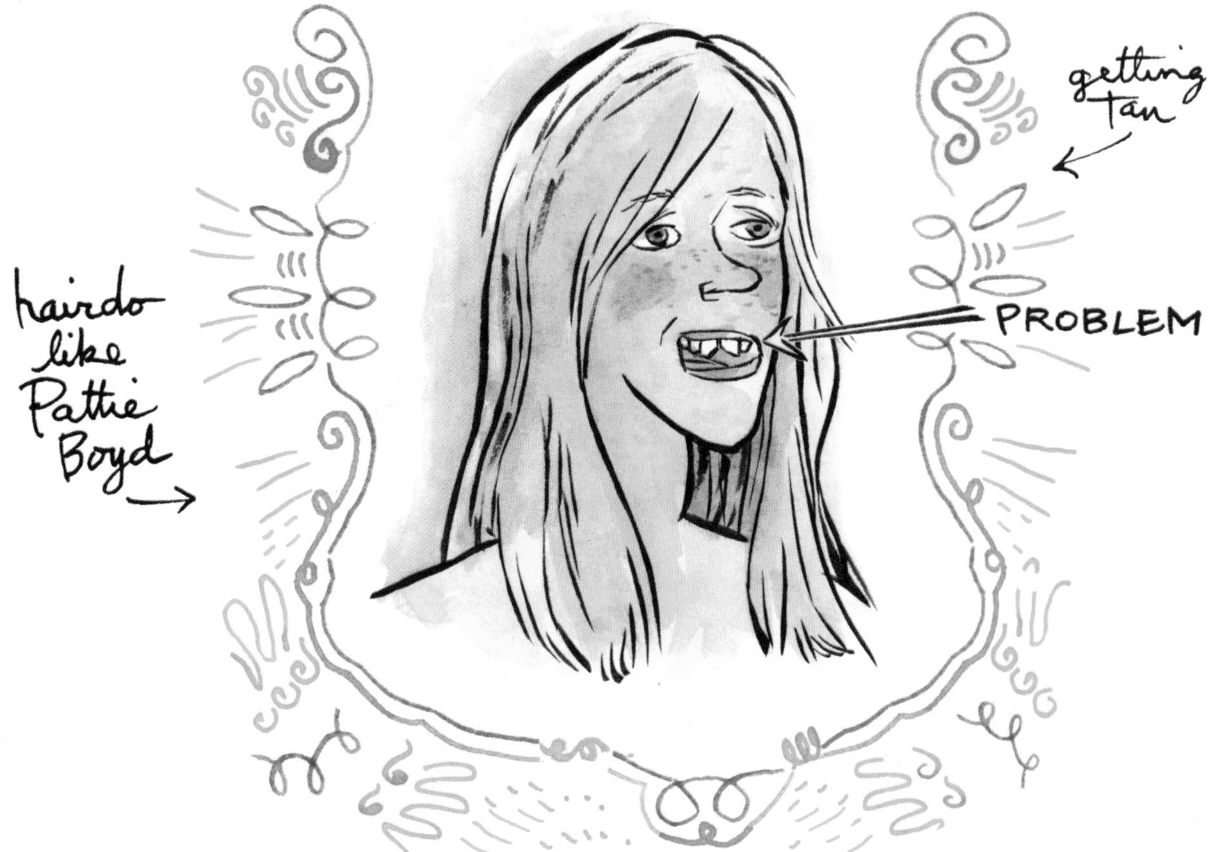
getting tan
hairdo like Pattie Boyd
PROBLEM

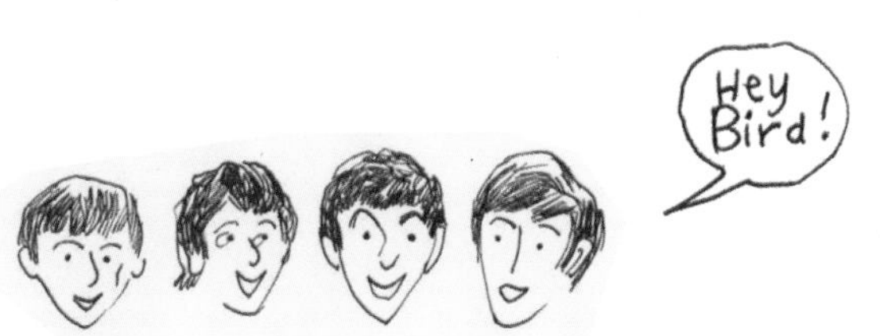
Hey Bird!

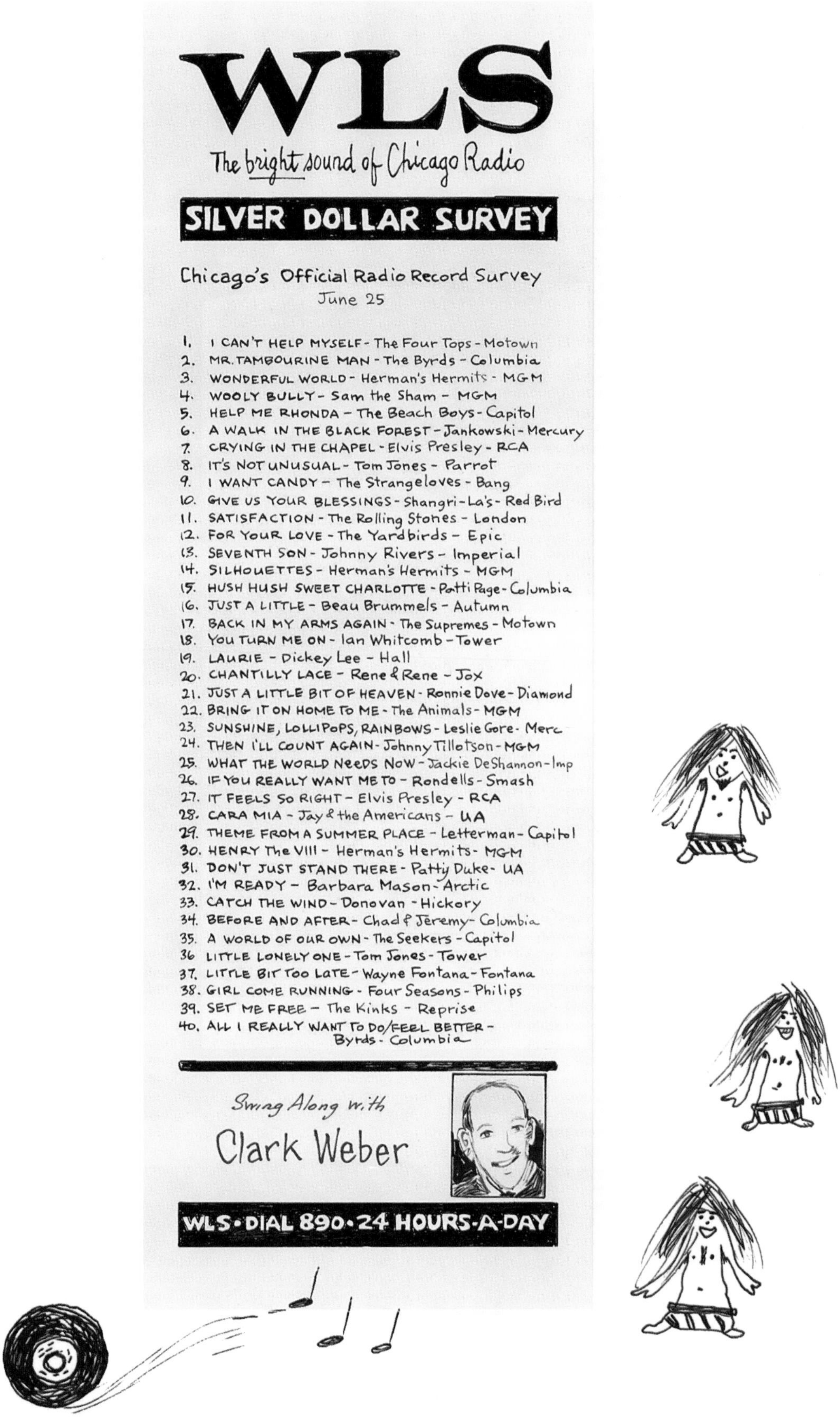

WLS

The bright sound of Chicago Radio

SILVER DOLLAR SURVEY

Chicago's Official Radio Record Survey

June 25

1. I CAN'T HELP MYSELF - The Four Tops - Motown
2. MR. TAMBOURINE MAN - The Byrds - Columbia
3. WONDERFUL WORLD - Herman's Hermits - MGM
4. WOOLY BULLY - Sam the Sham - MGM
5. HELP ME RHONDA - The Beach Boys - Capitol
6. A WALK IN THE BLACK FOREST - Jankowski - Mercury
7. CRYING IN THE CHAPEL - Elvis Presley - RCA
8. IT'S NOT UNUSUAL - Tom Jones - Parrot
9. I WANT CANDY - The Strangeloves - Bang
10. GIVE US YOUR BLESSINGS - Shangri-La's - Red Bird
11. SATISFACTION - The Rolling Stones - London
12. FOR YOUR LOVE - The Yardbirds - Epic
13. SEVENTH SON - Johnny Rivers - Imperial
14. SILHOUETTES - Herman's Hermits - MGM
15. HUSH HUSH SWEET CHARLOTTE - Patti Page - Columbia
16. JUST A LITTLE - Beau Brummels - Autumn
17. BACK IN MY ARMS AGAIN - The Supremes - Motown
18. YOU TURN ME ON - Ian Whitcomb - Tower
19. LAURIE - Dickey Lee - Hall
20. CHANTILLY LACE - Rene & Rene - Jox
21. JUST A LITTLE BIT OF HEAVEN - Ronnie Dove - Diamond
22. BRING IT ON HOME TO ME - The Animals - MGM
23. SUNSHINE, LOLLIPOPS, RAINBOWS - Leslie Gore - Merc
24. THEN I'LL COUNT AGAIN - Johnny Tillotson - MGM
25. WHAT THE WORLD NEEDS NOW - Jackie DeShannon - Imp
26. IF YOU REALLY WANT ME TO - Rondells - Smash
27. IT FEELS SO RIGHT - Elvis Presley - RCA
28. CARA MIA - Jay & the Americans - UA
29. THEME FROM A SUMMER PLACE - Letterman - Capitol
30. HENRY The VIII - Herman's Hermits - MGM
31. DON'T JUST STAND THERE - Patty Duke - UA
32. I'M READY - Barbara Mason - Arctic
33. CATCH THE WIND - Donovan - Hickory
34. BEFORE AND AFTER - Chad & Jeremy - Columbia
35. A WORLD OF OUR OWN - The Seekers - Capitol
36. LITTLE LONELY ONE - Tom Jones - Tower
37. LITTLE BIT TOO LATE - Wayne Fontana - Fontana
38. GIRL COME RUNNING - Four Seasons - Philips
39. SET ME FREE - The Kinks - Reprise
40. ALL I REALLY WANT TO DO/FEEL BETTER - Byrds - Columbia

Swing Along with

Clark Weber

WLS • DIAL 890 • 24 HOURS-A-DAY

You LIKE me TOO MUCH

July 1

Tureki came by today and asked if I would meet him at the show, and I shouted NO NO NO right in his face. I guess word has gotten around about the Towne Theatre.

What is it with boys? Smelly and loud. They love to act stupid when they're together. They love that dumb song WOOLY BULLY. Man, when that bunch gets together at my house, the TRINITY I'm talking about, they sing that over and over. All they know is the chorus, none of the inside lyrics, so they make up a bunch of glide-over words and then BARK OUT THE CHORUS like hounds. Yes, they are singing along to a record. No, I cannot play my albums when the Trinity is over. That's when I grab my transistor and head out to the middle of the lake in my favorite little wooden rowboat. The bad news is, I can still hear them out there!

And they've taken over my little brother!

Jamie
SSH!
Rudy
WOOLY WHAT?
Shut Up!!
Joe
Go away!
Stop it!
Jim

.. and it's nice when
you believe me.

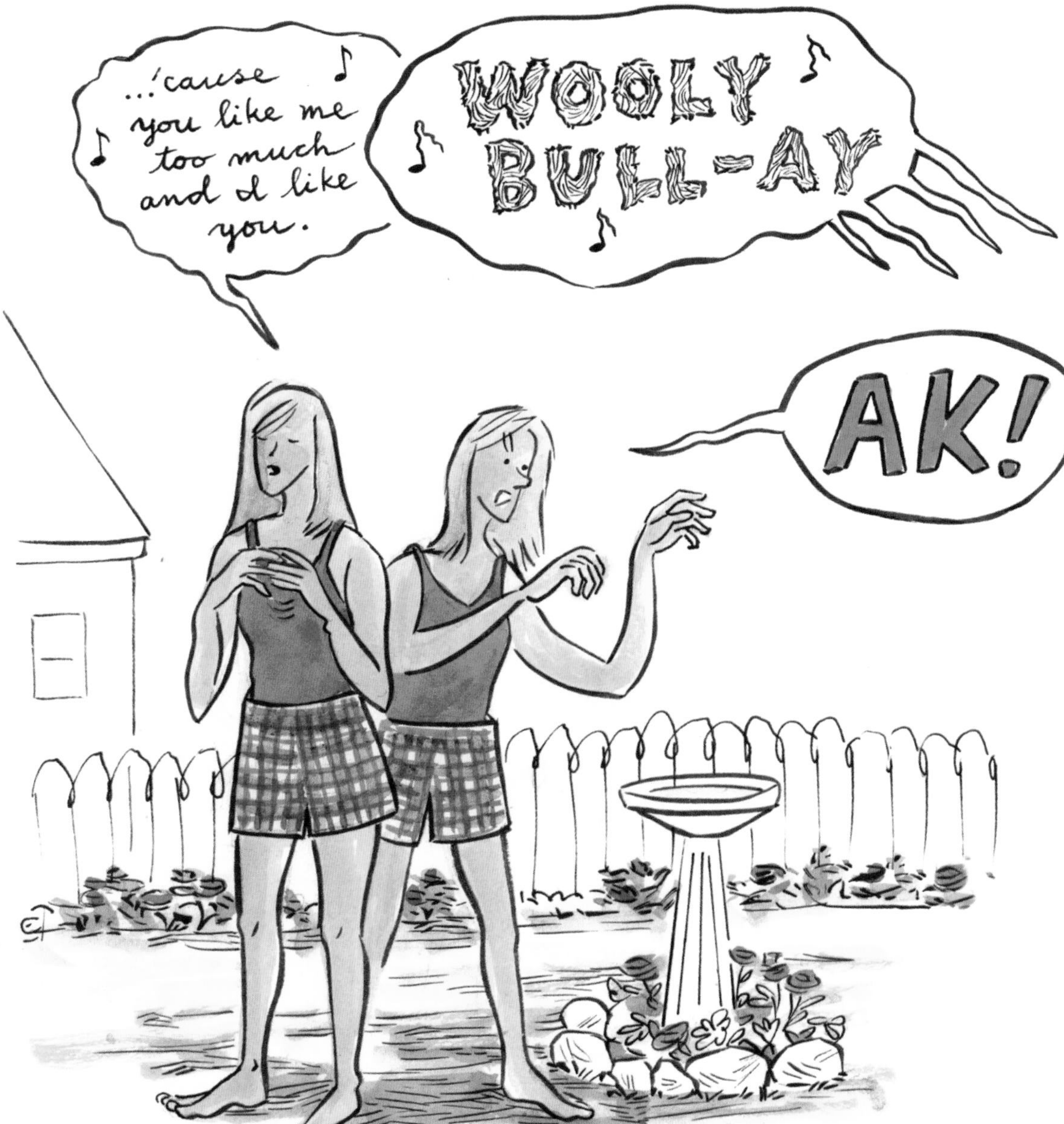
...'cause you like me too much and I like you.
WOOLY BULL-AY
AK!

WOOLY BULLY

♫ ..if you

♫ leave me...

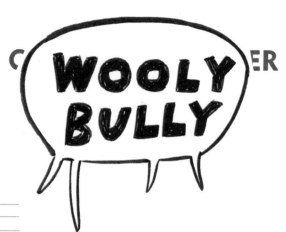

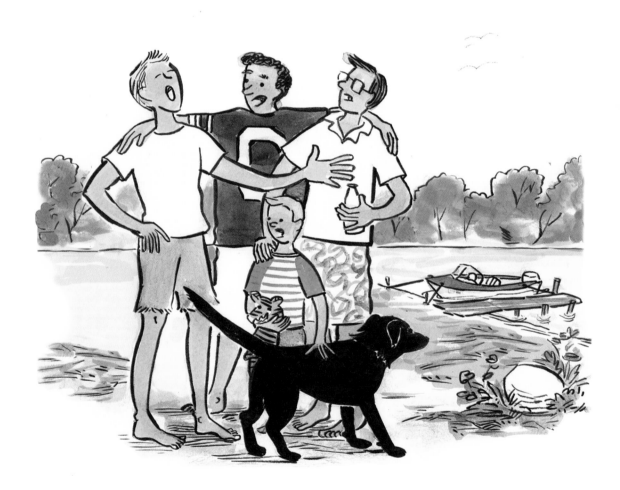

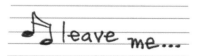

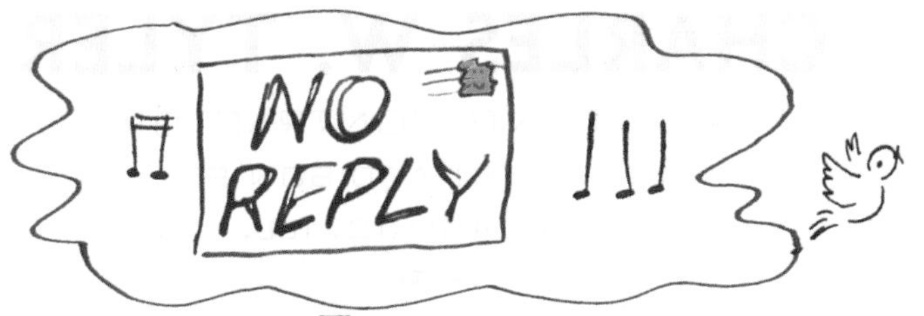
NO REPLY
!!!

JULY 2 uh

This is kind of sad. Just like that, Mary is gone. She was going to come over and listen to records and stuff, but she didn't show. So I decided to bike over there to her house, it's just past Tureki's, and the house was empty. Not only empty, the door was wide open. The lady who lives next door said they left at night. So much stuff was still in there, but they were definitely gone. A **TERRIBLE** mess, with broken walls and windows. No goodbye.

Where are my Tickets?

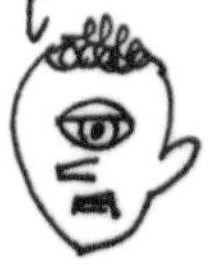

I've never seen anything like that. People living in such bad shape. I felt so sad for Mary. No wonder she came over so much, and she was hungry every time. I'm glad she liked the Beatles, and that Beatlemania brought happiness to her. On the way home, I ran into Tureki. He said that family was loud. All they did was fight.

I was thinking of giving her that extra ticket (<u>if they'd ever get here!</u>). She would've loved the concert.

Here's the sad part: When I got home, I went upstairs to fiddle around with my make-up-- but it was <u>GONE</u>. Eyeliner, shadow and mascara all missing. <u>BISQUICK!</u> When we had sandwiches, she said she forgot something and ran upstairs. Thank goodness, I had put my slicker in my pocket! Why would Mary do that after I was so nice to her?

OH NO!

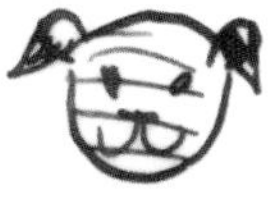

CHAPTER: And I Love Her.

JULY 3

Laying here tonight, looking out my window, I have about a thousand thoughts. It's a gigantic window that looks out on the lake and up at the sky. Dad dragged home 4 of these picture windows from some jobsite. My room has one. I can lay here at night and sometimes see shooting stars. It's my Wishes Window. (I wish I could meet the Beatles.)

All day, thoughts about Mary and what she did. I told Ginia about it. She reminded me that I did the same thing to Jamie. "How is it any different?" she asked. I guess it's not. All I knew was, I **HAD** to have that picture. I'd found something that made sense to me, and was exactly what I needed to lead me in the right direction. My direction. Maybe the make-up was like that for her. I'll never know. Maybe, but I'm still mad. I'm glad I have a friend like Laurie. She'll never steal from me. I need to confess to Jamie, that's for certain.

Seeing Mary's house like that, all torn up and with the front door wide open, made me see that there are other kinds of people out there with different lives. All kinds, not just troubled ones. Like I know that communism is terrible because people are not very free, but I bet there's a girl my age in Russia who, if given the chance to hear the Beatles, would Love them like I do. Or maybe there's some music she knows that's great for her and would be different for me. In fact--

ANOTHER COOL THING ABOUT MY BIG WINDOW IS THAT IT HAS A LEDGE UNDER IT WHERE I CAN SET MY TRANSISTOR AT NIGHT AND PICK UP RADIO STATIONS FROM FAR AWAY. Nashville, Canada, Detroit. BUT THE BEST, my favorite is **WVON**. THE VELVET-Y DEEP VOICES OF THE DJs REMIND ME THAT THIS SOUND OF SOUL IS COMING ACROSS THE DARK OF NIGHT FROM ANOTHER, DIFFERENT CHICAGO, DOWN BY COMISKEY PARK. I **LOVE** THIS MUSIC. IT'S LIKE DRINKING AN EXTRA-THICK CHOCOLATE MALT THAT'S TOTALLY DELICIOUS. The ONLY THING BETWEEN ME AND THE HIGH, COOL, CLEAR VOICE OF Curtis Mayfield IS THE OCCASIONAL AIR-WAVE CRACKLE OF INTERFERENCE DUE TO THE APPROACH OF A DISTANT THUNDERSTORM.

There's ONLY ONE GOOD THING I CAN SAY ABOUT Mary's FAMILY CHOOSING DARKNESS TO SLIP AWAY: NIGHT IS WHERE A WHOLE BUNCH OF GREAT MUSIC LIVES, JUST WAITING TO BE LISTENED TO AND LOVED A LOT. So, PEOPLE -- Get Ready! THERE'S A TRAIN a'COMIN.'

THERE'S A TRAIN A'COMIN'

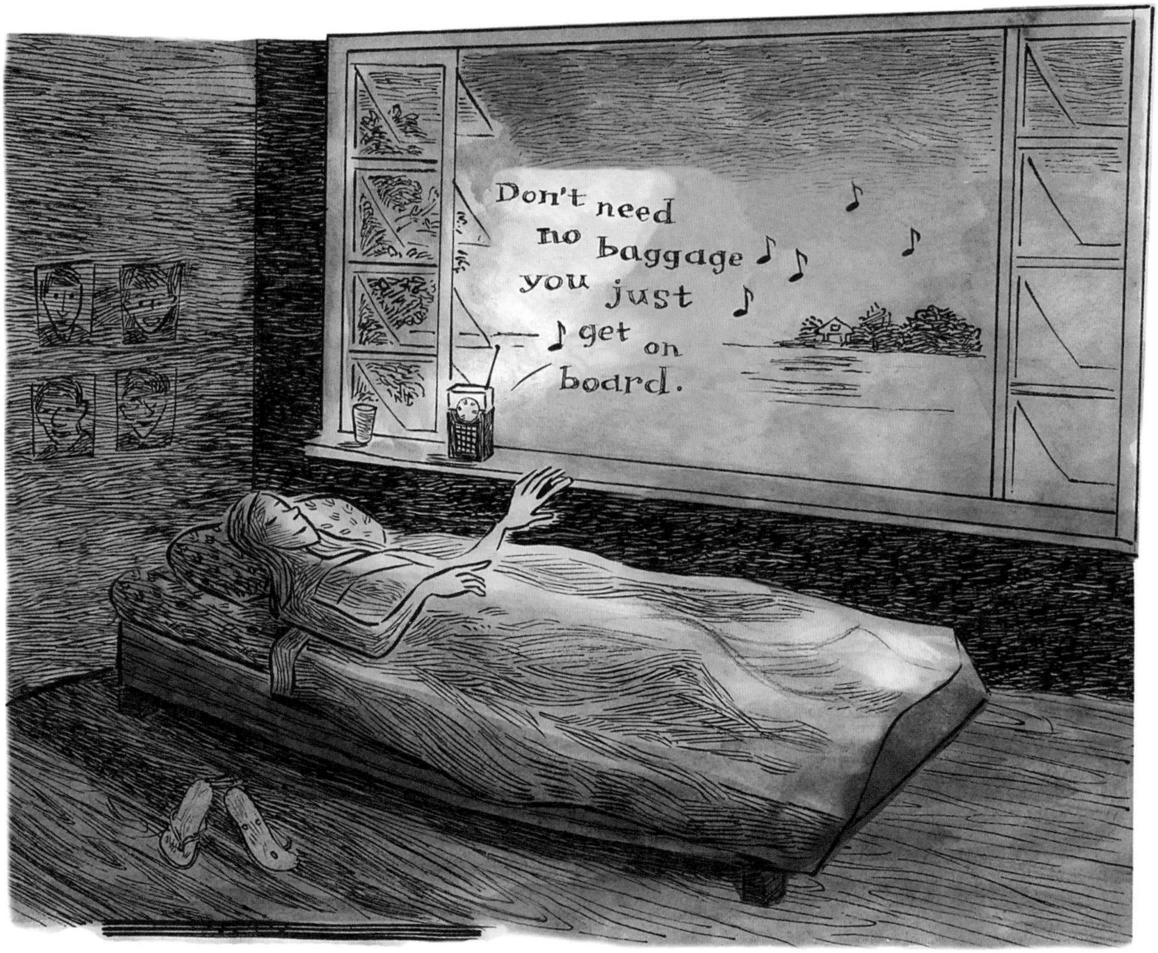
Don't need no baggage you just get on board.

I Feel Fine

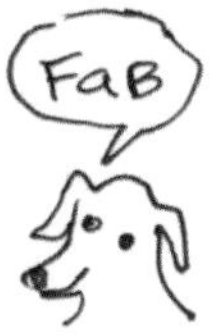
FaB

JULY 6

THEY CAME TODAY! THEY CAME TODAY! THE **TICKETS** CAME TODAY!

Beatles Beatles Beatles Beatles Beatles Beatles

When I opened the mailbox and saw that Triangle Productions envelope, it felt like a thousand lightning bugs of pure excitement hit my belly. Like John sings: "It's such a feeling that my love --- **I can't HIDE** --- **I can't HIDE** --- **I CAN'T HI-IDE!**

However, I absolutely <u>DO</u> have to hide around here because everyone likes to call me out and make fun of my genuine enthusiasm. I can hide. I can hide. I can hide!

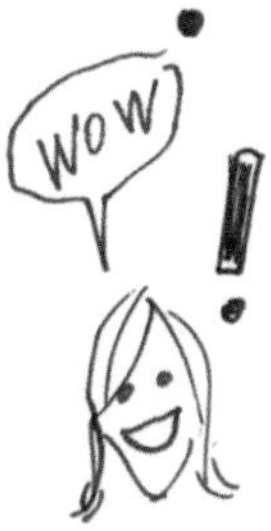
WOW

OK, so once I got the tickets out of the box, I ran inside and called the club members. Then, because I am the president, it is VERY important that I make sure nothing bad happens to these tickets (glad now they didn't come last week). I'm worried Joe might take them. Or Ginia. (actually nah. she won't do nothin.) Jim might get his greasy food fingers all over them. Gu might eat them. And then AAAH! Worries for the person in charge. So I went out in the garage, found an old piece of plastic sheeting, cut a custom size that fit the tickets, sealed the tickets inside, taped and stapled it all around and then pinned it to the center of my bulletin board next to a picture of JFK and Jackie.

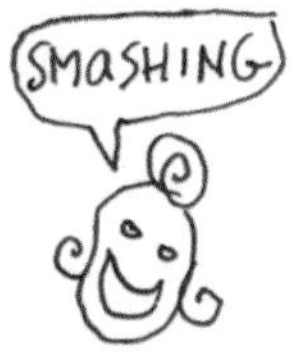
SMASHING

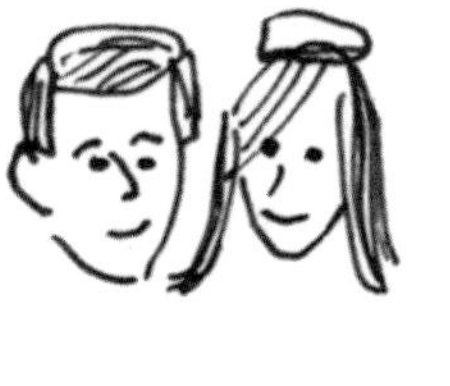

... I'm in love with her
and I feel fine.

This is, so far, the most important Beatle day of the year. To celebrate, I've been listening to Beatles VI. I'm really liking that song "You like me too much," that George sings. Wait— let me say that over. I **LOVE** that song. And I love looking at that rosy colored cover with George in that pink shirt ... **LOVE** him so. Except George, I have to disagree with you on something: You CAN'T like the Beatles too much!

It was the best day ever until Dad came home and boy was he mad because I cut that piece of plastic for my tickets out of something he needed for a job. And then Mom was mad because I didn't put her scissors back where I got them from. Ginia yelled at me for helping myself to her thumbtacks. Joe wasn't home or he would have found some way to torment me. He's still mad at me about last year (I broke a thermometer and put the red stuff in a shot glass and set it on the counter and he came home later, saw it there and drank it— thought it was kool-aid. Mercury! He had to go have his stomach pumped out).

Well, there's one good thing: the tickets are here, they are in my room, and I get to look at them whenever I want. The concert will be here before I know it: August 20, 1965.

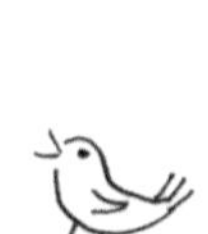

Can't WAIT!

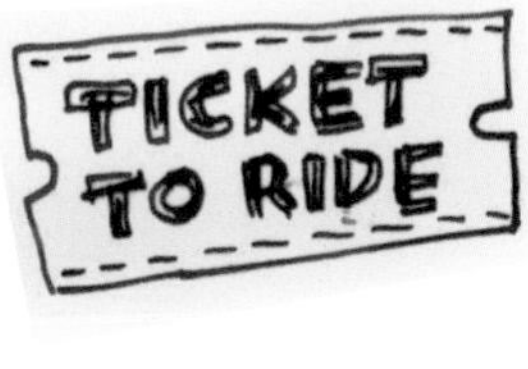
TICKET TO RIDE

I'm so glad..
That she's my
little gir-rl.

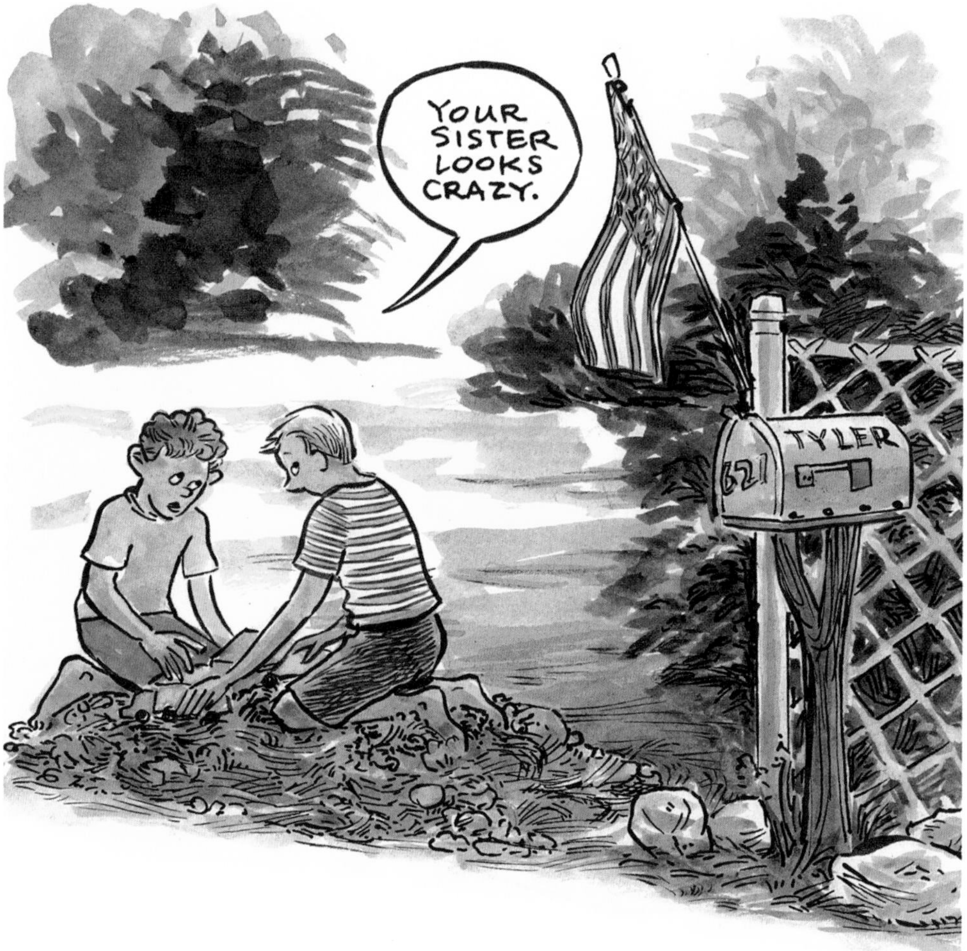
YOUR SISTER LOOKS CRAZY.
TYLER
621

SHE'S SO GLAD..
SHE'S TELLING ALL
THE WORLD.

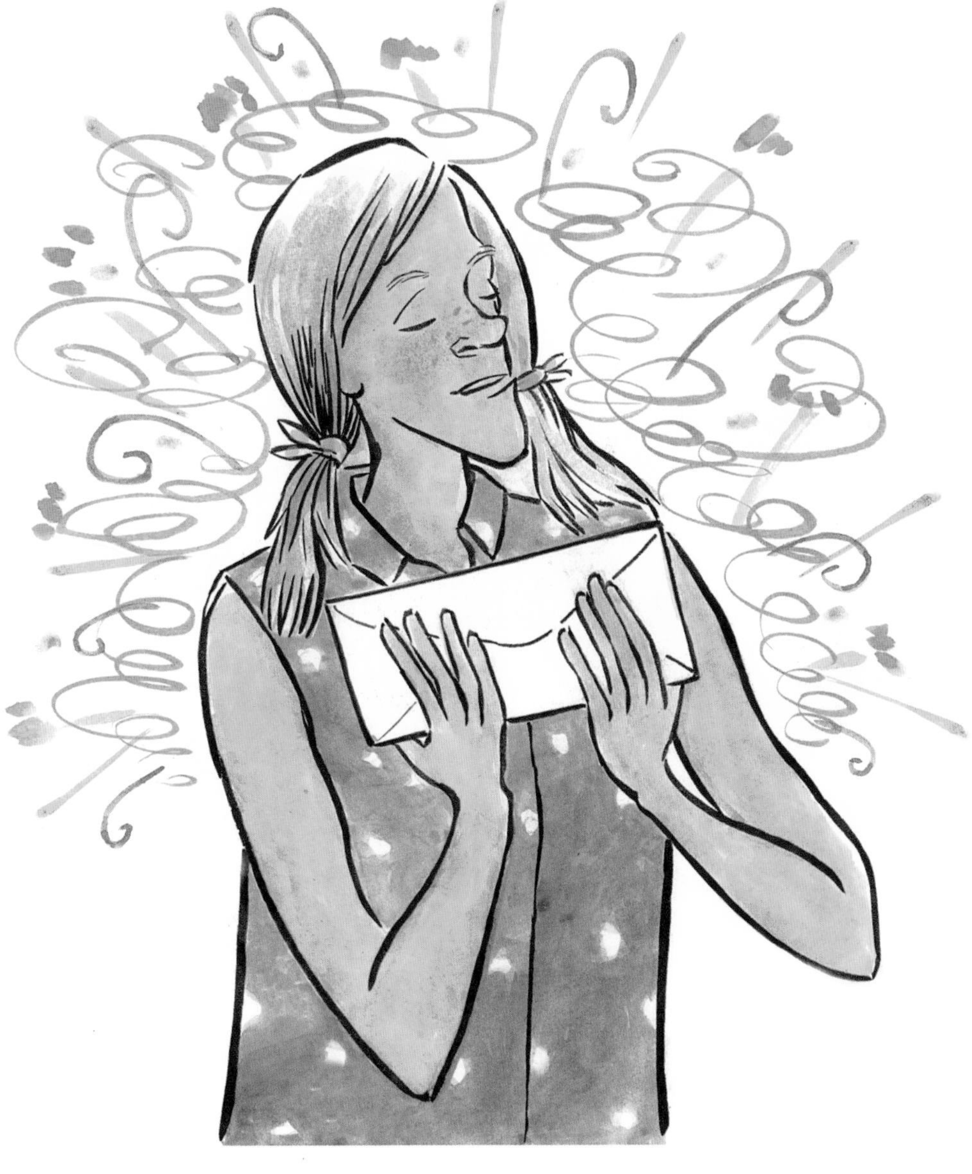

PLACE OF HONOR

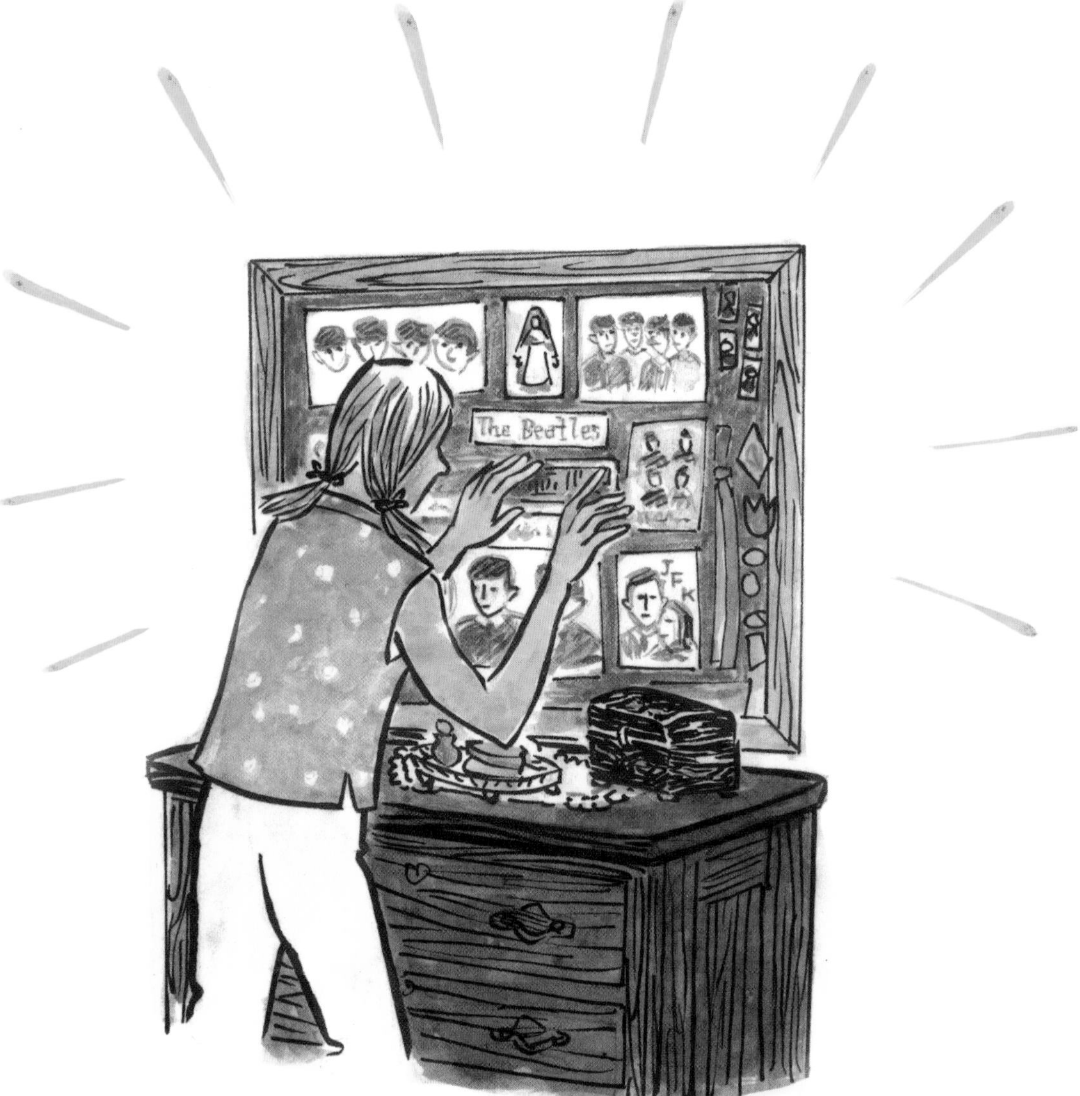
The Beatles
JFK

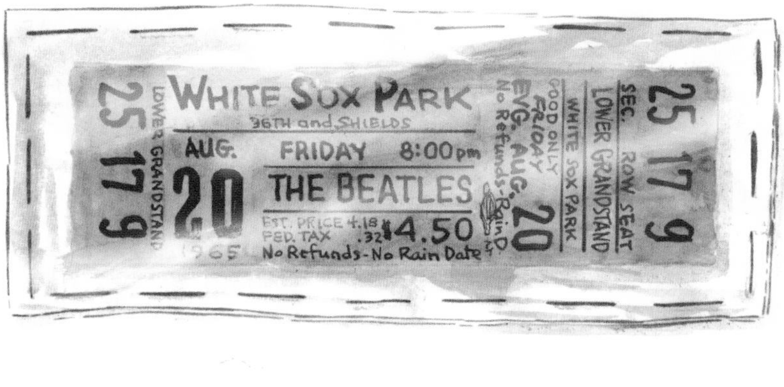
25 17 9
LOWER GRANDSTAND
WHITE SOX PARK
36TH and SHIELDS
AUG.
20
1965
FRIDAY 8:00pm
THE BEATLES
EST. PRICE 4.18
FED. TAX .32
$4.50
No Refunds-No Rain Date
GOOD ONLY
FRIDAY
EVG. AUG. 20
WHITE SOX PARK
LOWER GRANDSTAND
SEC. ROW SEAT
25 17 9

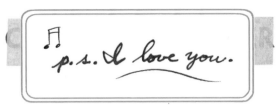

JULY 11

WELL, I HAVE MY TICKETS, AND THE DATE IS SET, AUG. 20. I STUDIED THE CALENDAR AND REALIZED THAT IT'S <u>40</u> DAYS FROM NOW. IT'S A *Long* WAYS AWAY, BUT IT WILL BE HERE BEFORE I KNOW IT.

IT ALSO POPPED OUT AT ME: 40 IS KIND OF LIKE THE TOP 40 HITS LIST. 40 DAYS AWAY. I NEED TO MAKE SURE I HAVE EVERYTHING I NEED, BECAUSE I'LL BE COUNTING DOWN THE DAYS. I NEED AN OUTFIT, SHOES, HAT, SOME SPENDING MONEY -- WHAT ELSE.. OH YEAH, NOW I NEED NEW MAKE-UP, THANKS TO MY OLD FRIEND *Mary*. THIS IS GOING TO BE THE HARDEST, BECAUSE MOM SAID THE OUTFIT I GET FOR THE CONCERT WILL BE WHAT I WEAR TO THE FIRST DAY OF SCHOOL SO SHE'LL PAY FOR THAT. I THINK I CAN WEAR MY SHOES FROM GRADUATION. MAKE-UP AND SPENDING MONEY. NO BABYSITTING MONEY IS COMING IN BECAUSE THE SAPKOS HAVE GONE TO MICHIGAN FOR THE REST OF THE SUMMER TO BE WITH THEIR GRANDPARENTS. I REALLY HAVE TO COME UP WITH SOME IDEAS BECAUSE I NEED *Yardley*!

WEIRD WONDERFUL Dream:

Last NIGHT I DREAMT I WAS AT THE LAUNDROMAT WITH THE MAN FROM THE BAIT SHOP. WE WERE EATING PEANUT BRITTLE. THEN I WENT OUT THE BACK, BUT IT WAS ACTUALLY IN FRONT OF OUR HOUSE AT THE LAKE. I WAS WEARING GEORGE'S PINK SHIRT FROM THE VI ALBUM, AND I DOVE INTO THE WATER. *Warm!*

SKYLARKIN'

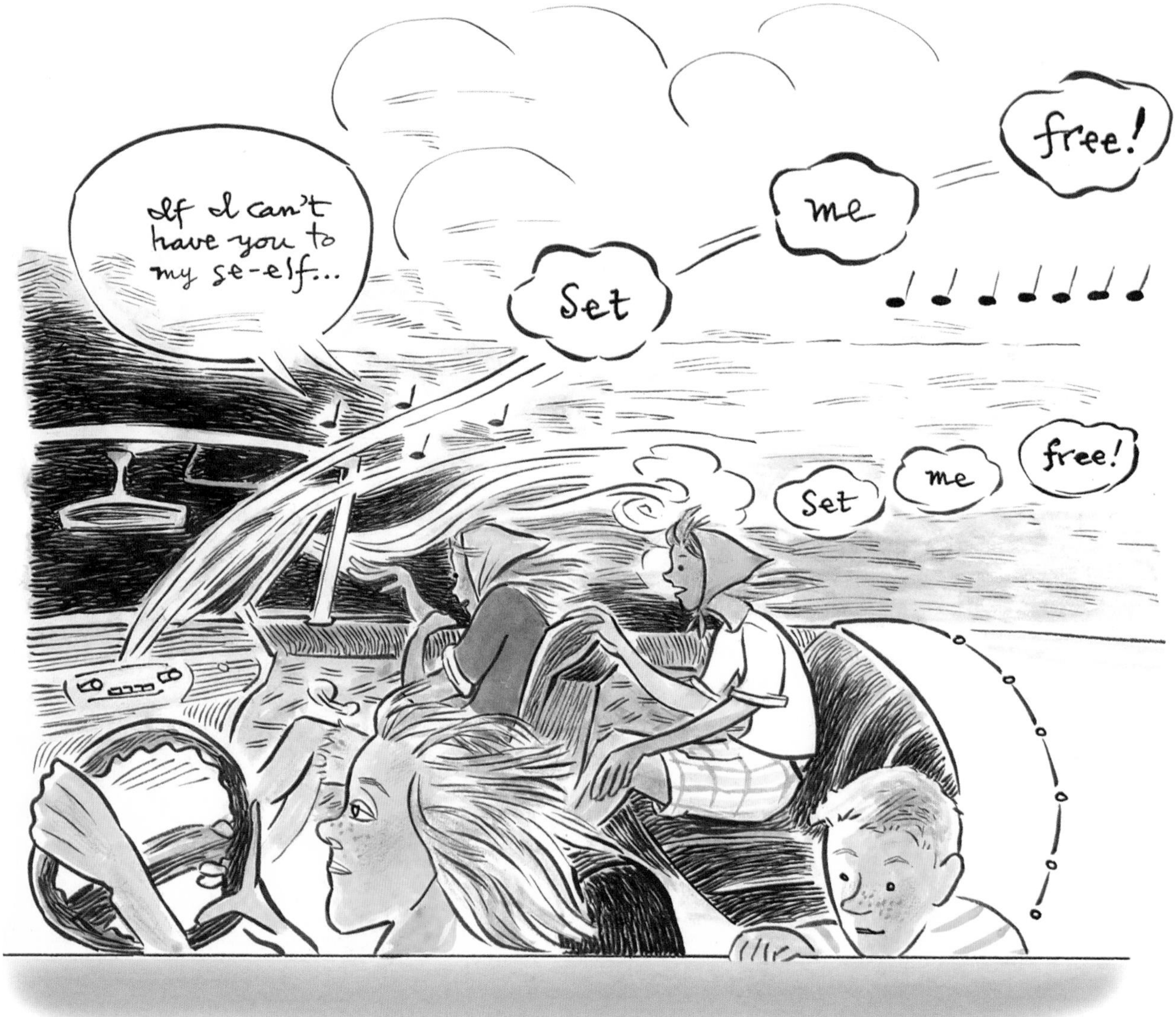
If I can't have you to my se-elf...
Set
me
free!
Set
me
free!

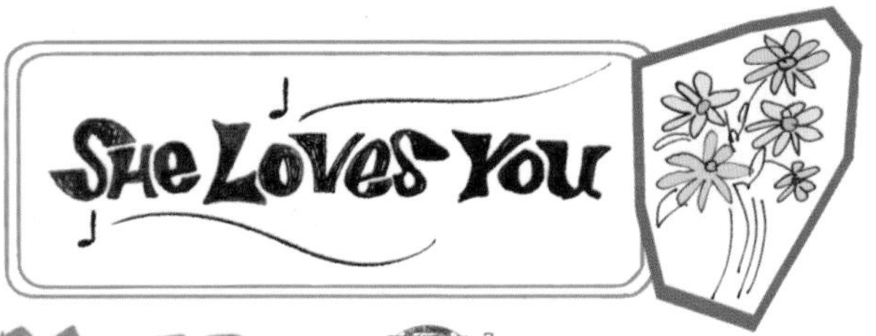
She Loves You

JULY 12

In an unbelievable gesture of being nice, my sister Ginia came home from her job at the Jewel and volunteered to take me, Laurie, and Jimmy to the D.Q. to get whatever we want! She put the top down on Mom's car and turned the radio up loud to my station. She's acting very strange. In about 2 months, she'll be heading off to the convent. Maybe it's starting to hit her that her life will be different. No more jumping in the car on a hot night to get a 15¢ cone. Glad I'm not joining the convent. I like boys too much. It just would not work. I'm also in love with doing what I want. Too many cool things are happening now. Lots of changes. I don't want to miss out on anything.

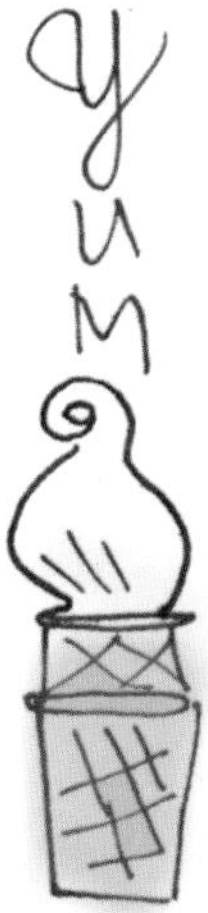
YUM

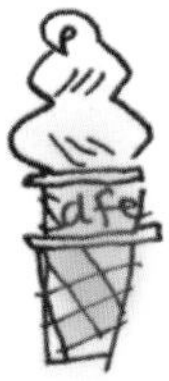

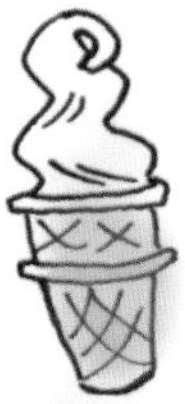

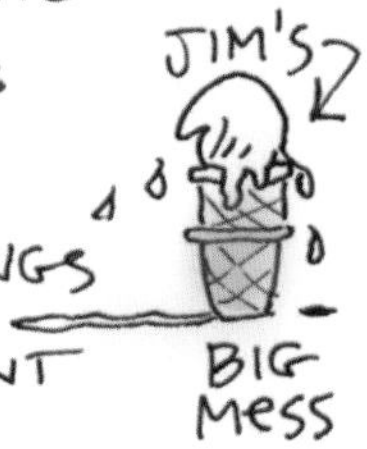
JIM'S
BIG MESS

Luckily, Laurie and I made triangle scarves today, PERFECT for riding with the top down. They're so easy to make, and are reversible, too. Good for in the boat. Good for church. I picked out a paisley fabric. Madras, too, although that's not for wet weather. Bleeds.

Blasting really loud in a car— great way to enjoy the hits.

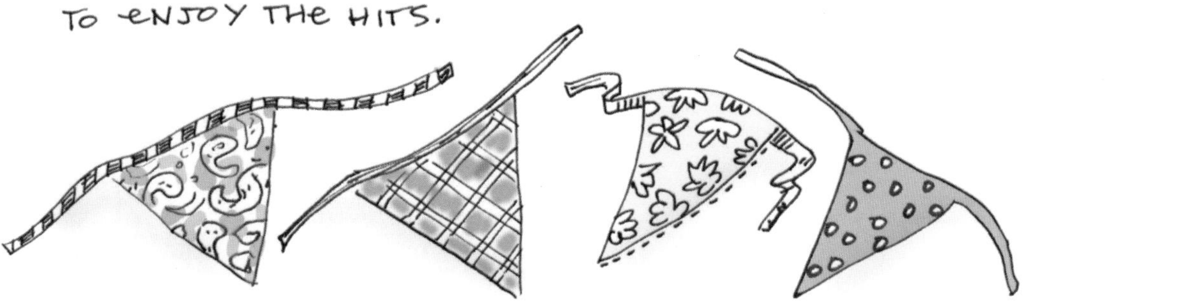

No flowers painted on the corners.

AND YOU KNOW THAT CAN'T BE BAD

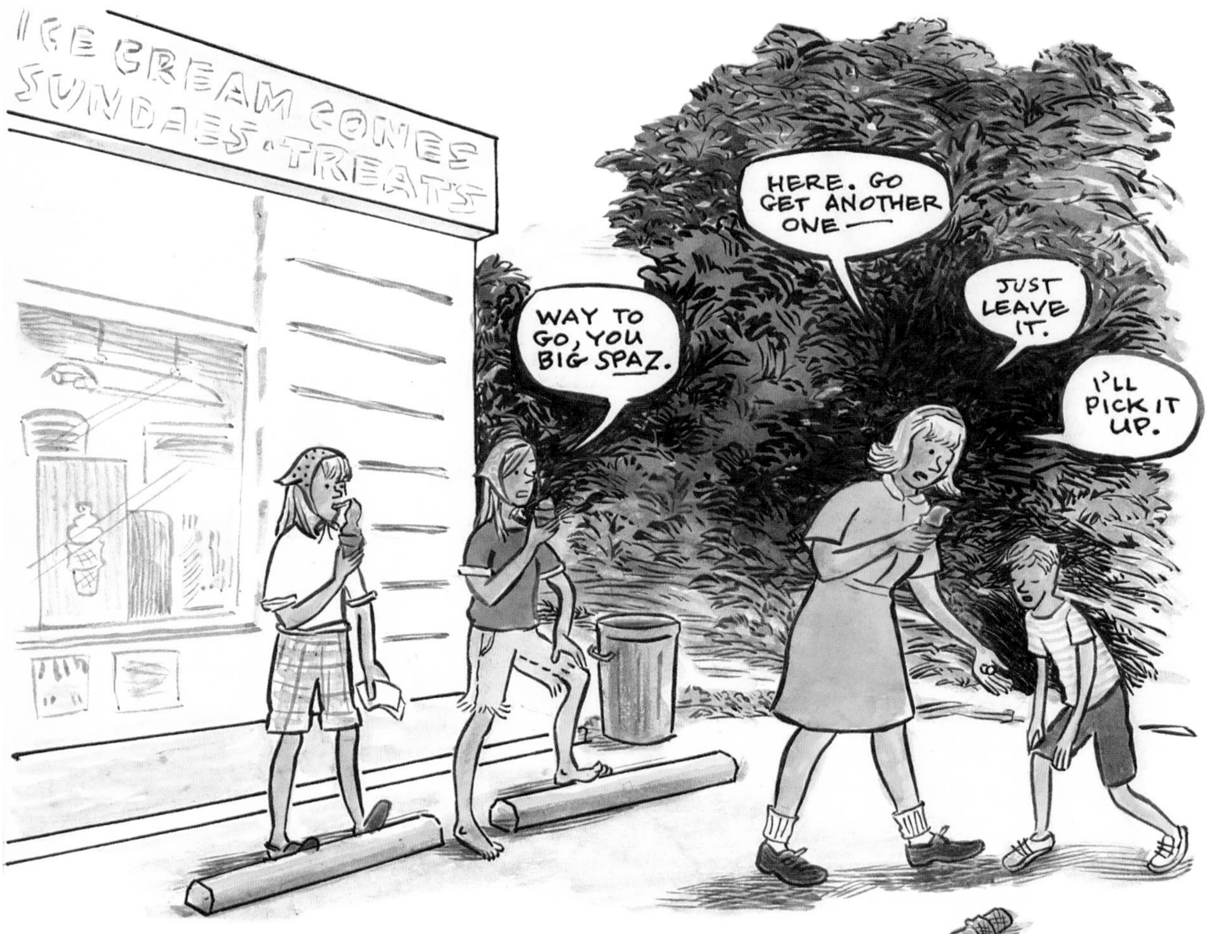
ICE CREAM CONES
SUNDAES·TREATS
WAY TO GO, YOU BIG SPAZ.
HERE. GO GET ANOTHER ONE—
JUST LEAVE IT.
I'LL PICK IT UP.

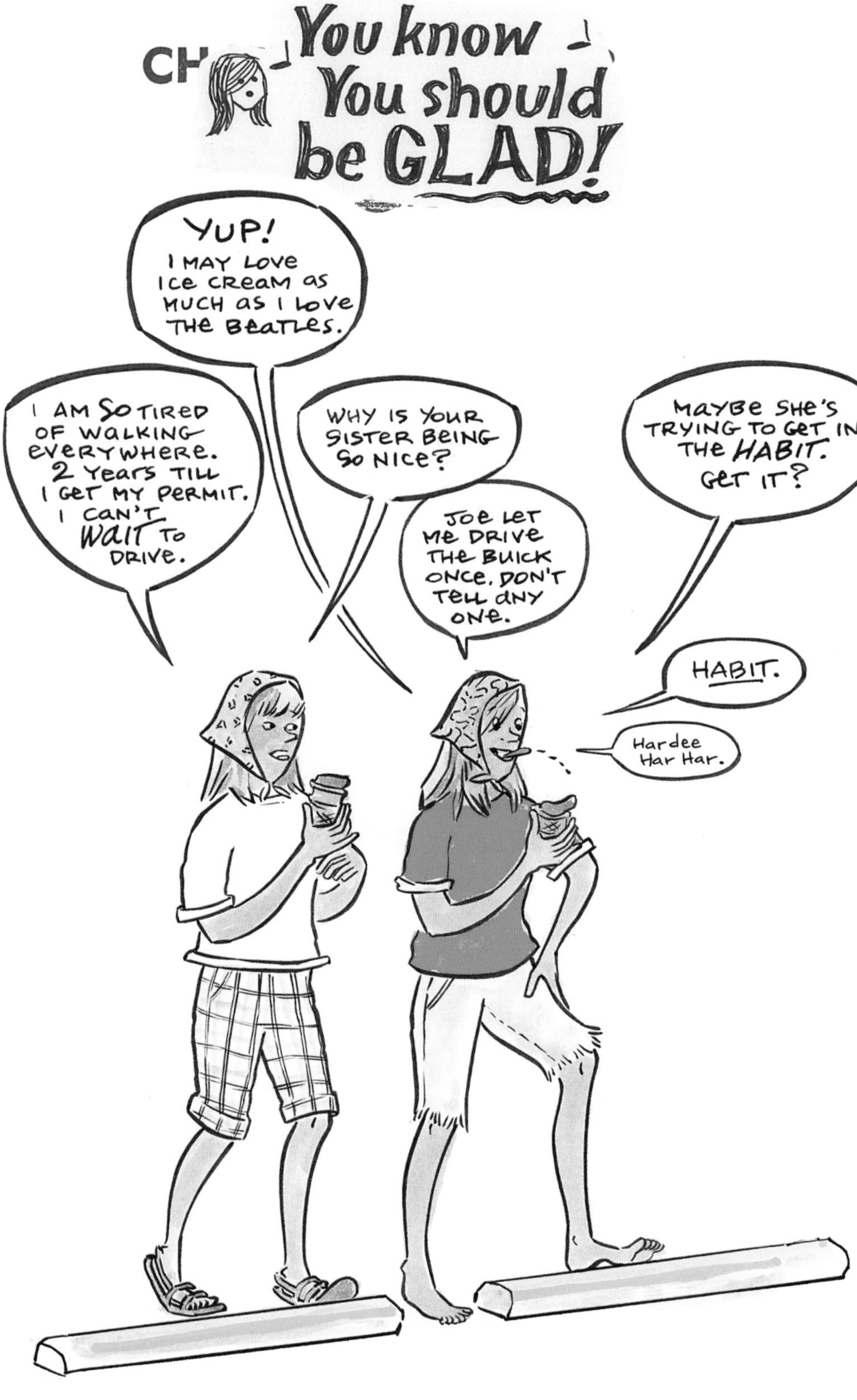
CH
You know You should be GLAD!
YUP! I MAY LOVE ICE CREAM AS MUCH AS I LOVE THE BEATLES.
I AM SO TIRED OF WALKING EVERYWHERE. 2 YEARS TILL I GET MY PERMIT. I CAN'T WAIT TO DRIVE.
WHY IS YOUR SISTER BEING SO NICE?
MAYBE SHE'S TRYING TO GET IN THE HABIT. GET IT?
JOE LET ME DRIVE THE BUICK ONCE. DON'T TELL ANY ONE.
HABIT.
Hardee Har Har.

Every Little Thing ♩

jooleye   thirteen-ager
38Days. So excited! But i'm
bothered by something
right now.

The Beatles have not been on the charts! I know they
have a movie coming out soon, so maybe they're
holding the songs back to co-incide with the
movie's debut. I don't know. all I can say is that
a Beatles song on the radio would make cone-getting
so much more fun.

In the mean time here's some songs from
the radio that I like:

♩ What the World Needs Now is love sweet love.
    Jackie De Shannon
♩ Baby I'm Yours — Barbara Lewis
♩ For Your Love — Yardbirds
♩ Yes I'm Ready — Barbara Mason
♩ Set Me Free — The KINKS
♩ What's New Pussycat — Tom Jones
♩ I Want Candy — Strangeloves
    (I want new make-up but I still don't
     have a JOB!)

I'll tell you what's dumb — Patty Duke's new
song "Please, Don't Just Stand There." It's copying
Leslie Gore. You know how I feel about copying.
She needs to go stand somewhere else!

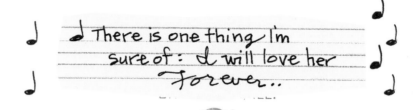

There is one thing I'm sure of: I will love her Forever...

ANOTHER DUMB SONG = "*Laurie*." HEY. *Laurie* IS MY BEST FRIEND. YOU'D THINK THEY COULD COME UP WITH SOMETHING NICE. ANYWAY, THE SONG IS ABOUT A GIRL THAT THIS FELLOW MEETS AT A DANCE AN SHE'S AN ANGEL TO HIM, BLA BLA BLA. BOY DID THEY HAVE A GOOD TIME. SHE LOST HER SWEATER AND IS GONE. NEXT THING YOU KNOW HE FINDS OUT SHE DIED ON HER BIRTHDAY "a year ago today" ≡SPOOKY≡ THEN FINDS HER SWEATER " Lyin' there upon her grave —STRANGE THINGS HAPPEN IN THIS WORLD. " HOPE NOTHING STRANGE HAPPENS TO ME BEFORE THE CONCERT!

a GEM

Why we have a new Buick Skylark:

MOM HAD TO WORK DOING SECRETARIAL TO MAKE THE PAYMENTS, WHICH IS WHY I'M BABYSITTING THIS SUMMER. AND JIM IS 5. SHE HAD MANY PROBLEMS WHEN SHE WAS EXPECTING AT AGE 40. THEY GATHERED US KIDS AROUND AND SAID THAT IF ANYTHING WENT WRONG, THEY WOULD LET HER DIE AND SAVE THE BABY. THANK GOODNESS ALL TURNED OUT WELL. BUT THEN THAT GOOFY FOOTBALL COACH DENTIST YANKED ALL HER TEETH OUT. AND THEY'D GIVEN HER A SURGERY AFTER JIM. NO MORE CHILDREN. BOY DID SHE FEEL OLD AND UGLY. THEN WE MOVED OUT OF THE CITY. LESS ATTRACTIVE WARDROBE NEEDS OUT HERE. BUT SHE LOVES TO LOOK NICE. SO EVENTUALLY, SHE DECIDED TO QUIT FEELING OLD. The Skylark CHANGED THINGS. RIDING AROUND IN THAT RIG IS Dreamy. EVEN IF IT'S ONLY TO GET GROCERIES OR ICE CREAM.

ALL OF THEM

Let's Go!

♫ Please don't wear Red tonight.

JULY 29

Yikes, it happened. Strange incident to report. I stepped on a hot coal yesterday. Why was it in the grass in the first place? It's cancelled about a thousand things. I can't walk. I can't go swimming. I can't listen to my transistor because it's out of batteries and I don't have a job to get new ones. I can't even get up to change the dial between WLS and WCFL. It's terrible right now. I'm stuck. Even Jim is mad at me because we have to stay in, so there's a lot of watching TV.

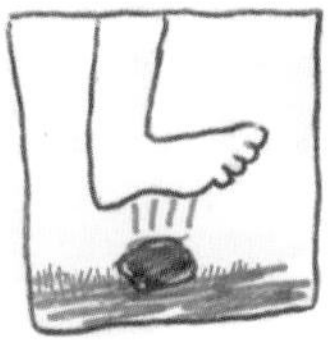

Here's how it happened. We were having a cookout. A bunch of my parents' friends came over — club girls and their families and men that Dad knew from plumbing with their bunch. Nice food. They brought cole slaw, Jello, baked beans, cake, chips, a case of pop, and beer. Mom and Dad did all the meat. And Mom made her specialty: deluxe watermelon basket. And potato salad.

Anyway, Dad had all the coals in a pit with big rocks around it to hold up the grate. All day the men fiddled with the fire, drank beer, and sat there talking about sewer lines. And concrete. And fuse boxes. And furnaces. I don't know what the ladies talked about because I was in the water all day. Gosh, I love to swim!

O.K. after everyone ate, cleaned up, and went home, the Trinity arrived. Like a tornado.

Yes it is

WHAT WERE YOU DOIN' OUT THERE IN BARE FEET? WATCH WHERE YOU STEP NEXT TIME.
THIS NEEDS UNGUENTINE OINTMENT.

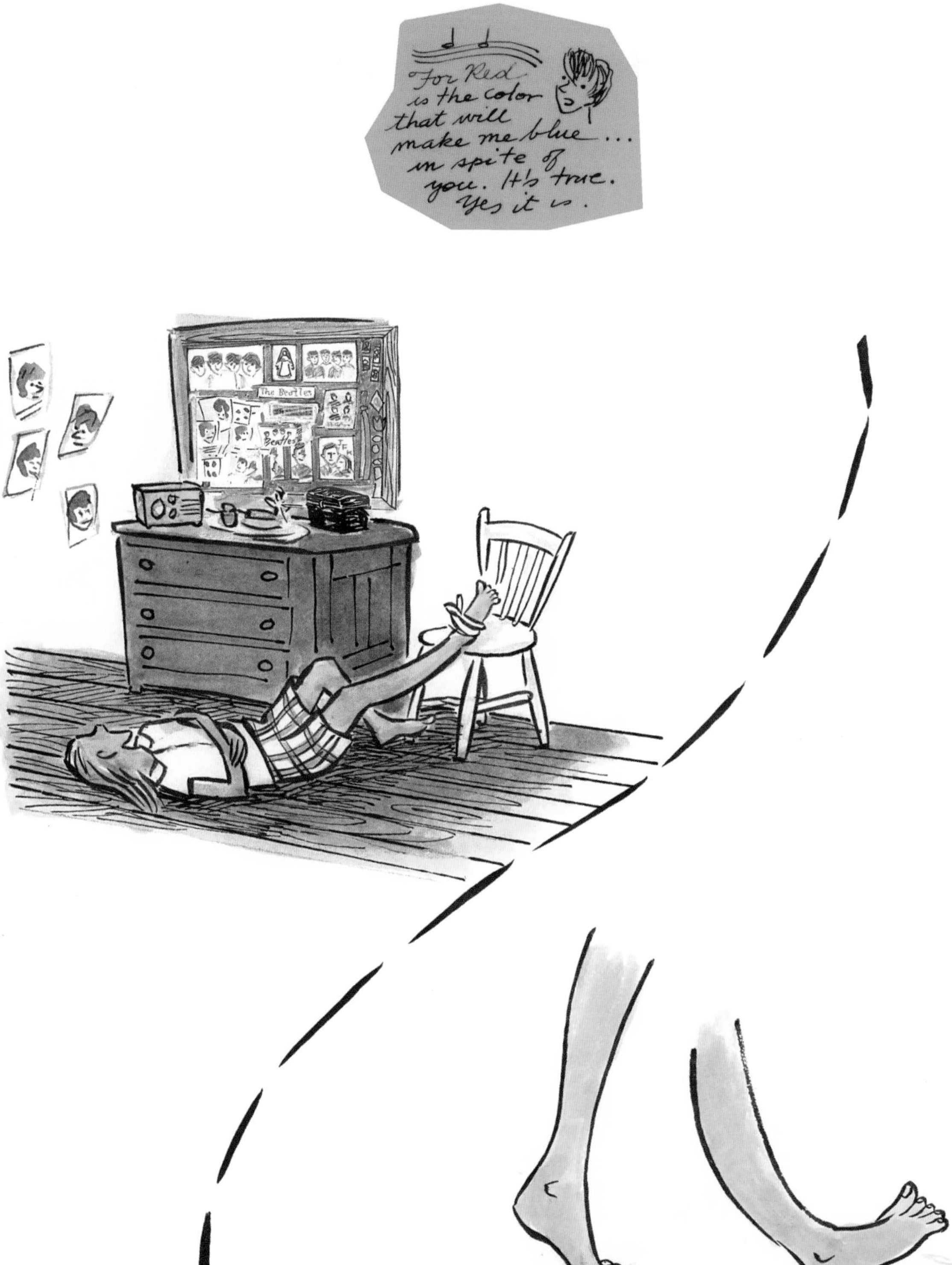
For Red
is the color
that will
make me blue...
in spite of
you. It's true.
Yes it is.
The Beatles
Beatles

SPUD THERAPY

PLI INTRACTOR
1 GON ST.
3, ILL.

They just came in from practice and inhaled all the left-overs like slobs. Then *ha ha* they went outside and were throwing hot coals at each other. So dumb. Dad hollered at them to put 'em all back in the pit, and then he doused it with water. *But,* the one they missed, my foot found. *Yeowch!* So now I'm stuck and this is really stupid. And the boys didn't get in trouble. They NEVER do.

Thing is– when I heard Joe and them come in, I thought 'Oh. Jamie's here. I need to confess.' He's been pretty nice to me lately, so I figured...

It's a really bad burn. When Mom was dressing it, she told me about a bad burn she had on her palms. She was running through the house and fell into the fireplace hearth at their one room cabin. Her dad sat her in a chair and he peeled Irish potatoes very thin and laid them across her burns. As soon as the layer warmed up, he'd take it off and put a new thin layer on. He did this over and over until her burn quit hurting. She never had a scar. I don't know why she didn't do that with my foot. Yeah I do. All the potatoes went into potato salad, just finished off by the Trinity! BUMS!

This foot better get healed up quick. I'm going to see my Beatles in 22 days and I don't care if I'm on crutches or I have to crawl -- I WILL NOT MISS THAT CONCERT!

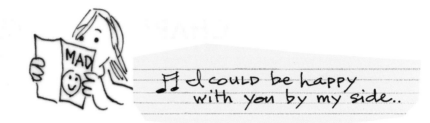

♫ I could be happy with you by my side...

So I'm laying around now, my foot hurts and I'm upset. There's so much to do to get ready for August 20. I don't even have a dress yet. Mom suggested that while I'm laid up, I could pick out a dress from one of the catalogs and we'll order it. Penneys, Wards, and Sears.

The problem with a catalogue is, you can't try anything on. I may have grown. I'll have to guess for now. The first one is sleeveless and I love it. Out of all of these, it's my favorite, but I'd have to bring a sweater along. Don't want to have to carry anything extra. The second one, Madras, would look good with penny loafers, but if it rains, well -- you know. (It's been raining on Fridays for the last 3 weeks!)

I like the blue one, with the ties. Here's the thing — I wore blue so much in school. I'm tired of it. I don't want to go to the concert looking like a school girl. I want to look more grown up and sophisticated. I want to look TOUGH! I'd really stand out in that yellow dress, but I'm afraid the bees will follow me thinking I'm a sunflower. Geez, I can't decide. I'll do it tomorrow.

Later: GLORY BE! My brother and sister just hatched a plan to go to Tennessee by themselves next week. Before she leaves for the convent and before football practice starts. I might have a little job opportunity because of it. More later.

FROM THE
JUNIORS SECTION
WARDS CATALOG,
SIZE 11

JULY 31

"WHAT LUCK! JOE SAID I COULD DO HIS MONDAY JOB FOR HIM ON THE MONDAY HE'S GONE IN TENNESSEE AND KEEP THE MONEY: MOP THE FLOOR OF THE TAVERN. I THINK I CAN DO THAT. HE'S GOING TO SHOW ME HOW THIS MONDAY. I'LL BE ON CRUTCHES. HOPE IT WORKS OUT. I REALLY NEED MAKE-UP.

PROBABLY ANOTHER WEEK WITH THIS FOOT PROBLEM. MOM KEEPS CHANGING BANDAGES AND ADDING OINTMENT. I'M SUPPOSED TO HAVE FAN CLUBBERS OVER FOR A SWIM NEXT SATURDAY. SHE SAYS IT'S HEALING NICELY, ALTHO I'M SICK OF BEING STUCK IN THE HOUSE WITH MY POOR FOOT AND THAT ADORABLE IMP JIM. THANK GOD FOR TV!

THERE'S A NEW SHOW ON AFTER BOZO. (I FORGOT TO EXPLAIN BOZO — JIM'S LUNCHTIME SHOW. BOZO THE CLOWN. THEN HE GOES TO NAP). BACK TO THE NEW SHOW: IT'S CALLED "Where the action is!" IT'S GOT THE VERY LATEST IN MUSIC AND DANCING. EVERYBODY ON THAT SHOW IS TOUGH. NOTHING IS STILL. THERE ARE A BUNCH OF PEOPLE AND BANDS I NEVER HEARD OF. THERE'S SOMETHING CONCERNING ABOUT IT, THOUGH. I'LL TRY TO DESCRIBE.

THE BEATLES ARE THE BEST. NOBODY EVEN COMES CLOSE TO BEATING THEM. NOBODY. MANY BANDS TRY TO DO THAT, TRY TO BE LIKE THEM, AND THERE ARE A WHOLE LOT OF OLDER PEOPLE OUT THERE WHO KEEP TRYING TO GIVE US ACCEPTABLE FAKE VERSIONS. TRYING TO FOOL US INTO THINKING IT'S EASY ENOUGH. LOOK HERE YOU DOPES: YOU CAN'T REPRODUCE THE BEATLES, OR THEIR MAGIC. Let me explain.

♩ ... I don't want to sound complaining... but

you know there's ♪ always rain in my heart.

EXPLAIN ➘

YOU KNOW HOW THE BLESSED VIRGIN MARY APPEARED TO THOSE CHILDREN FROM PORTUGAL? 3 LITTLE KIDS, AND ALL KINDS OF MIRACLES HAPPENED. SHE APPEARED AND THOSE KIDS WERE ON A CLOUD WITH HER. AFTER THAT, THE KIDS WERE CHANGED. THEY WERE DIFFERENT FOR THE BETTER. Well, THAT'S THE WAY I FEEL THINGS CHANGED FOR ME. The Beatles APPEARED ON Ed Sullivan AND THEY BROUGHT ME A CLOUD TO LIVE ON. Miracles happen, LIKE FEELING GREAT AND HAVING THINGS TO LOOK FORWARD TO. I WASN'T THE ONLY ONE. They CHANGED A LOT OF PEOPLE. The Beatles BROUGHT NICE, PUFFY CLOUDS TO US.

So THE PHYNQUES AND THE FAKERS TRY TO FOOL US INTO THINKING THEY GOT CLOUDS, WHEN IN FACT THEY NEVER LEAVE THE GROUND. AT LEAST I KNOW THIS GOING IN, SO THERE'S NO FOOLING ME. But SO MANY PEOPLE DON'T AGREE THAT CLOUDS ARE POSSIBLE, AND SO IT GOES. CLOUD BRINGERS ARE RARE — AS UNICORNS.

Because I KNOW THE DIFFERENCE, I'M FREE TO JUST ENJOY THE MUSIC. EVEN THOUGH I KNOW THAT THOSE BANDS AREN'T THE GREATEST, I STILL WATCH THE SHOW.

IT'S TIME FOR THE → ← GRAND PRIZE GAME!

Jim's Bozo Cloud

..I do all the pleasing with you
it's so hard to REASON---

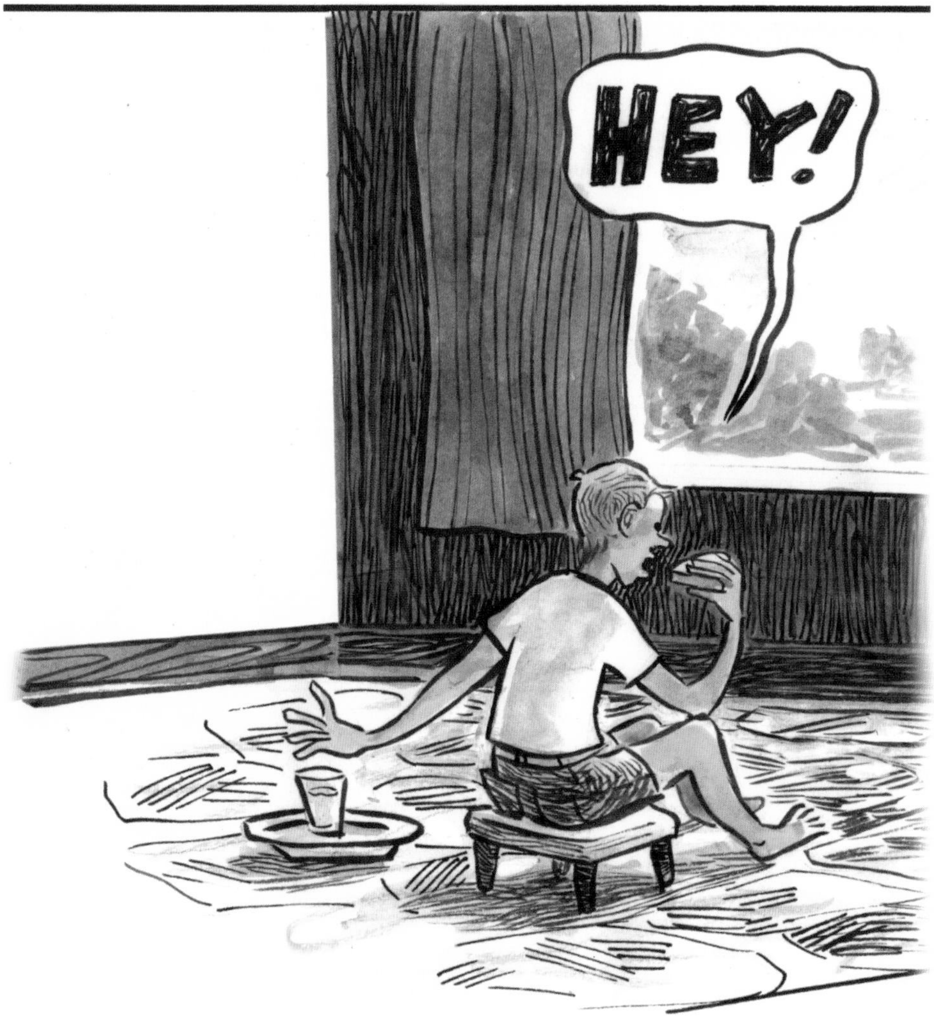
HEY!

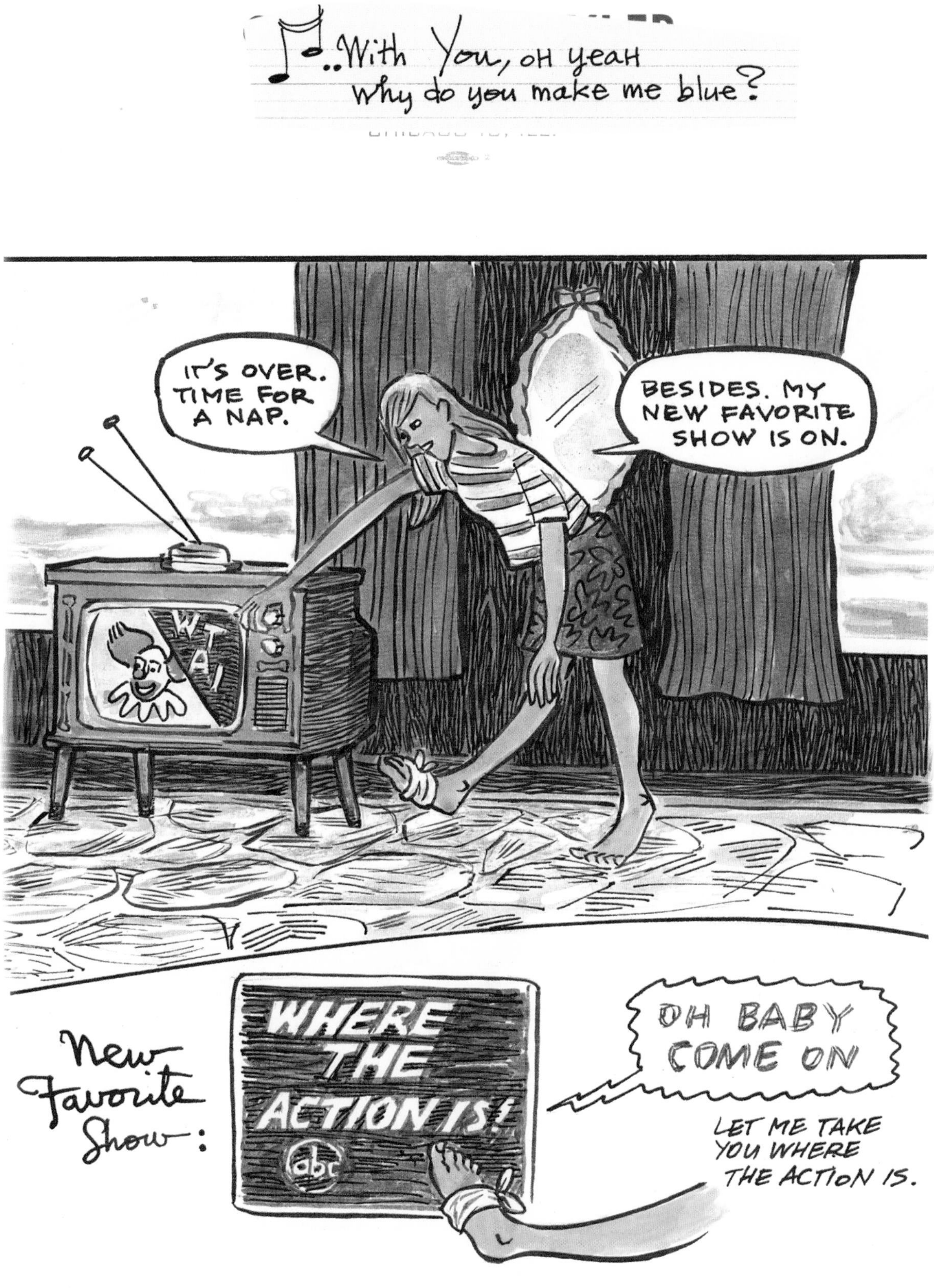
..With You, oH yeaH
Why do you make me blue?
IT'S OVER. TIME FOR A NAP.
BESIDES. MY NEW FAVORITE SHOW IS ON.
WTAI
New Favorite Show:
WHERE THE ACTION IS!
abc
OH BABY COME ON
LET ME TAKE YOU WHERE THE ACTION IS.

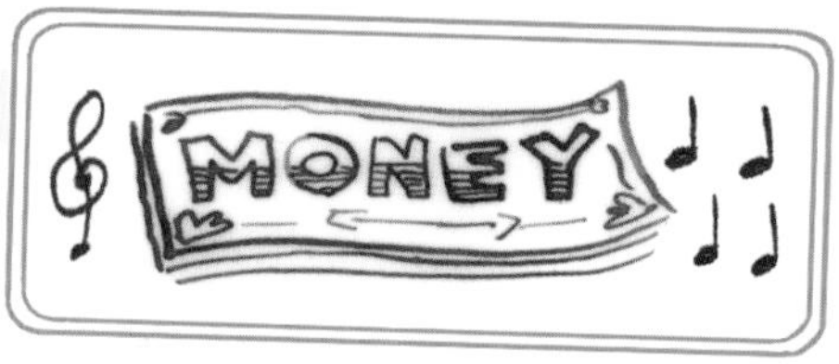
MONEY

AUGUST 6

Hooray. MY BROTHER AND SISTER JUST TOOK OFF FOR TENNESSEE FOR 10 DAYS. YAY! I HAVE THE WHOLE UPSTAIRS FOR MYSELF! NO HAVING THE THIRD DEGREE FROM Ginia EVERY TIME I GO IN MY ROOM. NO DOPEY BEHAVIOR FROM JOE. I'M THE OLDEST NOW. I'LL USE MY POWER WISELY.

GINIA WANTED TO BE GONE BEFORE Dollar Days AT THE Jewel. SHE'S SICK OF THAT PLACE. PEOPLE ARE CRAZY— LIKE THE LADY WHO RETURNED A ROLL OF TOILET PAPER BECAUSE IT DIDN'T TEAR STRAIGHT. JOE HATES HIS JOB, TOO, AND I CAN SEE WHY. YOU WOULD THINK THAT MOPPING A FLOOR WAS EASY. HE SHOWED ME. IT WASN'T THAT HARD. BUT MR. COZZI, WHO OWNS THE PLACE, IS PRETTY FUSSY. "WATCH OUT FOR HIM," JOE warned.

AUG 9 Mr. COZZI IS MEAN! I HOPED HE'D GO EASY ON ME BECAUSE OF MY CRUTCHES BUT HE DIDN'T. I HAD TO DO IT OVER TWICE. (I did ham it up a bit).

Then HE ASKED IF I WANTED TO MAKE SOME extra money. OF COURSE I SAID yes TO HAULING BOTTLES TO THE TRASH AND WASHING HIS FRONT WINDOWS. UP AND DOWN THE LADDER, INSIDE AND OUT, TAKING OUT STINKY BEER BOTTLES. JOE GETS $2 TO MOP — SO I FIGURED THAT I'D GET $6 BECAUSE I DID 2 extra JOBS. I ALMOST DIED WHEN Mr. COZZI GAVE ME $3 "Excuse me, but my brother gets $2 to MOP ONLY. I did 2 more jobs for you." AND DO you KNOW WHAT THAT HIPPO HONKED back at me? "That's 'cuz YOU'RE A GIRL."

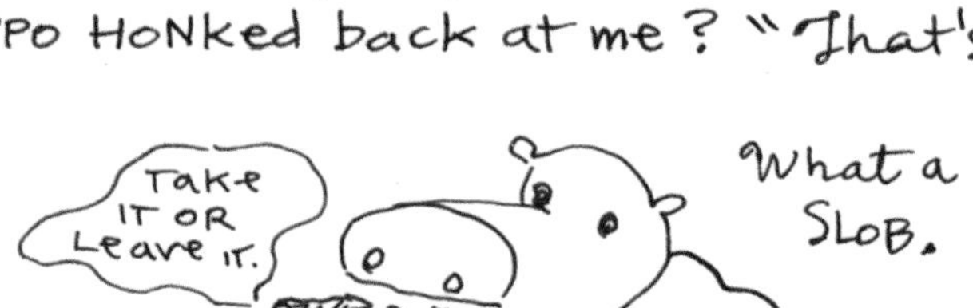
TAKE IT OR LEAVE IT.
What a SLOB.

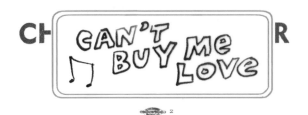

CAN'T BUY ME LOVE

I TOLD HIM I WAS GONNA TELL JOE WHEN HE COMES BACK, AND HE SAID "He don't work here no more. I fired him." JOE DIDN'T TELL ME THAT. I STOOD THERE ABOUT TO COME UNGLUED. I DID ALL THAT WORK WITH CRUTCHES AND HOPPING AROUND. I DIDN'T WANT TO STAY THERE AND ARGUE WITH HIM. DARN IT! I NEEDED AT LEAST $4. IT TOOK SEVERAL HOURS, TOO. Mom stayed home so I COULD COVER FOR JOE. What a mess! And HOW ON EARTH COULD I TELL MOM THAT JOE WAS FIRED?

Why was JOE FIRED? I HAD TO KNOW. "That CLOWN AND HIS BUDDIES CLIMBED UP MY FLAGPOLE OUT ON THE DOCK AND JUMPED IN THE LAKE. I CAN'T HAVE THAT HERE." So JOE WAS FIRED FOR BEING JOE.

Then SOMEBODY AT THE BAR SAID "That's the TYLER KID THAT WON THE AMERICAN LEGION." ANOTHER PERSON SAID "YOU'RE CHUCK TYLER'S KID?" Yes. "YOU SING GOOD IN CHURCH." BEFORE I KNEW IT, I HAD MY $4 BECAUSE THEY PITCHED IN QUARTERS. IF THERE WERE MORE BAR FOLKS, I WOULD HAVE MADE EVEN MORE MONEY. THEN, TO TOP IT OFF, ONE OF THE GUYS SAID "COZZI, YOU CHEAPSKATE. GIVE THE GIRL ANOTHER BUCK." "aw-rite, aw-rite," AND SO I LEFT WITH $5 DOLLARS. I've NEVER BEEN SO HAPPY AND SO TIRED AT THE SAME TIME.

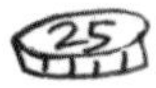
25
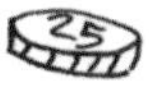
25
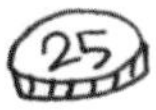
25
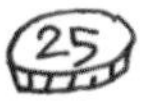
25

I HOBBLED HOME AND DECIDED NOT TO SAY ANYTHING ABOUT JOE. I'LL LEAVE THAT TO HIM. AND I FELT THAT MIRACLE THING, YOU KNOW. LIFE ON THAT Beatles cloud.

♪ *You don't realize how much I need you.*

AUGUST 12

So happy because my foot is better and I got to go swimming AND I got to go up town today and get my make-up. I rode up with Mom and Mrs. Oelerich, the lady she works with. I had just enough for what I needed from the tavern, and was surprised to learn that Mom was going to give me some money for all that babysitting I've been doing. So I've got my outfit and my spending money covered. But the dress that we ordered still hasn't come.

Jamie came over. He knows Joe's in Tenn. Wait— I have to discuss the DRAMATIC almost turn of events regarding that trip. They were supposed to be back today, but they called long distance last night to ask if they could stay a bit longer. Like another week. Thank God Mom said No, she needs the car to get to work. She didn't say "get back here and take your sister to get her outfit and to the concert." And my sister and brother never thought that either. I understand, though, how hard it is to leave Tennessee. But still, they need to get back here.

So Jamie came over and was just hanging around. He made himself a sandwich and played ball with the Stars and the Spits. If it's not swimming it's baseball all day long. I played on the Spits. Jim and Jamie were Stars. Spits won 5-4. Yay. We beat them. I thought Jamie would leave, but then he wanted to listen to <u>VI</u>. Honestly. He sat over

THERE IN HOUND DOG CORNER WHERE WE KEEP THE STEREO AND LISTENED WHILE I KIND OF STRAIGHTENED UP THE ROOM — NOT REALLY. I SAT ON THE OTHER SIDE OF THE ROOM NERVOUS. WAS THIS THE TIME TO TELL HIM? WITH NO TRINITY AROUND? HMMM. I WENT AND GOT A POPSICLE. "D'YOU WANT ONE?" HE DIDN'T.

ⓒ .... "I'm sorry, but I took your picture."

Ⓙ: "What?"   ⓒ: "Last year. Your record picture. You guys were looking for it."

Beatles: "Look what you're doin' --- I'm feeling blue and lonely. Could it be too much to ask of you what you're doing to me..."

Ⓙ: "What are you talking about?"

Beatles: "I've been waiting here for you. Wondering what you're gonna do. Should you need a love that's true, it's me-e-e-e-e..."

ⓒ: "The record jacket!"

Ⓙ: "That dumb thing? I don't care. You still have it?"

ⓒ: "Yeah."

Ⓙ: "Keep it!"

ⓒ: Keep it! I COULDN'T BELIEVE IT.

"So do you want to go to the concert. You know. That extra ticket. It's the least I can do to make it up to you."

And JUST THEN DAD CAME HOME FROM WORK.

— — — — — —

One OF THE THINGS I LIKE TO DO Late AT NIGHT, AFTER EVERYONE'S ASLEEP AND THE MOSQUITOES HAVE QUIT, IS SLIP INTO THE STILL WATER OUT IN FRONT OF THE HOUSE. THE WATER IS WARMER THAN THE AIR. LIKE IN A BATHTUB. THEN I LIKE TO LAY ON THE PICNIC TABLE AND TRY FOR SOME OF THOSE WISHING

♩ Please remember How
I feel about you...

STARS. USUALLY I HAVE SONGS SWISHING THROUGH MY HEAD — MY BRAIN'S A RADIO. BUT TONIGHT I'M PONDERING VI. JAMIE SITTING THERE LISTENING. ME TELLING HIM SORRY. HIM LOOKING AT ME. What was THAT. He KEPT Looking AT ME, NOT LIKE A TRINITY MEMBER, BUT TYPE OF GUY #3: NICE. I DON'T KNOW WHAT TO MAKE OF THAT. SO I DECIDED TO WALK OVER TO THAT TAVERN.

I STAND BACK BY THE TREES AND WATCH THE COUPLES COME AND GO FROM THE CLUB TO THEIR CARS. THE PARKING LOT IS WHERE THE ACTION IS. There's ALWAYS A FIGHT BETWEEN 2 DRUNKS OVER A GIRL, AT LEAST ONE A NIGHT. MOSTLY WHAT GOES ON IS STUMBLING ABOUT AND MAKING OUT.

The CROWD IS A BIT OLDER THAN ME, WITH DIFFERENT HAIRSTYLES. GREASY HAIR SLICKED BACK FOR THE BOYS, AND THE GIRLS WEAR CHIFFON SCARVES OVER THEIR BIG BOUFFANTS. ROCK AND ROLL AND ELVIS — NO BRITISH. THEY COME OUT FROM CHICAGO WITH SOUPED-UP CARS AND ON MOTORCYCLES. HOT RODS. THEY DON'T GIVE A DARN ABOUT US HAVING TO PUT UP WITH THE NOISE AND KNOCKED OVER MAILBOXES. (IT'S HAPPENED SO MUCH TO THE SAPKOS, THEY KEEP IT PERMANENTLY ON THEIR CHORES LIST. 'SET-THE-MAILBOX-BACK-UP'). THEY'VE CRASHED INTO FENCES, YARDS, AND GARAGES. Thankfully, THIS TAVERN IS NOT NEXT TO OUR HOUSE. HOW COULD WE GET ANY SLEEP? OF COURSE DURING THE SUMMER AND ON HOT NIGHTS ESPECIALLY, IT'S A BIG PROBLEM.

So I HIDE AND OBSERVE THE GREASY GUYS AND

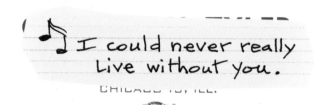

♪ I could never really
Live without you.

GALLOU-SHUS GIRLS KISSING AND THROWING THEMSELVES
ACROSS THE HOODS OF CARS, ROLLING ABOUT. IT'S FUNNY
AND THRILLING. SMOOCH SMOOCH PUSH THE BOY AWAY.
I HEAR LOTS OF PLEADING FROM THE BOYS AND GIVING IN
BY THE GIRLS, UNDER HALF-HEARTED PROTEST. I CAN'T
SEE EVERYTHING FROM MY VANTAGE POINT, AND I DON'T
LIKE STANDING THERE LIKE A CREEP, SO I KEEP IT SHORT.
ON THE WAY HOME, IN MY HEAD TONIGHT THERE'S A SONG
PLAYING IN MY HEAD.

"I dont e-ven know how-w
to L-LO-O-Ve e-you-oo-oo.
Just the way -- you want me
To-o-o.

But I'm Ready
To Learn
Yes I'm Ready
To Learn
To fall in love with e-you-oo.

"I don't even know how to Kiss Your Lips.
at a moment like this."

WELL, MY SLICKER LIPS ARE
READY, AND I'M —————— READY
TO LEARN.

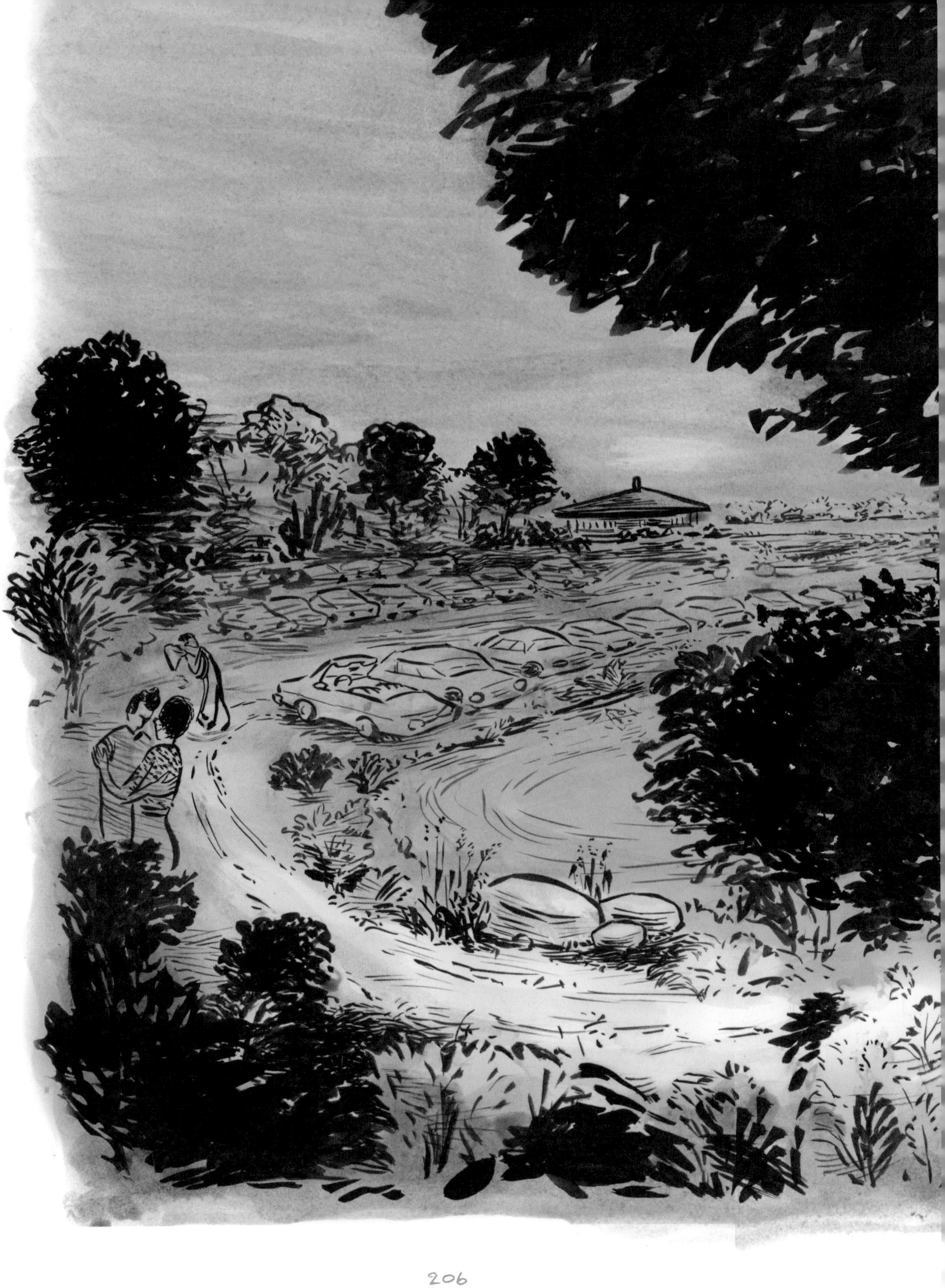

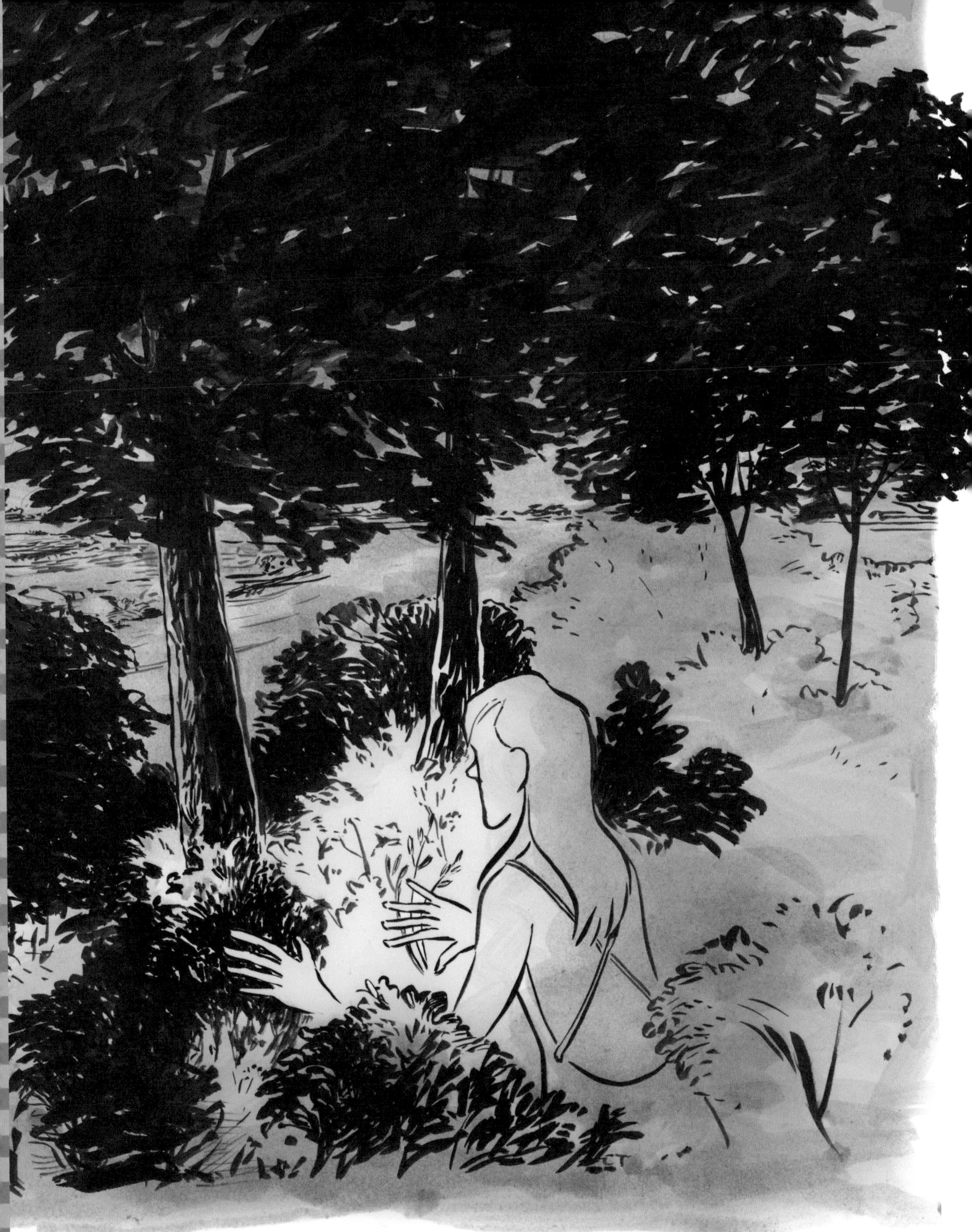

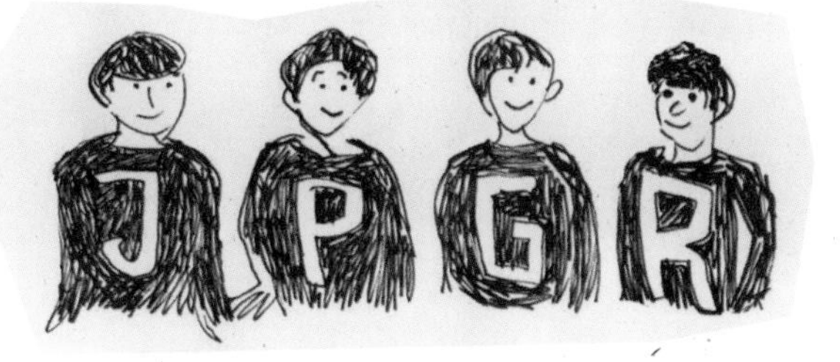
J
P
G
R

AUG. 14

Last NIGHT, Friday August 13 (Friday the 13th) I HAD a 'WEEK BEFORE THE CONCERT' Party. Janet, Barbara, and I. Laurie was SUPPOSED TO COME, BUT SHE GOT A LAST MINUTE CALL TO BABYSIT AT HER AUNT'S HOUSE. ANYWAY, BACK TO THE PARTY. It was REAL FUN. THEY ALL CAME OVER AT 7PM. WE HAD PIZZA AND COKES AND LISTENED TO THE RADIO UP IN MY ROOM. THE GIRLS STAYED OVERNIGHT. BARB BROUGHT A WINDOW SHADE AND WE WROTE "Beatles 4-ever" ON IT. WE USED ALL THE TECHNIQUES SISTER BERNADETTE TAUGHT US. IT'S VERY COLORFUL AND CLEVER. IT WAS SO HOT LAST NIGHT. HOT AND HUMID. WE DON'T HAVE AIR CONDITIONING, BUT WE MANAGED TO GET THROUGH IT.

I CALLED Laurie TO DISCUSS THE SITUATION WITH Jamie. SHE SAYS HE LIKES ME. I don't believe THAT FOR A MINUTE. I DON'T KNOW WHERE IN MY HEAD TO PUT THAT THOUGHT. HE'S JOE'S FRIEND AND THEY ARE A BUNCH OF IDIOTS. IT WAS HARD TO SLEEP, ALL SWEATY AND THINKING ABOUT THIS.

Everyone GOT UP LATE AND WANTED BREAKFAST ANYWAY. THAT'S WHAT CORNFLAKES ARE FOR. JANET AND BARBARA LEFT AT NOON. Laurie was GOING TO COME OVER, BUT I WAS FEELING QUEASY. UNEASY. DOWNRIGHT YUCKY. I HATE WASTING A DAY LIKE THIS. I WAS PLANNING ON BUILDING UP MY TAN. UGH – I'm going to bed.

SICK.

?ASK ME WHY

KEEP YOUR SHOES ON. THERE'S BROKEN BOTTLES AND OLD BEER CANS —
PROTECT YOUR DOGS NO MATTER WHAT!
... AND DON'T RUB UP AGAINST THE PIER. MIGHT GET A BLOOD SUCKER ON YOU.
BOY DO I HATE THIS BATHING CAP!
STOP IT, JIMMY. GO BE WITH YOUR LITTLE FRIENDS!
HA HA

YOU'RE GONNA LOSE THAT GIRL

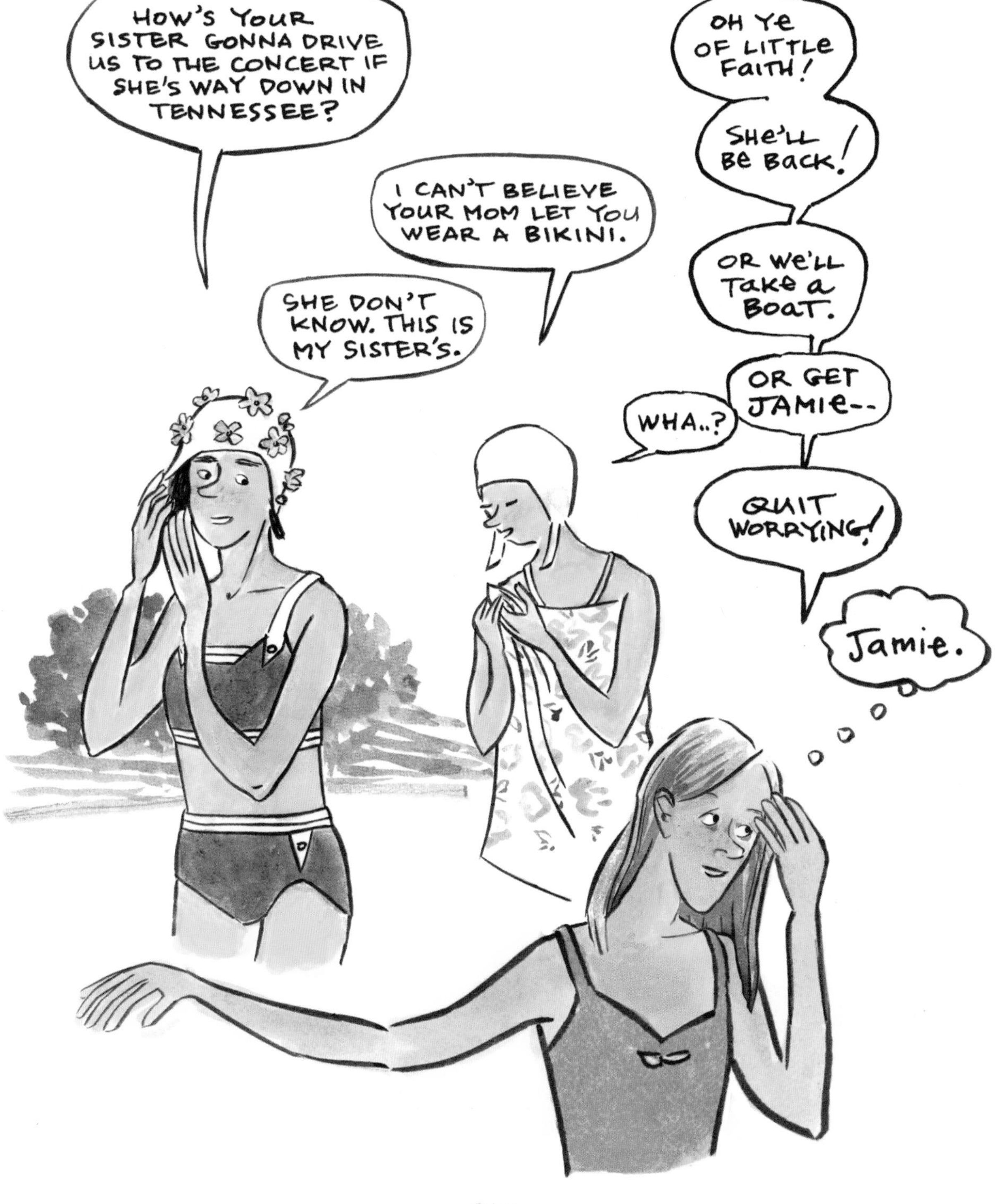
HOW'S YOUR SISTER GONNA DRIVE US TO THE CONCERT IF SHE'S WAY DOWN IN TENNESSEE?
I CAN'T BELIEVE YOUR MOM LET YOU WEAR A BIKINI.
SHE DON'T KNOW. THIS IS MY SISTER'S.
OH YE OF LITTLE FAITH!
SHE'LL BE BACK!
OR WE'LL TAKE A BOAT.
OR GET JAMIE--
WHA..?
QUIT WORRYING!
Jamie.

CHARLES W. TYLER

PLUMBING CONTRACTOR

1837 WEST ADDISON ST.

CHICAGO 13, ILL.

AUG. 16

Feeling much better now after a good night's sleep. It must have been the 24 hr. flu. I felt really bad just after they left. Too hot to be sick.

Today was rainy. Jamie came over, but I don't know when he got here because I slept in. Ginia and Joe came home yesterday, finally the car is back. They were down there 4 extra days. Lots of stories to tell. They went cave exploring, rock climbing, and touristing up at Lookout Mountain. Glenda went with them. Boy did they have a good time. On one of the days — the day that they all happened to be wearing madras shirts, they got caught in a downpour with the top down. Luckily, they got a picture of this — colorful drowned rats. So we're going we're going now up to town to get the pictures developed. I gotta see that one.

Later — I was able to get my roll of film back. Pictures taken of my Beatleish room. I asked them to develop them even if they were a trifle too fuzzy. Dad's bellows camera has a light leak. We had picked up Laurie and went around town looking for Beatles hats or jockey style hats or whatever you might call them. I bought some clay for sculpting and also Jimmy's birthday presents. By the way, his birthday was the 9th. I got him scissors, tape, crayons, paste, and a pencil case — for kindergarten. He wrote me a thank you note. 'KNAHT CURAOYL.'

4 MORE DAYS!

Another Girl

Hooray!

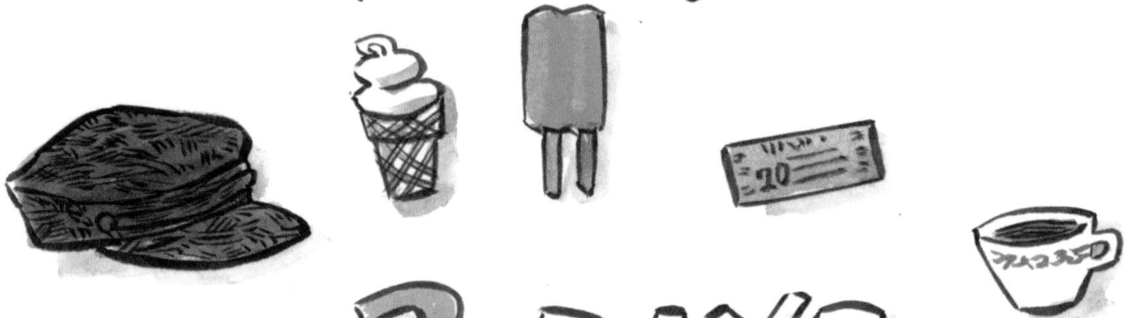

3 DAYS 2 GO!

♪ on the HELP album:

1. HELP
2. The Night Before
3. You've Got to Hide Your Love Away
4. I Need You
5. Another Girl
6. You're Going to Lose that Girl
7. Ticket to Ride

♪ on The Charts:

1. I Got You Babe
2. Satisfaction
3. California Girls
4. What's New Pussycat
5. HELP!

(and it's moving UP)

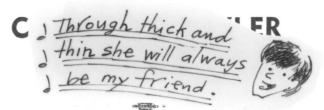

C **Through thick and thin she will always be my friend.**

AUGUST 17

It's TUESDAY. LAST NIGHT WAS THUNDERING SO LOUD IT WOKE ME UP. I THOUGHT SOMETHING EXPLODED. MY PICTURE WINDOW SHOOK SO MUCH, I WENT IN BY JIM. EVENTUALLY I CAME BACK TO MY OWN BED. I GOT UP THIS MORNING AT 10:30, AND AS ALWAYS, THE Beatles WERE LOOKING DOWN AT ME. No matter WHERE I'M AT IN MY ROOM, THEY'RE WATCHING WITH BIG SMILES. I LOVE THEM SO MUCH. ABOUT 1:30, AFTER WATCHING "Action," GINIA, JIMMY, HER HIGH SCHOOL FRIEND MARIJANE AND YOURS TRULY WENT UP TO TOWN. I BOUGHT AN ICE CREAM CONE, A POPSICLE, AND A HAT Finally. FINALLY FOUND WHAT I WANT. It's A DARK GREEN CRINKLED-UP LEATHER JOCKEY OR BEATLE STYLE HAT, THE ICE CREAM WAS WHITE, AND THE POPSICLE WAS RED. COLORFUL! I HAD TO BABYSIT THE SAPKOS FROM 3:30 – 5:30 (THEY'RE BACK. THEIR GRANDMOTHER COULDN'T STAND THEM). THEN I CAME HOME AND WASHED MY HAIR. I MADE A DUPLICATE OF MY BEATLE CONCERT TICKET. Maybe I CAN START A COUNTERFEITING RING AND MAKE A FORTUNE. MY TICKET IS GREEN. PLUS I HAD COCOA. (WHY IN THE World WOULD I Have Cocoa ON A Hot Day?) OH WELL. It TAKES ALL KINDS TO MAKE THE WORLD. TODAY, I WATCHED T.V. — TOO MUCH. 3 MORE DAYS! I'M GETTING ANTSY. AND WHAT I WROTE YESTERDAY WAS STUPID BECAUSE I WAS TIRED. I'M TIRED NOW, TOO. I GUESS I'LL NEVER GET CAUGHT UP ON MY SLEEP. NOT IF IT'S STORMY! So excited. So much left to DO!!!

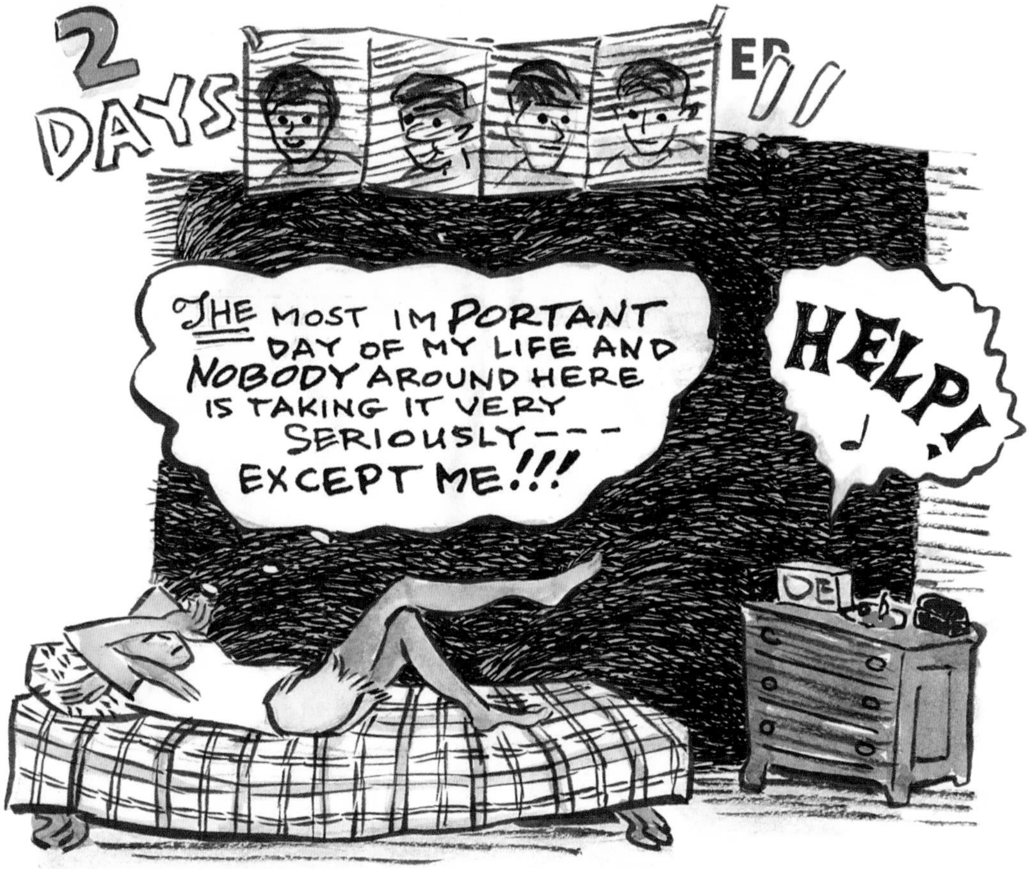
2 DAYS
THE MOST IMPORTANT DAY OF MY LIFE AND NOBODY AROUND HERE IS TAKING IT VERY SERIOUSLY--- EXCEPT ME!!!
HELP!
DE

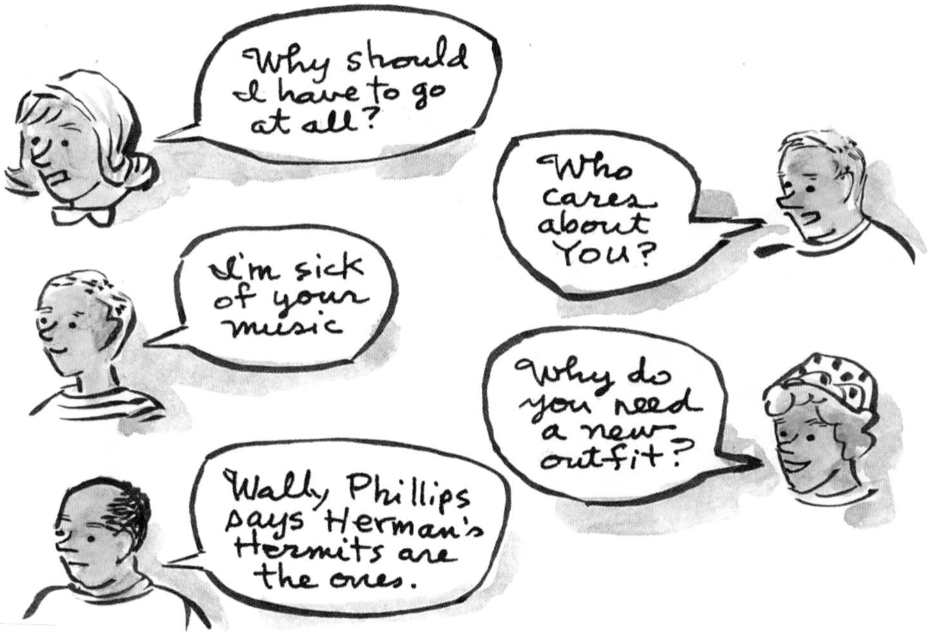
Why should I have to go at all?
Who cares about YOU?
I'm sick of your music
Why do you need a new outfit?
Wally Phillips says Herman's Hermits are the ones.

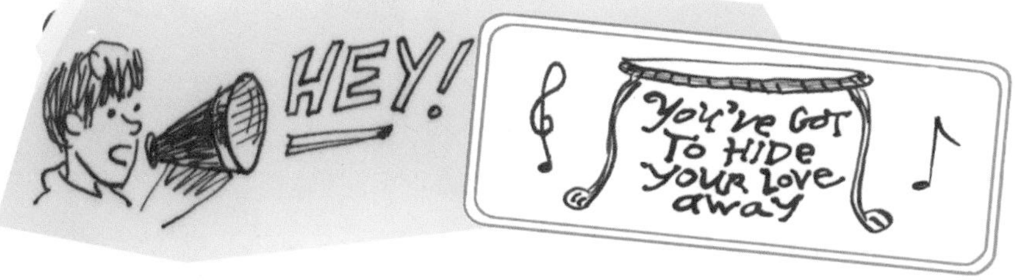
HEY!
You've Got To Hide Your Love away

AUG. 18 Today is Wednesday. I HAD a BUSY day. GOT UP THIS MORNING AT 9:00 TO THE SOUND OF THUNDER. We HAD WAFFLES. JUST THINK = THIS TIME AUG 20, 2 DAYS FROM NOW IS THE DAY.

Me AND Ginia and Laurie AND Jim AND Mom WENT TO Helen Domas' HOUSE IN LIBERTYVILLE FOR a LUNCHEON IN GINIA'S HONOR. Helen IS ONE OF THE CLUB GIRLS. THEY MEET EVERY MONTH AND HAVE SOME SORT OF HOY-FELOY TYPE THING. (HOW DO YOU SPELL THAT WORD?) We WERE GOING TO GO TO WARDS AND PICK UP THE DRESS I ORDERED SO I COULD WEAR IT TO THE LUNCHEON, BUT THEN WE FOUND OUT IT WASN'T GOING TO ARRIVE UNTIL August 30! IT'S TIME TO SHOP FOR ANOTHER DRESS, SHOES, AND PURSE. 2 DAYS TO GO AND I STILL DON'T HAVE a DRESS. TOMORROW IS THE DECIDED DAY TO GO. PRETTY MUCH. THERE'S NO DAYS LEFT.

Helen's HOUSE WAS THE RITZ. FANCY AND EXPENSIVE FURNISHINGS. LUNCH WAS ON THE LAWN, IT WAS SO LOVELY. THERE WERE WAITERS.

After THE FANCY LUNCH, I WENT TO Laurie's HOUSE AND SHE MADE ME GO TO 4-H. Laurie's LIKE ME, NO DRESS YET. What are we DOING AT 4-H? I DROPPED OUT LAST YEAR. NEEDED TO DEVOTE TIME TO MY WALLS AND TO MY MUSIC.

We ARE LEAVING FIRST THING TO GO SHOPPING SO I'D BETTER GET TO BED. I'M GETTING UP AT 7 TO WATCH G.T. 5 - EIGHT DAYS IN SPACE. It's LAUNCHING INTO ORBIT. Write MORE TOMORROW. Can't wait!

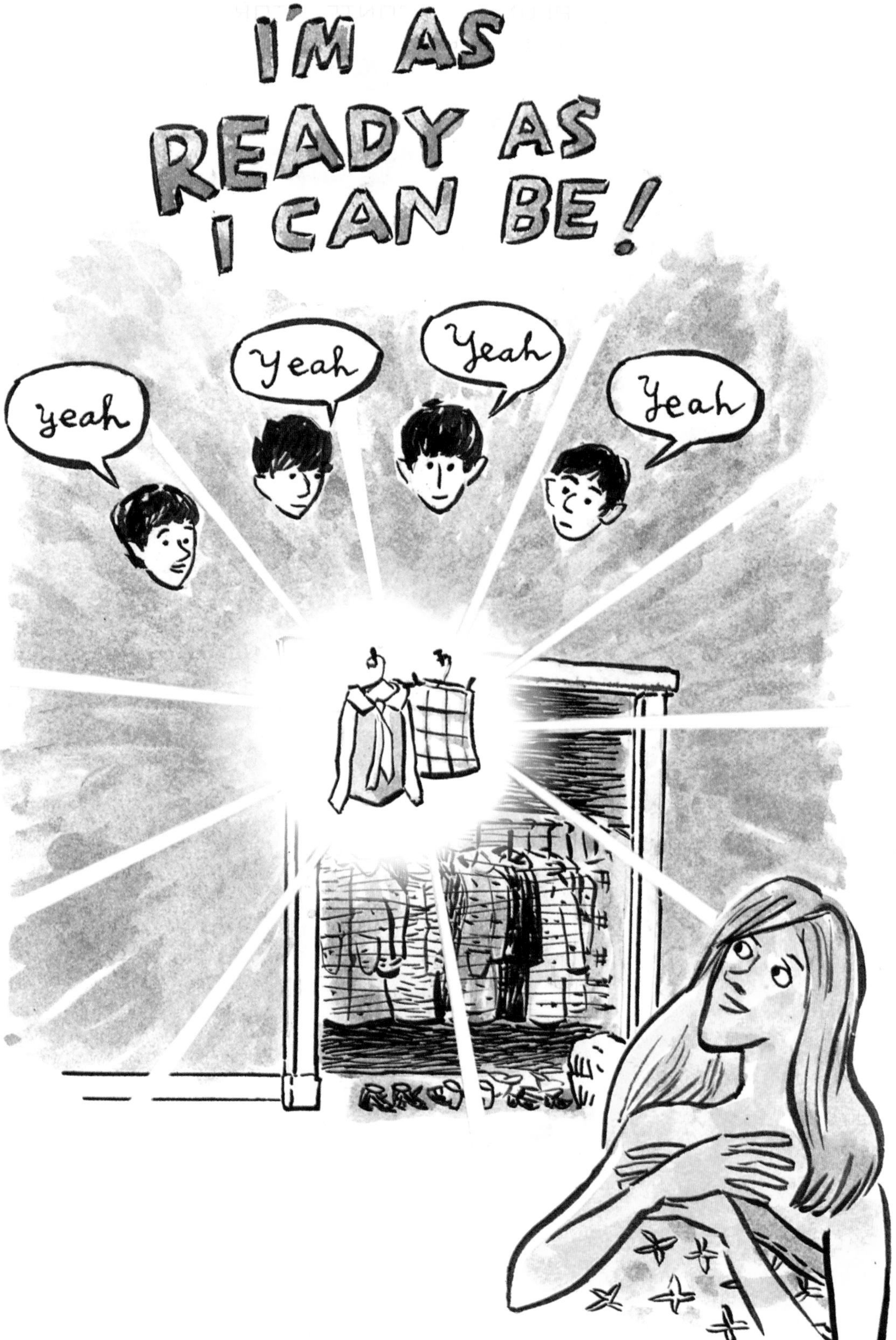
I'M AS READY AS I CAN BE!
yeah
Yeah
Yeah
Yeah

The Night Before

AUG 19

It's THURSDAY. THE DAY BEFORE THE CONCERT. ONE MORE DAY. Finally, I GOT MY DRESS TO SEE MY BOYS IN. IT HAS A GREEN, AND GRAY, AND BLACK PLAID STRAIGHT SKIRT, WITH A LONG SLEEVED, FULLY LINED WHITE CHIFFON BLOUSE AND A GREEN VEST-JAC. THE BLOUSE HAS TIES THAT COME OUT. I GOT BLACK SHOES WITH ONE INCH STACKED HEELS WITH A T-STRAP AND HOLES. LITTLE HOLES. (STILL HAD TO PAY FOR THE WHOLE SHOE, HA HA). I HAVE MY GREEN CRINKLED UP LEATHER HAT, BLACK SHOULDER BAG, AND THAT'S IT. THAT'S MY OUTFIT.

WE HAD MADE THAT BIG BEATLES-4-EVER SIGN. TO HIDE IT SO WE CAN TAKE IT INTO THE SHOW WITH US, WE ROLLED IT UP ON A CANE AND PUT MATERIAL OVER IT SO THAT IT LOOKS LIKE AN UMBRELLA. IT'S A CINCH TO GET THROUGH. OH I FORGOT — I GOT MY DRESS AT ROBERT HALL. $8.97. NOT BAD, HUH?

We TOOK LAURIE AND HER MOM TO GET MATERIAL FOR HER DRESS. SOMETHING LIKE MINE. She IS GOING TO BE UP ALL NIGHT.

At MY HOUSE, THE TRINITY DECIDED THEY NEEDED DANCE LESSONS. THEY BROUGHT JOHN AND HANK OVER FROM THE TEAM. PRACTICING TO IMPRESS THE GIRLS. FUNNY! BIG GUYS WHO DON'T KNOW HOW TO DANCE. RUDY IS CHICKEN. BUT JAMIE — — I'D BEEN TEACHING HIM TO DANCE ALL ALONG. HE AND I HAD A LOT OF LAUGHS, DANCING THE NIGHT AWAY. EVERYBODY HIT THE LAKE, THEN I HIT THE SACK. BIG DAY TOMORROW.

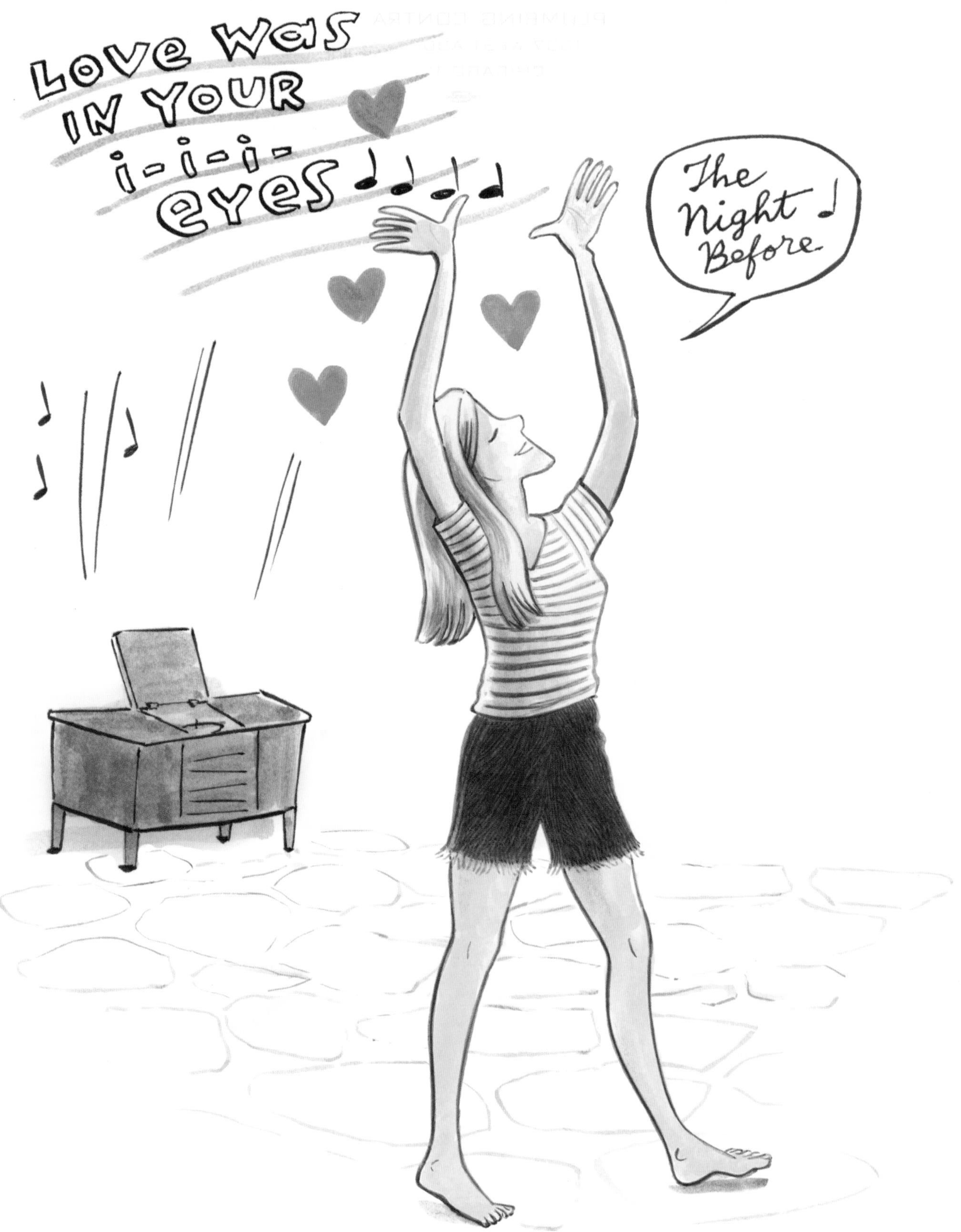
Love was in your i-i-i-eyes
The Night Before

4. 37 M/M

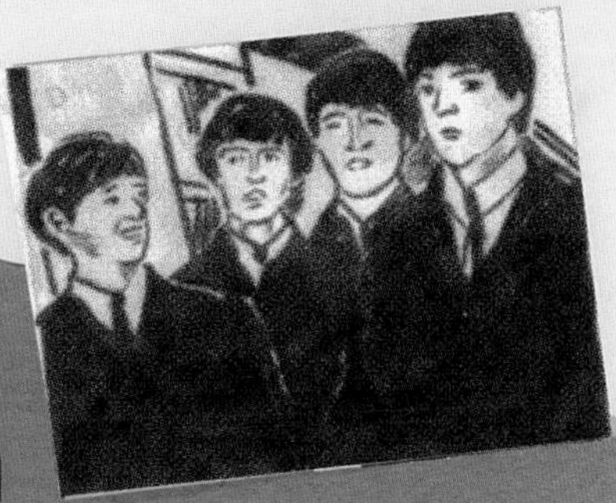

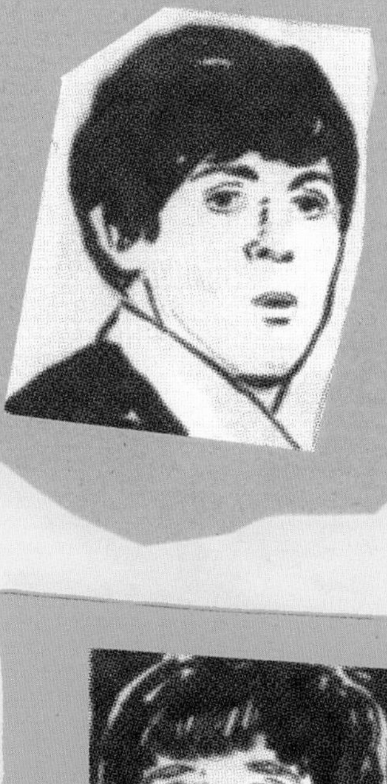

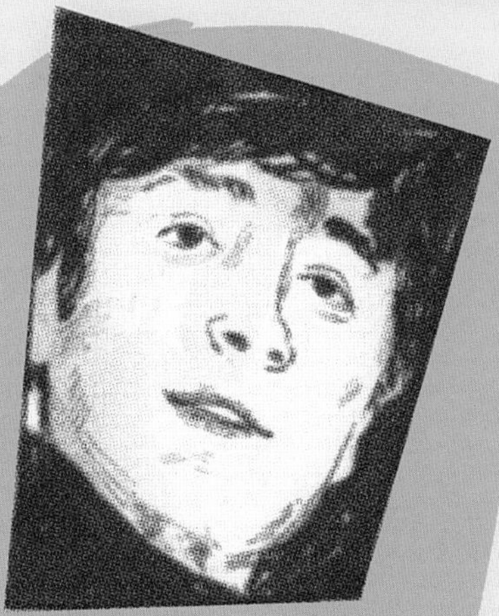

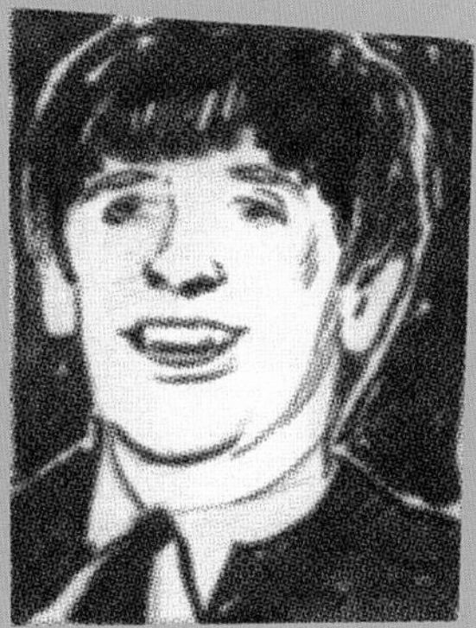

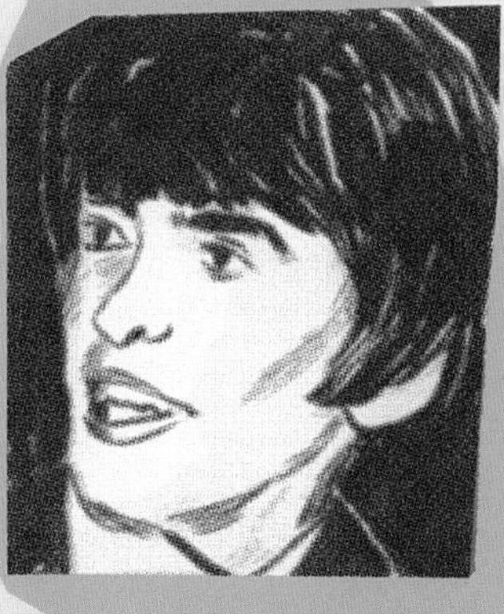

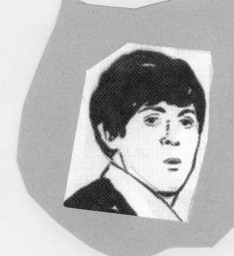

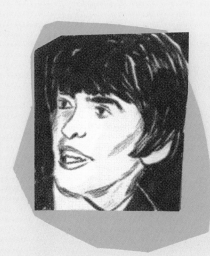

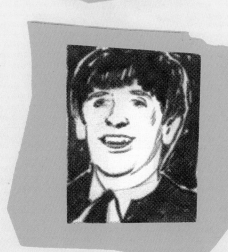

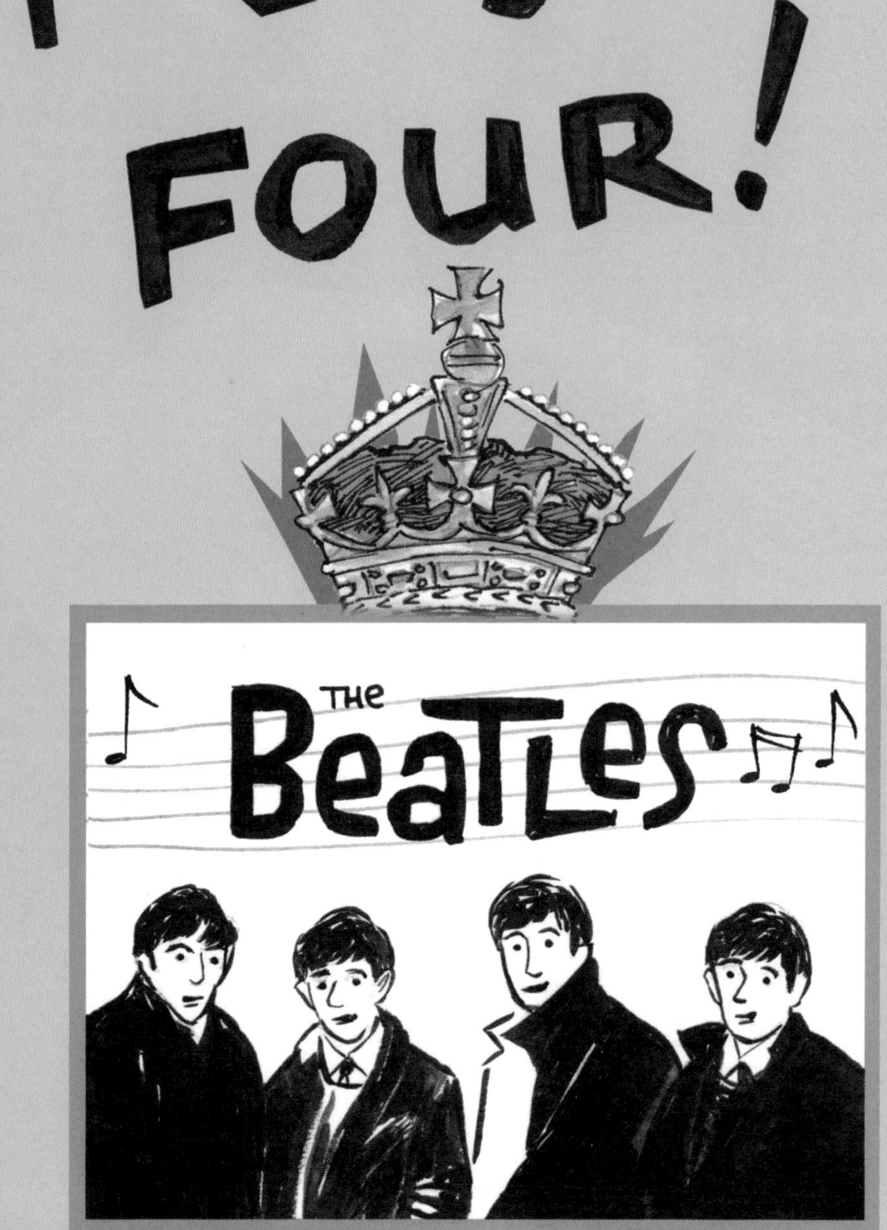
1-2-3-
FOUR!
THE
BEATLES

37 Minutes of Madness

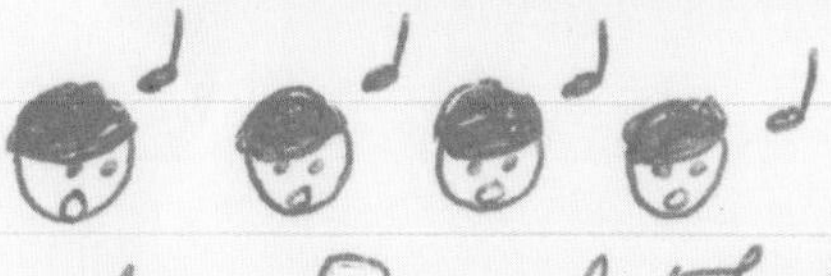

by Carol Tyler

Written ~~in~~ the day after all the excitement of the Beatles concert Friday evening August 20, 1965. Though it will not win the Pulitzer Prize, it is a little account of seeing the Beatles live in concert, right here in Chicago, Illinois, U.S.A.

I dedicate this to Ginia who spent her time to take us all the way down to White Sox Park, and who was so nice to put up with us yah-hoos.

AUG. 20, 1965
is finally HERE!

I got up about 10. I didn't feel good at all yesterday and couldn't get to sleep. Just ate a bowl of corn flakes. No time to write. So much to do. 9 hours until the concert. I can't believe it. The greatest day of my life is here!

AUG 21. I couldn't write anything last night because we didn't get home until 4 in the morning. So here is a recounting of the events. It really was the greatest day ever, which is why I'm using a red pen.

Started getting dressed about 2:00. Barbara was to come over at 2:30 and we were gonna leave about 3:00. Barb came on time and Laurie came at 10 to 3. We left to pick up Janet and Kathy Reardon. (She will be in 8th grade at St. Joe's in Round Lake. Ginia works with her Mom.)

We got to Chicago about 5:00 and parked

GLORIOUS ARRIVAL

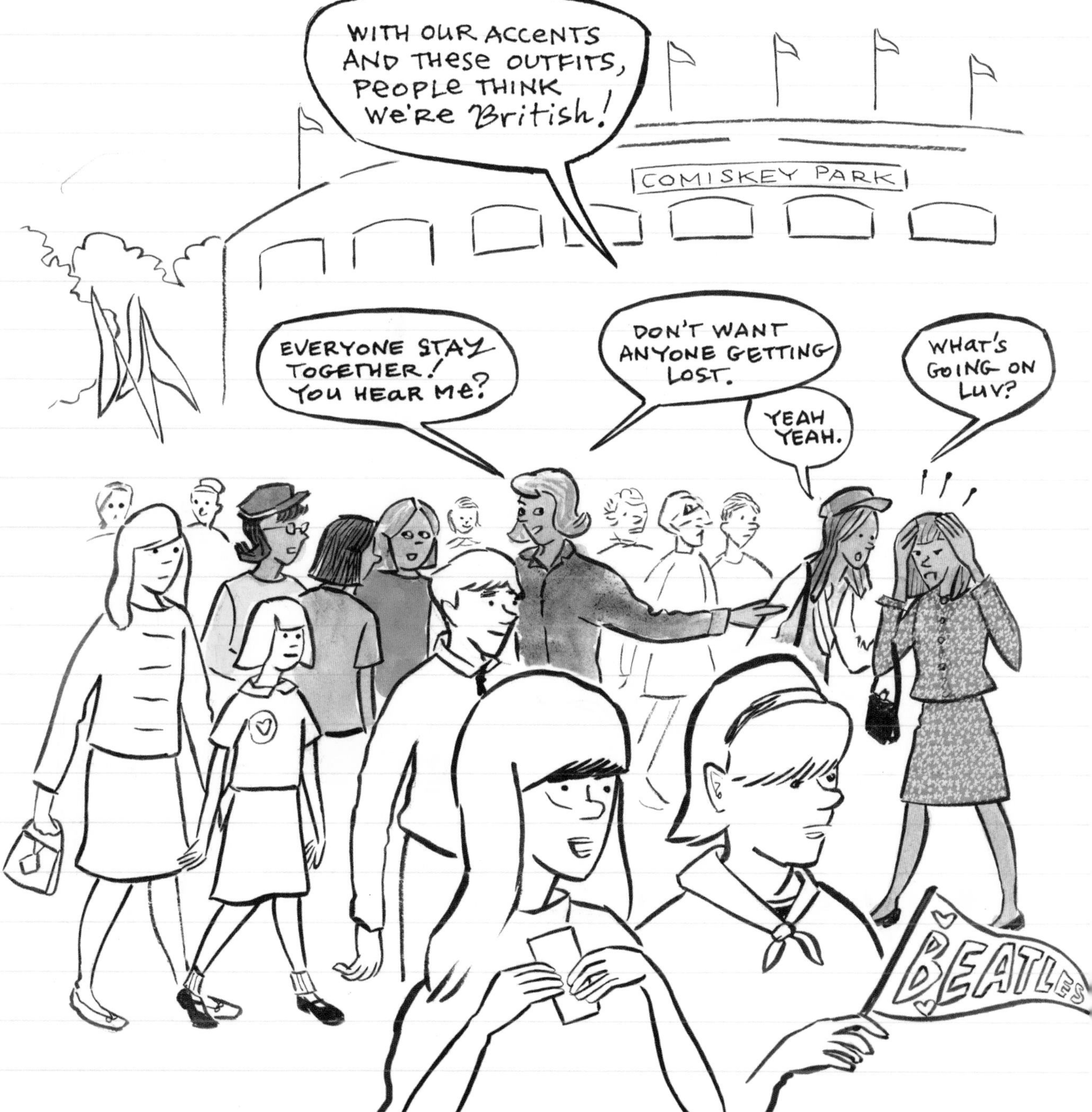
WITH OUR ACCENTS AND THESE OUTFITS, PEOPLE THINK WE'RE British!
COMISKEY PARK
EVERYONE STAY TOGETHER! YOU HEAR ME?
DON'T WANT ANYONE GETTING LOST.
YEAH YEAH.
WHAT'S GOING ON LUV?
BEATLES

next to my Grandmother's house on Eddy St. That's one block from the Addison St. "L" station. We caught the train at 5:15. We got to Sox Park by subway at 6:15.

You have to walk ~~one~~ two blocks from the subway to the ballpark. Those two blocks are described like this: Every 10 feet there was a Chicago policeman. In between, there were men selling Beatle pins, books, pictures, packages, penants, posters, oil paintings punch balls, buttons, necklaces, bracelets, and rings.

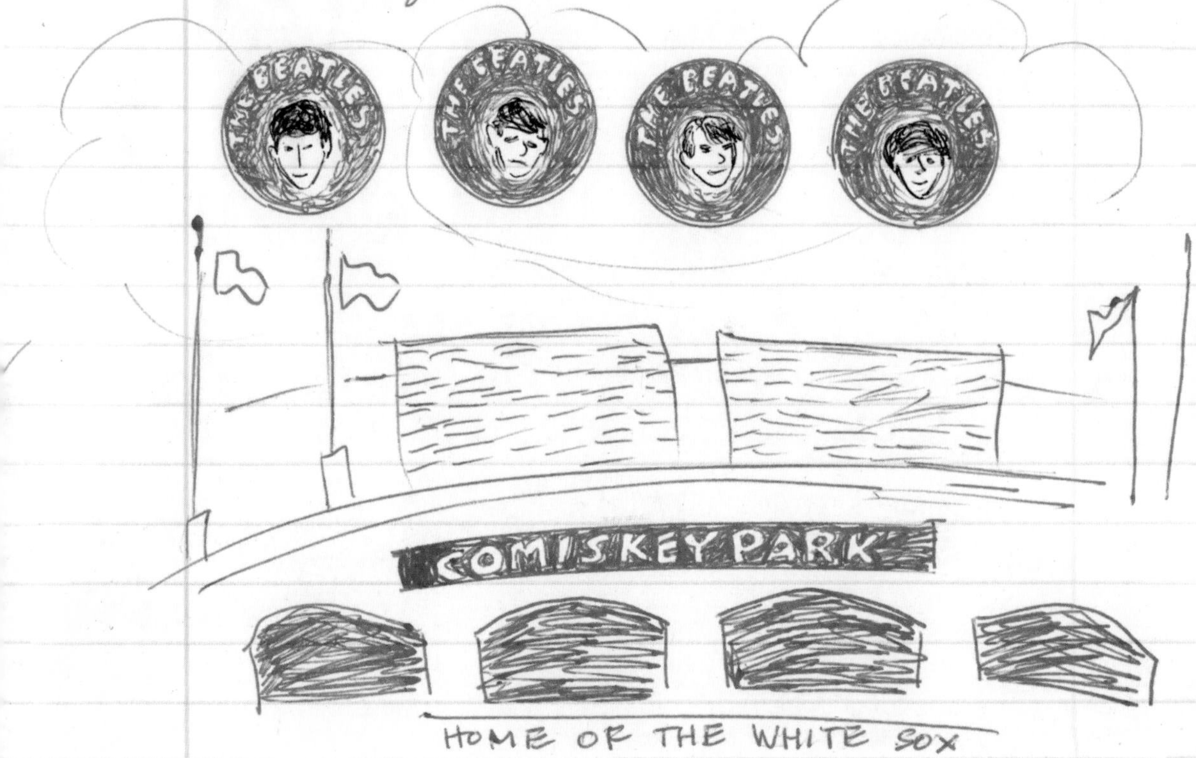
THE BEATLES
THE BEATLES
THE BEATLES
THE BEATLES
COMISKEY PARK
HOME OF THE WHITE SOX

STRICKEN

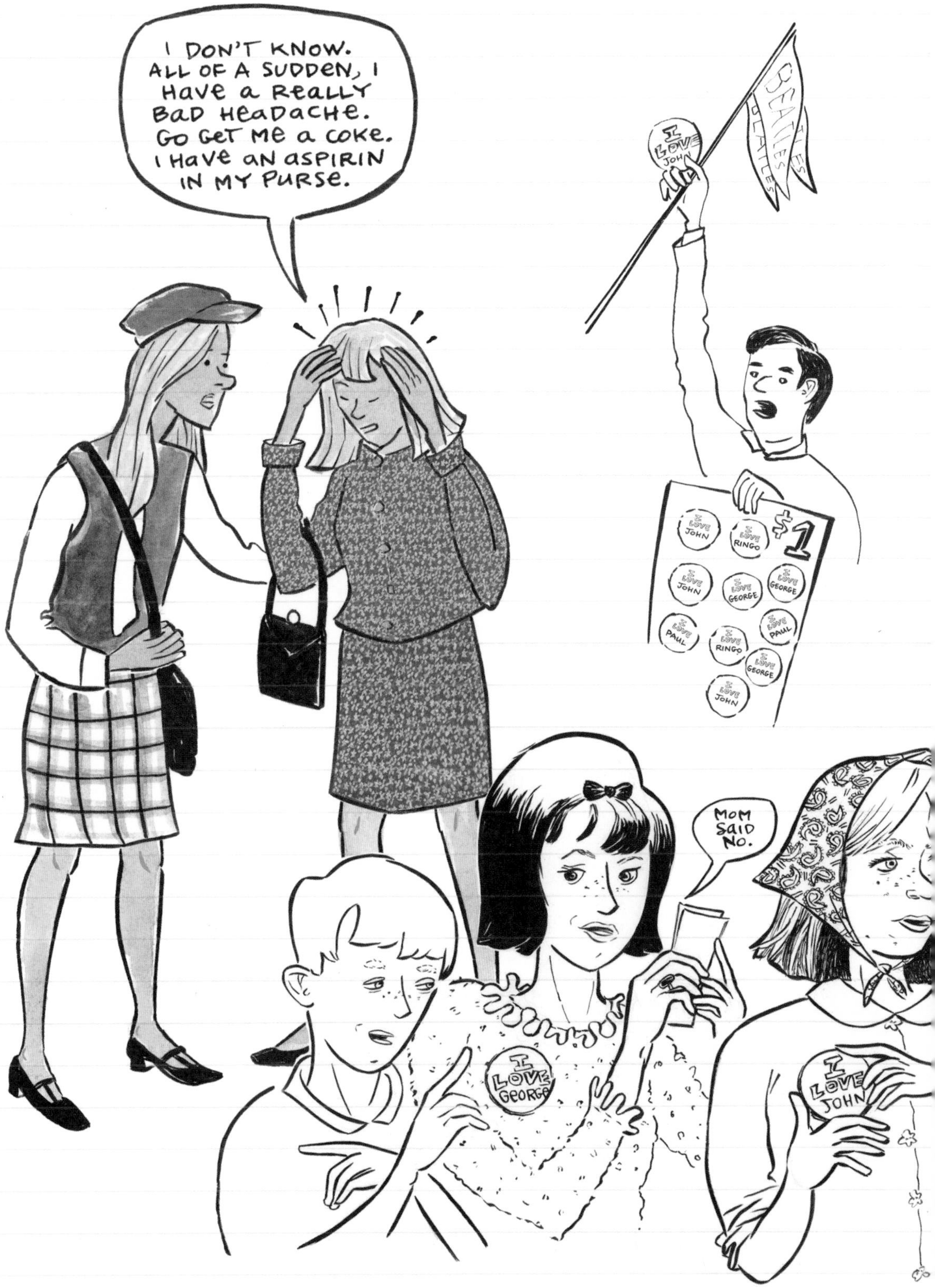

I DON'T KNOW. ALL OF A SUDDEN, I HAVE A REALLY BAD HEADACHE. GO GET ME A COKE. I HAVE AN ASPIRIN IN MY PURSE.
I LOVE JOHN
BEATLES
BEATLES
I LOVE JOHN
I LOVE RINGO
$1
I LOVE JOHN
I LOVE GEORGE
I LOVE GEORGE
I LOVE PAUL
I LOVE RINGO
I LOVE PAUL
I LOVE GEORGE
I LOVE JOHN
MOM SAID NO.
I LOVE GEORGE
I LOVE JOHN

It was such great weather. Just right and not hot like it's been. Perfect! And to think that they were already here in Chicago, breathing the same beautiful air. This was heaven.

The doors didn't open until 6:30. Girls were everywhere. I wanted to buy everything. Not really, but I really did want a penant. Too much money. I did get a pin.

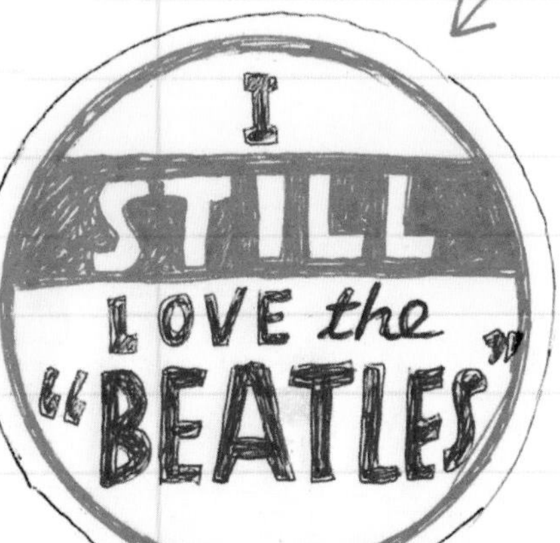
I
STILL
LOVE the
"BEATLES"

There were so many people and it was loud with lots of activity. Everybody was so excited. Laurie started to get a headache. She had to take an aspirin.

There were so many penants. I really wanted one.

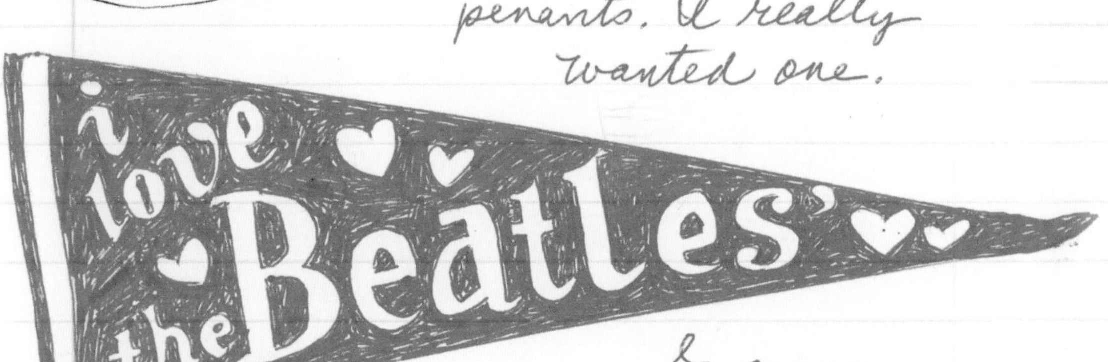
i love
the Beatles

So many faces everywhere!

We waited in line and finally the doors opened. Gate 7. That was us. The man ripped the bottom half of my ticket off. Just like that. I still have the top as a souvenir. I'll have to get used to seeing only half of it. As soon as you gave the man your ticket, you were inside. There was a big guy standing there with another man selling Beatles USA Ltd. Books - for one dollar. I bought one, of course Absolutely everyone had one. It was official.

We had terriffick seats in Sec. 25 Row 17 seats 7-11. I was seat 9. It was about 15 minutes to 7. That means we sat there waiting for the show to start at 8 for one hour and 15 minutes.

There were all these silly guys going by all the time selling stuff. Pepsi. Lemonade

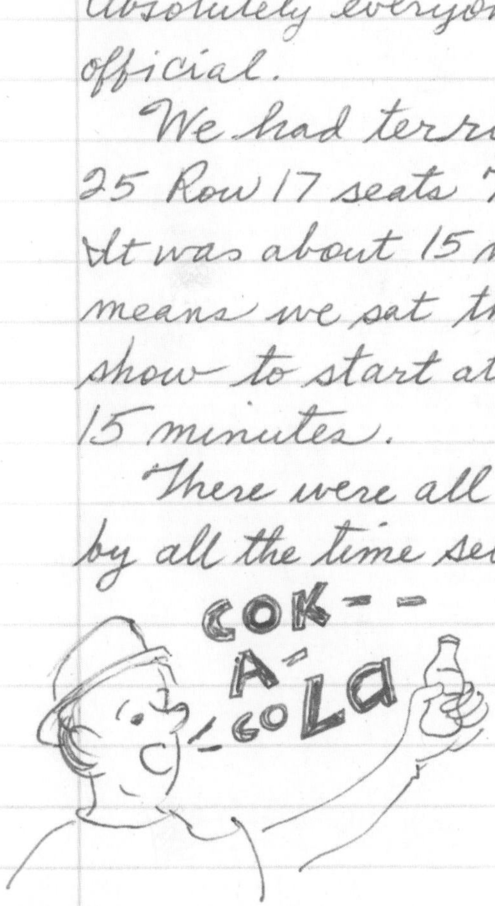
COK--
A-
COLA

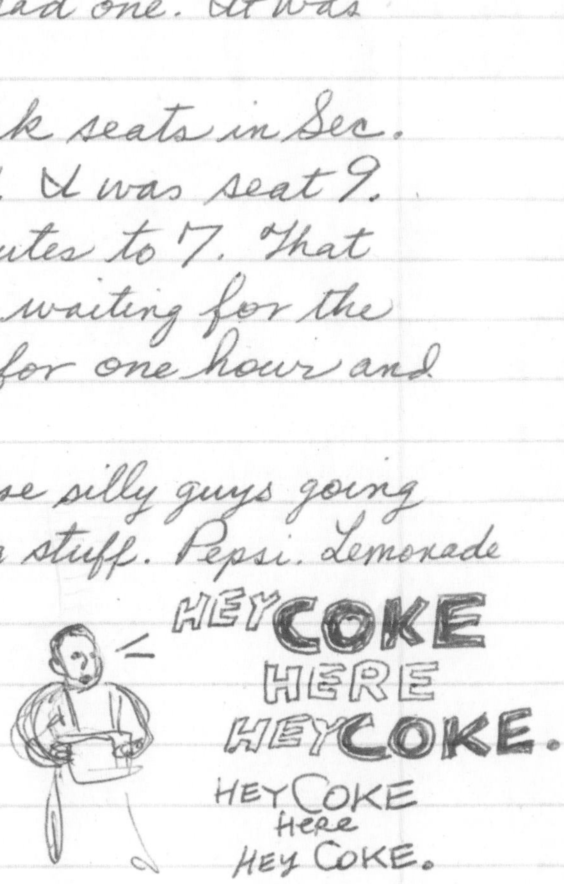
HEY COKE
HERE
HEY COKE.
HEY COKE
Here
HEY COKE.

'ELLO MATE!

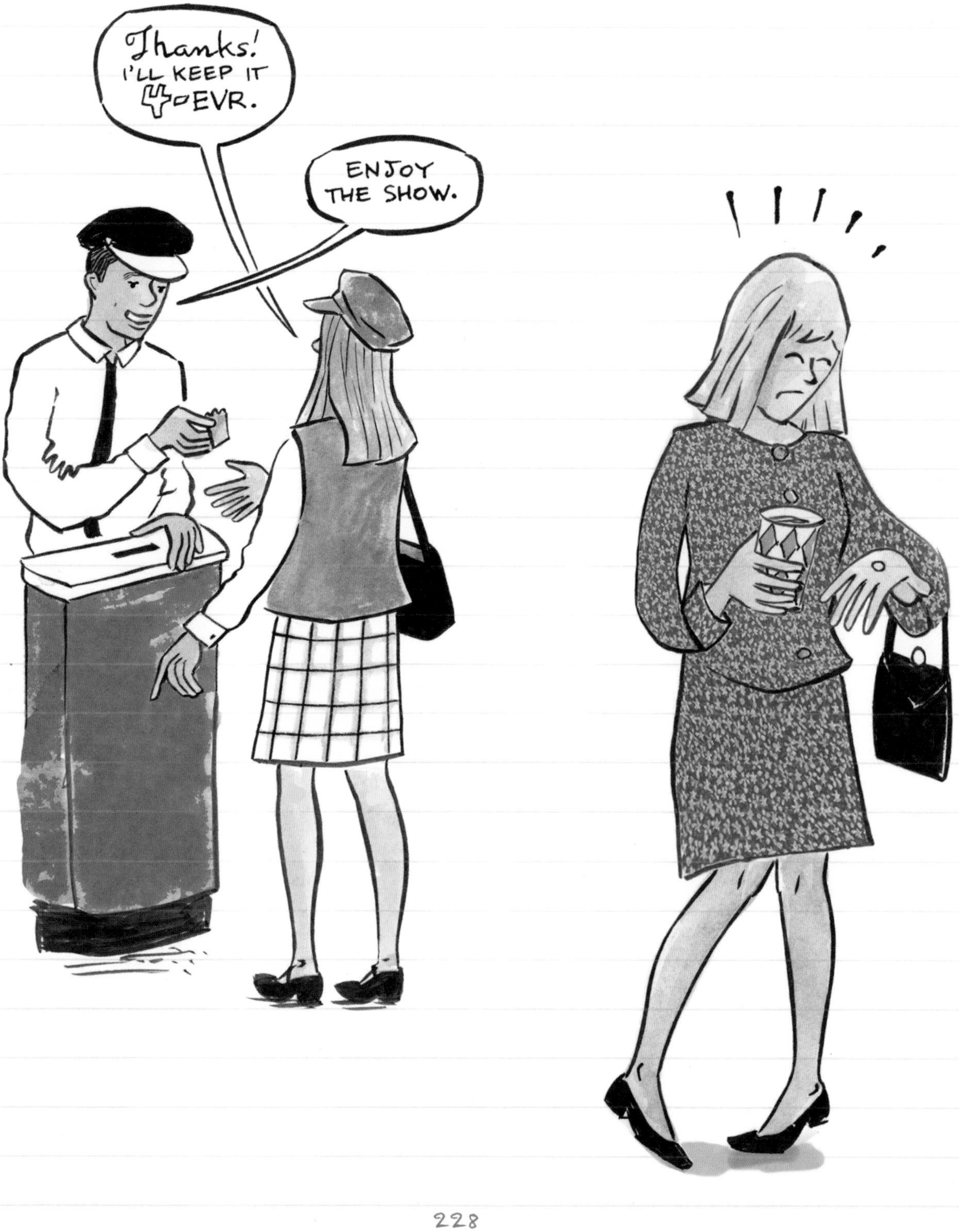
Thanks! I'LL KEEP IT 4-EVR.
ENJOY THE SHOW.

SWEET SPOT

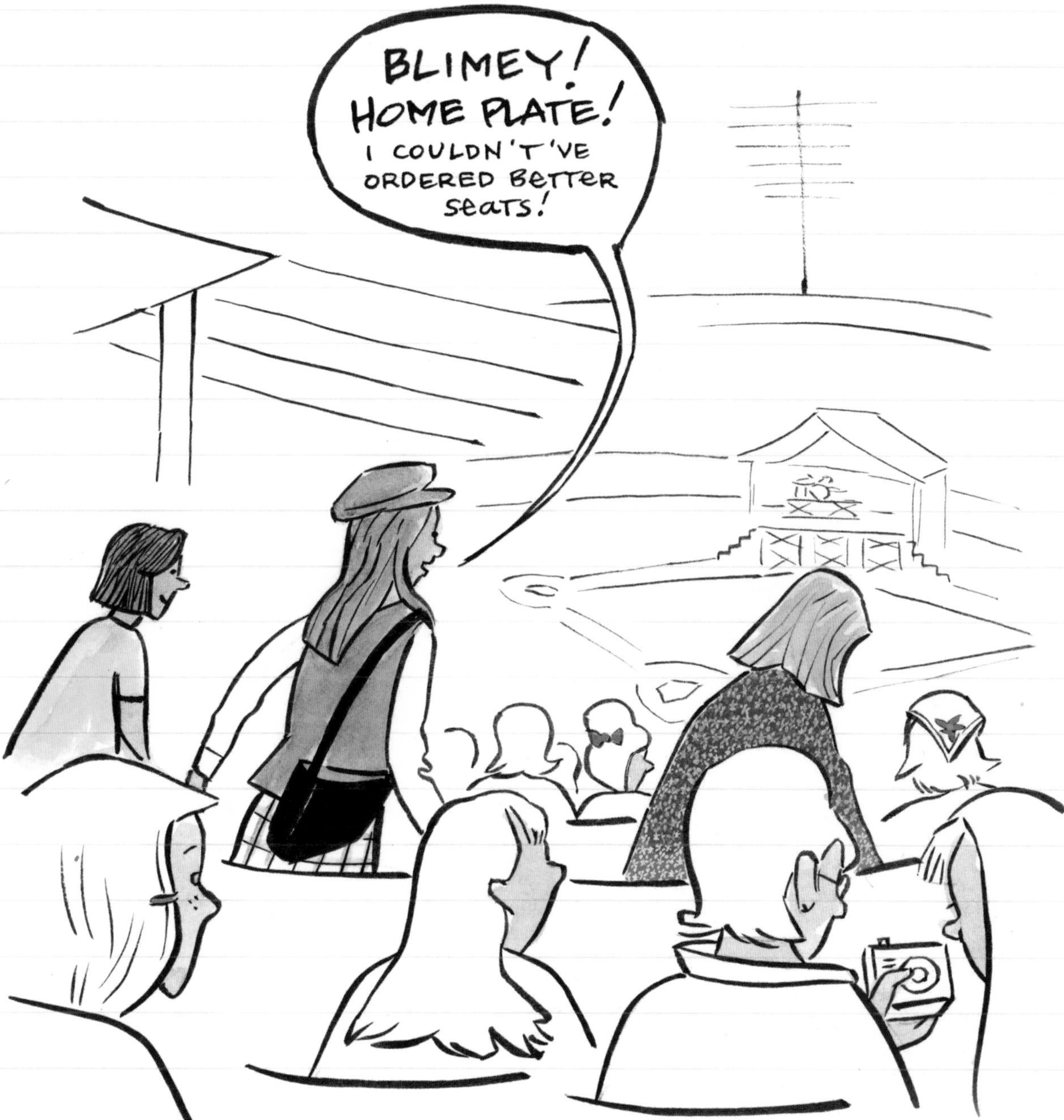
BLIMEY! HOME PLATE! I COULDN'T'VE ORDERED BETTER SEATS!

"$1.00 buys a pair of binoculars! Get your binoculars!" We met a bunch of nice kids who were absolutely great. This one girl let me use her pair and it made everything look right up close. I'd be able to see the Beatles real good.

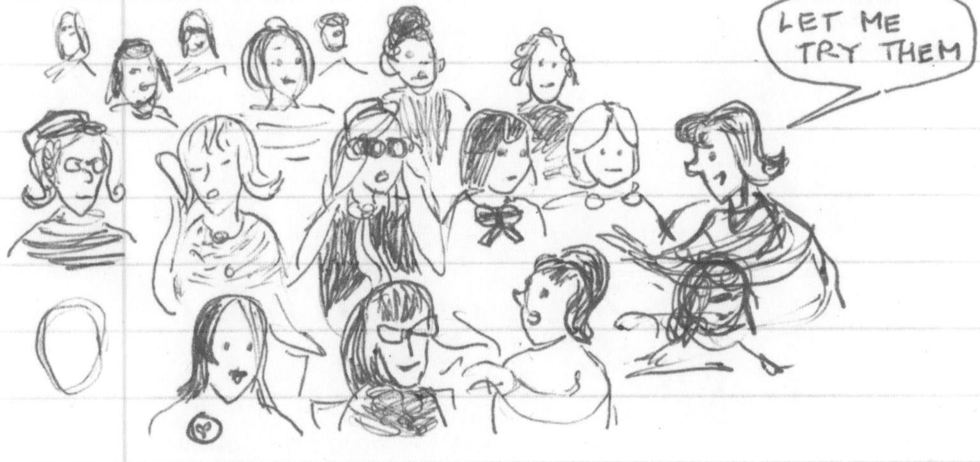
LET ME TRY THEM

Then all of a sudden they turned on the stadium lights. We almost died and the show hadn't even started.

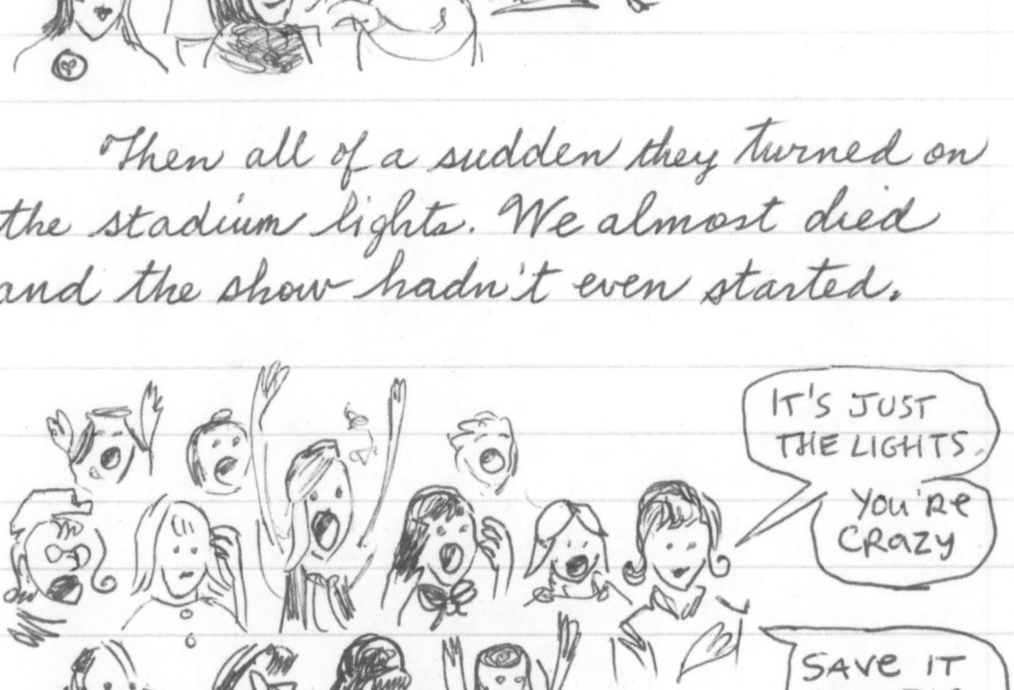
IT'S JUST THE LIGHTS.
YOU'RE CRAZY
SAVE IT FOR THE SHOW.

Finally the show started at 8:00. King Curtis and his Orchestra started out with the Star Spangled Banner. We all stood up and sang along. Then the Discoteque dancers came out on stage and danced to King Curtis. Everybody was squirming. Next up was Cannibal and the Head Hunters. They did their hit "Land of 1000 Dances." Hoo-wee- I knew them all. It was getting dark and the lights made the ballpark beautiful. C&THH are 4 guys who ~~don't~~ JUST sing, they don't have instruments. Then Brenda Holloway came on in a white chiffon flowing dress. God she looked like an angel. She sang with King Curtis's Orchestra. Motown songs. While she was singing, in the dugout to the left of us, there were a bunch of Andy Frain ushers and policemen. Louise Caldwell (George's sister) and Brian Epstein were standing there, too. Brian had a dark suit on with a very calm look on his face. He had his arms folded most of the time. Very business-like.

We were only 17 rows up from home plate, so we could see the dug-out activity pretty well.

Sounds Inc. took over the stage. They got everybody wound-up singing and clapping. They were the last act before the Beatles came on. Everybody was hollering when these policemen came out and Andy Frains started marching forward in a very uniformed manner. Now there was a triple thick wall to try to break through if you wanted to run out there. As soon as we saw the policemen, we knew the Beatles were on the way so we all started screaming "WE WANT THE BEATLES! WE WANT THE BEATLES!" Poor Sounds, Inc. were trying to keep singing with all these girls drowning them out completely.

I'M SCARED

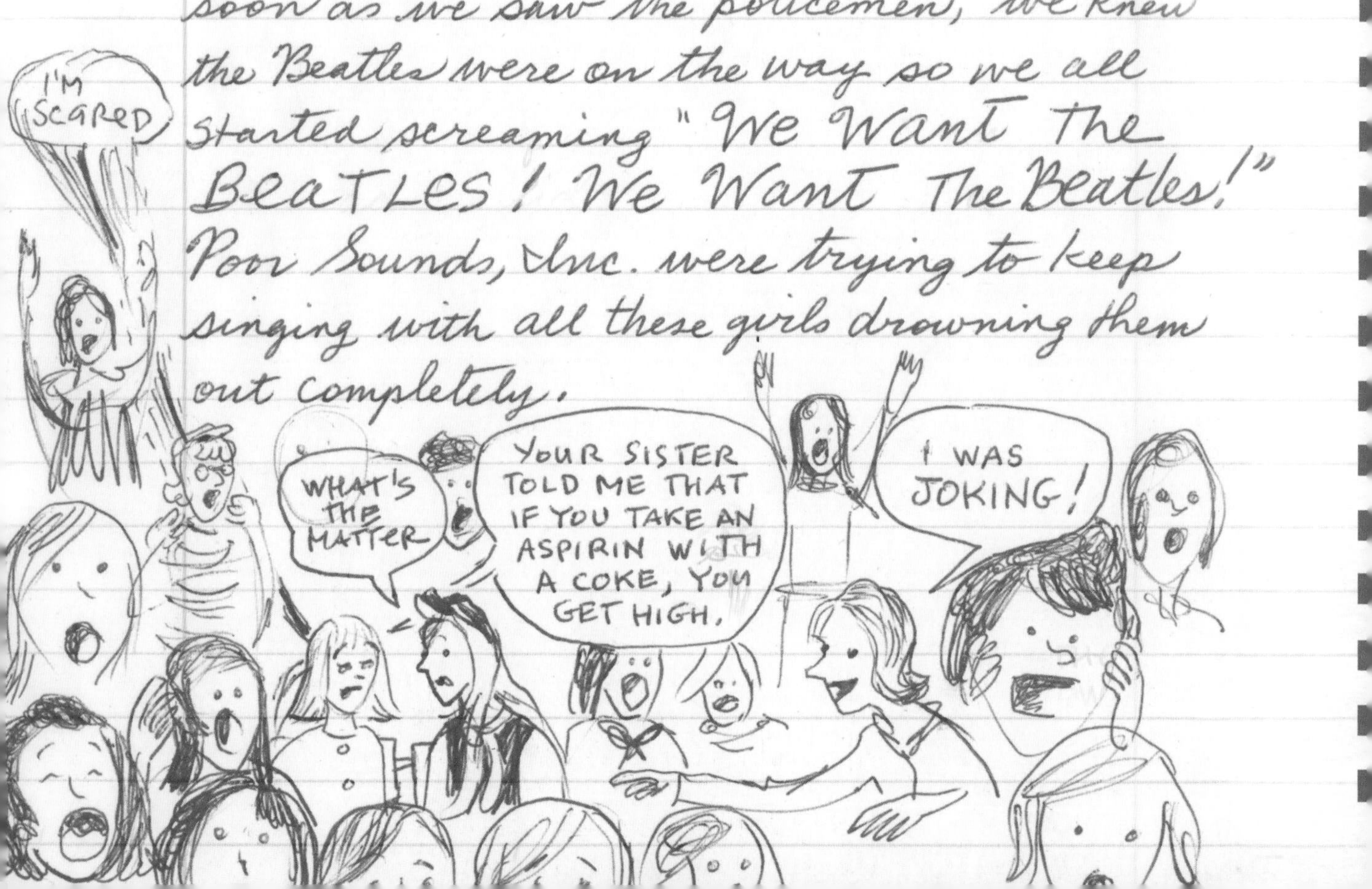
WHAT'S THE MATTER
YOUR SISTER TOLD ME THAT IF YOU TAKE AN ASPIRIN WITH A COKE, YOU GET HIGH.
I WAS JOKING!

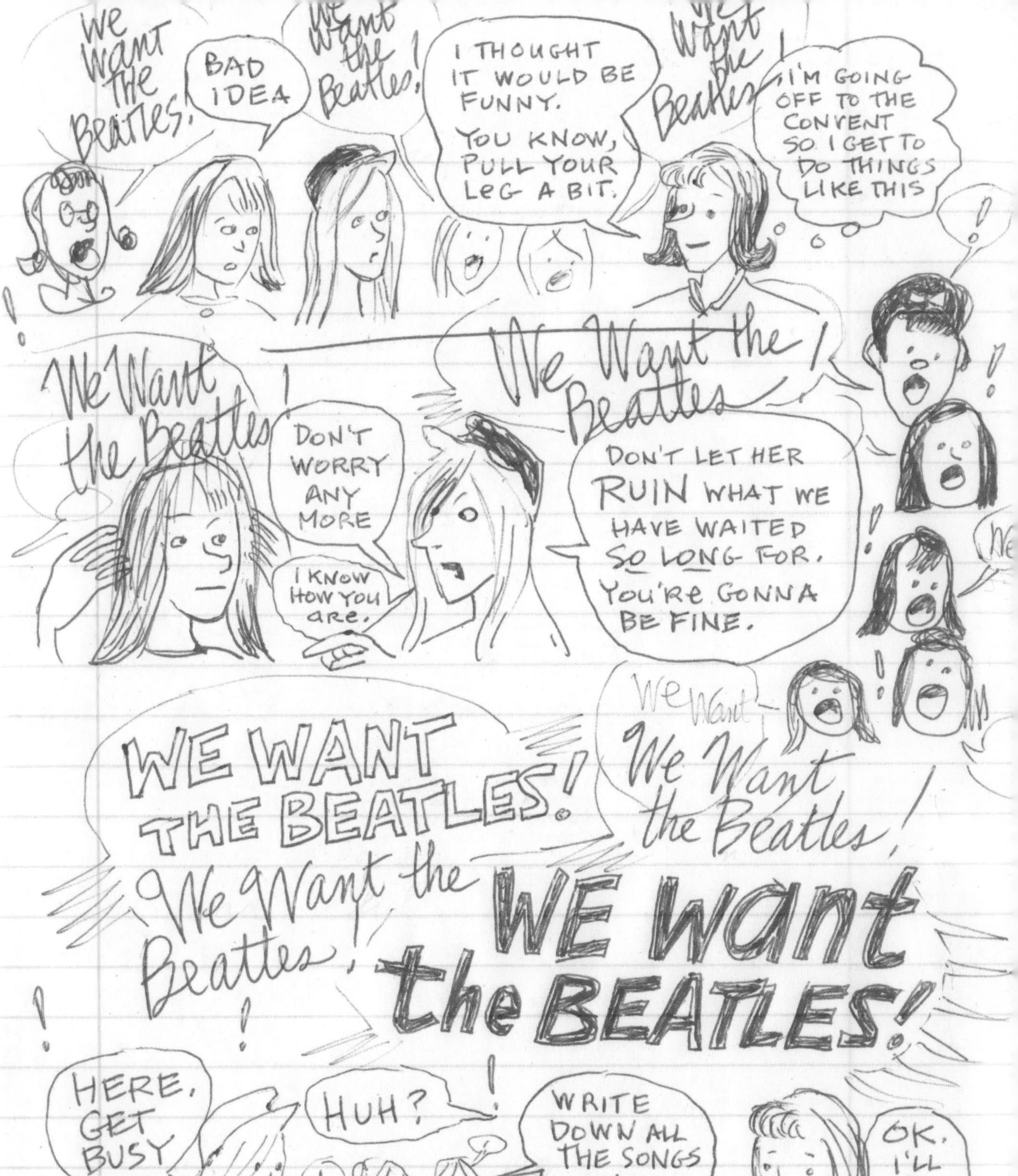

We want the Beatles!
BAD IDEA
We want the Beatles!
I THOUGHT IT WOULD BE FUNNY. YOU KNOW, PULL YOUR LEG A BIT.
We want the Beatles!
I'M GOING OFF TO THE CONVENT SO I GET TO DO THINGS LIKE THIS
We Want the Beatles!
DON'T WORRY ANY MORE
I KNOW HOW YOU ARE.
We Want the Beatles!
DON'T LET HER RUIN WHAT WE HAVE WAITED SO LONG FOR. YOU'RE GONNA BE FINE.
WE WANT THE BEATLES!
We Want
We Want the Beatles!
We Want the Beatles!
WE WANT the BEATLES!
HERE, GET BUSY
KEEP YOURSELF BUSY
HUH?
WRITE DOWN ALL THE SONGS GINIA.
OK. I'LL DO THAT

And then finally it came!

One of the DJs said "Here they are ---

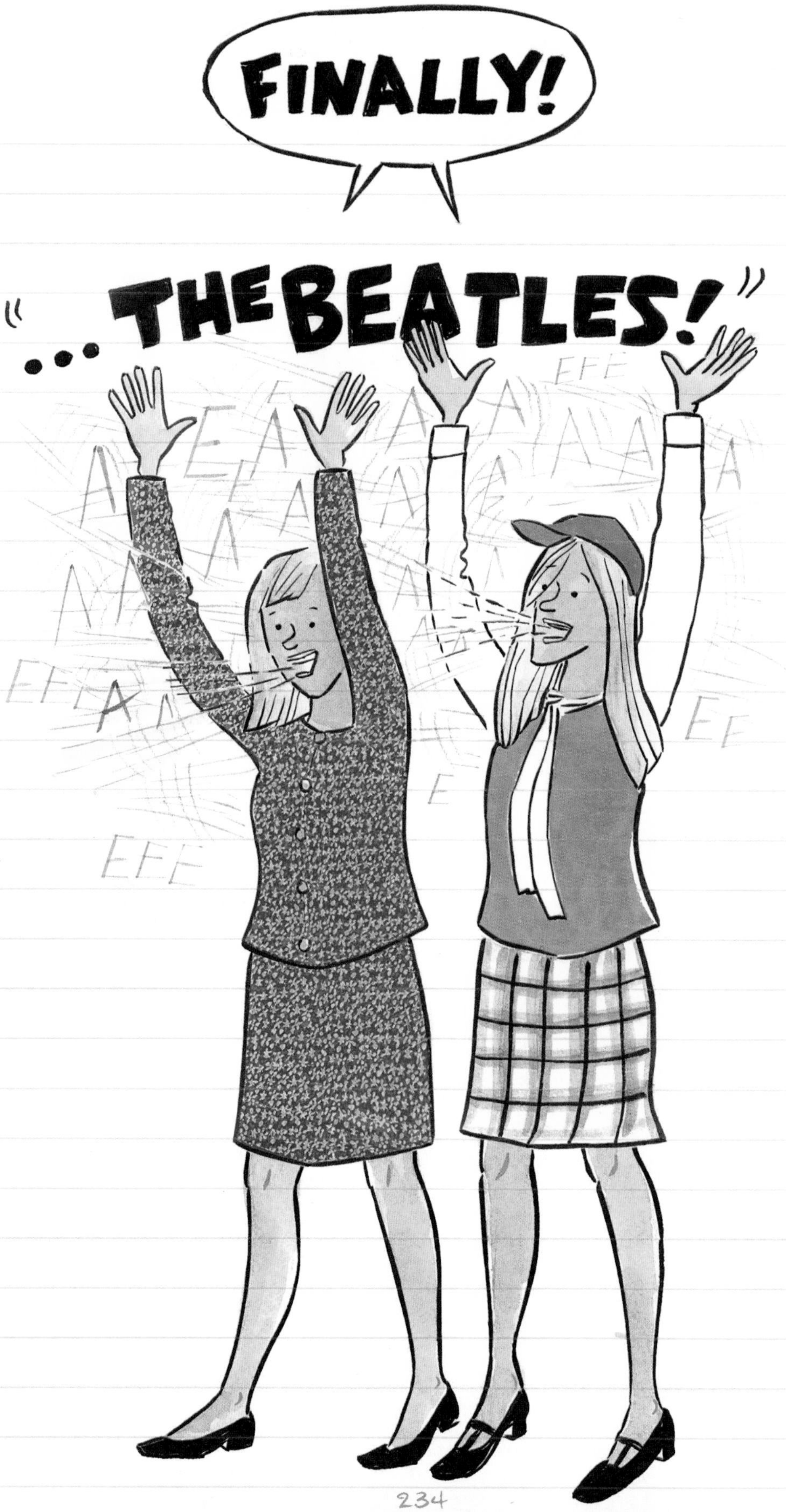
FINALLY!
"...THE BEATLES!"

"THE BEATLES!"

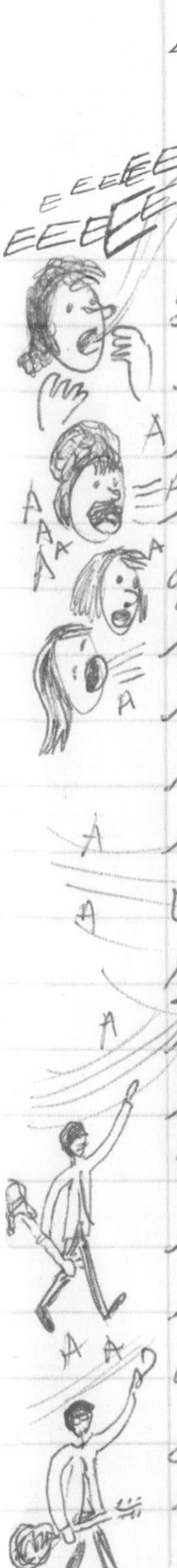

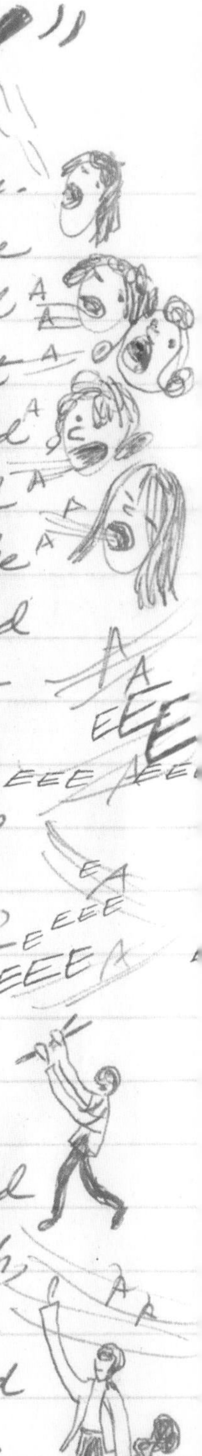

"They walked up to the stage so casually. 25 People right away fainted. Everyone was screaming and crying. We were all standing. They walked with a confident stride and bounced on their knees kind of as they walked to the stage at second base! It was so great. Beatles ~~sand~~ on the baseball diamond! Paul and John and George had their guitars and Ringo had his rings. It was definitely them, I could not believe my eyes. This was real! They had tan-ish light ~~or med~~ brown coats on. Cordureoy kind a little more brown than tan. ½ + ½. They also had on black pants with black ties and white shirts. Paul had his brown bass guitar, George had a black one to come walking out with, just like the ones I made for my wall. George also had a red one to sing Hard Days Night. John had his blue one and an old brown one. Ringo's drums were silver. Of course they had on their Beatle boots. They waved as they came in and got on stage. Screaming was getting louder and louder. And louder!

It was 9:23.

They Looked Smashing!

The first song they launched into was

1. **TWIST AND SHOUT**

After that number, right into

2. **SHE'S A WOMAN**

and then

3. **I FEEL FINE** "I'm in Love with her and I Feel FINE!"

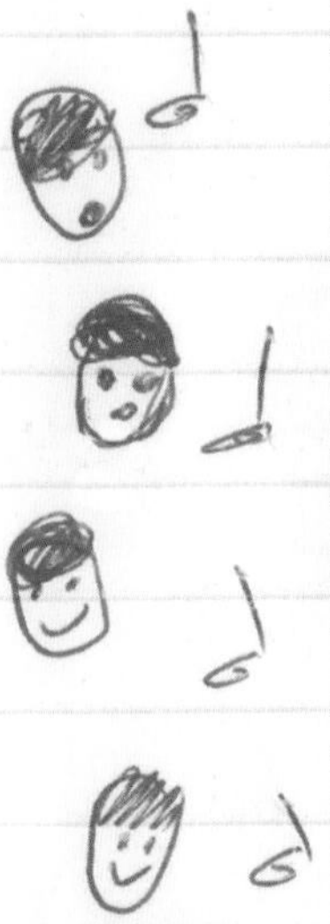

"She's a woman who loves her man." And then they bowed.

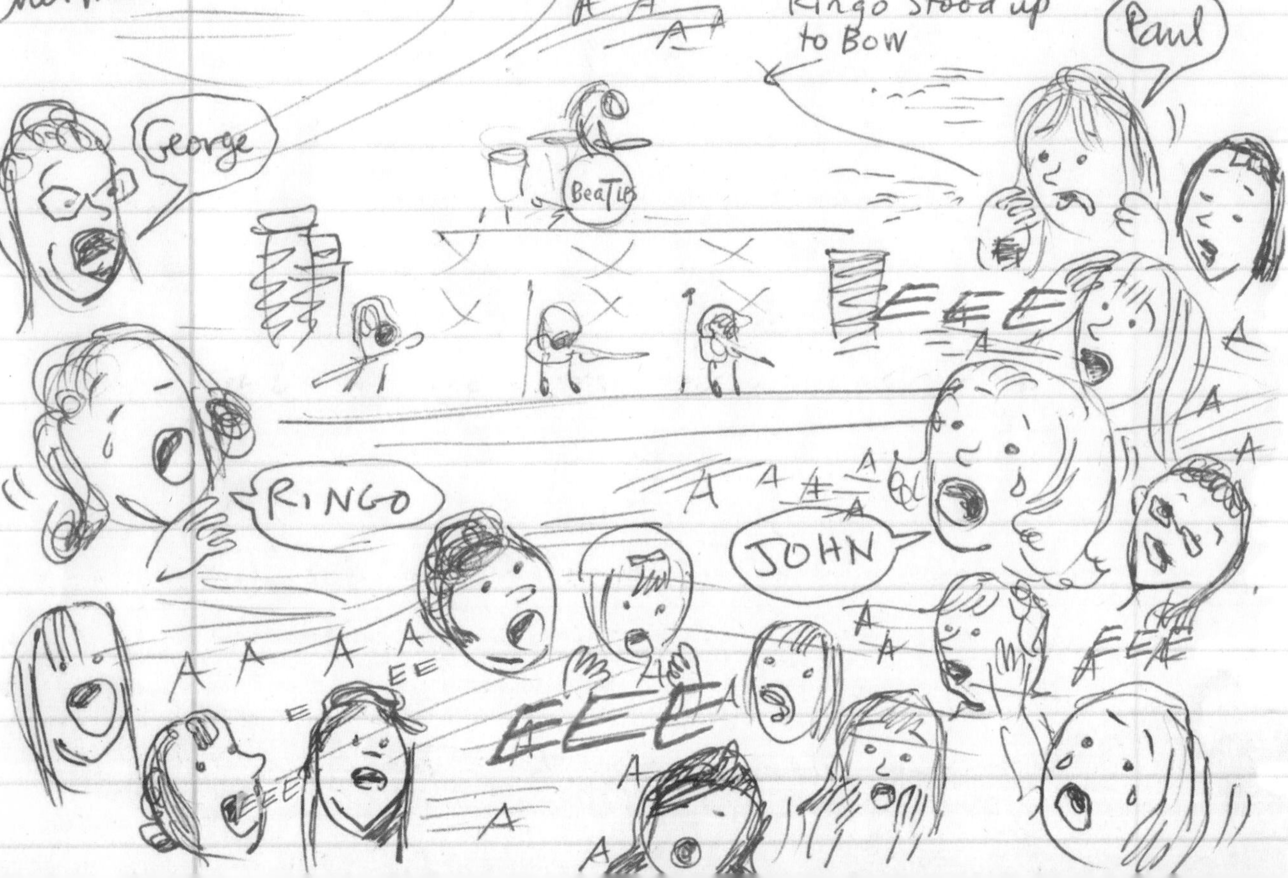

A A A A
Ringo stood up to Bow
Paul
George
BeaTLes
EEE
RINGO
JOHN
A A A A
EE
EEE

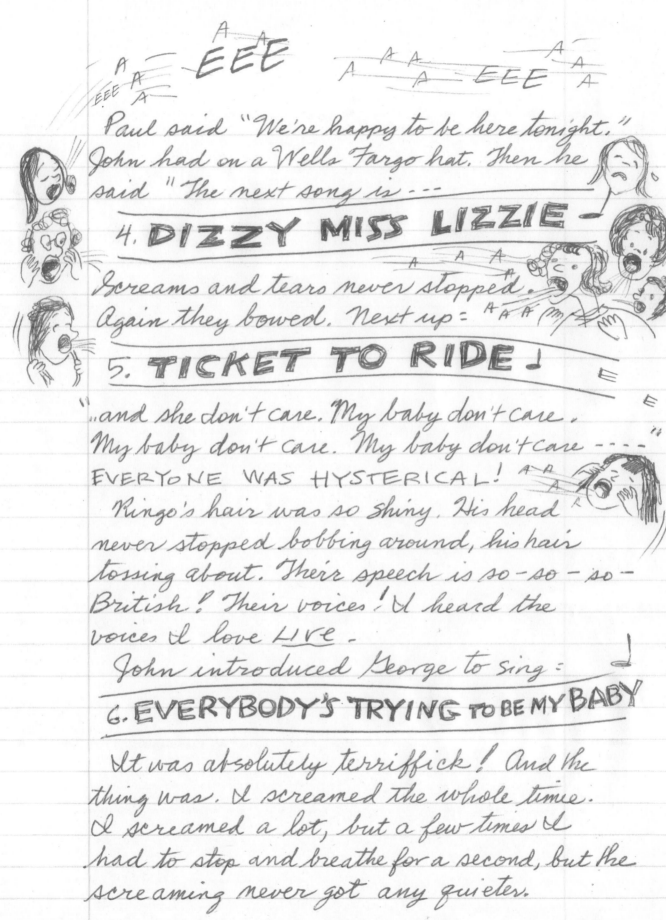

A — A A A EEE A A A A A EEE A A

Paul said "We're happy to be here tonight."
John had on a Wells Fargo hat. Then he
said "The next song is ---

4. DIZZY MISS LIZZIE —

Screams and tears never stopped. A A A
Again they bowed. Next up = A A A

5. TICKET TO RIDE ♪

E
E

"...and she don't care. My baby don't care.
My baby don't care. My baby don't care ----"
EVERYONE WAS HYSTERICAL! A A A A
    Ringo's hair was so shiny. His head
never stopped bobbing around, his hair
tossing about. Their speech is so-so-so-
British! Their voices! I heard the
voices I love LIVE.
    John introduced George to sing = ♪

6. EVERYBODY'S TRYING TO BE MY BABY

    It was absolutely terriffick! And the
thing was. I screamed the whole time.
I screamed a lot, but a few times I
had to stop and breathe for a second, but the
screaming never got any quieter.

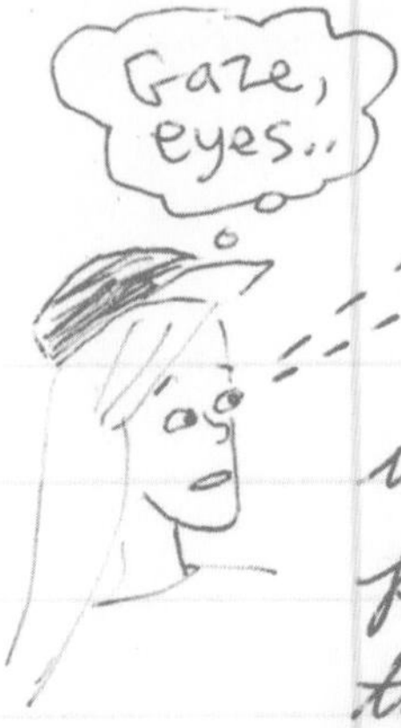
Gaze, eyes..

I took a moment to look around without screaming. There were so many people at the ballpark. And this was the second show—there was one in the afternoon. So it was a double-header. The Chicagoland area is obviously very big. Mostly it was girls and young women. Some kids were there. I was surprised to see so many boys. They wore ties. And most girls had on new outfits. Dresses mostly. No pants. Everybody was having a great time. One guy, though, I watched him. He just sat there the whole performance like a bump on a log-- didn't make a move. Why did he even come? And another lady, an old sourpuss looked the other way for the whole 37 minutes. But not me. I screamed and waved and jumped and pulled my hair.

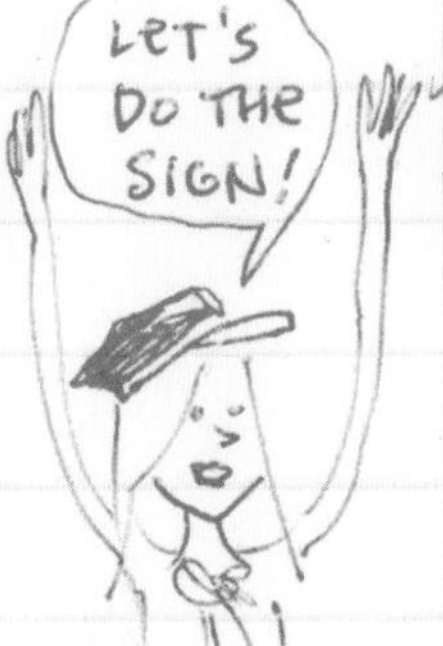
LET'S DO THE SIGN!

About this time we held our sign up. The one hidden in the umbrella. They looked at it. They looked right at it. They saw it! But then an usher came over and told us to put it away.

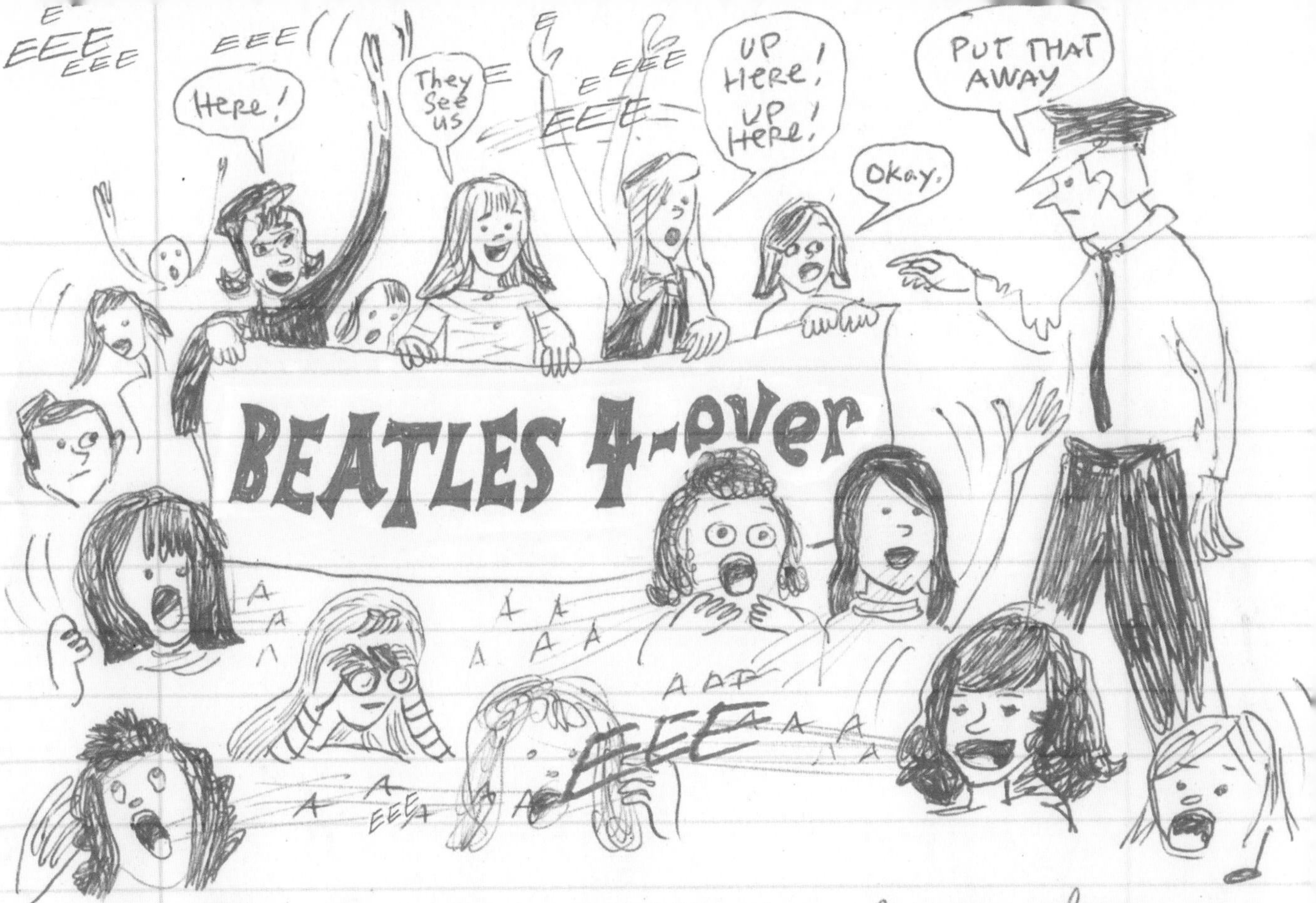
EEE EEE
Here!
They see us
UP Here! UP Here!
Okay.
PUT THAT AWAY
BEATLES 4-ever

But then the most screams for the show so far were pulled out at the 7th song.

7. CAN'T BUY ME LOVE

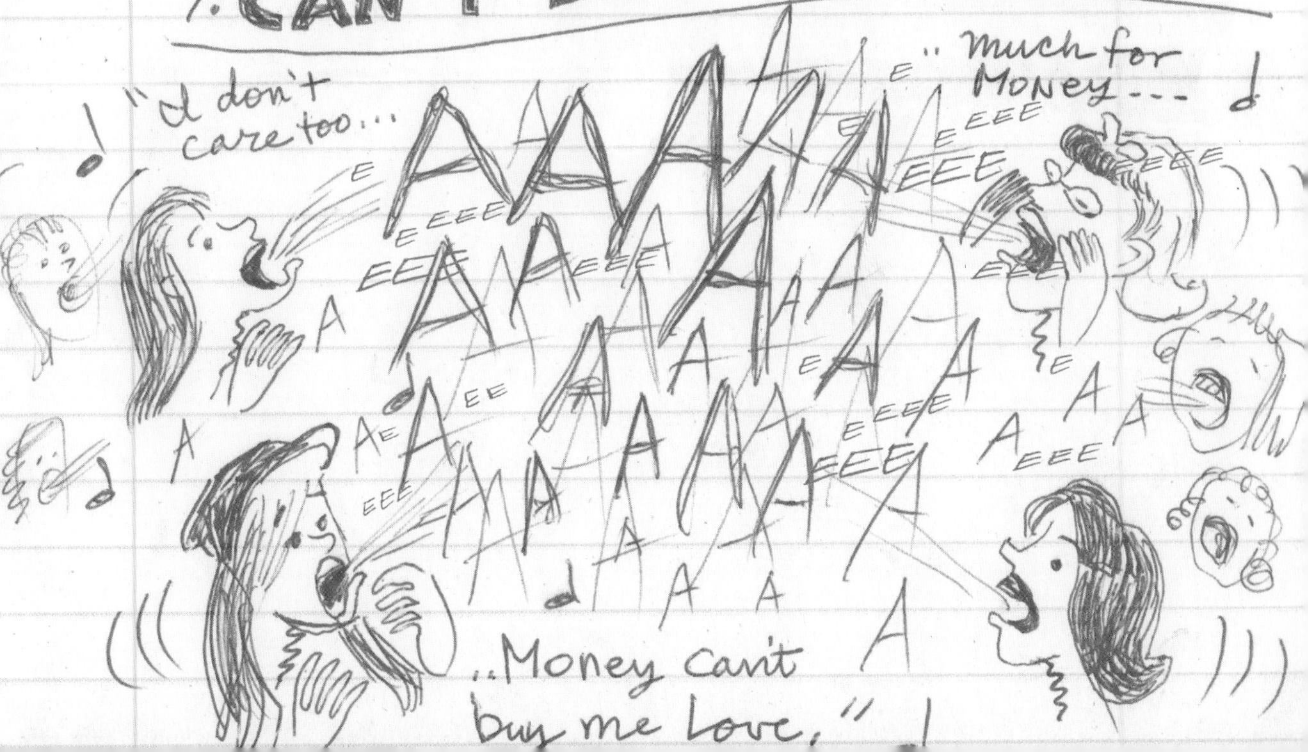
"I don't care too...
.. much for Money...
AAAA
..Money can't buy me Love."

When a plane went overhead, they took the end of their guitars and Ringo took his drumsticks and pretended they were shooting at the plane.

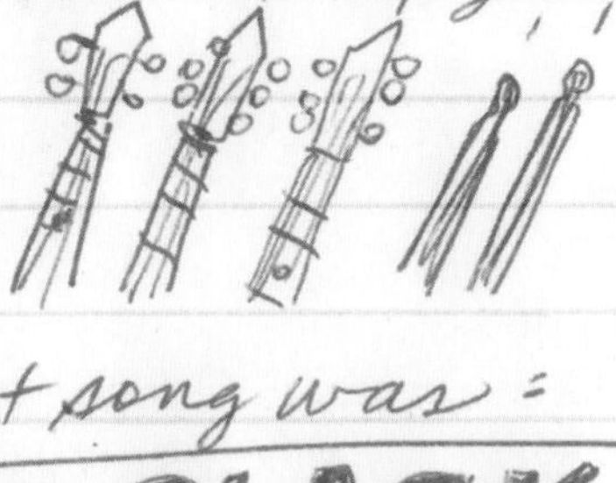

Ringo's rings look tough. They all look tough. Then the next song was:

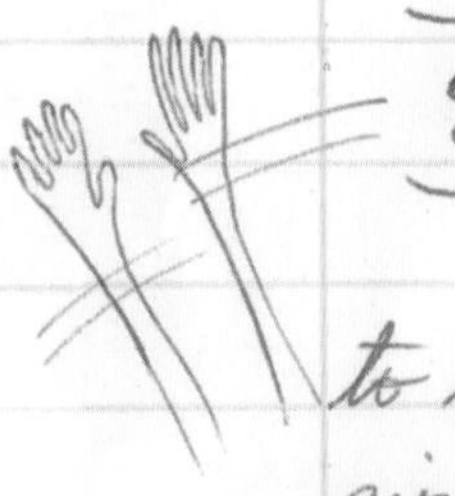

8. BABY'S IN BLACK

Even old people started clapping to the beat, along with us screaming. One girl near us had a tambourine. Some people were swaying. Madness.

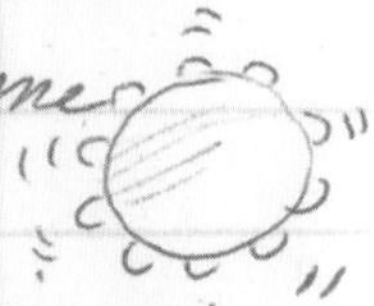

Paul said "Now we'll have Ringo sing..."

9. I WANNA BE YOUR MAN

I love the beat on that. I love how George twangs out the notes between Ringo's lyrics. I love how Ringo shakes about. Love Paul's bass run. John's rhythm. And he says he wants to be my lover.

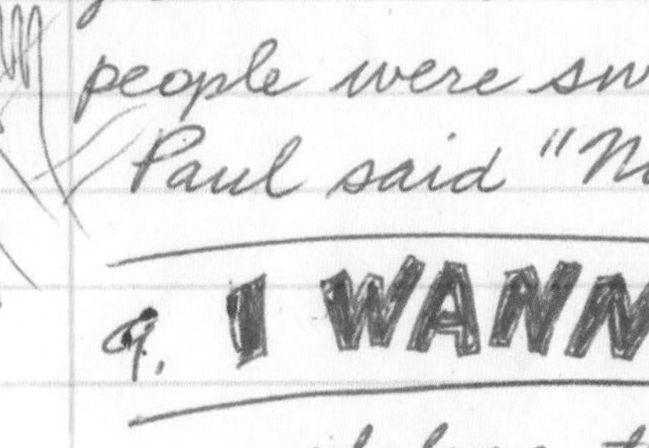
A A A A A A
EEE
EEE

translated means:

I LOVE EVERYTHING YOU DO AND WHAT YOU DO TO ME!

You are the GREATEST!!!

IT'S ALMOST MORE THAN I CAN BEAR!

They looked like they were having a good time, too. The stage had stairs on both sides so when song 3 was on, I Feel Fine, John started running down the stairs toward the crowd.

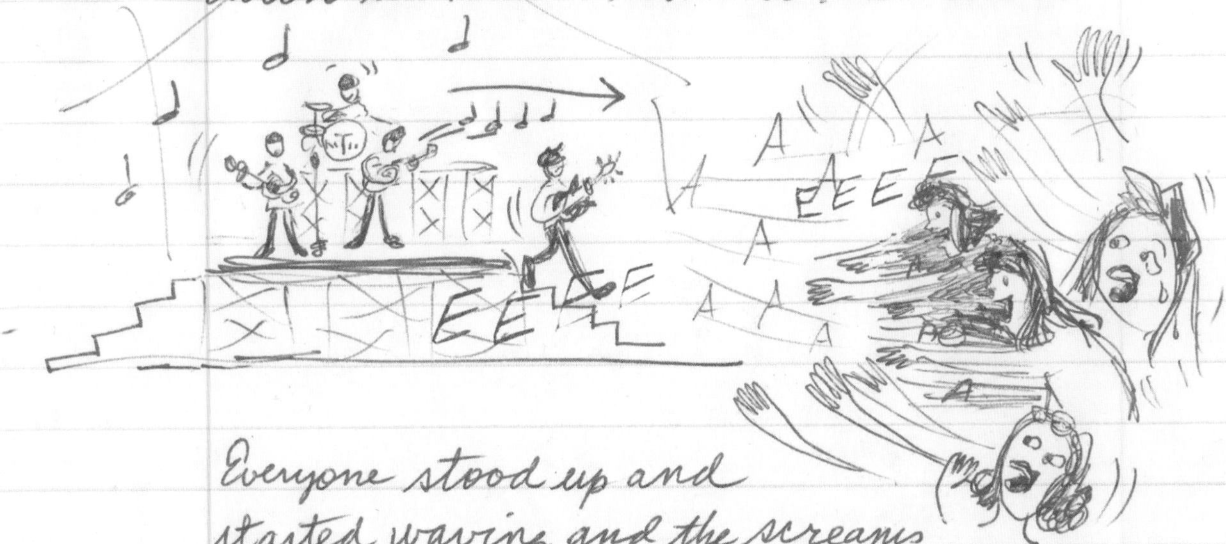

A
A
A
EEEE
A
A
A
A
A
A
EEEE

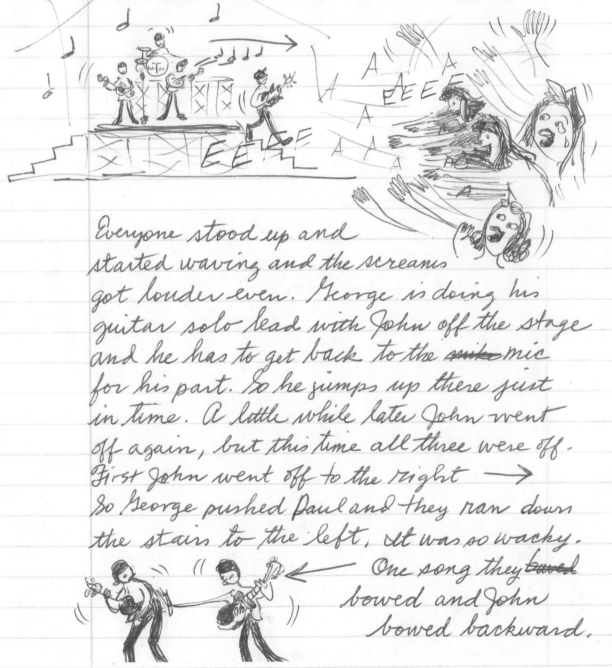

Everyone stood up and started waving and the screams got louder even. George is doing his guitar solo lead with John off the stage and he has to get back to the ~~mik~~ mic for his part. So he jumps up there just in time. A little while later John went off again, but this time all three were off. First John went off to the right → So George pushed Paul and they ran down the stairs to the left. It was so wacky.

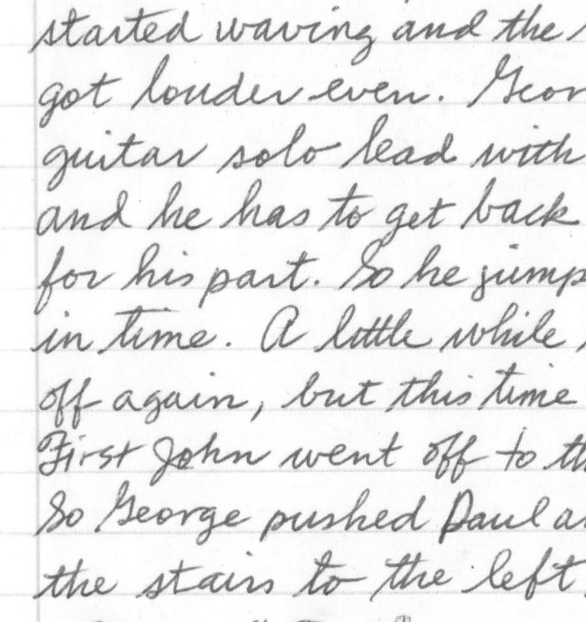

One song they ~~bowd~~ bowed and John bowed backward.

Then there was this Chord. And everybody knew instantly what it was

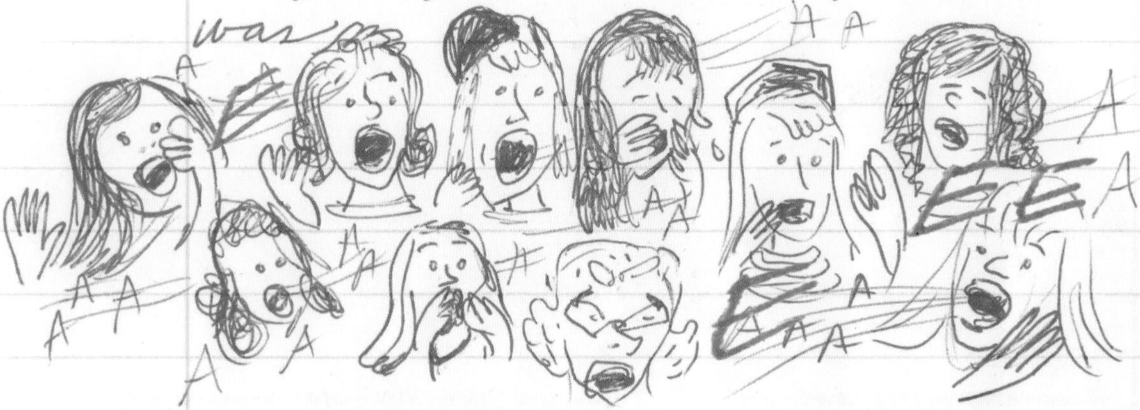

"It's been

10. A HARD DAY'S NIGHT

After 'night,' the screams did not cease. George then said "We're now going to sing the song from our latest movie. It's called "Help!""

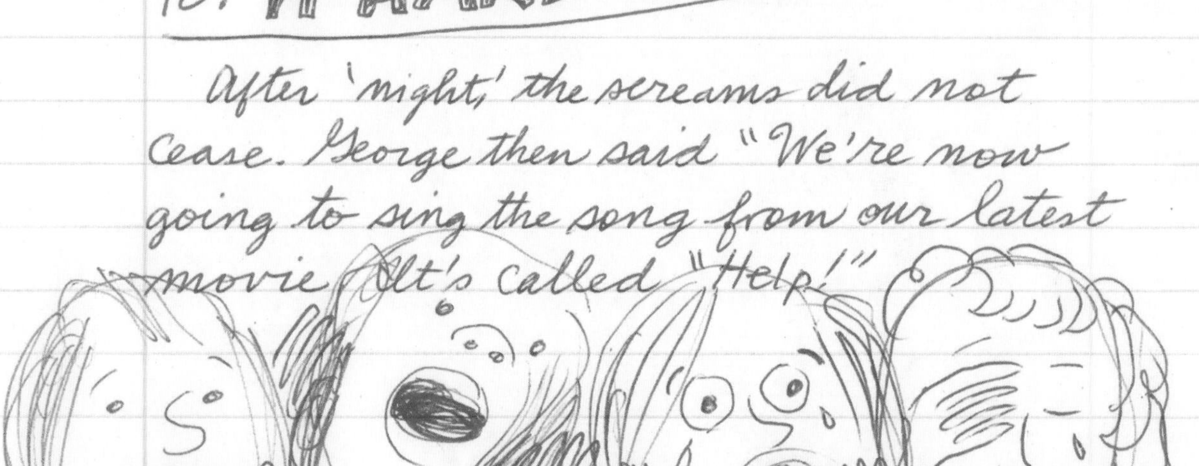

Paul said→ "one 1. two 2. three 3 four 4

11. HELP!

"Won't you Please Please help me."

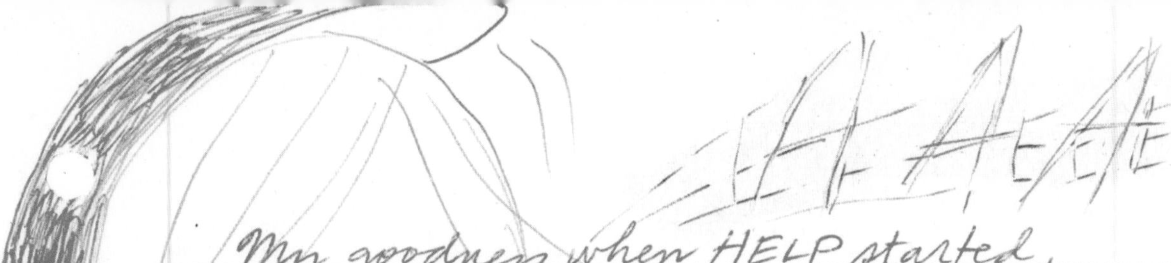

My goodness when HELP started, I started. Crying that is. I cried and cried and screamed and cried. It was so loud you could hardly hear the introduction or the song. I was crying and screaming so much I could only make out ~~what~~ where they were. Paul and George were on the left at one mic, John was on the left alone at his own mic and Ringo, of course is always sitting up there with his drums. They're perfect.

Paul said it had been a great evening and thanked us all for coming. "And now here is the last song of the evening:" I had never heard it before, but I NEVER EVER will forget it.

"YOU TELL LIES THINKING I CAN'T SEE — YOU CAN'T CRY 'CAUSE YOU'RE LAUGHING AT ME"

12. I'M DOWN!

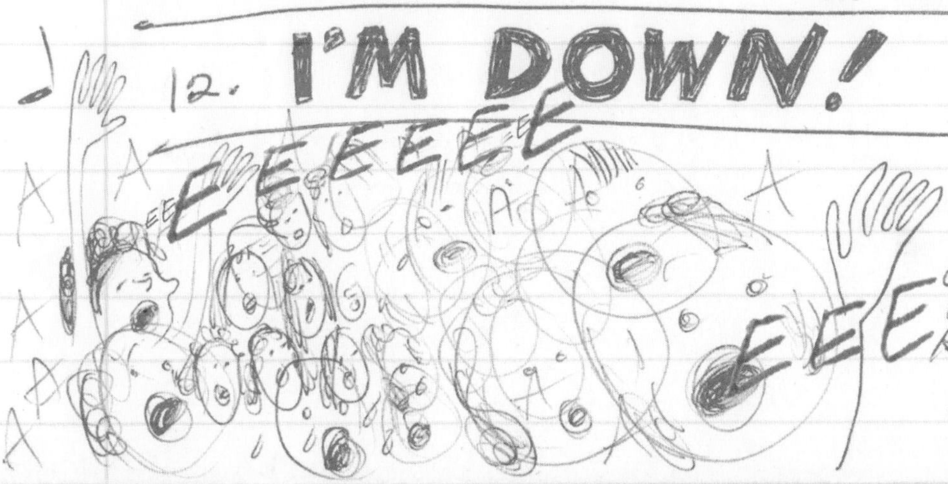

This song got the most screams of all!

After it was over, everyone stood up. We were all screaming and crying and waving and jumping in a frenzy of wild hysteria that felt like this

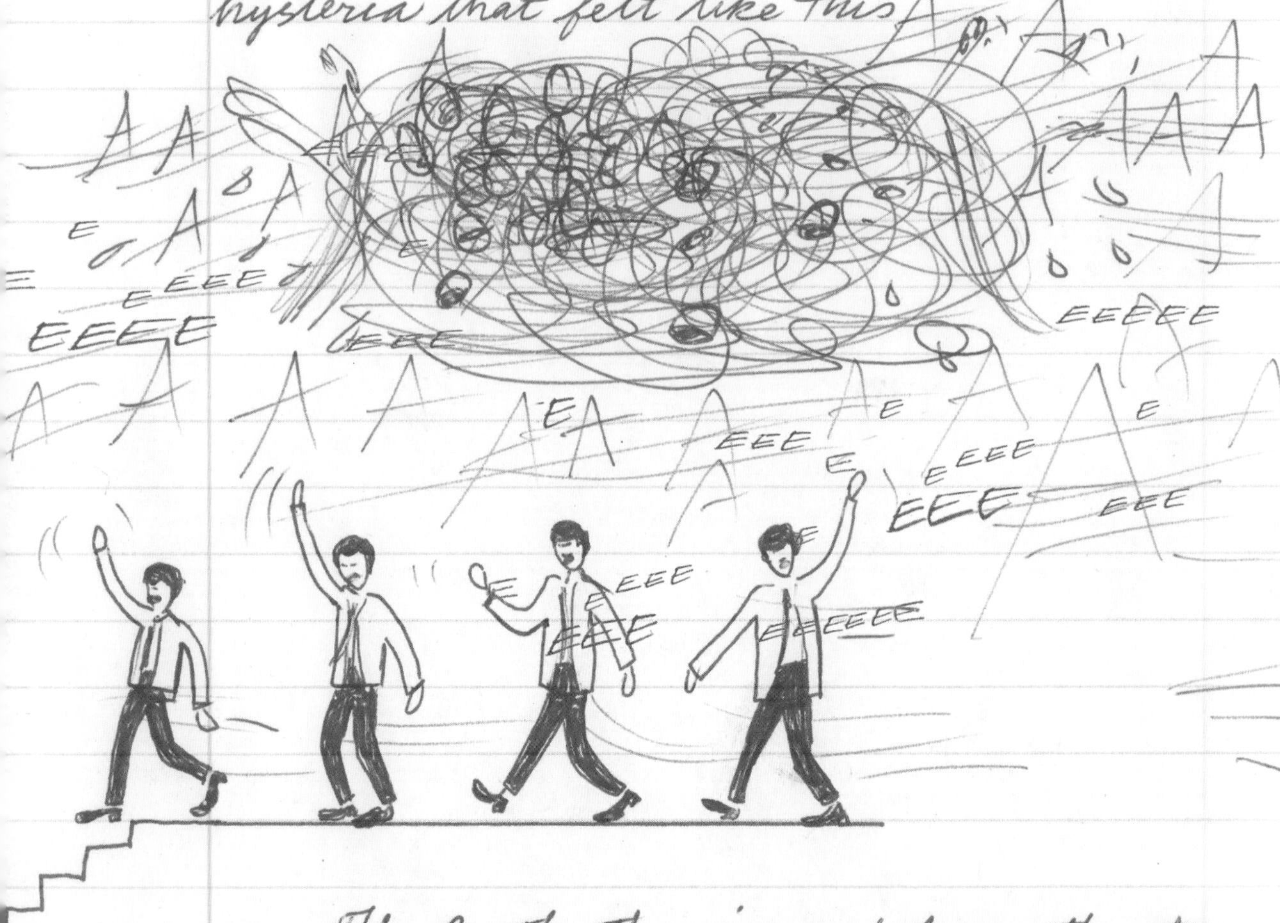

The Beatles then jumped from the stage onto a golf cart. A girl broke away from policemen and got within 20 feet of them when she was stopped. It was in the paper the next day. They asked her "Why did you run after the Beatles?" Any one of us could have answered that.

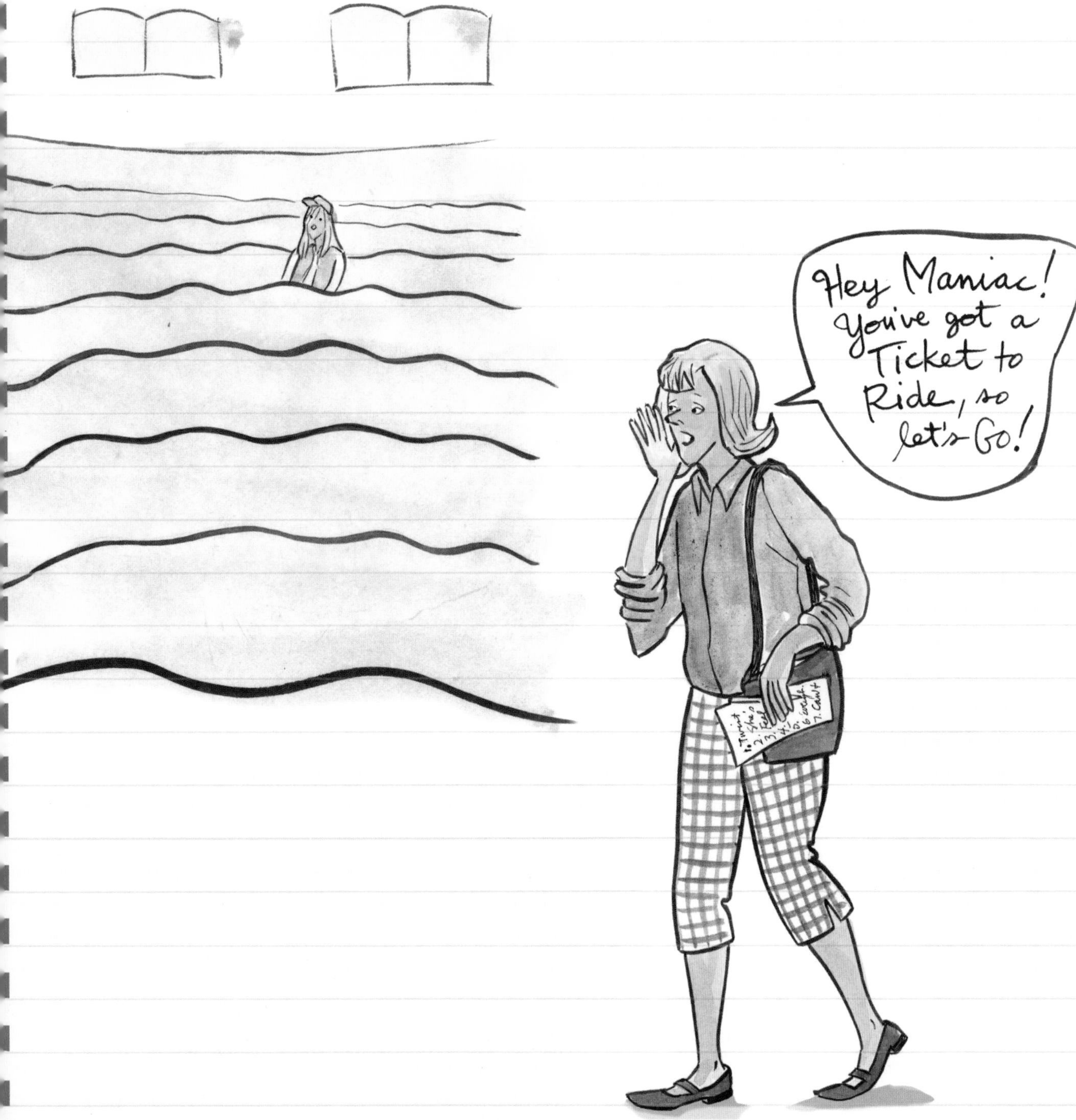
Hey Maniac! You've got a Ticket to Ride, so let's Go!

After the concert, it was time to go but I couldn't move. I never wanted to leave, the lights in the stadium were on, their stuff was still there on stage. The drum set. How could I say goodbye? The guitars. Their sweat. Paul was sweating like crazy at the end of I'm down. How do I hold onto this night forever?

We took the subway back to the car. I guess it was around 11:30. Ginia took us to the Buffalo Ice Cream Parlor. I had french fries and a coke. About 10 different people came up and said "Did you see the Beatles?" Yes. "How were they?" They don't call them the Fab 4 for nothing. "Could you hear them?" In my heart. It was hard to talk because I was hoarse. I met this really nice waiter in the swanky area of the place. We talked for a long time. I liked him. He thought I looked tough.

We were on our way home from the Buffalo about 1:15. There was still traffic, so we drove west out to O'hare Airport. We walked around and watched planes coming and going. Flights to London. Yes they exist and I could go there.

We felt like international travelers walking around. Laurie and I put on our British accents and tried to fool people. We got good at British accents from when we used to call information in London to ask for the fake Mr. Teddy Smythe. A lot of tired people from long trips. We were at the airport from about 15 minutes to 2:00 until about 2:30. We got home to Fox Lake at 3:30 and by the time we dropped everybody off and I got to bed, it was 4. So tired I was from my long trip.

I had butterflies for at least a week before the show and even still. It will give me a thrill till I am 64, I bet you. That's 50 years away.

One week later — Still excited!
The Beatles came on stage at 9:23 and were on until 10. 37 minutes. Whenever I hear a song from the concert they sang, I cry. Beatles 4-ever! Beatlemania 4-ever! I hope next year I get to meet them.

From Me to You

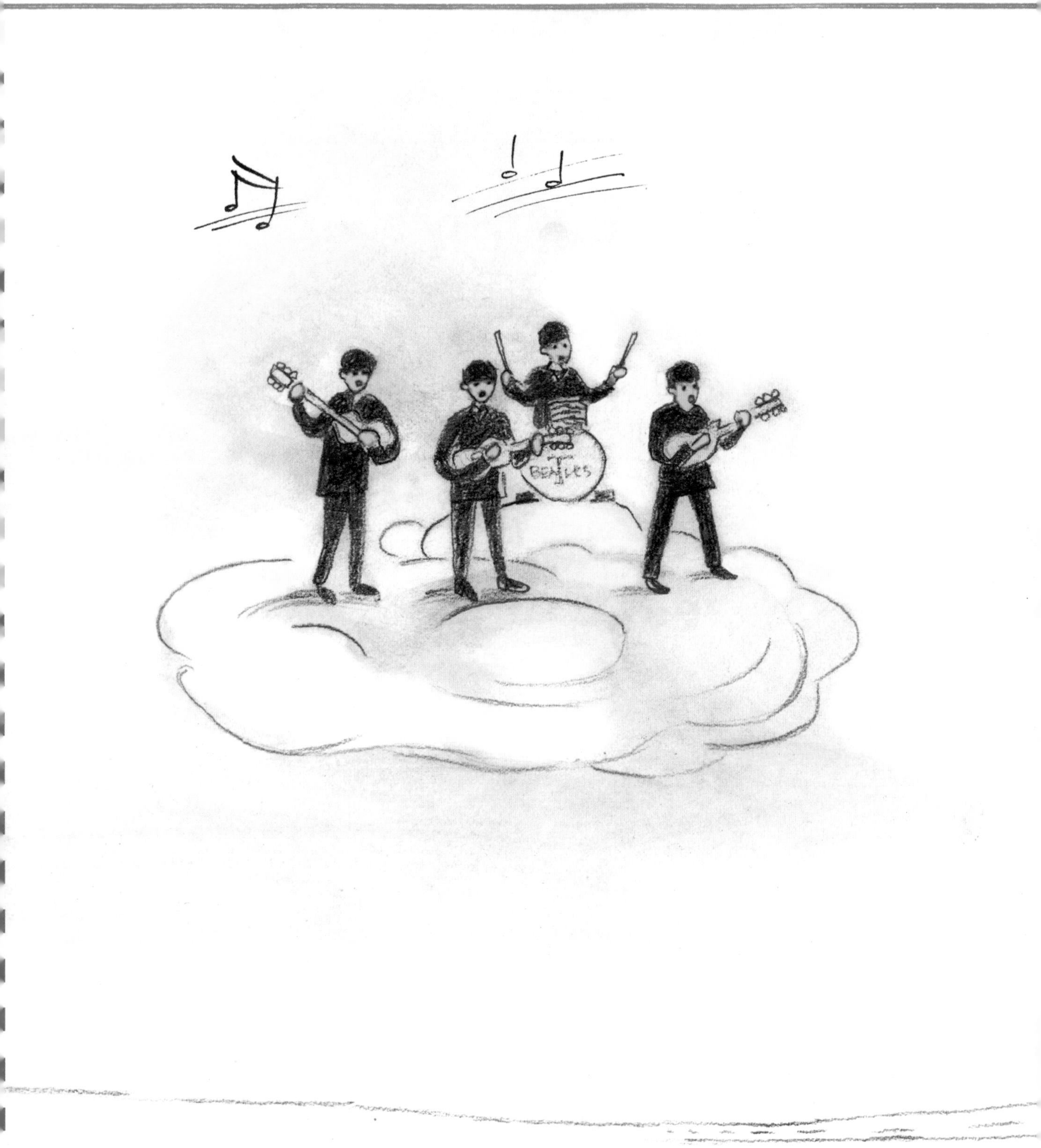
BEATLES

I HAVE SO MANY QUESTIONS NOW, ABOUT LIFE, ABOUT SCHOOL --- about Laurie and Jamie --- BUT THE BIGGEST QUESTION OF ALL IS
WHAT WILL THE LADS DO NEXT?

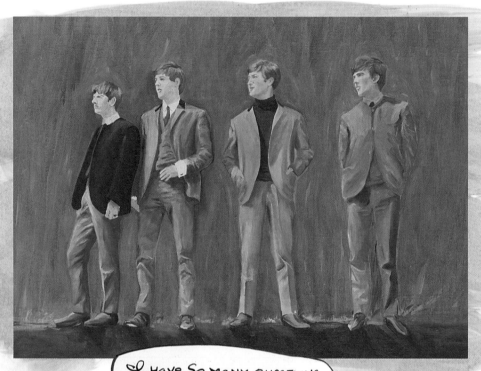

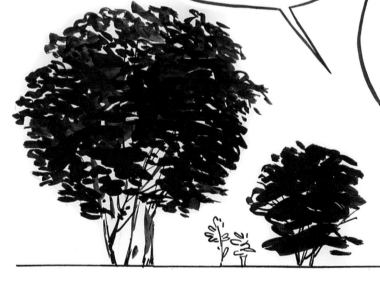

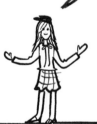

Carol Tyler